COSMECEUTICALS

COSMECEUTICALS

Editors

Prof. Y. Madhusudan Rao
M. Pharm, Ph.D

Centre for Biopharmaceutics and Pharmacokinetics,
University College of Pharmaceutical Sciences,
Kakatiya University, Warangal (A.P), India.

Dr. Shayeda
M. Pharm, Ph.D

Asst. Professor, University College of
Pharmaceutical Sciences,
Kakatiya University, Warangal (A.P), India.

PharmaMed Press
An imprint of Pharma Book Syndicate
A unit of BSP Books Pvt. Ltd.
4-4-316, Giriraj Lane,
Sultan Bazar, Hyderabad - 500 095.

Disclaimer

The information provided in this book is to provide helpful information on the Cosmeceuticals. This book is not meant to be used, to diagnose or treat any medical condition. The publisher and authors are not responsible for any specific health or allergy needs that may require medical supervision and are not liable for any damages or negative consequences from any treatment, action, application or preparation, to any person reading or following the information in this book. The publisher and authors are not responsible for the action/usage of the products mentioned in this book. Readers should be aware that the websites listed in the reference part of this book may change and they are given for information purpose only.

Published by

PharmaMed Press

An imprint of Pharma Book Syndicate

A unit of BSP Books Pvt. Ltd.

4-4-316, Giriraj Lane, Sultan Bazar, Hyderabad - 500 095.
Phone: 040-23445605, 23445688; Fax: 91+40-23445611
E-mail: info@pharmamedpress.com

ISBN: 978-93-85433-11-5 (HB)

Dedication

I dedicate this book to my father

Sri. Y. Vishnu Janardhan

who took all the pains to educate me and bringing me to this level

and

My life partner

Usha Rani

PREFACE

It was my long desire to write a book on Cosmetics and Cosmeceuticals ever since I started teaching Cosmetic Technology to B.Pharm students. After working as consultant to National Soap Company, Tripoli, Libya during 1987-1990 the desire built up as various techniques employed in industry were known. Previous students used to rely on the notes given by me and many of them approached and encouraged me to write a book on Cosmetics. My interest further increased when I assigned Sunscreens, Hair Dyes as M.Pharm project work. The first student (Shayeda) has successfully completed the Ph.D. in Cosmeceuticals and the thesis was very well appreciated by the examiners. The rewards were excellent. She could get 2 patents and one of them was commercialized. All these prompted me to write the book seriously.

Cosmetic industries are powerful and rich. Most of the details are kept as secrets are not fully disclosed. The evaluation part of the products was mostly not disclosed. Herbal and Natural Cosmetics and Cosmeceuticals are not discussed properly in the few texts available. Regulatory aspects also differ in various countries as far as Cosmeceutical is interpreted differently. In some countries they are equated as Cosmetics, in others they are considered as OTC drugs/drugs. We tried to include or consider all these aspects in our text. As this is my first venture in writing the book on Cosmeceuticals there may be few lapses. Constructive criticism is welcome and I seek this from experts in industry and academia.

The topics included in this book are not complete. After getting the feedback we wish to bring out volume II of this book with chapters like Alopecia, Moisturizers, Eczema etc. We are already in the process of bringing out two volume series in Cosmetics. If things go as expected, in a year we will bring out these volumes.

The intention of this book is to serve as both reference and text book to students of pharmacy (under graduate and post graduate), teachers and people in industry and allied fields. Based on the feedback and criticism obtained, we wish to refine and bring about the upcoming books. The book is already subjected to plagiarism check and I wish to thank all those who have helped me in bringing out this book including the publishers who were after us. Any comments about the book may be sent to the e mail: yamsani123@gmail.com.

- Editors

ACKNOWLEDGEMENTS

I wish to thank Dr. Shayeda who was my Ph.D. scholar earlier and now a colleague for her interest in Cosmetics. Three chapters of this book are from the topics of her Ph.D. work. She has done a marvellous job with cosmetic products. I profusely thank Mr. D. Sathish and his wife S. Himabindu. Mr. D. Sathish is a scholar working with me for his Ph.D. for his tremendous contribution in bringing out this book. His untiring efforts for patiently going through the data including the one generated from various websites and internet made it possible to bring out this book. I also take this opportunity to thank Dr. P.K. Laxmi, Mrs. P. Renuka and Dr. T. Ashok for their contribution in bringing out this text either directly or indirectly.

I also take this opportunity to thank my wife Usha for her constant encouragement and making it possible to spare my time sacrificing her time.

- Editor

CONTRIBUTORS

Prof. Y. Madhusudan Rao, M.Pharm, Ph.D is currently working as senior professor in University College of Pharmaceutical Sciences, Kakatiya University, Warangal. He with 35 years of experience in teaching and research, 155 research publications, 15 review articles, guided 27 scholars for Ph.D, is having 6 national and 1 international patent. He taught cosmetic technology for B.Pharm and M.Pharm students for more than 13 years. He guided the research work for 3 students at M.Pharm and 1 student for Ph.D in the field of Cosmetics and Cosmeceuticals. He acted as consultant to many industries producing cosmetics and few of the products developed are commercialized and launched. A few more cosmetic products are to be launched this year. Apart from his interest in cosmetics, he has considerable experience and publications in Novel drug delivery systems, Biopharmaceutics and Pharmacokinetics. He received research projects from various funding agencies.

Dr. Shayeda, is working as Asst. Professor at University College of Pharmaceutical Sciences, Kakatiya University, Warangal. She got two research projects from UGC and AICTE, INDIA. She has publications in national and international journals. Now she is guiding M.Pharmacy and Ph.D students in the field of pharmaceutics. She has completed her Ph.D in cosmetics and has European patent in the field of cosmetics.

Dr. P.K. Lakshmi, Former Director, Drug Information Center, Karnataka State Pharmacy Council, Bangalore and currently she is Professor and Head of the department, Department of Pharmaceutics, G.Pulla Reddy College of Pharmacy, Hyderabad. She has undergone many international trainings by WHO on Rational Use Drugs. Visited many countries to learn working of DICs abroad. (Singapore, France, Switzerland, Australia, Malaysia). She has guided many M.Pharm students of pharmaceutics and Pharmacy practice. She has edited 5 books and published many articles in national and International journals.

Dr. Y. Shravan Kumar, Associate Prof. at Vagdevi College of Pharmacy, Warangal has guided several M.Pharm students, has written many chapters in various text books. He completed his Ph.D. from University College of Pharmaceutical Sciences, Kakatiya University, Warangal and has publications in national and international journals.

Mr. D. Sathish is a research scholar at University College of Pharmaceutical Sciences, Kakatiya University, Warangal under the guidance of Prof. Y. Madhusudan Rao.

Mrs. S. Himabindu is a research scholar at University College of Pharmaceutical Sciences, Kakatiya University, Warangal under the guidance of Dr. Shayeda.

Mrs. P. Renuka has completed her M.Pharm in the field of cosmetics under the guidance of Prof. Y. Madhusudan Rao and now working as Asst. Prof. at Vagdevi College of Pharmacy, Warangal.

CONTENTS

CHAPTER 2
ACNE AND ITS TREATMENT OPTIONS

CHAPTER 3

ANTI-AGING

CHAPTER 4

ANTIPERSPIRANTS AND DEODORANTS

CHAPTER 5

SUNSCREENS

Chapter 6

Hair Dyes

Chapter 7

Psoriasis

CHAPTER 8

LEUCODERMA AND ITS TREATMENT

CHAPTER 9

HYPERPIGMENTATION AND ITS TREATMENT

CHAPTER 10

MEDICATED AND ANTIDANDRUFF SHAMPOOS

CHAPTER 1

COSMECEUTICALS

Y. Madhusudan Rao[1], Y. Shravan Kumar[2], D. Sathish[1]

[1]Center for Biopharmaceutics and Pharmacokinetics, University College of Pharmaceutical Sciences, Kakatiya University, Warangal-506 009, Andhra Pradesh, India.

[2]Vaagdevi College of Pharmacy, Ramnagar, Hanamkonda, Andhra Pradesh, India.

1.1 History and Background

Cosmeceuticals have become the fastest-growing segment of the personal care industry. About 25 years ago Dr. Albert Kligman of the University of Pennsylvania originally coined the term 'cosmeceutical', describing a hybrid category of products found on the spectrum between drugs and cosmetics that exert a pharmaceutical therapeutic benefit but not necessarily a biological therapeutic benefit.[1]

The difference between a drug and a cosmeceutical is that the former is defined by having a biological effect on living tissue. Another important distinction is that cosmeceuticals are not regulated by the U.S. Food and Drug Administration (FDA) and, thus, are not subject to premarket requirements for proof of safety or efficacy. Cosmeceutical products often are tested through *in vitro* studies using silicone replicas of skin and, at best, clinical trials are small, open-label studies usually supported by the cosmetic companies themselves. The rigorous testing required for pharmaceuticals is not mandatory for cosmeceutical products.[2]

There are approximately 400 cosmeceutical manufacturers, including companies that supply the cosmeceutical chemicals and/or manufacture the products in the U.S. market. The largest companies in the industry for finished products are Procter & Gamble, Johnson & Johnson, L'Oréal, Estée Lauder, Avon and Allergan, which together represent nearly one-half of the U.S. market.

1.1.1 Skin Protection

The efficacy of a cosmetic product depends not only on the active ingredients but also on the delivery system to improve its efficacy. We have to remember that skin is more than an assembly of several layers of cells as corneocytes, keratinocytes, fibroblasts and complementing each other. Chemical products, pollution, stress, irradiation from infrared (IR) and ultraviolet (UV) sources, and abrasion are involved in skin aging. The consequences can be visible or invisible: inflammation, burns, edema, long-term illness, actinic damage, and premature aging. The aging of the skin manifests itself in many ways: drying out, loss of elasticity and texture, thinning, damaged barrier function, appearance of spots, modification of surface line isotropy, and finally, wrinkles.

Most of the cosmeceuticals have been developed with claims of antiwrinkle and firming, moisturizing and lifting, skin toning and whitening activity; the antiaging category of skin care products shows presently the highest growth rates.

1.2 Regulations

In India, a well defined Drugs and Cosmetics Act (1940) operates the regulations of cosmetics under the authority of Central Drugs Standard Control Organization (CDSCO). For the manufacture of cosmetics for sale or distribution the manufacturer should build the factory premises according to the Schedule M-II. Rapid growth of Pharmaceutical Industry has revamped and modernized the regulatory set-up of the country. Many areas including the production and distribution of healthcare products are brought under the same ambit of regulatory framework. Bioproducts, food additives and medical devices are all been regulated by regulating committee. Conducive environment in India also encourages substantial growth in all departments. With the introduction of Patent Act 2005, many new manufacturers are able to patent their products and market them effectively. The new regulatory guidelines have facilitated Research and Development activities to ensure the standard and quality of new drugs. It has also given an opportunity for the new players to invest in the emerging market of drugs and cosmetics manufacturing. Market friendly changes in the policies have also boosted up the market of Pharmaceutical Industry.

According to Drugs and Cosmetics Act (1940), "cosmetic" means any article intended to be rubbed, poured, sprinkled or sprayed on, or introduced into, or otherwise applied to, the human body or any part thereof for cleansing, beautifying, promoting attractiveness, or altering the appearance, and includes any article intended for use as a component of cosmetic.

In 1938, the U.S. Congress enacted a statue that officially defined cosmetics and drugs in detailed terms, setting up formal criteria for classifying a product as either a drug or a cosmetic. No intermediate category exists, although it was appreciated that a topical could be both a cosmetic and a drug at the same time. This remains the law to this very day. It defined a cosmetic, in pertinent part, as an ''article intended for beautifying and promoting attractiveness.'' In contrast, a drug was defined as a substance for use in the diagnosis, cure, treatment, or prevention of disease, intended to affect the structure and function of the body. This last clause legally determines whether a formulation is a drug or a cosmetic. Most skin care products lie somewhere in between drugs and cosmetics.

They comprise a continuous spectrum of substances intermediate between the two polar categories defined by Congress. Some traditional cosmetics are more drugs like in their beneficial effects and some drugs impact principally on appearance. It is this intermediate, broad-spectrum range of substances that consists of both drugs and cosmetics which justifies the fusion term cosmeceuticals. This is simply a biological concept that recognizes the new realities of skin care products.[3] Cosmeceutical is a pragmatic term that enables us to state without pretense the benefits of a product. It is not an invitation to pass new laws. There are three main trading blocks, the United States, Europe, and Japan. Obviously globalization as an integrated free-trade network cannot work if each block classifies and regulates skin care products differently. Unfortunately, no international consensus currently exists, inevitably sparking disputes and trade practices that may place some producers at a grave disadvantage. The situation is more complex and far more demanding in Europe. This is made obvious in the European Economic Cosmetic (EEC) Directive of 1993. The requirements for labeling cosmetics are formidable and daunting.[4] The product information that must be made available to officials encompasses the following: qualitative and quantitative composition of the product: specifications of raw materials; methods of manufacture; safety assessments; and proof of effectiveness.

In the United States, manufacturers are not required to demonstrate either safety or efficacy prior to marketing, as is the case for drugs. On top of all this, the EEC has prohibited testing on animals after January 1998. Japanese authorities have created their own laws in response to the problem that many skin care products are neither pure drugs nor pure cosmetics in the traditional sense, but mixtures of the two. The category we call cosmeceuticals they call 'quasi drugs.' They allow cosmetics to include pharmacologically active ingredients, provided that the medicinal effects are mild and the products have been demonstrated to be safe. The legal wording leaves a lot of room for ambiguities and ad hoc interpretations that some perceive as a trade restraint.

In the United States, the following agents are regulated as drugs while in Europe (according to the European commission on cosmetics) they are sold as cosmetics.

1. Antiperspirants
2. Antidandruff shampoos
3. Sunscreens

This classification is detrimental to industry in the United States, especially in the case of sunscreens, which are more advanced and more effective in Europe because there is greater choice of ingredients. Paradoxes also abound in the United States. For example, retinol (vitamin A) can be sold as a cosmetic, but its oxidation product, retinoic acid, is regulated as a drug. However, the product is still only available by prescription. On the other hand, minoxidil, a drug that purports to grow hair and improve attractiveness, satisfies the basic definition of a cosmetic and is available without a prescription. New insights about the function of the skin, as well as the development of new products for skin care, make it necessary to question or redefine the definitions of cosmetics and drugs. Moreover, in the United States, Europe, and Japan, different definitions of cosmetics are used. The definition of a drug is more or less equivocal on these countries.

According to the Food, Drug and Cosmetic (FDC) Act, a drug is defined as an article intended for use in the diagnosis, mitigation, treatment, or prevention of disease or intended to affect the structure or any function of the body. In the United States, according to the FDC act of 1938, a cosmetic is defined as an article intended to be rubbed, poured, sprinkled, or sprayed on, introduced into, or otherwise applied to the human body or any part thereof for cleansing, beautifying, promoting attractiveness, or altering the appearance without affecting structure or function.[6] It is noteworthy that in this definition the cosmetic is not allowed to have any activity (i.e., without affecting structure or function). In Europe, the definition of a cosmetic was re-evaluated and described by the council directive 93/35/EEC of June 14th, 1993.[7] The cosmetics directive contains 15 articles. The definition of a cosmetic is described in article 1 and is as follows:

A 'cosmetic product' shall mean any substance or preparation intended to be placed in contact with the various external parts of the human body epidermis, hair system, nails, lips and external genital organs or with the teeth and the mucous membranes of the oral cavity with a view exclusively or mainly to cleaning them, perfuming them, changing their appearance and/or correcting body odours and/or protecting them or keeping them in good condition.

According to the pharmaceutical affairs law, the Japanese definition of a cosmetic is as follows:

The term cosmetic means any article intended to be used by means of rubbing, sprinkling or by similar application to the human body for cleansing, beautifying, promoting attractiveness and altering appearance of the human body, and for keeping the skin and hair healthy, provided that the action of the article on the human body is mild.

The Japanese definition is only slightly different from the definition of a cosmetic within Europe. Both definitions allow a cosmetic to have mild activity and possess pharmaceutical activity. This is in sharp contrast to the definition of a cosmetic in the United States. The introduction of the term "cosmeceutical" enables to classify more precisely a product with an activity that is intended to treat or prevent a (mild) skin (abnormality). In order to avoid introducing new definition criteria, cosmeceuticals are only regarded as a subclass within the domain of a cosmetic or drug. In Europe and Japan, cosmeceuticals can be regarded as a subclass of cosmetics; however, in the United States cosmeceuticals can only be regarded as a subclass of drugs. Cosmeceuticals could be characterized as follows:

1. The product has pharmaceutical activity and can be used on normal or near-normal skin.
2. The product should have a defined benefit for minor skin disorders (cosmetic indication).
3. As the skin disorder is mild the product should have a very low-risk profile (see Table 1.1).

Table 1.1 Cosmeceuticals as a Subclass of Cosmetics (Europe and Japan) and as a Subclass of Drugs (U.S.).

	Cosmetic	Cosmeceutical	Drug
Pharmaceutical activity	+	+	+
Intended effect in skin disease	–	+	+
Intended effect in mild skin disorder	–	+	+
Side effects	–	±	+

The procedure for registration of a cosmeceutical should not be as cumbersome as for drugs. The intended activity of the cosmeceutical for treatment of a minor skin disorder should be demonstrated by clinical studies within the framework of good clinical practice. Moreover, it should be shown that safety requirements are optimal and that no side effects can be expected.[8] The safety evaluation is mandatory for cosmetics in Europe, according to articles 2, 12, and 13. In the United States, this would mean that a subclass of drugs (cosmeceuticals) are registered in a similar manner as over-the-counter products.[9] It would be beneficial if these countries could agree on the definitions of cosmetics and drugs and, in so doing, define cosmeceuticals as a subclass of cosmetics. This would prevent the current situation in which certain products are registered as drugs in the United States (sunscreens) and as cosmetics or cosmeceuticals in Europe and Japan. Clearly cosmeceuticals are the fastest growing segment of the skin care market and are currently the driving force in the field of skin care research.

Table 1.2 Summary of cosmetic regulations- USA, EU and INDIA[10].

CONTENTS	USA	EU	INDIA
Authority	FDA	EMEA	CDSCO
Rules and regulations	Food Drug and Cosmetic Act	Council Directive 76/768/EEC	Drugs and Cosmetic Act
Pre-market approval	Not required	Not required by Cosmetic Directive	Required under state govt. licensing
Labelling	Should comply with the FD&C and FP&L	Based on Council Directive 76/768/EEC	Should comply with part XV of the D&C rules 1945
Expiry date	No date required	Date of minimum durability if durability is <30 months. Period after opening if durability is >30 months	Indicated as 'use before date'
Post marketing reporting system	Yes (voluntary cosmetic registration programme)	N/A	N/A

Table 1.3 Regulations specifically prohibit or restrict the use of the following ingredients in cosmetics[11].

Ingredient	Activity
Bithionol	Because it may cause photo-contact sensitization.
Halogenated salicylanilides (di-, tri-, metabromsalan, and tetrachlorosalicylanilide)	Because they may cause photocontact sensitization.
Chloroform	Because of its animal carcinogenicity and likely hazard to human health.
Vinyl chloride	As an ingredient of aerosol products, because of its carcinogenicity
Zirconium-containing complexes	In aerosol cosmetic products, because of their toxic effect on lungs, including the formation of granulomas.
Methylene chloride	Because of its animal carcinogenicity and likely hazard to human health.
Chlorofluorocarbon propellants	The use of chlorofluorocarbon propellants (fully halogenated chlorofluoroalkanes) in cosmetic aerosol products intended for domestic consumption is prohibited.

1.3 Types of Cosmeceuticals

Based on their function cosmeceuticals are classified as follows-

- Skin-whitening and/or depigmenting cosmeceuticals
- Moisturizing cosmeceuticals
- Antiwrinkle cosmeceuticals
- Sunscreen cosmeceuticals
- Antiphotoaging cosmeceuticals

Based on various products presently on the market, cosmeceuticals can be divided into the following broad categories:

- Antioxidants
- Growth factors
- Peptides
- Metals
- Anti-inflammatories/botanicals,
- Polysaccharides
- Pigmentlightening agents.

1.3.1 Antioxidants[12]

Oxidative stressors create inflammatory molecules that lead to the formation of free radicals species. These free radicals are highly reactive molecules with unpaired electrons, and they can cause cellular damage to cell membranes, lipids, proteins, and DNA. Damage to DNA eventually results in collagen breakdown. Free radicals also play a role in 3 additional detrimental processes: inflammation, photodamage, and carcinogenesis. Antioxidants neutralize damaging free radicals by quenching reactive molecules and, thus, protecting cells from both endogenous stress (by-products of cellular energy) and exogenous stressors (ultraviolet light, pollution, cigarette smoke).

Antioxidants comprised a group of diverse molecules including, but not limited to, vitamins (A, B, C, and E), alpha lipoic acid (ALA), Coenzyme Q-10 (CoQ-10), idebenone, polyphenols, and kinetin. They vary in their abilities to protect against inflammation, photodamage, and carcinogenesis.

1.3.1.1 Vitamin A

Forms

Several forms of vitamin A are used cosmetically, in particular retinol, retinyl esters (e.g., the acetate, propionate, and palmitate esters of retinol), and retinaldehyde. Through endogenous enzymatic reactions, these are all ultimately converted to trans-retinoic acid, which is the functional form of vitamin A in skin.

Mechanisms

Interaction of trans-retinoic acid with nuclear receptor proteins leads to interaction with specific DNA sequences to affect transcription, resulting in either increased or decreased expression of specific proteins/enzymes. Among the many gene expression changes induced by retinoids, some specific ones that are likely relevant to skin antiaging effects are those leading to thicker skin, which likely contributes to diminish fine lines and wrinkle appearance, for example, increased epidermal proliferation and differentiation (epidermal thickness increase), increased production of epidermal ground substance (glycosaminoglycans [GAG] that bind water, thus increasing epidermal hydration and thickness), and increased production of extracellular dermal matrix components such as collagen (dermal thickness increase). In addition to stimulatory effects, retinoids also have inhibitory effects. For example, retinoids are reported to reduce production of collagenase and inhibit production of excess ground substance in photoaged dermis, an important mechanism because reduction in excess GAG is associated with reduced skin wrinkling. Retinoids also reduce expression of tyrosinase, a key enzyme in the conversion of tyrosine to melanin. Because the epidermal effects of a topical retinoid such as trans-retinoic acid (e.g., epidermal thickening) occur within days after initiation of treatment, skin effects such fine line reduction can begin to appear quickly. In general, retinoids are very potent, so topical doses of less than 1% are typically sufficient to obtain significant effects.

Working with retinoids presents two substantial challenges. The first is their tendency to induce skin irritation. Choice of retinoid can reduce this issue. Retinol is better tolerated by skin than trans-retinoic acid, 2-retinaldehyde has irritation potential similar to retinol and retinol esters are better tolerated than retinol. The second key concern is instability, especially in the presence of oxygen and light. To increase retinoid stability in finished product, formulation and packaging should ideally be done in an environment with minimal exposure to oxygen and light.

1.3.1.2 Vitamin B3

Forms

The primary forms of vitamin B3 that have been used in skin care products are niacinamide (nicotinamide), nicotinic acid, and nicotinate esters, such as tocopheryl nicotinate, myristoyl nicotinate, and benzyl nicotinate.

Mechanisms

Vitamin B3 is an essential vitamin. It is a precursor to a family of endogenous enzyme cofactors, specifically nicotinamide adenine dinucleotide (NAD), its phosphorylated derivative NAD(P), and their reduced forms NAD(H) and NAD(PH), which have antioxidant properties. These cofactors participate in many enzymatic reactions in the skin and thus can potentially influence many skin processes. The diversity of processes in which these cofactors participate may be the mechanistic basis for the diversity of cosmetic effects observed from the topical use of a precursor such as niacinamide. Fairly high doses (2% to 5%) of vitamin B3 have been used to achieve these desired effects like improved skin color, skin barrier improvement, reducing skin sensitivity and responsiveness to environmental insult, such as from surfactant exposure.

The key challenge for working with niacinamide and nicotinate esters is avoiding hydrolysis to nicotinic acid. Nicotinic acid, even at low doses, can induce an intense skin reddening (flushing response). Formulating in the pH range of 4 to 7 is preferred to avoid hydrolysis. Most of the esters, unfortunately, induce a skin flushing response, some within seconds or minutes of topical application even at very low concentrations of less than 1%. Some of the esters, such as tocopheryl nicotinate and myristoyl nicotinate, apparently are less prone to cause this flush response and thus appear to be more suitable for aesthetic use topically.

1.3.1.3 Panthenol

Form

Panthenol, or provitamin B5, is also known as pantothenol and pantothenyl alcohol. The D optical isomer of panthenol is termed dexpanthenol. It is a precursor to pantothenic acid (vitamin B5).

Mechanisms

Because panthenol is a precursor to pantothenic acid, its skin effects may derive from this precursor role. Pantothenic acid is a component of coenzyme A, which is critical in cellular metabolism, including in acyl group transfer during fatty acid biosynthesis and gluconeogenesis. By increasing synthesis of stratum corneum lipids, improved barrier could result. Panthenol also promotes fibroblast proliferation and epidermal reepithelialization in vitro, effects that might promote wound healing. Because panthenol is water soluble and hydroscopic, it has skin moisturization potential, especially when combined with the widely used moisturizing agent glycerol.

High temperatures must be avoided when formulating with D-panthenol, which is the active form of the material, to avoid conversion to DL-panthenol. The only other challenge in working with this water-soluble material can be product stickiness if high levels are used.

1.3.1.4 Vitamin C

Forms

There are many forms of this vitamin. Some commonly used ones are ascorbic acid, ascorbyl phosphate (magnesium or sodium salt), ascorbyl palmitate, and ascorbyl glucoside.

Mechanisms

Vitamin C has been used as a skin lightener because of its antioxidant activity and tyrosinase inhibition effect. It has also been described as an anti-inflammatory agent because it reduces the erythema associated with postoperative laser resurfacing. In addition, ascorbic acid serves as an essential cofactor for the enzymes lysyl hydroxylase and prolyl hydroxylase, both of which are required for posttranslational processing in collagen (types I and III) biosynthesis. Thus, by stimulating these biosynthetic steps, ascorbic acid has potential to increase collagen production for wrinkle appearance reduction. Ascorbate compounds have been reported to have skin anti-aging effects in the topical doses range from 3% to 17%.

The primary challenge with vitamin C and derivatives is stability (oxygen sensitivity), particularly with ascorbic acid, where loss of nearly half of the ascorbic acid in a month can occur. This is accompanied by rapid product yellowing, which is likely an aesthetic negative for the consumer. Various stabilization strategies can be attempted to address the issue, such as exclusion of oxygen during formulation, oxygen-impermeable packaging, encapsulation, low pH, minimization of water, and inclusion of other antioxidants. Despite these strategies, ascorbate stability remains a challenge, and some of these approaches, such as very low pH, can lead to unwanted aesthetic skin effects. One family of ascorbic acid derivatives is the ascorbyl phosphate salts (Mg and Na). The stability of these salts is substantially better than for ascorbic acid. Another challenge is skin delivery. Penetration of ascorbic acid across skin is generally poor, and typically less than 1% of the topical dose enters the skin. For the phosphate derivatives of ascorbate, skin penetration can be an even greater challenge due to the negative charges on the phosphate moiety. Thus, the use of approaches to enhance skin penetration is desired.

1.3.1.5 Vitamin E

Forms

In addition to the more commonly used forms of vitamin E, in particular tocopherol and tocopheryl acetate, several other esters, for example, succinate, nicotinate, linoleate, and phosphate, are used in the cosmetic arena. Natural tocopherol also has several isomers (alpha, beta, gamma, and delta) that differ in some of the side chains and have somewhat different potency. The more cost-effective among these is synthetic alpha-tocopherol.

Mechanisms

Vitamin E is an oil-soluble antioxidant. Because oxygen radicals are involved as a factor in many skin problems, both acute and chronic, vitamin E has the potential to prevent and improve skin problems caused by these radicals, in particular, those caused by UV exposure such as sunburn, skin photoaging (wrinkling), and hyperpigmentation. Topical vitamin E is effective in presenting UV-induced skin redness. Vitamin E, at relatively high doses, provides significant effects.

Because tocopherol and tocopheryl acetate are oil soluble, using high levels can present some challenge in developing an aesthetically elegant (nongreasy) formulation. There is some oxidative stability concern with tocopherol; thus, tocopheryl acetate is often used to avoid this issue. Tocopheryl acetate appears to be less effective, however, due to apparently slow hydrolysis to the functional free tocopherol.

1.3.1.6 Alpha lipoic acid

Alpha lipoic acid (ALA) is a lipoamide synthesized in the mitochondria of plants and animals. It is a scavenger of reactive oxygen species and a metal chelator. ALA regenerates endogenous antioxidants such as vitamins C and E, glutathione and ubiquinol. ALA is both water and lipid soluble, allowing it to penetrate lipophilic cell membranes and enter the aqueous intracellular matrix. The molecule prevents lipid peroxidation, has anti-inflammatory properties, and acts as an exfoliant. ALA does not protect against UV-induced erythema or reduce the number of sunburn cells.

1.3.1.7 Ubiquinone

CoQ-10, or ubiquinone, is a fat-soluble antioxidant located in the inner mitochondrial membrane of nearly all living cells that is necessary for steps in adenosine triphosphate (ATP) production for cellular energy. It acts by downregulating MMPs. CoQ-10 also inhibits lipid peroxidation in plasma cell membranes. There is good in vitro evidence that CoQ-10 can decrease periorbital wrinkles. Idebenone is a more potent synthetic analog of CoQ-10 that is a powerful antioxidant. Idebenone shows highest anti-inflammatory properties, photoprotective effects, and prevention of UV immunosuppression. It may repair mitochondrial DNA and decrease nuclear thymine dimer photoproducts. Like other antioxidants, idebenone downregulates MMP expression. Overall, it may improve roughness, dryness and fine lines, and increase hydration.

1.3.1.8 Polyphenols

Polyphenols are plant-derived antioxidants that have anti-inflammatory, photoprotective, and anticarcinogenic properties. Flavonoids are a subgroup of polyphenols that are popular ingredients in many cosmeceuticals. They include grape seed extract, green tea extracts, and soy isoflavones. Grape seed extract can induce vascular endothelial growth factor expression on keratinocytes to enhance dermal wound healing. Green tea extracts such as epigallocatechin 3-allate have been shown to decrease levels of UVB damage, DNA damage, sunburn, and erythema.

1.3.2 Growth Factors

Growth factors comprise a large group of regulatory proteins that attach to cell surface receptors to mediate inter- and intracellular signaling pathways. Wound healing relies on a complex interaction of various cytokines and growth factors.

Growth factors relevant to wound healing may induce new collagen, elastin, and glycosaminoglycan formation and mediate angiogenesis.

One human growth factor presently used in cosmeceuticals is transforming growth factor-1, which is derived from cultured fibroblasts harvested from neonatal foreskin. Advances in biotechnology have lead to further products such as processed skin cell proteins (PSPTM) harvested from fetal cell lines. Other growth factors include placental extract, recombinant epidermal growth factor, and platelet- derived growth factor.

1.3.3 Peptides

Forms

With variations in amino acid sequence, number of amino acids, and use of derivatives of these acids, the array of possible peptides is limitless. A few peptides with known sequences have been of particular interest to the cosmetic industry, such as palmitoyl-lysine-threoninethreonine- lysine-serine (pal-KTTKS; Matrixyl), acetyl-glutamate-glutamate-methionine-glutamine-arginine-arginine (Ac-EEMQRR; Argireline), and the tripeptide copper glycine-histidine-lysine (Cu-GHK).

Mechanisms

The peptide pal-KTTKS is a fragment of human dermal collagen that stimulates new collagen production and has been proposed for wound healing. The synthetic pal-KTTKS is also functional in stimulating collagen production in vitro. In addition, at extremely low levels (parts per billion) in culture, pal-KTTKS reduces excess dermal GAGs which contribute to an antiwrinkle appearance effect. Like KTTKS, GHK is also a fragment of dermal collagen. Copper is a required factor for activity of lysyl oxidase, an enzyme involved in collagen synthesis. Ac-EEMQRR is described as a mimic of botulinum neurotoxin (Botox), which functions by inhibiting neurotransmitter release, thus "relaxing" the muscles involved in defining facial wrinkles.

An important challenge is delivery into skin because peptides are poorly penetrating, especially as the number of amino acid residues increases. An approach to that problem is the addition of a lipophilic chain (e.g., palmitate), which can increase skin penetration several fold over the underivatized peptide. An additional challenge is the cost. As the number of amino acid residues increases, the cost of the peptide can increase dramatically. The consequences are that only low levels of a peptide can be used in the product, which is acceptable if the peptide is potent or the finished product cost to the consumer must be high.

Sugar amines

Forms

Many materials fall within the broad category of sugar amines, with some widely known ones being the hexose amines glucosamine and N-acetyl glucosamine (NAG).

Mechanisms

Glucosamine and NAG are precursors to the biopolymer hyaluronic acid, which is an important water-binding structural component of skin in the epidermis and the dermis. Topical use of the hexose compounds thus can improve skin moisturization and also fine lines/wrinkle appearance by building skin structural matrix. NAG has been discussed as an exfoliant, interfering with the cross-linking between corneocytes. Glucosamine has inhibited protein glycosylation in vitro, inhibiting activation of protyrosinase to the active enzyme tyrosinase and thus inhibiting the production of melanin. These materials also have anti-inflammatory properties.

For glucosamine, the challenge is stability. It readily undergoes a Maillard reaction leading to a brown polymeric product. This can be managed to some extent by use of antioxidants and acidic pH. NAG is substantially more stable and thus lacks this challenge. Both materials at high doses (e.g., above 2%) can be sticky in formulation, which can impart aesthetic negatives.

Ceramides

Forms

There are many ceramides and ceramide analogs. This contribution will not focus on any particular material but rather discuss them as a group.

Mechanisms

Ceramides are lipids essential for a normal stratum corneum water barrier. The other key lipid components of the barrier are cholesterol and fatty acids. All three are required and occur in an approximately equimolar mixture in the intercellular space in stratum corneum, but ceramides have received more attention. Externally supplied ceramides function by incorporating into the intercellular lipid of stratum corneum to replace the depletion that occurs with aging and environmental damage such as from surfactant exposure. The most effective therapy is described as a mixture of ceramides with the other two barrier lipid components.

Ceramides are oil-soluble. As long as the dose of ceramide is not high, it should incorporate into the oil phase of a formulation without difficulty. Ceramides can be expensive though, such that use of high concentrations is a cost challenge.

1.3.4 Metals

Forms

Of the many metals, cosmetic products typically contain only a few, among them zinc, copper, selenium, strontium, magnesium, and manganese, as salts and complexes with organic compounds. A few examples are zinc oxide, copper peptide, and selenomethionine.

Mechanisms

Metals have specific functions in the skin, often associated with their role as required cofactors in the activity of metalloenzymes, and therefore, the mechanisms associated with individual metals are widely varied. Certain metalorganic compound complexes such as pyrithione-zinc and selenium sulfide are antifungal agents that are effective as antidandruff agents.

Zinc is also associated with the antioxidant proteins superoxide dismutase and metallothionein, so zinc oxide has antioxidant potential as a source of zinc for synthesis of these proteins. Copper is a cofactor for many proteins, including lysyl oxidase and prolyl hydroxylase, enzymes that are important in collagen synthesis. Selenium is a cofactor for the antioxidant enzymes glutathione peroxidase and thioredoxin reductase.

Some metals and their complexes are colored (e.g., copper is blue-green), so that can be an aesthetic challenge at higher doses. Metal salts also can negatively affect product thickeners, requiring substantial adjustment of the formulation. The presence of zinc, for example, can complex with materials such as avobenzone, a common UVA sunscreen, resulting in the avobenzone crystallizing out of solution, causing a yellowing of the product, and significantly decreasing the sunscreen's efficacy.

1.3.5 Anti-inflammatories/Botanicals

Numerous cosmeceuticals have been researched to treat sensitive skin, skin affected by rosacea, and photodamage to reduce the redness associated with inflammation. Licochalcone A, from the licorice plant *Glycyrrhiza inflata,* has anti-inflammatory properties. The mechanism of action is thought to be dual inhibition of cyclo-oxygenase and lipoxygenase, thereby reducing proinflammatory cytokines and UVB-induced prostaglandin E2 release by keratinocytes. In this book we are going to discuss about botanicals in individual chapter according to the topic.

1.3.6 Polysaccharides

Polysaccharides include the family of hydroxy acids: alpha hydroxy acids (AHA), beta hydroxyl acids (BHA), and polyhydroxy acids (PHA). The AHAs include glycolic acid (grapes), lactic acid (milk), malic acid (apples), and citric acid (citrus fruits) among others. They are considered to be keratolytics because they diminish corneocyte adhesion in the lower levels of the stratum corneum, allowing exfoliation and improvement in skin dullness. They also function as humectants, possibly by increasing dermal glycosaminoglycans, as well as improve stratum corneum barrier function. The exact mechanism of action of AHAs is not known. BHAs, such as beta-lipohydroxyacid and tropic acid, are exfoliants appropriate for acne prone and oily skin. Salicylic acid was once thought to be a BHA, but it is structurally a phenolic aromatic acid. Its lipophilic structure allows it to penetrate into the sebaceous follicles, thus making it useful for patients with oily skin. Salicylic acid is available in a wide range of concentrations. PHAs can hydrate, moisturize, as well as exfoliate the skin. They include gluconolactone, which may protect against UV radiation in vitro and lactobionic acid, which is both an antioxidant and a humectant. Because of their large size, PHAs do not penetrate the skin as easily and are therefore less irritating to sensitive skin.

1.3.7 Pigment Lightening

The popularity of pigment-lightening cosmeceuticals is because of their effect on out skin tone. The most commonly used pigmentlightening agent is hydroquinone, which works by inhibiting tyrosinase activity. Tyrosinase is the rate-limiting, essential enzyme in the biosynthesis of melanin. It is available both in over-the-counter and in prescription strengths, and it is often combined with other agents such as retinol, AHAs, vitamin C, and topical steroids. Side effects include an irritant contact dermatitis and, more rarely, exogenous ochronosis. Kojic acid is a fungal derivative commonly used in Japan that has been shown to decrease melanin content via tyrosinase inhibition in vitro. It also decreases melanin content in melanocytes and is an antioxidant. One disadvantage is that it can be irritating and is known to cause true hypersensitivity. Like hydroquinone, it is often combined with other cosmeceutical agents or with topical steroids to reduce irritation. Glabridin is the main active ingredient in licorice extract and can inhibit tyrosinase activity. In addition, glabridin has anti- inflammatory properties attributed to cyclooxygenase inhibition. Ellagic acid is a polyphenol widely found in plants such as pomegranates, which inhibits tyrosinase by chelating copper at the active center of this enzyme. It may selectively inhibit melanin synthesis only in UV-activated melanocytes. Fatty acids such as linoleic acid act by tyrosinase degradation without toxic effects on melanocytes.

1.4 Marketed size

According to the study conducted by Indian Cosmetic Sector Analysis the cosmetic market is around INR 356 billions. Most of the international companies have introduced their products in India in 1990s. The total Indian beauty and cosmetic market size currently stands at INR 422.3 Billion in 2010 and showing growth between 15–20% per annum, in the US it is about $6.5 billions. Skin care products occupy half of the cosmeceuticals industry through out the world. Among the skin care products anti-aging market plays major role driven by an aging population seeking to maintain the appearance of youth. Antioxidants will remain the largest chemical category while botanicals and enzymes stay among the best opportunities. Injectables and skin care products will register the fastest growth.

According to Confederation of Indian Industries (CII) report, US$0.68 per capita is spent for cosmetics, which might be lower than some other countries, but this indicates a growing awareness among consumers. There are two major factors that are saying the buying decision among women here. First obviously is the television and media exposure they have today. The other not so obvious one is the corporate dressing culture, which slowly is evolving in the Indian market.

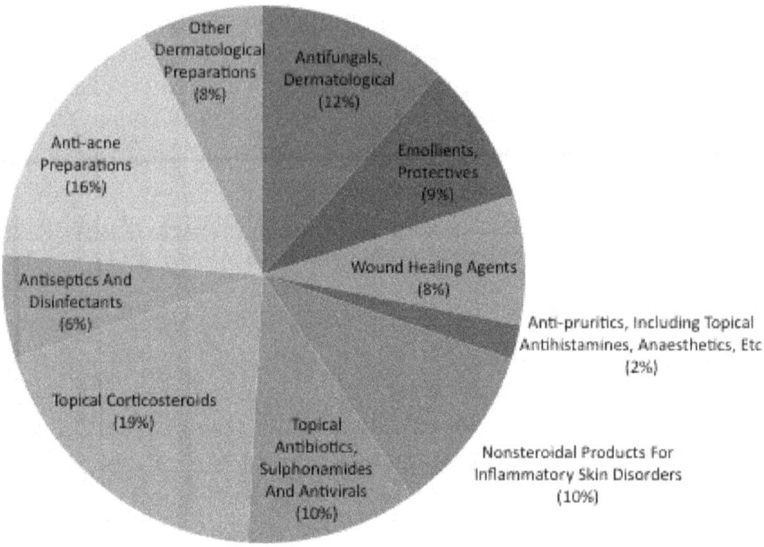

Fig. 1.1 Global Therapeutic Dermatology Marketsplit by Product Class.

[Colour Fig. on page 393]

1.5 Conclusion

The cosmetics industry today holds a unique position. It is characterized by highly competitive marketing strategies and depends on the ability to introduce rapidly new innovative products into the market place. On the other hand, dermatological research may also proceed in the cosmetic field while in-depth research may be conducted with regard to therapeutic applications. Cosmetic companies are permitted to create and market products that are known to have an effect on the structure and function of skin, with little regulation. Most consumers believe that cosmeceuticals are regulated and tested as drugs. Consumers trust that ingredients have been tested for safety and that claims made in advertisements are real.

One can easily conclude that cosmeceuticals will continue to evolve in parallel with advances in our understanding of skin biology, along with improved methods of measuring the benefits that may be provided by well-engineered skin care products. But we have to consider the changes in the science and technology, so clinicians, scientists and dermatologists have to update their knowledge in this field to produce high quality products with safety.

References

1. Fredric S. Brandt, M.D., Alex Cazzaniga, Michael Hann, Cosmeceuticals: Current Trends and Market Analysis. *Semin Cutan Med Surg*, 2011; **30**:141-143.
2. Christine M. Choi, M.D., Diane S, Berson, MD. Cosmeceuticals: Current Trends and Market Analysis. *Semin Cutan Med Surg*, 2006; **25**: 163-168.
3. Peter Elsner, Howard I. Maibach Cosmeceuticals-Drugs vs Cosmetics, Marcel Dekker, Inc. New York. 2000; **23**:1-11.
4. Noonan F.P., De Fabo EC. Immunosuppression by ultraviolet B radiation, initiation by urocanic acid. *Immunol Today* 1992; **7**:250–254.
5. Mertz P.M., Davis S.C., Ovington L.G. Cosmeceuticals: predicting their influence on compromised skin. *Cosmet Toilet* 1992; **107**:43–44.
6. Vermeer B.J., Gilchrest B.A. Cosmeceuticals: A proposal for rational definition, evaluation and regulation. *Arch Dermatol* 1996; **132**:337–340.
7. Editorial supervision by Pharmaceuticals and Cosmetics Division, Pharmaceutical Affairs Bureau, Ministry of Health and Welfare. *Guide to Quasi-Drug and Cosmetic Regulations in Japan*. Tokyo: Yakuji Nippo, 1992.
8. Stern R.S. Drug promotion for an unlabeled indication: the case of topical tretinoin. *N Engl J Med* 1994; **331**:1348–1349.
9. De Salva S.J. Safety evaluation of over-the-counter products. *Regul Toxicol Pharmacol* 1985; **5**:101–108.

10. Srikanth.T., Syed sajjad Hussen, Anand Abha, Vasantharaju SG, Sandeep G. A comparative view on cosmetic regulations: USA, EU and INDIA. *Der Pharmacia Lettre* 2011; **3(1)**: 334-341.

11. Larry E. Millikan, M.D. Cosmetology, Cosmetics, Cosmeceuticals: Definitions and Regulations. *Clinics in Dermatology* 2001; **19**:371–374.

12. Donald L. Bissett. Common cosmeceuticals. *Clinics in Dermatology* 2009; **27**: 435–445.

CHAPTER 2

ACNE AND ITS TREATMENT OPTIONS

Y. Madhusudan Rao, Shayeda, D. Sathish, S. Himabindu

Center for Biopharmaceutics and Pharmacokinetics, University College of Pharmaceutical Sciences, Kakatiya University, Warangal-506 009, Andhra Pradesh, India.

2.1 Introduction

Acne is one of the most common skin disorders seen in dermatology practice and affects an estimated 85% of adolescents and young adults.[1] Although it is most common in patients aged 12 to 24 years, it also affects other age groups, with a prevalence of 8% in adults aged 25 to 34 years and of 3% in those aged 35 to 44 years.

Before entering into the chapter we are proudly saying that we got a patent on antiacne cream and it is launched successfully in market with trade name Teracne from the Leads Pharma Pvt. Ltd. company. Our review on Acne and its treatment options was published in current drug delivery (Bentham Science Publishers, USA).

2.1.1 Pathogenesis of Acne

There are four primary pathogenic factors, which interact in complex manner to produce acne lesions:

1. Sebum production by the sebaceous gland;
2. *Propionibacterium acnes* (*P. acnes*) follicular colonization;
3. Alteration in the keratinization process; and
4. Release of inflammatory mediators into the skin.

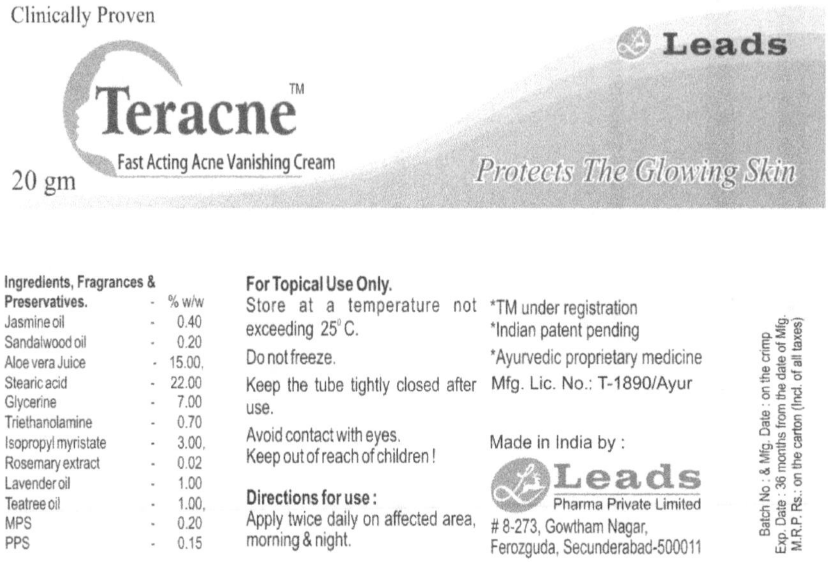

2.1.1.1 Sebum production by the sebaceous gland

Sebum production is more in patients with acne. Sebum is composed of fats or a variety of different lipids, including cholesterol, glycerides, fatty acids, squalene and wax and cholesterol esters, but the exact composition of sebum varies with a person's age. Among these, triglycerides play major role in the pathogenesis of acne. *P. acnes* convert triglycerides into free fatty acids which encourages colonization of *P. acnes* and forms the microcomedone. Thus the sebaceous gland is a neuroendocrine inflammatory organ that likely coordinates and executes a local response to stress and normal functions. Androgens play an essential role in acne pathogenesis. As most of the patients with acne have normal circulating androgen levels, acne severity does not correlate with serum androgen levels. It is postulated that androgens may play only a permissive role in priming or initiating acne development, or it may be the local overproduction of androgens in the skin and/or the high expression and responsiveness of androgen receptors that determines the formation of acne lesions.

The main influence of androgen on acne pathogenesis concerns the proliferation/differentiation of sebocytes and infrainfundibular keratinocytes.[2]

2.1.1.2 *Propionibacterium acnes* (*P. acnes*) follicular colonization

Propionibacterium acnes is a normal inhabitant of skin that colonizes the pilosebaceous follicle. In persons prone to acne, the inflammatory response to *P. acnes* results in damage to the follicle and release of follicular contents into the surrounding tissue, where they induce further inflammatory reaction, resulting in erythematous papules, pustules, and nodules.

Various antimicrobial peptides are expressed in healthy skin without any visible signs of inflammation, suggesting that antimicrobial peptides may be induced in the absence of proinflammatory cytokines/chemokines and resident skin microbiota may facilitate antimicrobial peptide induction without inflammation. It was recently proposed that the beneficial effects of resident microbiota may come from their ability to induce antimicrobial peptide expression. The identification of *P. acnes* proteins, inducing solely antimicrobial peptide and not proinflammatory cytokine/chemokine expression, would promote stimulation of maintenance levels of antimicrobial peptides. Consequently, increased resistance to abnormal *P. acnes* colonization could be facilitated.[2]

2.1.1.3 Alteration in the keratinization process

One of the crucial events in the development of acne lesions is hyperkeratinization in the follicular infundibulum and sebaceous duct resulting in microcomedones. The pathogenesis of follicular hyperkeratinization is still unclear. IL-1a has been reported to induce hyperkeratinization in follicular infundibulum *in vitro* and *in vivo*. In addition, abnormal infundibular keratinization has been associated with a disorder in terminal differentiation of infundibular keratinocytes, which is related to increased filaggrin (filament aggregating protein) expression. In case of the hormonal response, increased DHT may act on infundibular keratinocytes leading to abnormal hyperkeratinization. Follicular keratinization may be triggered by relative deficiency of linoleic acid and peroxides in sebum. Recently, *P. acnes* extracts have been implicated in the formation of the microcomedo. However, the pathogenesis of closed and open comedo formation remains ambiguous.[2]

2.1.1.4 Release of inflammatory mediators into the skin

Acne vulgaris is accepted as an inflammatory disease occurring as an immune reaction to the *P. acne* bacteria. When bacteria proliferates in the hair follicle, follicular hyperkeratinization results and leads to the formation of *Propionibacterium acnes*. In this event, the production of pro-inflammatory cytokines and tumor necrosis factor [alpha] by the T cells and keratinocytes increases. It leads to an even greater increase of bacteria and creates small lumps (microcomedones) on the skin composed of dead skin cells and oil. Microcomedones worsen and aggravate inflammation, leading to severe acne formation.

2.2 Clinical Classification of Acne

Grade 1 (Mild)	:	Comedones, occasional papules. (Comedones or black heads are wormlike masses of hardened sebum).
Grade 2 (Moderate)	:	Comedones, papules, few pustules.
Grade 3 (Severe)	:	Pustules, nodules, abscess.
Grade 4 (Cystic)	:	Cyst formation

2.2.1 The Degrees of Acne[3]

- White heads (closed comedones): Little closed bumps in the skin due to blocked pores that have not opened into the skin surface **(Fig. 2.1).**
- Black heads (open comedones): Visible, blocked pores **(Fig. 2.2).**
- Zits: Pus- filled spots (Pustules).
- Red pimples or lumps under the skin (papules), containing inflamed tissue.
- Hard lumps: Under the skin that can be very painful, go deep into the skin and often cause scars. **(Fig. 2.3).**
- Open sores or pimples with the tops scratched off.
- Marking (macules) and scarring.
- Non-inflammatory acne: This is seen as few black heads or white heads and a pimple now and then. Pimples usually do not scar unless squeezed or picked which may lead to infection. It can injure skin and underlying tissue.
- Inflammatory acne: In this white heads become inflamed pimples and pustules develop and there will be a constant outbreak covering the face and sometimes the neck, back, chest and groin. These pus filled pimples can cause disfiguring cysts deep pitting and scarring.

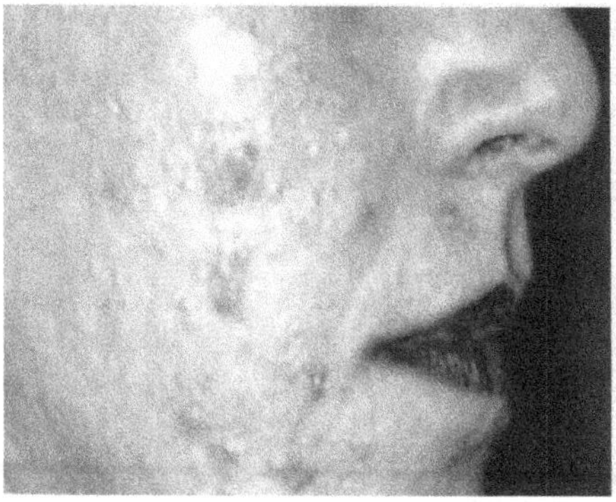

Fig. 2.1 Multiple closed comedones (white heads).[Colour Fig. on page 394]

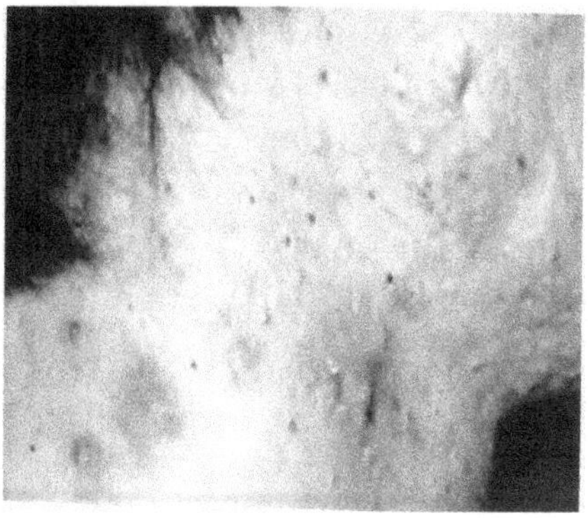

Fig. 2.2 Multiple open comedones (Black heads). [Colour Fig. on page 394]

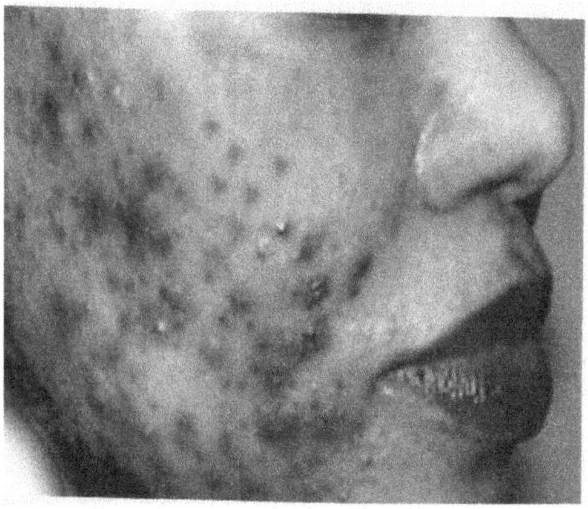

Fig. 2.3 Papular and cystic acne and the figure also shows post inflammator hyperpigmentation. [Colour Fig. on page 394]

2.2.2 What Makes Acne Worse

Usually acne is associated with the increase in the amount of hormones secreted during puberty. Hormones increase the oil secretion from skin and bacteria developing in the secreted oil can add to the redness and inflammation which makes acne get worse. Acne will not result from dirt, poor hygiene, diet, sexual activity, greasy foods or chocolate. Acne is aggrevated by soap and too much scrubbing or use of abrasive products and strong cleansers and picking or squeezing pimples and black heads (which can delay healing, spread infection deep into the skin and cause scars).

Exactly why some people get acne and some do not? is not fully understood. It is known to be partly hereditary. Several factors are known to be linked to acne such as

- Family/Genetic history: The tendency to develop acne runs in families.[4]
- Hormonal activity, such as menstrual cycles and puberty. During puberty, an increase in male sex hormones called androgens cause the glands to get larger and make more sebum.[5]
- Stress, through increased output of hormones from the adrenal (stress) glands.
- Hyperactive sebaceous glands, secondary to the three hormone sources above.
- Accumulation of dead skin cells.
- Bacteria in the pores. *Propionibacterium acnes* (*P. acnes*) is the anaerobic bacterium that causes acne.[6]
- Skin irritation or scratching of any sort will activate inflammation.
- Use of anabolic steroids.
- Any medication containing halogens (iodides, chlorides, bromides), lithium, barbiturates, or androgens.
- Exposure to certain chemical compounds. Chloracne is particularly linked to toxic exposure to dioxins, namely Chlorinated dioxins.
- Several hormones have been linked to acne: the androgens testosterone, dihydrotestosterone (DHT) and dehydroepiandrosterone sulfate (DHEAS), as well as insulin-like growth factor 1 (IGF-I).
- Acne-prone skin has been shown to be insulin resistant.
- True acne vulgaris in adults may be a feature of an underlying condition such as pregnancy and disorders such as polycystic ovary syndrome or the rare Cushing's syndrome.
- Menopause-associated acne occurs as production of the natural anti-acne ovarian hormone, estradiol fails at menopause. The lack of estradiol also causes thinning of hair, hot flashes, thin skin, wrinkles, vaginal dryness, and predisposes to osteopenia and osteoporosis as well as triggering acne (known as acne climacterica in this situation).

2.3 Acne Treatment

Acne treatment mostly aims to interrupt the acne cycle and prevent the formation of more acne. It includes reduction in sebum production, correcting the abnormal ductal keratinization, reducing the colony of *Propionibacterium acne* and prevent the release of inflammatory mediators that are basically responsible for the pathogenesis of acne.

Many treatments aim to prevent new outbreaks, they need to be applied to the whole area of affected skin, not just at affected area. Any type of treatment may take 6 to 8 weeks to show any benefit so it is usually worth before leaving one treatment and going for another one.[7]

2.3.1 Treatment Options

1. OTC (Over The Counter) Preparations or Topical Preparations
2. Prescription drugs or Systemic drugs

2.3.1.1 Commercial over the counter preparations

(a) Cleansing products, such as special soaps, lotions and scrubs.

(b) Astringents or toners to reduce surface oil on the skin.

(c) Antiseptic washes and wipes.

- Scrubbing brushes, pads or loofahs.
- Special tape to apply on the skin and liftout black heads.
- Cosmetics and special formula sunscreens and make-up.
- Gels, Creams and lotions to treat acne.

The ingredients which are allowed in the treatment of acne are

(a) Benzoyl peroxide (BPO) 2.5-10%

(b) Salicylic acid (SA) 0.5-2%.

(c) Sulphur 3-10% alone, or 3-8% in combination with resorcinol.

(d) Resorcinol 2% or resorcinol monoacetate 3% in combination with Sulphur 3-8%.

Table 2.1 Examples of Over-the-Counter Salicylic Acid Products.

Name of the medication	Commonly used brand names
Benzoyl Peroxide	Acne.org Treatment Neutrogena On-the-Spot Clearasil Oxy-10 Fostex Clear by Design Persa-Gel
Salicylic Acid	Stri-dex Clearasil Clearstick Oxy Night Watch
Sulphur	Clearasil Adult Care
Resorcinol	Clearasil Adult Care

2.4 Topical Treatment

Topical treatments aimed at preventing the formation of new comedones take several months to show maximal benefit.

The different groups of topical drugs available are

1. Comedolytics [8,9] : Tretinoin, isotretinoin, adapalene, azelaic acid, benzoyl peroxide, tazarotene.
2. Keratolytics : Salicylic acid, Sulphur and alfa-hydroxy acids.
3. Anti-inflammatory agent : Adapalene, nicotinamide, topical steroid.
4. Antimicrobials : Tetracycline, erythromycin, clindamycin, lincomycin, benzoyl peroxide and azelaic acid.
5. Antiandrogens : Cyproterone acetate and flutamide.
6. Combined preparations : Erythromycin with zinc, erythromycin with benzoyl peroxide, clindamycin with tretinoin etc.
7. Miscellaneous drugs : Herbal medicines and home remedies.

2.4.1 Comedolytics

Comedones or blackheads are wormlike masses of hardened sebum, appearing most frequently on the face, especially the forehead and nose. The Drugs which prevents the formation of comedones are called comedolytics. The commonly available topical retinoids are tretinoin, isotretinoin, adapalene and tazarotene. The efficacy of topical therapeutic agents is based on their direct or indirect influence on the pathogenetic factors of acne. The adequate topical agent should be selected in accordance to the predominant type of acne vulgaris lesions. In general, by combining different topical agents, efficacy of the therapy can be enhanced and toxicity can be reduced.

2.4.1.1 Topical retinoids

The retinoids are classically described as a group of compounds with similar chemical structures exerting similar biologic effects i.e., many synthetic retinoids have dissimilar structures but still have retinoid activity. Therefore, function, the ability to bind retinoid receptors and activate the retinoid pathway, truly dictates what a retinoid is. The naturally occurring retinoids all work along the vitamin A pathway. They are considered vitamins in that they are necessary in small amounts for the body to function properly.

The metabolites of vitamin A work as hormones. They bind to specific receptors, exert their effects, and are subsequently metabolized to inactive forms. There are 2 distinct types of retinoid receptors in the human body: RAR (retinoic acid receptors) and RXR (retinoid X receptors). RAR is composed of 3 isoforms, RARα, RARβ, and RARγ, each encoded by separate genes. These receptors are ligand-dependent transcriptional factors that belong to the steroid-thyroid hormone family. The concentration and activity of each type of retinoid receptor varies by tissue type throughout the body. RARγ is the most abundant type seen in cutaneous epithelium, whereas RARβ is not found in the skin. Different retinoid isomers also exhibit different binding affinities for these retinoid receptors. 9-cis-retinoic acid is a ligand for both RAR and RXR, whereas all trans-retinoic acid (tretinoin) has binding affinity only for RAR. 13-cis-retinoic acid (isotretinoin) does not bind retinoid receptors directly, making its mechanism of action still unclear. These possible combinations make the effects of retinoids vital and varied throughout the entire body.

There are four physiologic functions of retinoids in the body.

1. To ensure normal embryonic development, the importance of which is evidenced by the well described effects of an excessive retinoid state during pregnancy, isotretinoin-induced embryopathy.
2. Role of retinoids in the body is to normalize epithelial differentiation in varying tissue types, including the skin. This effect is used in the treatment of acne as well as the ichthyoses.
3. Retinoids maintain healthy vision through the production of rhodopsin, an 11-cis-retinaldehyde-containing eye pigment that enables night vision.
4. Retinoids are required for adequate immune function and lymphocyte survival.

There are three generations of retinoids based on their chemical structure.

I generation : It includes retinol, tretinoin, and isotretinoin and are available in the strengths of 0.025%, 0.05% and 0.1%.

II generation : These retinoids are etretinate and its metabolite acitretin.

III generation : These retinoids are synthetically produced tazarotene, adapalene and bexarotene and are available as 0.1% formulations.

Tretinoin

Tretinoin was the first retinoid used for the treatment of acne. The efficacy of the early preparations of tretinoin were somewhat limited by cutaneous irritation. However, newer formulations afford much greater tolerability than the early prototypes. Advances in drug-delivery systems have also yielded good results with less irritation. Tretinoin is the only topical retinoid available in generic formulations, often making it the drug of choice for patients with limited financial means or highly restrictive formularies.

Generic tretinoin is available in 0.025%, 0.05% and 0.1% cream, and a 0.01% and 0.025% alcohol based gel. Generic tretinoin 0.05% liquid is currently the only available topical retinoid in a liquid form. Retin-A Micro® was the first formulation with a modified vehicle developed to combat the inherent irritancy of tretinion. Inert microspheres embedded with tretinoin rest on the cutaneous surface and slowly release the retinoid. It is available in a 0.04% and 0.1% non alcohol gel formulation. It is also the only retinoid that comes in a pump dispenser.

Avita®, like Retin-A Micro®, takes advantage of new vehicle technology, making improvements on the original tretinoin formulations. In this product, the tretinoin is enmeshed within a polyoylprepolymer, creating a delayed, controlled release of the medication. Avita® is available as a 0.025% cream and gel. Atralin™ is a retinoid formulated to have less irritation. It is available as a 0.05% aqueous gel containing the moisturizers, soluble collagen and sodium hyaluronate, as well a humectant, glycerin. It should be noted that the collagen in Atralin™ contains soluble fish proteins and should not be used in any patients who have a known fish allergy.[10]

Table 2.2 Topical Retinoid Preparations

Drug	Trade
Tretinoin	Tretinoin 0.025% cream Avita® 0.025% gel Retin-A Micro® 0.1% gel Atralin™ 0.05% gel
Adapalene	Differin® 0.1% gel
Tazarotene	Tazorac® 0.1% cream
Tretinoin/clindamycin	Ziana™ 0.025%/1.2% gel

Adapalene

Adapalene, a naphthoic acid, is a synthetic retinoid that possesses some of the biologic activities of tretinoin, but with distinct physiochemical properties. The most distinctive of these properties is its increased chemical and light stability, rigidity, and high lipophilicity.

In vitro and *in vivo* studies have shown that adapalene affects the cellular differentiation, keratinization, and inflammatory processes that are abnormally present in acne vulgaris. Adapalene also possesses anti-inflammatory properties. Its unique chemical structure imparts a high melting point and low solubility, causing adapalene to have low flux through the skin and to attain high concentrations in the stratum corneum and hair follicle. These characteristics are potentially beneficial in the treatment of acne.[11]

Tazarotene

Tazarotene (Tazorac®) is another synthetically produced retinoid commonly used in the treatment of acne. It is quickly hydrolyzed to its active metabolite, tazarotenic acid and is able to bind all 3 RARα/β/γ. Although its affinity is for RAR β/γ, its primary effects include regulation of cell differentiation and down-regulation of proinflammatory mediators (IL-6, migration inhibition factor-related protein). Taking advantage of its antiproliferative properties through AP1 and the down-regulation of ornithine decarboxylase and keratins 6/16, tazarotene is also used topically in the treatment of psoriasis.

Azelaic acid (Skinoren)

Azelaic acid is a naturally occurring dicarboxylic acid with modest antibacterial and comedolytic effects. It may be tolerated when retinoids and benzoyl peroxide are not. It can cause hypopigmentation and this can be used to advantage in darker skins when post-inflammatory hyperpigmentation has become a cosmetic problem.

Benzoyl peroxide

This is the staple ingredient of many over-the-counter preparations and is available in strengths ranging from 2.5 to 10%. It has comedolytic activity and is good at treating inflammatory acne, both through direct antibacterial and anti-inflammatory mechanisms. It does often cause some dryness and irritation which may be minimized by building up the concentration to the limit of tolerance. It can also bleach clothes and hair. Despite this, it is a safe and proven therapy which is well tolerated by most.

Side effects

Retinoids work by increasing the rate of desquamation of the stratum corneum, patients often notice a fine peeling on the surface of the skin not associated with erythema. This side effect can be controlled by gentle exfoliation with a washcloth, followed by application of a bland moisturizer. The peeling is generally temporary or sporadic in nature and is usually self-limited. Another well-described side effect is a flare of acne within the first few weeks of starting a topical retinoid. This flare-up will resolve with continued use of the medicine. By informing patients of this possible flare at the onset of therapy, knowing that it will resolve with continued treatment, goes a long way to ensure continued compliance. Although retinoids are not true photosensitizers, some patients experience increased photosensitivity to the sun while on retinoids. Most topical retinoids carry a Food and Drug Administration pregnancy category of C, with the exception of tazarotene. Because tazarotene is also approved for psoriasis, a condition where the total body surface area affected can exceed 35%, the risk of fetal exposure is higher. Thus, it carries a pregnancy category rating of X.[10]

2.4.2 Keratolytics

Alpha-Hydroxy acids include glycolic acid, lactic acid, pyruvic acid, citric acid and glucuronic acid which are good keratolytics and decrease the thickness of the stratum corneum by reducing the cohesion between corneocytes. They are effective in treatment of acne as they reduce follicular hyperkeratosis. Salicylic acid and sulphur also come under this category.

Alpha hydroxy acids are an entire class of organic, water-soluble acids. The most common of the alpha hydroxy acids are glycolic acid and lactic acid. Alpha hydroxy acid at concentrations of 10% works by preventing cells from adhering to one another on the skin surface, which then causes the top layer of skin to peel and shed, revealing new and smoother skin underneath. But the side effects that its use for acne can generate make it less appealing than some other ingredients. There is only one beta hydroxy acid-salicylic acid. The main difference between alpha hydroxy acids and beta hydroxy acid is their lipid (oil) solubility. Alpha hydroxy acids are water soluble only, while beta hydroxy acid is lipid (oil) soluble. This means that beta hydroxy acid is able to penetrate into the pore which contains sebum and exfoliate the dead skin cells that are built up inside the pore. Because of this difference in properties, beta hydroxy acid is better used on oily skin with blackheads and whiteheads. Alpha hydroxy acids are better used on thickened, sun-damaged skin where breakouts are not a problem.

The following alpha hydroxy acids are used as house hold treatment in acne :

- Glycolic acid : derived from sugarcane
- Lactic acid: from fermented milk
- Citric acid: citrus fruits
- Maleic acid: from unripe apple
- Mandelic acid: bitter almonds
- Tartaric acid: from fermented grapes

2.4.3 Anti-inflammatory Agents

Topical steroids usage is limited in the treatment of acne in the sense that it induces acne form eruptions by itself. These should be used for short duration. Example: Clobetasol propionate (0.05%) applied twice daily can reduce inflammatory lesions in nodulocystic acne. Nicotinamide gel (topical) in 4% concentration has been used to reduce inflammation in grade II and grade III acne.

2.4.4 Antimicrobials

Erythromycin is active against Gram-positive and Gram-negative bacilli. It interferes with the formation of the polypeptide chain and inhibits protein synthesis in the organism. It also prevents the chemotaxis of neutrophil by preventing the formation of comedogenic free fatty acids and thereby exhibits anti-inflammatory properties. It is available as 2%, 3% and 4% creams, gels and lotions. It is also available in combination with benzoyl peroxide, which helps in slowing of development of bacterial resistance. It is also available in combination with zinc acetate (1.2%). It has a very low sensitization potential. Clindamycin is topically used as 1% gel, solution or lotion. It inhibits bacterial protein synthesis very similar to erythromycin. It has low sensitization potential.

2.4.5 Antiandrogens

Topical cyproterone acetate (2 mg/ml) applied once daily for three months is found to be effective in treating acne. Topical flutamide (2.5%) used continuously for a period of four months was found to be useful in inflammatory acne.

2.4.6 Combination Therapy

Drugs with different modes of action are combined to achieve better results. Usually an antibiotic is combined with either a comedolytic or an anti-inflammatory drug. Two topical drugs can also be used. Combinations of benzoyl peroxide and antibiotic, or retinoid and antibiotic may work marginally better and be nomore irritant than the agents used alone. This may be because the multifactorial pathophysiology of the underlying problem is addressed. There is also some evidence to suggest that using antibiotics in combination with non antibiotic agents puts less selective pressure behind the development of antibiotic-resistant strains of *P. acnes*.

2.5 Systemic Therapy

Systemic drugs for acne vulgaris are classified as

1.	Antibiotics	:	Tetracycline, erythromycin, co-trimoxazole.
2.	Hormones	:	Spironolactone, estrogens,
3.	Retinoic acid derivatives	:	Isotretinoin.
4.	Enzyme inhibitors	:	Zileuton
5.	Miscellaneous group	:	Dapsone, zinc sulphate, chlofazemine, vitamin A.

2.5.1 Antibiotics

Oral antibiotics are usually reserved for more severe acne, acne predominantly on the trunk, acne unresponsive to topical therapy, and in patients at greater risk of scarring. Although antibiotics have shown effectiveness in terms of reducing the number of inflammatory lesions, but none clear acne completely. There is no conclusive evidence that one antibiotic is more effective than another (including first and second generation tetracyclines) or that oral antibiotics are more effective than topical preparations for mild-to-moderate facial acne. There is no evidence that higher doses are more effective than lower doses or that controlled-release preparations are necessary. The choice of antibiotic should therefore be based on the patient's preference, the side effect profile and cost.

2.5.1.1 Tetracyclines

The tetracycline family of antibiotics is extremely useful in acne because they have multiple modes of action, functioning as antibiotics that reduce bacterial populations and as anti-inflammatory drugs that attack acne from a second front. These drugs exert their antibacterial properties by blocking the 30S ribosomal subunit and in turn inhibiting translation during protein synthesis. The tetracyclines also have many antiinflammatory effects. The generation of reactive oxygen species and the oxidative burst in neutrophils is decreased by the tetracyclines. Nitric oxide production is modulated and matrix metalloprotease and collagenase activity is inhibited. Nonantibiotic derivatives of doxycycline have been recently developed that are highly antiinflammatory and even antineoplastic through inhibition of angiogenesis and may be of use in acne and other inflammatory diseases. A general problem with the tetracyclines is the potential for photosensitivity which, unfortunately, is enhanced in the nonantibiotic derivatives. Tetracycline dose is 500 mg twice daily for acne, must be taken on an empty stomach (1 hour before eating or 2 hours after eating). Ingestion with food and especially dairy products can block the absorption of tetracycline in the gut. Tetracycline can frequently cause gastrointestinal upset and may very rarely cause esophagitis and pancreatitis. Caution should be advised when going out in the sun as tetracycline may cause sun sensitivity or even induce pseudoporphyria. Rarely, a painful photo-onycholysis may also be caused by tetracycline.

Doxycycline, a second-generation member of the tetracycline family, is often dosed at 100 mg twice daily to give optimal antibacterial effects. Unlike tetracycline, doxycycline may be taken with food. However, doxycycline has more potential to induce a phototoxic reaction than tetracycline and extreme care should be used when prescribing doxycycline in the summer months. Another second-generation tetracycline, minocycline, is also commonly dosed at 100 mg twice daily for acne, although 1 mg/kg has been shown to be an effective dosage for the average acne patient and one with fewer side effects. Like doxycycline, minocycline can be taken with food. Unlike the other tetracyclines, the minocycline chemical structure has a large side chain that increases its side effect profile. Because of the high lipophilicity of minocycline, it can cross the blood-brain barrier and may induce vestibular disturbances, such as dizziness, vertigo, and ataxia. A blue-gray discoloration of the skin may be seen with long-term minocycline use. This hyperpigmentation may be distributed in scars, on sun-exposed skin, or diffusely. Hyperpigmentation seems to be dose and duration related. Tetracycline has multiple disadvantages, including greatest effect of diet on absorption, lower anti-inflammatory and antibacterial activity, and lower effect on acne lesions.

2.5.1.2 Macrolides

Erythromycin, clindamycin, and azithromycin are 3 members of the macrolide family that are used for treating acne. All exert their antibacterial effect by irreversibly binding to the bacterial 50S ribosomal subunit, thus inhibiting translocation during protein synthesis. Oral erythromycin is administered at 500 mg twice daily. It should be taken with food because it commonly causes gastrointestinal distress. Although erythromycin is safe in pregnancy and in lactating women, erythromycin estolate should be avoided in these patients because it my cause cholestatic jaundice. As an inhibitor of the cytochrome P450 system, erythromycin may cause reduced clearance of theophylline, warfarin, carbamazepine, and cyclosporine. Although topical clindamycin is often used in the treatment of acne, the use of oral clindamycin is much more limited due to its side effect profile. A total of 20% to 30% of patients taking oral clindamycin will experience diarrhea. Oral clindamycin may also promote the overgrowth of *Clostridium difficile* in the gastrointestinal tract in turn causing pseudomembranous colitis.

Topical and oral erythromycin and topical clindamycin have been well-established acne treatments for decades but have become much less effective in the past 15 years or so as a result of the acquisition of resistance by *P. acnes*. Resistant bacteria are now induced quickly by macrolide therapy because most patients have a portion of their normal skin flora that is genetically resistant, and that subgroup expands under the selective pressure of therapy. Resistance can be combated by the addition of benzoyl peroxide to topical macrolide regimens. It has been clearly shown that such combination products are not only more effective than monotherapy with macrolides but also do not permit the survival of resistant populations of *P. acnes*.

Ciprofloxacin and trimethoprim-sulfamethoxazole are both sometimes useful in acne. Trimethoprim–sulfamethoxazole works by blocking dihydrofolatereductase/dihydropteroatesynthetase, thus impeding bacterial DNA purine and pyrimidine synthesis. Potential side effects include anemia, thrombocytopenia, and agranulocytosis. Because trimethoprim–sulfamethoxazole has a sulfa moiety, a hypersensitivity reaction may occur.

There have been numerous case reports of apparent contraceptive failure when administered along with antibiotics (rifampin). The basis for this concern is that antibiotics might change the bowel flora and alter the metabolism and absorption of contraceptives. In 2004, a report was published in the general medical literature that asserted that long-term antibiotic use roughly doubled the risk of breast cancer in women. The risk was similar for all antibiotics studied and did not differ based on the diagnosis that was treated.[12]

2.5.2 Hormones

Drugs used for hormonal therapy can be divided into four main groups.

- Androgen receptor blockers (spironolactone, cyproterone acetate, and flutamide);
- Adrenal androgen production blockers (glucocorticoids);

- Ovarian androgen blockers (oral contraceptives);
- Enzyme inhibitors (dutasteride) (discussed separately)

The main goal of these therapies is to oppose the effects of androgens on the sebaceous gland.

2.5.2.1 Androgen receptor blockers

Spironolactone

Its main mechanism of action is as a steroidal androgen receptor blocker, which competes with testosterone and dihydrotestoterone for androgen receptors and decreases androgen-stimulated sebocyte proliferation. It is also known to inhibit androgen biosynthesis by decreasing type II 17β hydroxysteroid dehydrogenase, therefore halting the conversion of androstenedione to testosterone. Other proposed actions of spironolactone include inhibition of 5α reductase and increased steroid-hormone binding globulin. Together, this results in a 30-50% reduction in sebum excretion.

Cyproterone acetate

It is a synthetic derivative of 17-hydroxyprogesterone that works as an androgen receptorblocker. It has also been shown to decrease the production of adrenal androgens by inhibiting the conversion of dehydroepiandrosterone to androstenedione by 3β hydroxysteroid dehydrogenase isomerase. Several studies have confirmed the efficacy of cyproterone acetate, with overall improvements of 75-90%. Its effectiveness in the treatment of acne is thought to be related to its ability to reduce sebum production and comedogenesis. It has also been shown to decrease testosterone, gonadotropin, and androstenedione, as well as improve acne and seborrhea in as little as 3 months. As a sole agent, it is used in doses of 50 to 100 mg daily given on days 5 to 14 of the menstrual cycle, however, it is more commonly incorporated into oral contraceptive pills in doses of 2 mg combined with 35 mcg of ethinyl estradiol (Diane-35™ and Dianette™).

Flutamide

Flutamide is a nonsteroidal androgen receptor blocker approved by the FDA for use in the treatment of prostate cancer but also is effective in treating hirsutism and acne in women. It is converted to its highly potent metabolite, 2-hydroflutamide, which acts to selectively inhibit the binding of dihydrotestosterone to the androgen receptor. Because flutamide has less affinity for the androgen receptor than spironolactone, greater doses are usually needed. Monitoring of liver function with flutamide is necessary as cases of fatal hepatitis have been reported. Hepatotoxicity seems to be dose and age related. Addition of an oral contraceptive pill and use of lower doses can reduce these side effects and decrease concerns over pregnancy risk.

Table 2.3 Hormonal Treatments for Acne.

Drug	Mechanism of Action	Standard Dose	Side Effects
Spironolactone	Androgen receptor blocker	25 to 200 mg daily	Menstrual irregularities, breast tenderness, hyperkalemia, hypotension, birth defects
Cyproteroneacetate	Androgen receptor blocker	50 to 100 mg daily on days 5 to 14 of menstrual cycle or 2 mg combined with 35 mcg of ethinylestradiol	Breast tenderness, headache, nausea, and breakthrough bleeding, hepatotoxicity, birth defects
Flutamide	Androgen receptor blocker	250 to 500 mg daily	Hepatotoxicity, breast tenderness, gastrointestinal upset, hot flashes, and decreased libido, birth defects
Oral contraceptives	Ovarian androgen blocker	Depends on specific pill	Menstrual irregularities, breast tenderness, gastrointestinal upset, weight gain (see text for contraindications)
Glucocorticoids	Adrenal androgen production blocker	2.5 to 5 mg of prednisone at bedtime	Adrenal suppression (higher risk with dexamethasone)

2.5.2.2 Adrenal androgen-production blockers

Glucocorticoids

Androgen production can be blocked by the administration of low dose glucocorticoids. This treatment is usually reserved for those patients with late-onset congenital adrenal hyperplasia (CAH). CAH is caused by an inherent defect in the enzymes 21-hydroxylase or less commonly 11-hydroxylase, resulting in build up of androgen precursors. Typical doses are 2.5 to 5 mg/day of prednisone taken at bedtime. Serum dehydro-epiandrosterone sulphate (DHEAS) levels can be monitored and should decrease or normalize with therapy. An ACTH stimulation test may be necessary to check for adrenal suppression. ACTH is injected with subsequent blood monitoring of cortisol levels 30 minutes later. An increase in plasma cortisol indicates the adrenal gland is functioning properly.

2.5.2.3 Ovarian androgen blockers

Gonadotropin-releasing agonists

Agents such as buserelin, nafarelin, and leuprolide are effective in the treatment of acne and hirsutism in women with and without endocrine abnormalities. They work by blocking androgen production by the ovary. These gonadotropin releasing agonists disrupt the cyclic release of FSH and LH from the pituitary, therefore blocking ovulation. These agents are available as a nasal spray or an injection. Because these drugs also suppress the production of estrogens patients can develop menopausal symptoms, headaches, and bone loss which may limit the use of this medication for acne.

2.5.2.4 Oral contraceptive

Oral contraceptives contain an estrogen (usually ethinyl estradiol) and a progestin to decrease the risk of endometrial cancer associated with unopposed estrogens. The first combination pills had high concentrations of estrogen in the 100-to 150 mcg range, and carried a high risk of thromboembolic disease, stroke, and myocardial infarction. Therefore, newer formulations contain estrogen doses ranging from 20 to 35 mcg of ethinyl estradiol (EE).

Oral contraceptives reduce the production of androgens and sebum by inhibiting LH and FSH, thereby suppressing ovulation and ovarian androgen production. In addition, circulating levels of testosterone are decreased by the estrogen induced increase in steroid hormone binding globulin. The second component in oral contraceptives is progestin. Many progestins have the inherent ability to interact with androgen receptors, aggravating acne, hirsutism, and androgenetic alopecia; however, the newer third-generation progestins, desogestrel, norgestimate, and gestodene, have the lowest intrinsic androgenic activity. One of the most promising recent developments is the novel progestin drospirenone. Drospirenone is a 17-alpha-spironolactone derivative that possesses both antiandrogenic and antimineralocorticoid activity. A 3 mg dose of drospirenone is equivalent to 25 mg of spironolactone. This has the added benefit of off-setting the estrogen-related fluid retention and weight gain associated with some oral contraceptives.[13]

2.5.3 Retinoic Acid Derivatives

2.5.3.1 Isotretinoin

Oral Isotretinoin is used in severe, nodulocystic acne if other treatments fail including antibiotics. Isotretinoin's exact mechanism of action is unknown. It is believed that 13-cisretinoic acid exerts its action by isomerization to all-trans-retinoic acid, which then interacts with the retinoid receptors. It is the only acne medicine available which affects all four pathogenic factors of acne. Dose of isotretinoin varies from 0.1 to 2 mg/kg. Typically, 0.5-2 mg/kg/day is recommended for 16-20 weeks to reach a total cumulative dose of 120-150 mg/kg.

2.5.4 Enzyme Inhibitors

By maintaining a higher intake of protein in relation to carbohydrates we can reduce the activity of 5-α reductase and thus the formation of the more potent dihydrotestosterone.[14-17] There are two ways to prevent the negative effects of dihydrotestosterone on the body. Either we have to inhibit the activity of 5-α reductase or we have to increase the breakdown of dihydrotestosterone via liver. Those nutrients that reduce the activity of 5-α reductase include zinc, soy, flaxseed, pumpkin seed and evening primrose oil and enzyme inhibitor like finasteride. To enhance the detoxification capability of your liver, thereby reducing dihydrotestosterone a diet high in garlic, broccoli, cabbage and cauliflower would be beneficial.

Zileuton is an orally active inhibitor of 5-lipoxygenase is proved as a new efficient and safe systemic anti-acne drug.[18]

Consuming lots of berry fruits such as strawberries and blackberries, as well as taking supplements of the vitamins A, C and E and the herb St Mary's thistle (*Silybum marianum*) would further augment liver function.[19]

Physical treatment

To achieve the maximum therapeutic response physical treatments are used in combination with topical or systemic therapy.

Lesion removal

Comedones

Open and closed comedones can be removed mechanically with a comedone extractor and a fine needle or a pointed blade (to open closed comedones). Such physical treatment is often temporary, and new comedones may form to replace those removed. Comedone removal may be done by a dermatologist, a nurse, an esthetician. A topical retinoid may be applied before mechanical extraction to make the procedure easier and also prevent formation of new comedones.

Active Deep Inflammatory Lesions (Cysts and Sinus Tracts)

Aspiration of deep inflamed lesions may be necessary; this procedure is frequently followed by an in situ injection of cortisone (diluted corticosteroid, 25 mg/ml) in cysts and sinus tracts. Oral isotretinoin is ineffective on these lesions. It is preferable to first aspirate from the bottom of the lesion, then inject the steroid into the top of the lesion. This procedure leads to improvement within several days, with flattening of the lesion. It is often used in combination with either a systemic antibiotic or oral isotretinoin.

Phototherapy

Visible Light

This is usually indicated for patients with mild or moderate inflammatory acne. *In vitro* and *in vivo* exposure of acne bacteria to 405–420 nm of ultraviolet (UV) free blue light results in the photodestruction of these bacteria through the effects on the porphyrins produced naturally by *Propionibacterium acnes*.

Photodynamic therapy

The porphyrins produced by *P. acnes*, as shown on high-performance liquid chromatography, are mostly coproporphyrin. The addition of delta-aminolevulinic acid (ALA) enhanced intracellular porphyrin synthesis and yielded higher amounts of coproporphyrin.[20]

Now a days plant products are used in the treatment of acne which show more patient compliance.

2.6 A Brief Description of the Plant Products used in the Formulation of Anti-acne Creams

2.6.1 Sandalwood Essential Oil

Botanical source: Sandalwood oil is extracted from *Santalum album* of the Santalaceae family.

Fig. 2.4 Sandal Wood Plant.
[Colour Fig. on page 395]

Fig. 2.5 Sandal Wood Chips.
[Colour Fig. on page 395]

Oil properties: The oil has a woody, exotic smell, subtle and lingering and the color is pale yellow to pale gold.

Extraction: Sandalwood oil is extracted from the chipped heartwood by steam distillation and yields 4-6%.

Chemical constituents: The main chemical components are santalol, santyl acetate and santalene. Our essential oil contains 90% santalol.

On the skin, sandalwood oil relieves itching and inflammation of the skin, and is most effective in relieving dehydrated skin, making it great for anti-ageing skincare and the astringent action has a great toning effect and is also used with great results in oily skin conditions and to prevent the skin from forming ugly scars and for fighting dry eczema.

Sandal wood oil blends well with bergamot, black pepper, geranium, lavender, myrrh, rose, vetivert and ylang-ylang.

2.6.2 Ylang Ylang Essential Oil

Botanical source: Ylang ylang oil is extracted from *Cananga odorata* var. genuina plant belonging to family Anonaceae and also known as "flower of flowers".

Fig. 2.6 Ylang ylang oil. [Colour Fig. on page 395]

Oil properties: Ylang ylang oil has an exotic, sweet smell and is slightly yellow in colour.

Extraction: Ylang ylang oil is extracted from the freshly picked flowers by water or steam distillation. The first distillation is called ylang ylang extra, which is the top grade. An absolute and concrete are also produced by solvent extraction.

Chemical constituents: The main chemical components are benzoic, geraniol, lonalol, eugenol, safrole, benzyl acetate, farnesol and pinene.

Ylang ylang oil could have a soothing effect on the skin and its stimulating effect on the scalp could promote more luxurious hair growth.

Ylang ylang oil blends well with bergamot, grapefruit, lavendor and sandalwood.

2.6.3 Tea Tree Essential Oil

Botanical source: Tea tree oil is extracted from *Malaleuca alternifolia* belonging to family Myrtaceae and also known as ti-tree, ti-trol and melasol.

Fig. 2.7 Tea tree plant. [Colour Fig. on page 395]

Oil properties: Tea tree oil has a light spicy, rather pungent smell and is very pale in colour. The viscosity is watery.

Extraction: Tea tree oil is extracted from the leaves and twigs by steam distillation. The yield is 1.8%.

Chemical constituents: The main chemical components of Tea tree oil are terpinene-4-ol, cymene, pinene, terpinene, cineole etc.

Uses: Tea tree oil is very important in helping the immune system to fight off infectious diseases.

- It is active in all three varieties of infectious organisms: Bacteria, fungi, viruses.
- It can help with influenza, cold sores, catarrh, glandular fever and gingivitis.

It is used many cosmetic products like moisturizing creams, foundation creams. Tea Tree oil could help clear abscesses, acne, burns, dandruff, herpes, and oily skin, also valuable for athlete's foot, cold sores, blemishes, diaper rash, warts, sunburn and infected wounds.

Tea Tree oil blends well with - cinnamon, clary sage, clove, geranium, lavender, lemon, myrrh, nutmeg, rosewood, rosemary and thyme.

2.6.4 Camomile Oil

Botanical source: Camomile oil is extracted from the flowers of Roman camomile or German camomile.

Fig. 2.8 White Camomile Plant. [Colour Fig. on page 395]

Fig. 2.9 Yellow camomile plant. [Colour Fig. on page 395]

Oil properties: Camomile oil has a sweet, apple-like fragrance and is very clear blue in colour with a watery viscosity, while the German camomile oil is sweet and straw-like fragrance, is dark blue in colour and its viscosity is medium.

Extraction: Camomile oil is extracted from the flowers by steam distillation and yields 1-7% from Roman camomile and 0.2-0.4% from German camomile

Chemical constituents: The main chemical components of Roman chamomile oil are alfa-pinene, camphene, b-pinene, sabinene, myrcene, 1,8-cineole, y-terpinene, caryophyllene, propyl angelate and butyl angelate.

The main chemical components of German camomile oil are chamazulene, alfa-bisabolol, bisabolol oxide A, bisabolol oxide B and bisabolone oxide.

For the skin it can be used to calm acne, eczema, rashes, wounds, dermatitis, dry and itchy skin and other allergic conditions in general.

Camomile oil blends well with - Bergamot, geranium, clary sage, lavender, jasmine, tea tree, grapefruit, rose, lemon and ylang ylang.

2.6.5 Bergamot Essential Oil

Botanical source: Bergamot oil is extracted from the tree *Citrus aurantium* var. bergamia (also known as *C. bergamia*), of the Rutaceae family and is also known as Bergamot orange.

Oil properties: Bergamot oil is basically citrus, yet fruity and sweet, with a warm spicy floral quality. The color ranges from green to greenish-yellow and the oil has a watery viscosity.

Fig. 2.10 Bergamot Plant. [Colour Fig. on page 396]

Extraction: Bergamot oil is extracted by expression from the rind of both ripe and unripe fruit and yields about 0.5%.

Chemical constituents: The main chemical components are alpha-pinene, myrcene, limonene, alpha-bergaptene, b-bisabolone, linalool, linalyl acetate, nerol, neryl acetate, geraniol, geraniol acetate and alpha-terpineol.

Precautions: Bergamot oil can cause burns when used on a sensitive skin which is then exposed to sunlight, as the high content of bergaptene can cause photo-toxicity. It is advisable to keep out of the sun if this oil is used on the skin.

Uses: Bergamot oil can be used in the treatment of depression, stress, tension, fear, hysteria, infection, anorexia, psoriasis, eczema and general convalescence.

Bergamot oil blends well with sandalwood, black pepper, clary sage, cypress, frankinsense, geranium, jasmine, mandarin, nutmeg, orange, rosemary, vetiver and ylang-ylang.

2.6.6 Lavender Essential Oil

Botanical source: Lavendor oil is extracted from the tree *Lavandula angustifolia* of the Lamiaceae family.

Fig. 2.11 Lavender Flowers. [Colour Fig. on page 396]

Oil properties: Lavendor oil has a light fresh aroma, is clear in color and watery in viscosity.

Extraction: Lavendor oil is extracted by steam distillation from the flowering tops and yields 1.4% - 1.6%.

Chemical constituents: The main chemical components of lavender oil are Alpha-pinene, linalool, linalyl acetate, limonene, 1,8-cineole, cis-ocimene, trans-ocimene, 3-octanone, camphor, linalool, linalyl acetate, caryophyllene, terpinen-4-ol and lavendulyl acetate.

Precautions: This oil may have allergic reactions.

Uses: Lavender oil has a soothing and calming effect on the nerves, relieving tension, depression, panic, hysteria and nervous exhaustion in general and is effective for headaches, migraines and insomnia.

On the skin, lavender oil tones and revitalizes and it is useful for all types of skin problems such as abscesses, acne, oily skin, boils, burns, sunburn, wounds, psoriasis, lice, insect bites, stings and also acts as an insect repellent.

Lavender oil is one of the few essentials oils that can be used neat on the skin, and this is especially useful when treating a minor burn wound.

Lavender oil blends well with cedarwood, clary sage, geranium, pine, nutmeg and all the citrus oils.

2.6.7 Patchouli Essential Oil

Botanical source: Patchouli oil is extracted from *Pogostemon cablin* of the Labiatae family.

Oil properties: Patchouli oil has a rich musky-sweet,strong spicy and herbaceous smell. It is light yellow to dark brown in colour and is a thick oil.

Extraction: Patchouli oil is extracted from the young leaves which are dried and fermented prior to steam distillation and yieds 2-3%.

Fig. 2.12 Patchouli Plant. [Colour Fig. on page 396]

Chemical constituents: The main chemical components of patchouli oil are b-patchoulene, a-patchoulene, seychellene, a-bulnesene, norpatchoulenol, patchouli alcohol and pogostol.

Precautions: It is non-toxic, non-irritant and non-sensitizing, but the smell of patchouli oil may be a little persistent for some people and large doses may cause loss of appetite in some individuals.

It is effective for fungal and bacterial infection and is of great help for insect bites. It could also be used as an insect repellant and is also used as a support for dealing with any substance addiction. Furthermore, it has a great deodorizing action, and helps when feeling hot and bothered, while cooling down inflammations and assisting with wound healing.

On the skin, this oil is one of the most active and is a superb tissue regenerator, which helps to stimulate the growth of new skin cells. In wound healing, it not only promotes faster healing, but also helps to prevent ugly scarring when the wound heals.

Patchouli oil is very effective in sorting out rough, cracked and overly dehydrated skin and is used to treat acne, acne, eczema, sores, ulcers, any fungal infections, as well as scalp disorder.

Patchouli oil blends well with - bergamot, clary sage, geranium, lavender and myrrh.

2.6.8 Jasmine Essential Oil

Botanical source: Jasmine oil is extracted from Jasminum officinale of the Oleaceae family.

Oil properties: Jasmine essential oil has a sweet, exotic and richly floral smell.

Extraction: Jasmine oil is extracted from the flowers by steam distillation. 1,000 lbs of flowers yield approximately one pound of liquid concrete, which yields 0.2% aromatic molecules.

Chemical constituents: There are well over 100 constituents found in jasmine oil, but the main chemical components are benzyl acetate, linalool, benzyl alcohol, indole, benzyl benzoate, cis-jasmone, geraniol, methyl anthranilate and trace amounts of p. cresol, farnesol, cis-3-hexenyl benzoate, eugenol, nerol, ceosol, benzoic acid, benzaldehyde, y-terpineol, nerolidol, isohytol, phytol etc.

Fig. 2.13 Jasmine Flower. [Colour Fig. on page 396]

Fig. 2.14 Jasmine Plant. [Colour Fig. on page 396]

Precautions: The therapeutic properties of jasmine oil are anti-depressant, antiseptic, aphrodisiac, anti-spasmodic, cicatrisant, expectorant, galactagogue, parturient, sedative and uterine.

Uses: It is a valuable remedy in cases of severe depression and soothes the nerves, producing a feeling of confidence, optimism and euphoria, while revitalizing and restoring energy.

Jasmine oil tones dry, greasy, irritated and sensitive skin, increases elasticity and is often used to assist with stretch marks and to reduce scarring.

Jasmine oil blends well with bergamot, rose, sandalwood and all citrus oils.

2.6.9 Geranium Essential Oil

Botanical source: Geranium oil is extracted from *Pelargonium odorantissimum* of the Geraniaceae family.

Fig. 2.15 Geranium Plant. [Colour Fig. on page 396]

Oil properties: Geranium oil is a strong smelling oil with a floral aroma and a hint of mint. The oil is mostly colorless, but can have a slight light green color to it. It has a watery viscosity.

Extraction: Geranium oil is extracted from the leaves and stalks through steam distillation.

Chemical constituents: The essential oil is composed of various chemical constituents and includes a-pinene, myrcene, limonene, menthone, linalool, geranyl acetate, citronellol, geraniol and geranyl butyrate.

Uses: Geranium oil can be used to help in the treatment of acne, bruises, burns, cuts, dermatitis, eczema, hemorrhoids, lice, as a mosquito repellant, ringworm, ulcers, breast engorgement, edema, poor circulation, sore throat, tonsillitis, PMS, menopausal problems, stress and neuralgia.

Geranium oil blends well with - angelica, basil, bergamot, carrot seed, cedarwood, citronella, clary sage, grapefruit, jasmine, lavender, lime, neroli, orange and rosemary

2.6.10 Sage Essential Oil

Botanical source: Sage oil is extracted from *Salvia officinalis* of the Labiatae family and is also known as garden, true and Dalmatian sage.

Oil properties: Sage oil has a sharp, herbal smell, and is watery in viscosity.

Fig. 2.16 Sage Plant.
[Colour Fig. on page 397]

Fig. 2.17 Sage Flower.
[Colour Fig. on page 397]

Extraction: Sage oil is extracted from the dried leaves by steam distillation.

Chemical constituents: The main chemical components of sage oil are a-pinene, camphene, b-pinene, myrcene, limonene, 1,8-cineole, a-thujone, b-thujone, camphor, linalool, bornyl acetate and borneol.

Precautions: Sage is a powerful oil and should be used with care. It is classified as an oral toxin and should be used with great care in aromatherapy. It should not be used during pregnancy, or by persons suffering from epilepsy or high blood pressure.

Sage oil also stimulates the lymphatic system and thereby boost glandular function while it also has value to treat dermatitis, atonic wounds, sores, ulcers, as well as insect bites and reducing large pores.

Sage oil blends well with bergamot, lavender, lemon and rosemary.

2.6.11 Aloe Vera Juice

Botanical source: *Aloe vera* juice is extracted from *Aloe barbadensis* (Miller) belonging to family Liliaceae.

Fig. 2.18 Aloe leaf. [Colour Fig. on page 397]

Fig. 2.19 Aloe vera plant. [Colour Fig. on page 397]

The meaning "bitter and shiny substance", derives from the Arabic word "alloeh".

Extraction: *Aloe vera* gel is derived from tissue that comprises the inner portion of the leaves.

Aloe vera leaves are fleshy, stiff and spiny along the edges, grow in a rosette. Each plant has 15 to 30 tapering leaves, each up to 50 cm long and 8 to 10 cm wide. Beneath the thick cuticle of the epidermis lies the chlorenchyma, between this layers a parenchyma layer which is colorless, mucilaginous pulp containing the aloe gel and numerous vascular bundles and inner bundle sheath cells from which a bitter yellow sap exudes when the leaves are cut (Reynolds, 1977). Red, yellow or paler-striped flowers rise from the heart of the leaves, hanging from a rather tall stem, branched or unbranched, as a cluster of narrow tubes. Aloe plants can withstand high temperature and long periods of drought, due to their ability to store water in their succulent leaves, at the same time they are very sensitive to freezing temperature, which can damage or kill the plants (Wendell, 2001).

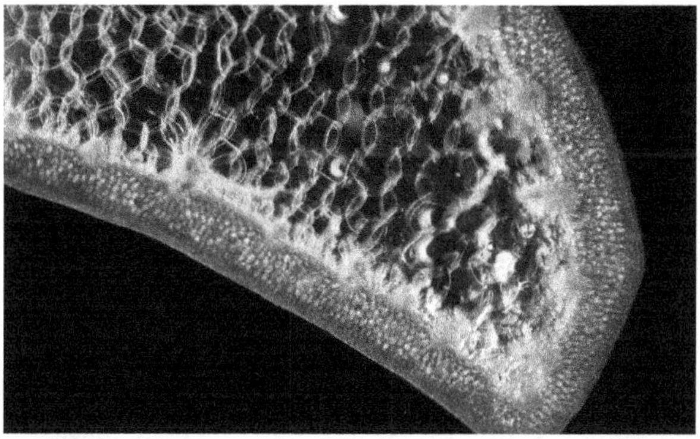

Fig. 2.20 Cross section of Aloe leaf. [Colour Fig. on page 397]

Collection of gel

Aloe vera gel was prepared by various methods according to their need. The gel has been collected from the mature, old leaves towards the base of the plant, because the barbaloin content was more in young leaves. The gel can be prepared by taking only the parenchyma layer or whole leaf as such. In the first method, the parenchyma layer was separated from the leaves, liquefied and filtered to remove the cells. But in the second method the whole leaves were liquefied and filtered to remove the cells, to the filtrate activated charcoal was added to remove the color in gel.

The collected gel degrades very rapidly at room temperature or when exposed to air. This degradation can be prevented by drying the gel or by adding suitable preservative and antioxidant or an addition algal sulphated polysaccharide.

Freeze drying or spray drying can dry the *Aloe vera* gel. The spray drying was done by spraying the gel with a suitable matrix to form powder, which retain stable in air for long term storage.

Chemical constituents: The components of *Aloe vera* can be divided into the following groups:

1. Vitamins: It is rich in all vitamins excluding vitamin D, especially the antioxidant vitamins A (betacarotene), C and E and even contains a trace of vitamin B12.

2. Enzymes: Several different types of these biochemical catalysts when taken orally aid digestion by breaking down fat and sugars. Bradykinase helps to reduce excessive inflammation when applied to the skin topically and therefore reduces pain, whereas others help digest any dead tissues in wounds. Lipases and proteases which break down foods and aid digestion are present.

3. Minerals: Calcium, sodium, potassium, manganese, magnesium, copper, zinc, chromium and the antioxidant selenium.

4. Sugars: These are derived from the mucilage layer of the plant which surrounds the inner gel, and are known as mucopolysaccharides, which enhance the immune system and help to detoxify. Aloe vera contains both mono and polysaccharides. Most important ones are the long chain sugars involving glucose and mannose or the gluco-mannans. These sugars are ingested whole from the gut, not broken down like other sugars, and appear in the bloodstream in exactly the same form by pinocytosis. Then in the blood stream they are able to exert their immune-regulating effect.

   Some of these polysaccharides are not absorbed but stick to certain cells lining the gut and form a barrier preventing absorption of unwanted material so helping to prevent a 'leaking' gut syndrome. In topical preparations the sugars are also the main moisturizers.

5. Anthraquinones: It contains twelve phenolic compounds which are exclusively in the plant sap. They have purgative effect. The important anthraquinones are aloin and emodin. In small concentrations they act as painkillers. They also function as antibacterials and antivirals.

6. Lignin: This in itself is an inert substance but when included in topical preparations it endows Aloe vera with a singular penetrative effect so the other ingredients are absorbed into the skin.

7. Saponins: These soapy substances form about 3% of the Aloe vera gel and are capable of cleansing, having antiseptic properties. These act powerfully as antibacterials against bacteria, viruses, fungi and yeasts.
8. Fatty Acids: It contains cholesterol, campesterol, b-sisosterol and lupeol. These four plant steroids are important anti-inflammatory agents.
9. Salicylic acid: It is having anti-inflammatory and antibacterial properties.
10. Amino acids: The body needs 22 amino acids the gel provides 20 of these. More importantly, it provides 7 out of the 8 essential amino acids which the body cannot synthesize.

Therapeutic properties: *Aloe vera* has many beneficial effects on different systems of the body.

Digestive system: *Aloe vera* juice consumed orally reduces acidity, detoxes, reduces pH levels, alleviates heartburn, alleviates constipation and alleviates the inflammation of the digestive tract.

Immune system: *Aloe vera* juice consumed orally reduces fever. *Aloe vera* gel applied topically for long periods prevents detrimental bacteria and fungi from penetrating the skin.

Musculoskeletal system: *Aloe vera* gel applied topically accelerates the healing of canker sores due to acemannan. It also accelerates the healing of burns, healing of Herpes simplex lesions. *Aloe vera* gel applied topically alleviates the itching associated with insect bites and stings. *Aloe vera* gel applied topically prevents scarring, temporarily improves the appearance of the skin and cleanses the skin.

Bioavailability: *Aloe vera* gel is able to penetrate the skin when applied topically.

Cosmetic uses: *Aloe vera* gel when applied topically it acts as moisterising agent. Because of this reason it is used in cosmetic creams like body creams, massage creams, facial creams (Bunyapraphatsara et al., 1996). When applied on to the scalp it removes dandruff and it gives conditioning effect to the hair. Hence aloe gel has been added to shampoos, bubble baths, after-sun lotions, burn relief products, local antiseptic products, sunscreen products, dryskin lotions, hydrocortisone preparations, antifungal liquids and even to the plastic edges of disposable razor catridges (Larry, 1995).

Adverse effects of *Aloe vera* gel

There are some unwanted reactions which occur with aloe gel on topical applications as well as on internal consumption. In some cases severe burning sensations were noted followed by long-term erythema (Hunter and frumkin, 1991). If aloe gel was contaminated with anthraquinone and administered orally causes symptoms of abdominal cramps and diarrhea. Several reports on aloe gel say that the plasma glucose level was lowering in human and also in laboratory animals (Ghannam et al., 1986; Ajabnoor, 1990). It was postulated in one study that this hypoglycaemic effect was mediated through the stimulation and release of insulin from the B-cells of pancreas (Ajabnoor, 1990). Therefore care should be taken when using oral *Aloe vera* gel in patients with diabetes.

Table 2.4 Chemical constituents of aloe vera.

Amino Acids:	Alanine	Arginine	Aspartic acid	Glutamic acid	Glycine
	Hydroxyproline	Isoleucine	Histidine	Leucine	Lysine
	Methionine	Serine	Threonine	Tyrosine	Proline
	Valine	Phenylalanine	Cystine		
Carbo hydrates:	Arabinose	Galactose	Glucose	Mannose	Xylose
Poly-saccharides:	Acemannan				
Minerals:	Calcium	Chlorine	Copper	Germanium	Iron
	Manganese	Potassium	Silicon	Magnesium lactate	Sulphur
Organic Acids:	Chrysophanic Acid	Cinnamic acid	Salicylic acid	Succinic acid	Uric acid
Quinones:	Anthraquinones	Barbaloin	Isobarbaloin		
Vitamins:	Vitamin B_1& B_2	Vitamin B_3	Vitamin B_6	Vitamin C	Choline
Aloewater: 96,000%					
Enzymes:	Bradykininase				
Other:	Resitannol	Resin	Ethereal Oil	(Aloe emodin)	Aloenin

Now-a-days most of the companies are making anti-acne preparations by using plant products. Examples,

- Zap-it!® acne treatment system

Each product contains salicylic acid, the most recommended anti-acne medicine. Zap-it!® products contain high-quality T36-C5 melaleuca oil, guaranteed to contain at least 36% terpinen and no more than 5% cineole. These compounds are beneficial to skin because they contribute to the oil's antiseptic and antibacterial properties.

Facial Wash
[Colour Fig. on page 398]

Deep Cleaning Astringent
[Colour Fig. on page 398]

Pore Clarifying Cream [Colour Fig. on page 398]

- V-actives anti-acne complex

  It is a ready to use 20% w/w standardized salicylic acid extraction blend of Meadowsweet (*Spiraea ulmaria*) flowers and White Willow (*Salix alba*) bark.

- Anti-acne products consist of *Eucalyptus globulus* and *Psidium guajava* oil[21]

Table 2.5

Excipients	% w/w	
	2% Eucalyptus	4% Guava
Stearic acid spermaceti	4.0	0.5
Glycerylmonostearate	4.0	0.5
White petrolatum	6.0	0.05
Silicone oil	6.0	0.05
Carbopol 940	1.0	0.1
Glycerine	1.0	0.1
PEG 1500	9.0	0.1
Citric acid	7.0	0.1
Sodium citrate	0.3	0.01
Sodium metabisulfate	0.3	0.01
Methyl paraben	2.0	1.5
Propyl paraben	2.0	1.5
Triethanolamine	1.0	68.5
Water	1.0	68.5

- Topical formulations (Gel) have been developed containing hydro-alcoholic extract of *Ocimum sanctum*, ethanolic extract of *Tabernaemontana divaricata*, *Aloe vera* concentrate gel powder and tea tree oil. (22)

Sample 1

Ingredients	Wt. %
Stearic acid	16.22
Paraffin oil	0.95
Cetyl alcohol	0.95
Triethnol amine	0.51
Propylene glycol	4.77
Isopropyl-myristate	0.95
Glycerin	1.90
Propyl paraben	0.095
Derma soft	1.90
Sulphur	0.38
Borax	0.76
Vitamin E (tocopherol)	0.56
Zinc oxide	0.76
Bismuth subnitrate	1.90
Extracts of *Aloe vera*	0.63
Salix alba bark	0.63
Sugar-cane	0.63
Distilled water	65.7
Fragrance qs	

Sample 2

Ingredients	Wt. %
Stearic acid	24.2
Cetyl alcohol	1.2
Triethnol amine	1.32
Propylene glycol	0.95
Isopropyl-myristate	1.2
Glycerin	2.0
Sulphur	1.90
Borax	1.90
Vitamin E (tocopherol)	0.56
Honey	3.5
Menthol	0.76
Distilled water	49.95
Extracts of *Azadirachta indica* (neem)1.76	1.76
Ocimum sanctum (tulsi)	1.76
Cucumis sativus (cucumber)	1.76
Mentha sylvestris (wild mint)	1.76
Mentha piperita (mint)	1.76
Aloe vera	1.76
Fragrance qs	

Sample 3

Ingredients	Wt. %
Stearic acid	22.2
Cetyl alcohol	1.5
Triethnolamine	0.67
Isopropyl-myristate	1.5
Methyl paraben	0.02
Benzoyl peroxide (5% soln)	8.0
Mineral oil	1.90
Vitamin E	0.56
Distilled water	63.65
Lemon essence qs	
Fragrance qs	

Sample 4

Ingredients	Wt. %
Stearic acid	22.2
Cetyl alcohol	1.5
Triethnolamine	0.67
Propylene glycol	6.5
Isopropyl-myristate	1.5
Propyl paraben	0.02

Ingredients	Wt. %
Derma soft	1.90
Glycerin	1.90
Sulphur micronized	0.38
Erythromycin	12.0
Zinc oxide	1.9
Ditilled water	50.03
Fragrance qs	

Sample 5

Ingredients	Wt. %
Stearic acid	22.2
Cetyl alcohol	1.5
Triethnolamine	0.67
Propylene glycol	1.5
Isopropyl-myristate	1.5
Glycerin	1.90
Propyl paraben	0.2
Borax	0.51
Lactic acid	10
Salicylic acid	5.0
Sodium hydroxide	1.8
Disodium EDTA	0.75
Distilled water	53.1
Fragrance qs	

Sample 6

Ingredients	Wt. %
Stearic acid	22.2
Paraffin oil	1.5
Cetyl alcohol	1.5
Triethnolamine	1.5
Propylene glycol	1.5
Isopropyl-myristate	1.5
Glycerin	2.0
Sulphur	0.67
Zinc oxide	2.0
Glycolic acid	16.0
Almond oil	4.0
Distilled water	45.63
Fragrance qs	

- DOW CORNING® cosmetic powder (for men) contains *Copaifera Officinalis* (Balsam Copaiba) Resin, *Carapa Guaianensis* Seed Oil and *Euterpe Oleracea* Pulp Oil.

- KUHS KOSMETIK has introduced an anti-acne Nanoemulsion which contains *Tea Tree Oil*

- CHEMIÉ ALLIANCE has introduced Cytobiol Iris A, is an active ingredient created from Iris extract, Vitamin A and Zinc salt. Cytobiol Burdock, active principle extracted from the roots of *Arctium majus* and its activity is due to the presence of polyphenols.

- noveon The Specialty Chemicals Innovator™ Anti-Acne Cream Gel for Sensitive Skin contains *Melaleuca Alternifolia* (Tea Tree) Leaf Oil, Water-Soluble Tea Tree Oil.

We have successfully formulated, evaluated and patented the anti-acne herbal formulation which contains different blends of oils like lavender, bergamot, geranium, tea tree oil etc.

Some marketed anti-acne products are given below

2.7 Conclusion

Plant-derived compounds have the ability to deliver real benefits. There are multiple herbs currently incorporated into cosmeceuticals with valid scientific rationale and supported with human clinical studies or have documented biologic activity by *in vitro*, *in vivo*, or animal studies. The cosmeceutical only has scientific integrity if the herbal components are stable, of therapeutic concentrations, and can be adequately delivered across human stratum correum.

References

1. Ribera M et al. Treatment of Acne in Daily Clinical Practice: an Opinion Poll Among Spanish Dermatologists. *Actas Dermosifiliogr* 2011; **102(2)**:121–131.
2. Ichiro Kurokawa et al. New developments in our understanding of acne pathogenesis and treatment. *Experimental Dermatology* 2009; **18(10)**: 821–832.
3. Lehmann HP. Agen. Health. *Res. Qual.*, 2001; **01**:17
4. F. Ballangera, P. Baudrya, J.M. N'Guyenb, A. Khammaria, B. Dréno Heredity: *A Prognostic Factor for Acne* 5/2/2005
5. US Dept Health and Human Services January 2005
6. National Guideline Clearinghouse 11/12/2007
7. Webster, G.F. *Brit. Med. J.,* 2002, **325**, 475-479.
8. Lalla JK, Nandedkar SY, Paranjapee MH, Talreja NB. *J Ethnopharmacol* 2001; **78**: 99-102.
9. Bhupendra G. *Antisept* 2005; **97**: 221-225.
10. Andrea L. Zaenglein, MD. Topical Retinoids in the Treatment of Acne Vulgaris. *Semin Cutan Med Surg* 2008; **27**: 177-182.
11. Jonathan S. Weiss, MD, and Joel S. Shavin, MD *Snellville, Georgia*. Adapalene for the treatment of acne vulgaris. *J Am Acad Dermatol* 1998; **39**: S50-4.
12. Guy F. Webster, Emmy M. Graber. Antibiotic Treatment for Acne Vulgaris. *Semin Cutan Med Surg* 2008; **27**:183-187.
13. Rosalyn George, Shari Clarke, and Diane Thiboutot. Hormonal Therapy for Acne. *Semin Cutan Med Surg* 2008; **27**:188-196.
14. Heudes AM, Laroche L. Muscular damage during isotretinoin treatment. *Ann Dermatol Venereol* 1998; **125**: 94–97.
15. DiGiovanna JJ. Isotretinoin effects on bone. *J Am Acad Dermatol* 2001; **45**: S176–S182.
16. McLane J. Analysis of common side effects of isotretinoin. *J Am Acad Dermatol* 2001; **45**: S188–S194.
17. Acne Treatment by inhibiting 5-Alpha Reductase Enzyme http://www.acne-rx-skincare.com/acne-diet.html (10 May **2003**).

18. Christos C. Zouboulis, Zileuton, a new efficient and safe systemic anti-acne drug, Review, *Dermato-Endocrinology* **1**:3, 188-192; May/June 2009.

19. Acne Treatment by inhibiting 5-Alpha Reductase Enzyme http://www.eternalhealth.org/womens_health/acne.htm (10 May **2003).**

20. Brigitte D. Acne: Physical Treatment. *Clinics in Dermatology* 2004; **22**:429–433.

21. Sirivan Athikomkulchai, Rith Watthanachaiyingcharoen, Sujimon Tunvichien, Panida Vayumhasuwan, Paisarn Karnsomkiet, Prapan Sae-Jong, Nijsiri Ruangrungsi, The development of anti-acne products from *eucalyptus globulus* and *psidium guajava* oil, *J Health Res* 2008; **22(3)**: 109-113.

22. Muhammad Athar Abbasi, Ayesha Kausar, Aziz-ur-Rehman, Hina Saleem, Sadia Muhammad Jahangir, Sabahat Zahra Siddiqui and Viqar Uddin Ahmad, Preparation of new formulations of anti-acne creams and their efficacy, *Afr. J. Pharm. Pharmacol.* 2010; **4(6)**: 298-303.

CHAPTER 3

ANTI-AGING

Y. Madhusudan Rao, Shayeda, D. Sathish, S. Himabindu
Center for Biopharmaceutics and Pharmacokinetics, University College of Pharmaceutical Sciences, Kakatiya University, Warangal-506 009, Andhra Pradesh, India.

3.1 Introduction

Anti-aging is simply not preventing getting old and the aging process is inevitable; anti-aging must mean something more. The whole process of life is that of maturation. We are born with plump cherubic round faces punctuated by eyes too large and noses too small for our facial proportions. With childhood, the surface area of the face increases, the nose enlarges, and the eyes appear relatively smaller. As adolescence approaches, the jaw line begins to assume prominence, and the round face becomes elongated with an increase in the size of the forehead. Young adulthood is characterized by carefully sculpted cheekbones, growth of the ears, and development of a mature hairline. And, finally, adulthood sees drooping of the nasal tip, lines of expression around the eyes and on the forehead, and loss of the creamy texture of the skin. These changes are completely due to intrinsic aging effects and do not represent extrinsic photo-aging. Anti-aging means removing undesirable lines from the face and leaving those behind that are attractive. For example, lines around the eyes that are indicative of a smile should remain, but frown lines indicative of worry and scorn should be treated. Lips should not be enlarged on a mature face, but the down-turned corners should be corrected to remove an unhappy face from a generally happy person. Looking and feeling wonderful at a mature age is anti-aging. This is the broad goal that we should work towards in our practices and in our research.[1]

The number of nonsurgical anti-aging procedures have increased in recent years. Reasons for this trend are various: The World Wide Web distributes an immense amount of information throughout the world within seconds, which in turn generates a great demand on information. Active and aggressive medias, which were almost absent 50 years ago, have made our society ambitious; the perception of which is attractive, desirable, and sexy gets globalized. In addition, our lifestyle has changed with the fast-growing offer of leisure activities. Wrinkles, fat deposits, and sun-damaged skin do not fit into our neat society. The increasing demand for aesthetic treatments has prompted many physicians without any knowledge in aesthetic medicine to offer various nonsurgical aesthetic treatments with the danger that aesthetic dermatology stands to lose its scientific relevance. Evidence-based medicine should be applied not only in medical procedures but also in aesthetic dermatology.[2]

Aging of human beings is a physiological process corresponding to a progressive loss in homeostatic capacity of the body systems, ultimately increasing the vulnerability to environmental threats and to certain disease states. Nobody can escape from aging. However, it is evident that the process progresses differently among individuals of the same age. In any given subject, senescence is heterogenous among organs and also among their constitutive tissues, cells, and subcellular structures.[3] Each and every organ of the human body develops and fails at its own rate, which is referred to as its age.[4] This systematic aging occurs throughout the entire body from the time of about 30 to 45 years of age (Table 3.1). To further complicate the situation, there is regional variability of skin aging over the body. It is indeed quite evident that at any time in adult life, the face, scalp, forearms, trunk, and other body sites show different manifestations of aging. In addition, scrutinizing skin aging at the tissue level (epidermis, dermis, hypodermis, hair follicle), and further, at the cellular level (keratinocytes, melanocyte, fibroblast, dermal dendrocyte, etc.) shows a patchwork of aging severity.

Table 3.1 Age Markers of Each of the Body System (4).

Type of Aging	Pause decline in	Typical onset age
Pineal Pause	Melatonin	20
Biopause	Neurotransmitters	Dopamine: 30, Acetylcholine: 40
Pituitary Pause	Hormone feedback loops	30
Psychopause	Personality health and mood	30
Sensory Pause	Touch, hearing, vision, and smell sensitivity	40
Cardiopause/Vasculopause	Ejection fraction and blood flow	40
Nephropause	Erythropoietin level and creatine clearance	40
Gastropause	Nutrient Absorption	40
Pancreopause	Blood sugar level	40
Insulopause	Glucose tolerance	40
Menopause	Estrogen, progesterone, and testosterone in women	40
Onchopause	Finger and toe nails	40
Genopause	DNA	40
Electropause	Electrical activity of brain waves	45
Andropause	Testosterone in men	45
Uropause	Bladder control	45
Parathyropause	Parathyroid hormone	50
Pulmonopause	Lung elasticity and function with increase in blood pressure	50
Thyropause	Calcitonin and thyroid hormone levels	50
Adrenopause	DHEA	55

3.1.1 Hormesis in Aging

In the fields of biology and medicine hormesis is defined as an adaptive response of cells and organisms to a moderate (usually intermittent) stress. Hormesis in aging is represented by mild stress-induced stimulation of protective mechanisms in cells and organisms resulting in biologically beneficial effects. Single or multiple exposure to low doses of otherwise harmful agents, such as irradiation, food limitation, heat stress, hypergravity, reactive oxygen species and other free radicals have a variety of anti-aging and longevity extending hormetic effects. Detailed molecular mechanisms that bring about the hormetic effects are being increasingly understood, and comprise a cascade of stress response and other pathways of maintenance and repair. Although the extent of immediate hormetic effects after exposure to a particular stress may only be moderate, the chain of events following initial hormesis leads to biologically amplified effects that are much larger, synergistic and produces multiple effects. A consequence of hormetic amplification is an increase in the homeodynamic space of a living system in terms of increased defence capacity and reduced load of damaged macromolecules. Hormesis counter-balances the progressive shrinkage of the homeodynamic space, which is the ultimate cause of aging, diseases and death. Healthy aging may be achieved by hormesis through mild and periodic, but not severe or chronic, physical and mental challenges, and by the use of nutritional hormesis incorporating mild stress-inducing molecules called hormetins.[5]

3.2 Skin Aging: Mechanisms

Elie Metchnikoff, a 1908 Nobel laureate for immunology said in his book, *The Prolongation of Life*, that aging could be slowed by eating yogurt or by the removal of the large intestine. Another well-known scientist, Brown-Sequard, regarded as the father of modern endocrinology, made claims of revitalization through self-injections of extracts made of sheep testes. These historical episodes have taught us the need of a far better understanding of the basic mechanisms of the aging process.[6]

Conceptually, human aging is one single chronological process of physiological decline progressing with age. This basic process exhibits multiple facets affecting differently the organs, tissues, and cells. This is particularly true in the skin. Over the past decades, the understanding of aging skin has considerably expanded, with a welcome emphasis on differentiating the intrinsic chronological aging changes from photoaging resulting from habitual chronic sun exposure.[7] According to this concept, the changes observed in the skin appearance as a result of aging reflect two main processes. Firstly, the intrinsic changes in the skin are caused by the passage of time modulated by hereditary factors, along with modifications occurring inherently in the structure, physiology, and mechanobiology. Secondly, photodamage is a result of the cumulative exposure of the skin to ultraviolet (UV) exposure. Clinically, these two types of aging are manifested differently, with intrinsic aging giving rise to smooth, dry, pale, and finely wrinkled skin, and photoaging giving rise to coarse, roughened, and deeply wrinkled skin accompanied by pigmentary changes such as solar lentigines and mottled pigmentation. Differences between these two types of aging can be seen within one individual when comparing an area of skin commonly exposed to the sun, for example, the face, the neck, and the dorsal forearms, with an area commonly masked from the sun, for example, buttock skin.

This concept that is based on a duality in skin aging has been challenged because it may appear as an oversimplification in clinical practice.[8] Thus, another classification of skin aging in several distinct types was given below. The important variables included the endocrine and overall metabolic status, the past and present life style, and several environmental threats, including cumulative UV and infrared exposures, and repeated mechanical solicitations by muscles and external forces such as earth gravity. In this framework, the past history of the subject is emphasized.

Accordingly, the global aging is considered to represent the cumulative or synergistic effects of specific features, each of them being independent from the others. Such a concept allows to individualize or integrate typical processes, including, among others, menopausal aging and smoking effects. Increased awareness of the distinct age associated physiological changes in the skin may allow for more effective and specific skin care regimens, preventive measures, and dermatological treatment strategies in the elderly. As a consequence, the immutability of skin aging can be challenged.[3,9] However, factors of skin aging share some common mechanisms.[10] For instance, molecular mechanisms imply hyaluronate-CD44 pathways in the control and maintenance of epithelial growth and the viscoelastic properties of the extracellular matrix that offer new opportunities for preventive intervention.[11]

3.3 Types of Aging

1. Environmental aging
2. Chronologic aging
3. Photo-aging
4. Ethnic aging
5. Endocrine aging
6. Catabolic aging
7. Gravitational aging
8. Gentical aging

3.3.1 Environmental Aging

The skin is the body's first line of defense against the environment and many people are getting aging due to the effects of exposure on outer layer of the skin. Advance aging can come from the sun and heat, cold and wind, low or high humidity. In addition, geographical, occupational, religious, cultural, or socioeconomic factors also will dictate what type of environmental insults and damage will supplement the aging process of the skin of a particular individual. The strong development of various industries and the rapid growth of the world population in the last decades led to a rather heavy pollutant-overloading of the atmosphere and water resources.[12]

The combustion of fossil fuels (coal, oil, gas) in the industry and in caloric plants, as well as in private households are associated not only with the emission of NO_2, SO_2/SO_3 (acid rain precursors) in addition to CO_2 in the atmosphere (green house effect and damaging of the world climate), but also with a number of polycyclic aromatic hydrocarbons (PAHs). The last ones are content in the air and even in trace amounts they are highly carcinogenic. By rain and snow they can be brought also to ground water. PAHs can be incorporated in the human organism (e.g. in DNA), leading to strong biological changes, accelerating the aging process, inducing carcinogenesis, etc. As a sequence of several oxidation/hydratization reaction steps in the liver, the resulting carcinogenic oxacyclopropane of DPE can react with the NH_2-group, e.g. of the guanine base, leading to a DNA modification and initiation of tumour. This process can also occur on adenine or cytosine groups of the DNA, likewise.

Type I collagen is the most abundant protein in skin connective tissue, which also contains other types of collagen (III, V, VII), elastin, proteoglycans, fibronectin, and other extracellular matrix proteins. Newly synthesized type I procollagen is secreted into the dermal extracellular space where it undergoes enzymatic-processing, arranging itself into a triple helix configuration. The triple helix complexes associate with other extracellular matrix proteins such as leucine-rich small proteoglycans, to form regularly arranged fibrillar structures. This process, called fibrillogenesis, results in formation of collagen bundles that are responsible for the strength and resiliency of the skin.[13]

3.3.2 Chronologic Aging

Historically, photoaging and chronological skin aging have been considered to be distinct entities. Although the typical appearance of photoaged and chronologically aged human skin can be readily distinguished, recent evidence indicates that chronologically aged and UV-irradiated skin share important molecular features including altered signal transduction pathways that promote matrix-metalloproteinase (MMP) expression, decreased procollagen synthesis, and connective tissue damage. This concordance of molecular mechanisms suggests that UV irradiation accelerates many key aspects of the chronological aging process in human skin. Based on this relationship between UV irradiation and chronological aging, acute UV irradiation of human skin may serve as a useful model to study molecular mechanism of skin chronological aging.

Chronologically aged skin appears thin, smooth, dry, unblemished, with some loss of elasticity. Comparison of skin surface makings between young and aged sun-protected skin reveals a modest age-related loss of architectural regularity. At the histological level, chronologically aged skin shows general atrophy of the extracellular matrix reflected by decreased number of fibroblasts, and reduced levels of collagen and elastin The organization of collagen fibrils and elastin fibers is also impaired. This impairment is thought to result from both decreased protein synthesis that particularly affects types I and III collagens in the dermis and increased breakdown of extracellular matrix proteins.[13]

3.3.3 Photo-Aging

The skin-damaging effects of solar radiant energy can be attributed to the cumulative effects of most of the UV (i.e. both UVB, UVA) and IR radiation that passes through the Earth's atmosphere. During the summer, about 20-30% of the total daily UV radiation is received from 11 am to 1 pm, with 75% between 9 am and 3 pm. In the temperate zones, UVB intensity at the Earth's surface varies more noticeably with the different seasons. These seasonal variations occur much less nearer the equator, because the farther north or south one goes from the equator (ie the greater the degree of geographical latitude) the greater the degree of the angle of incidence of earthbound solar radiation and the greater the decrease in UV radiation that reaches the Earth's surface.

Oxidative stress is thought to play a central role in initiating and driving the signalling events that lead to cellular response following UV irradiation. UV irradiation of skin increases hydrogen peroxides and other reactive oxygen species (ROS) and decreases anti-oxidant enzymes. These features are also observed in chronologically aged human skin. In both cases, increased ROS production alters gene and protein structure and function, leading to skin damage. Superoxide anion, O_2^-, is produced by energy transfer from several endogenous UV-absorbing chromophores, including NADH$^-$/NADPH, tryptophan, riboflavin or trans-urocanic acid to molecular oxygen. O_2^- is then converted by superoxide dismutase to H_2O_2 which, in the presence of transition metal such as iron and copper, undergoes conversion to the highly reactive hydroxyl radical (HO•). These compounds have the ability to activate several downstream proteins such as Raf, protein tyrosine phosphates (PTPs), and means mitogen-activated-protein kinase kinase 1 (MEKK1).

One of the earliest detectable responses of human skin cells to UV irradiation is activation of multiple cytokine and growth factor cell surface receptors, including epidermal growth factor receptor (EGF-R), tumor necrosis factor (TNF)-α receptor, platelet activating factor (PAF) receptor, insulin receptor, interleukin (IL)-1 receptor, and platelet derived growth factor (PDGF) receptor. Activation of growth factor and cytokine receptors (EGF, IL-1, and TNF-α) by UV irradiation, leads to clustering and internalization of the receptors. Interestingly, whereas activation of EGF, IL-1, or TNF-α receptors alone by its cognate ligand resulted in relatively modest activation of downstream signalling pathways, co-administration of EGF, IL-1, and TNF-α results in a strong synergic response similar to that caused by exposure to UV irradiation clinical changes seen in sun-exposed and sun-protected skin were given in Table 3.2.

Table 3.2 Clinical Changes Seen in Sun-Exposed and Sun-Protected Skin[14].

Exposed Skin	Unexposed Skin
Thickened and nodular	Thinned and smooth
Yellow and sallow	Clear, almost transparent
Coarse wrinkling	Fine wrinkling
Rough	Smooth
Frequent telangiectasia and ecchymoses	Less frequent telangiectasia and ecchymoses
Multiple lentigines	Minimal lentigines
Mottled pigmentation	Even pigmentation
Elastotic, lax skin	Inelastic, saggy, redundant skin
Comedones	Milia
Decreased sweating	Decreased sweating
Marked dryness and scaliness	Dryness and some scaliness
Easy tearing and shearing of skin	Fragile skin
Increased numbers of seborrheic and other keratoses	A few seborrheic and other keratoses
Increased numbers of premalignant lesions	Occasional premalignant lesions
Increased numbers of malignant lesions	Occasional malignant lesions

3.3.4 Ethnic Aging

People of colored skin comprise the majority of the world population, and Asian subjects comprise more than half of the total earth population. Ethnic skin difference related to skin color, which is dominated by the presence of melanin. The photoprotection derived from this polymer influences the rate of the skin-aging changes between the different racial groups. However, all racial groups are eventually subjected to the photo-aging process. Generally, Caucasians have an earlier onset and greater skin wrinkling and sagging signs than other skin types, increased pigmentary problems are seen in colored skin, although East Asians, living in Europe and North America, have less pigment spots. Induction of a hyperpigmentary response is thought to be through signaling by the protease-activated receptor-2, which together with its activating protease, is increased in the epidermis of subjects with colored skin. Biophysical property changes in skin with age demonstrate that the more darkly pigmented subjects retain younger skin properties compared with the more lightly pigmented groups.

3.3.5 Endocrine Aging

The biological change of adrenal gland in aging is accompanied by low serum levels of androstenedione (ASD), dehydroepiandrosterone (DHEA), DHEA sulphate (DHEAS), progesterone and aldosterone. The biological change of gonadotropins in aging is demonstrated by low serum levels of 17β-estradiol (female) and testosterone (male). Decreased serum levels of growth hormone and insulin-like growth factor are typical for somato-senescence and calcium-senescence is demonstrated by low serum levels of calcitonin and vitamin D but elevated levels of parathyroid hormone. In conclusion, during aging there is a tremendous decrease of peripheral hormones and an increase of some pituitary hormones (not growth hormone). However, cortisol decrease is smaller in relation to the decline of other peripheral hormones. This may result in a increased influence of cortisol effects in relation to other hormones of the adrenal glands.[15]

3.3.6 Catabolic Aging

In our standard diet many of the nutrients are essential to maintain health. Due to lack of protein-containing food, changes occurred in the skin, by age-related hormone deficiency. Lack of intake of fruits and vegetables causes vitamin C deficiency leading to scurvy. In this condition, there is a defect in coagulation resulting in purpura, particularly in a punctate perifollicular pattern on the legs. In elder people, anemia, generalized pruritus, and some diffuse hair loss is possible due to iron deficiency. Xerosis may also occurs due to the deficiency of essential fatty acid and vitamin A. Many of the elder people are deficient in zinc, and it has been suggested that this may be an important factor in preventing wound healing. Chronic hemodialysis is another example of catabolic aging affecting the mechanical properties of skin.

3.3.7 Gravitational Aging

Gravitational force of earth is one of the important mechanical forces which influences skin folding during aging. So information of any force which is generated by the skin may pass to different cells and it is evidenced in case of melanocytes, fibroblasts, dermal dendrocytes and keratinocytes. These forces will affect cell mechanosensitive ion channels which alter the structure of the dermal extracellular matrix.

3.3.8 Gentical Aging

Genetics is an important tool for identifying key molecular events that are involved in specifying biological functions. Along with understanding of oncogenesis, cell cycle genetic approaches are also used for the analysis of organismic aging and senescence. Genetic approach involves the analysis levels from the molecule to intact organism. But there are so many problems with genetic approaches. First, because of the lack of clear definitions of what constitutes aging, care must be taken to distinguish valid end points. Second, the cost of obtaining strains with significant alterations in age-related processes, the time necessary to construct such strains and the length of time necessary to analyze these strains are major constraints to progress. Third, one must choose an organism in which genetic technology is well developed. The human genome project has also made the analysis of human genes increasingly possible, and several studies aimed at identifying disease genes related to aging are in progress. Fourth, life span and other senescent processes are very sensitive to genetic background so that appropriate care must be taken to avoid both inbreeding and the accumulation of mutations in model systems.[16]

3.4 Agents which are Reported to have Anti Aging-Activity

3.4.1 Natural Products

A number of natural products with widely differing chemical structures have been reported to exert their anti-aging effects through varied mechanisms.

β-Carotene is a precursor of vitamin A; it has antioxidant activity and has been studied for its protective properties in a number of age-related disorders.

Lycopene is present in high concentrations in tomatoes and has been claimed to provide protection against many diseases, including cardiovascular diseases and some cancers, particularly prostate and is capable of directly blocking ultraviolet rays.

Lutein, present in vegetables and fruits decreases the chances of developing macular degeneration.

Laetrile (amygdalin; vitamin B7; chemically laevo-mandelonitrile-glucoside), commonly found in apricots, is a powerful hydroxyl radical scavenger. This property supports the rationale for its role in anti-ageing supplement programs.

Coenzyme Q10 (CoQ10; ubedecarenone) acts as an antioxidant and improves both rate and efficiency of energy production in cells.

Lipoic acid (ALA; thioctic acid), chemically 5-(1,2-dithiolane-3-yl)valeric acid is a potent antioxidant and anti-crosslinking agent; it is purported to reduce hardening of arteries, wrinkling of skin and stiffening of joints. Glucosamine acts as an important nutrient supplement for old people as it stimulates manufacture of glycosaminoglycans, important components of the cartilage needed for healthy joints.

Carnosine, chemically b-alanyl-L-histidine, is a naturally occurring dipeptide found in large amounts in skeletal muscle and also in brain, cardiac muscle and kidney. It acts as an antioxidant, an anti-crosslinking and anti-glycating agent and protects against cataracts and neurodegeneration.

Epitalon, synthetic tetrapeptide, which has been found to have an anti-aging profile associated with pineal gland products, such as melatonin. It is reported to induce telomerase activity and telomerase elongation in human somatic cells. Melatonin has been shown to have a range of anti-ageing effects, including regulation of reproductive function, suppression of certain types of tumours and effects on mitochondrial function.

Resveratrol is a phytoalexin present in a number of plants. This polyphenol is also present in red wine and appears to be beneficial in protecting against age-related macular degeneration, possibly through its antioxidant, anti-proliferative properties. Resveratrol. Although the exact target of resveratrol remains elusive, there are at least three possible mechanisms of action. First, resveratrol might be an antioxidant. Second, resveratrol activates SIRT1. Third, resveratrol suppresses mitogen-induced phosphorylation of S6K (a target of TOR) and subsequent cell hypertrophy, which is exactly what rapamycin does. Perhaps resveratrol is an indirect inhibitor of the TOR Pathway. Similar to metformin, resveratrol activates the kinase AMPK and induces PPARg coactivator-1a (PGC-1a). It has been suggested that resveratrol induces PGC-1a by activating SIRT1. Alternatively, AMPK is known to activate PGC-1a. In fact, both resveratrol and metformin activate AMPK and induce PGC-1a .[17]

Table 3.3 Other popular 'natural' ingredients for ageing skin without published studies in a Medline search.

Ingredient	Proposed mechanism
Seaweed extract	Antioxidant activity
Peppermint extract	Promotes circulation and relieves swelling
Algae extract	Unclear, possible antioxidant activity
Cucumber extract	Relieves swelling, suggested anti-inflammatory effects
Aloe vera	Anti-inflammatory effects
Wheat protein	Unclear
Witch hazel	Anti-inflammatory effects
Penthanol	Humectant

Along with above mentioned agents some foods like avocado, berries, green vegetables, garlic, ginger, nuts, yogurt, whole wheat pasta, brown rice, melons were reported as anti-aging foods. The safed musli (*Chlorophytum borivilianum*) traditionally used for the curing various diseases like aphrodisiac, adapatagen, restorative, health promotive tonic and anti-aging property has been reported.

3.4.2 Synthetic Drugs[17]

Aspirin

One of the most common causes of disability and death can arise from blood clots that develop inside a vessel. When dislodged, they may cause heart attack, or stroke. Aspirin (acetylsalicylic acid) is an analgesic, anti-inflammatory and antipyretic drug. It acts through inhibition of cyclooxygenase, the enzyme responsible for synthesis of prostaglandins and thromboxanes from arachidonic acid. Aspirin inhibits platelet aggregation and has an immediate and long-lasting effect on blood platelets, making them less likely to clump, hence reducing the risk of further clots. It is reported that aspirin delays the onset of endothelial senescence by preventing reduction of NO formation/generation and has also been found to inhibit senescence-associated beta-galactosidase activity and increased telomerase activity.

Doxycycline

Doxycycline is a derivative of tetracycline that retains antibacterial properties. Doxycycline hyclate (hydrochloride hemiethanolate hemihydrate) is reported to act as a skin rejuvenator through inhibition of matrix metalloproteinases (MMP). Its use was established in periodontal disease, where it is thought its action on connective tissue helps strengthen the gums. So theoretically, it may help to treat wrinkles if used topically, but studies are needed to determine safety and efficacy of such use.

Idebenone

Idebenone, a benzoquinone closely structurally related to CoQ10, is a potent agent in the treatment of wrinkles. It acts as an antioxidant and is more soluble than CoQ10. It can perform the same functions as CoQ10, but without autooxidation.

Inosine pranobex

Inosine pranobex (isoprinosine) is an immunostimulant complex formed from the p-acetamidobenzoate salt of dimethylaminoisopropanol and inosine in a 3:1 molar ratio. It has antiviral properties and is reported to restore immune responses in ageing humans.

Meclofenoxate

Meclofenoxate (centrophenoxine) possible anti-ageing benefits include protection against free radical damage in the brain, increased potential lifespan, reduction and prevention of age spots on the skin, increased mental energy, improved memory and learning ability, and prevention and treatment of stroke and brain injury. Animal studies have found that centrophenoxine is effective at removing lipofuscin (potassium age pigment) from the brain, heart, and skin. It has generally been prescribed for the treatment of cognitive deficits in the elderly. It is an agent with similar effects on learning and memory to vinpocetine and hydergine.

Metformin

Metformin is an antidiabetic drug, which works through enhancing the sensitivity of cell surface insulin receptors of muscle and fat cells to insulin involved in gluconeogenesis in the liver and thus reduce the risk of glycation and other age-related damage. Metformin also modulates stress responses through activation of adenosine monophosphate-activated protein kinase (AMPK) that exerts its effect through switching on pathways capable of preventing and repairing cell damage by producing a sudden bout of energy production concomitant with suppressing those energy demanding processes not directly essential for the survival of the organism. This is exactly what happens during calorie restriction when the body is in 'survival mode' and when nutritional stress of a low calorie diet activates pathways that increase cell repair. Therefore, metformin can act as a calorie restriction mimic.

Nimodipine

Nimodipine, a dihydropyridine calcium channel blocker developed for the treatment of high blood pressure. Nowadays, it is not generally used for this indication, but is frequently used for the treatment of vasospasm, a major complication of subarachnoid haemorrhage.

Picamilon

Picamilon is a proprietary name for sodium N-nicotinylgamma-aminobutyrate, and structurally it is a combination of GABA and niacin. It appears to be more effective than either hydergine or vinpocetine in improving blood flow in cerebral vessels that, in turn, produces cognitive enhancement. This effect is due to the synergy between the niacin and GABA molecules present in the hybrid structure, which readily crosses the blood brain barrier where it protects neurons against the effects of diminished oxygen during neurological ageing.

Piracetam

Piracetam[19], chemically 2-(2-oxopyrrolidin-1-yl)acetamide, is a nootropic that protects cerebral cortex from hypoxia, perhaps through enhancing blood flow. It increases the sensitivity of receptors in the brain involved in memory and learning and, hence, may help to slow down brain ageing.

Procaine

Procaine is a local anaesthetic, used in the treatment of arthritis and pain conditions. It reduces depression and provides a feeling of greater vitality and youthfulness. Procaine, however, has a stability problem and it rapidly hydrolyses in the body and remains active only for a comparatively short time. In order to improve its effect, a combination of procaine with benzoic acid as a preservative, and potassium metabisulfite as an antioxidant is used under the name of Gerovital H3 (GH3). Another combination, named Aslavital, has pyridoxine (vitamin B_6), mesoinositol and glutamic acid further supplementing those additives found in GH3. Aslavital is reported to have an even more powerful and beneficial effect on memory, atherosclerosis and other degenerative conditions than the original Gerovital H3. Gerovital H3 (GH3) also appears to be a relatively safe, yet weak MAO inhibitor and represents a major advance in the field of antiageing. Procaine, as Gerovital H3 and Aslavital, has numerous documented mechanisms of action. These include inhibition of monoamine oxidase (an enzyme in the brain that increases with age); nootropic properties and antioxidant action. It can be a useful adjuvant to other longevity agents and may be able to potentiate their effectiveness. When procaine enters the body, it is broken down into para-aminobenzoic acid (PABA), and diethylaminoethanol (DEAE), both of which are naturally present in the body. Both of these substances are biologically active and have numerous beneficial effects of their own. Although the majority of the research involving Gerovital and Aslavital attributes the benefits to the procaine molecule itself, there is still controversy as to whether the effects are due to procaine molecule itself, or its metabolites, PABA and DEAE.

Dimethylaminoethanol (deanol; DMAE)

It is an analogue of DEAE, is a precursor of choline and is a naturally occurring nutrient found in foods such as anchovies and sardines. It stimulates the production of choline, which, in turn, allows the brain to optimize production of acetylcholine. Acetylcholine is the primary neurotransmitter involved in learning and memory. DMAE inhibits the formation of ageing pigment (lipofuscin) and flushes it from the body. Lipofuscin is believed to be formed by the inefficient metabolism of fatty acids, and it accumulates with age in all body tissues, acting as intracellular garbage. Dimethylaminoethanol supposedly also has a positive effect on periorbital oedema (swelling of the eyelids) and on skin tightness. p-Aminobenzoic acid (PABA) has been used as a component of many commercially available sunscreens, due to its ability to block damaging ultraviolet rays. PABA, both topically and orally, is truly an anti-ageing substance with respect to its ability to protect skin from the sun. This versatile substance also has the potential to restore hair to its natural colour and encourage hair regrowth. PABA also acts as an antioxidant, protecting cellular membranes and mitochondrial DNA from free radical attack and oxidative stress. With respect to its other actions on ageing, it also acts as an anti-crosslinking agent by slowing and, in some cases, even reversing crosslinking in connective tissue proteins, such as collagen, and thus may enhance flexibility in normally ageing individuals.

Pyritinol

Pyritinol promotes the uptake of glucose by the brain. It is used in the treatment of various cerebrovascular and mental disorders. It produces an even more pronounced enhancement of cognitive function than ergolines and has been used for the treatment of a wide variety of neurologic disorders.

Selegiline

Selegiline (deprenyl), an antiparkinsonian drug, is an irreversible inhibitor of monoamineoxidase type B, an enzyme involved in the metabolic degradation of dopamine. Inhibition of the enzyme thereby elevates dopamine levels in the brain and central nervous system. In addition to its use as a drug for Parkinson's disease, it has also proved clinically useful for the treatment of depression and dementia. Selegiline is also noteworthy for its ability to upregulate antioxidant enzyme activities while simultaneously suppressing hydroxyl radical formation in the Substantia nigra.

Sirtuin activators

It has been suggested that calorie restriction extends the replicative lifespan of yeast by increasing the activity of SIR2, a member of the conserved sirtuin family of NAD(+)-dependent protein deacetylases that includes SIRT1, a human deacetylase. Drug screening has revealed three classes of small molecules that activate sirtuins. The effects of SIR2 on chronological lifespan are, however, are opposite to those on replicative lifespan and suggest that the relevant activities of SIR2-like deacetylases might be also complex in higher eukaryotes. Humans contain nine sirtuins. SIRT1 seems to antagonize the TOR pathway downstream of TOR. In fact, TOR activates the fat regulator PPAR-g, which is essential for adipocyte differentiation and fat accumulation. By contrast, SIRT1 represses genes controlled by PPAR-g, thus antagonizing TOR downstream. In addition, whereas TOR induces rDNA transcription, SIRT1 silences it.

Rapamycin

Rapamycin is an antifungal antibiotic a natural product that, in low nanomolar concentrations, selectively and effectively inhibits TOR. Because TOR is evolutionarily conserved, rapamycin inhibits TOR in both yeast and human cells. Moreover, TOR is antagonistically pleiotropic; thus, rapamycin inhibits yeast growth, while decelerating yeast senescence. Similarly, TOR is essential for the developmental growth but might be dispensable later in life. If so, rapamycin must be well-tolerated in humans. Indeed, rapamycin is used in combinations with other drugs to prevent organ rejection after renal transplantation. Renal transplant patients who receive rapamycin daily for several years do not seem to have obligatory problems from sustained blockage of TOR. Among the side-effects of rapamycin, there are no pronounced immunosuppressive problems (viral, bacterial and fungal infections, Kaposi's sarcoma or osteoporosis). Furthermore, rapamycin can be used to treat invasive fungal infections and HIV. The antifungal antibiotic rapamycin is not a classic immunosuppressant; rather, it modulates the immune response. Ironically, it was assumed that rapamycin would predispose patients to osteoporosis and cancer, but instead it turns out that rapamycin has anti-cancer and bone-sparing activities.[18]

3.5 An overview on Treatment Options for Skin Aging

3.5.1 Products

Sunscreen, Moisturizers, Tretinoin

3.5.2 Injectables and Fillers

- Botox cosmetic, Dysport
- Zyderm (bovine collagen)
- Restylane (hyaluronic acid)
- Juvederm (hyaluronic acid)
- Radiesse (hydroxyapatite)
- Evolence (porcine collagen)
- Sculptra (poly-L-lactic acid)

3.5.3 Peels and Microdermabrasion

- Light "lunchtime" peels: glycolic, beta, Jessner
- Medium depth peels: trichloroacetic acid
- Microdermabrasion: high pressure crystals delivered to skin which remove dead skin cells

3.5.4 Thermage

- Radiofrequency waves delivered to deeper skin layer which causes tightening of skin
- Produces heat in deeper layers of skin while maintaining cool on surface of skin
- Little recovery and not successful in all patients!

3.5.5 Laser

- Vascular lasers and intense pulsed light remove tiny blood vessels and brown spots
- Q switched lasers (Ruby, Versapulse, Medlite) remove brown spots
- Fraxel (fractionated erbium laser)
- Fractional CO_2 (fractionated CO_2 laser)

3.5.6 Intense Pulsed Light

Intense Pulsed Light uses different wavelengths of light to target "broken" blood vessels and superficial brown spots. The light energy is changed to heat energy, which gradually fades the targeted pigment or vessels.

3.5.7 Fraxel

- Multiple tiny microscopic columns of erbium laser light treat a fraction of the skin at one treatment, making recovery much easier than resurfacing treatments.
- Requires multiple treatments.
- Decreases fine lines, wrinkles, scars and skin blotchiness but not good for deep lines and sagging skin.

3.6 Formulations[19,20]

Sample 1 (Himalaya Anti-Wrinkle Cream)

Aloe vera (Barbados Aloe, Kumari) contains enzymes, polysaccharides and skin nutrients which exhibit antibacterial and antifungal action. It also has a natural sunscreen effect.

Papaver rhoeas (Red Poppy, Rakta-posta) acts as an emollient and a soothing agent.

Vitis vinifera (Grapes, Draksha) contains vitamins and minerals, which nourish the skin.

Citrus limon (Lemon, Nimbaka) and *Solanum lycopersicum* (Tomato, Raktamaci) are rich sources of vitamin C and A respectively and both have an antioxidant and natural sunscreen effect.

Santalum album (Sandalwood Tree, Chandana) has been used in skin diseases to alleviate itching and inflammation.

Sample 2 (Revitol Anti Aging Solution Ingredients)

Argireline

Dermox SRC

DMAE (Dimethylaminoethanol Bitartrate)

Edelweis extract

Evening primrose oil

Hyaluronic acid

Hydrolyzed wheat gluten and *Ceratonia siliqua*

LipoLight OAP

Macrocystis pyrifera

Matrixyl

Pentacare NA

Shea Butter

Skin tightener ST

Squalene

Vitamin A

Vitamin E

Home remedies for anti-aging

1. There are many benefits of honey, one being its anti-aging property. Take ½ tablespoon of honey and mix it with 1-2 tablespoon of rose water. Apply this mixture on face, neck, and other dry skin area. Leave it for about 15-20 minutes. Now wash it off with tepid water. Honey moisturizes and soothes dry skin. This mixture will clean the skin and tone it to give you a glowing complexion with wrinkle free skin.
2. Quit smoking: Cigarette smoke ages skin by releasing an enzyme that breaks down elastin and collagen- vital components of skin.
3. Drink lots of water during the day to provide optimum supply of moisture to the skin.
4. Do not over-wash the face. Washing face too often removes skin off its natural barrier oils and moisture that protect against wrinkles.

5. Turmeric powder when combined with sugar cane juice gives a paste that is quite effective in controlling wrinkles and prevents the skin from aging.
6. Milk is one of the gentlest and effective ways of removing dead skin cells. This will give a glowing skin naturally. Lactic acid in milk helps generate new skin cells. This home remedy also helps to improve the skin's texture and does wonders to even out the tone of the skin. Apply a little milk each night after washing your face.
7. Apply vitamin E oil or cod liver oil to the discolored area. If we do this daily the age spots will fade.
8. Many wrinkles are caused by the skin staying immobile for long periods of time. By doing regular expression exercises, we will increase the elasticity in your skin and reduce wrinkles.

3.7 Evaluation of the Anti-wrinkle Efficacy of Cosmetic Formulations [21]

We can determine both the width and depth of the wrinkles with the apparatus Clinipro Antiaging SD, using the IMAGE DB system. It has a flat probe. We can determine the amount of water present in the surface layers of the skin with a flat probe. With the help of values obtained, the percentage of reduction during the study period was calculated. Photographs were taken of these wrinkles on all the volunteers before starting the test and after 30 days of application of the product.

Accurate and fixed amount of the formulation was deposited with syringe, onto the entire surface of the faces of volunteers aged between 40 and 57 years. The face was then gently and uniformly massaged for 30 seconds, until complete absorption of the formulation. The volunteers were divided into two groups, those with dry skin and those with oily skin, 50% of the volunteers in the study had oily skin and the other 50% dry skin. The study was always carried out by the same person in order to reduce possible experimental errors, during the experiment period the volunteer should not use other preparations. The environmental conditions were between 23°C-25°C and relative humidity of 60%.

Two types of trials were carried out

Short-term trial: The formulation is applied for every 12 hours and measurements were taken 24 hrs after application.

Long-term trial: In this, the volunteers were treated with the formulation for one month, twice a day. Then the aqueous content of the skin was determined after 7, 15, 21 and 30 days.

Sensorial evaluation

In order to obtain volunteer's personal perceptions, the volunteers were asked about the product during its application and its action at the end of the study

The tests for sensorial evaluation

Based on the absence or presence of sensorial properties acceptability of the products is determined. The organoleptic characteristics like thick, hard, creamy, smooth, soft, dry, thin, spreadable, cool or warm were evaluated.

Adequacy was assessed by the patients themselves, who classified them within the following categories: Satisfactory, Passable, Non-satisfactory.

Improvement in the texture and elasticity of the skin: evaluated in terms of the appearance and feel of the skin, assigning one of the following categories: Very Good, Good, Passable, Bad. The parameters were visually assessed by the researchers.

The researchers assigned points to the reduction in the wrinkles, comparing each time point with the photograph taken at the start of the study:

1. No reduction,
2. Slight reduction,
3. Medium reduction,
4. Considerable reduction.

Other methods available for Instrumental and clinical evaluations[22]

Skin elasticity

Skin elasticity measurement is based on the suction/elongation method with the subsequent release of the skin inside the opening of the instrument device. The instrument used for measuring is the cutometer (CUTOMETER® MPA 580). In this study the skin elasticity is calculated by the ratio between the residual deformation and the maximum elongation of the skin. This ratio indicates the ability of the skin to return to its original state of recovery after a stressing event. Closer the value is to 1, more elastic the skin is.

Skin profilometry

Decrease of wrinkle depth is measured by means of Visioscan VC 98; a camera used for in vivo analysis of skin surface. The parameters valued in the image analysis are:

SEw: skin micro-wrinkleness

SESm: skin smoothness

Wrinkle volume

Digital photography

The camera was set up to the best quality of image (2304 x 1728 pixel, 4.0 Mp). Red and blue components of the skin were measured using a software dedicated for image analysis.

Self assessment

After 60 days of product use the subjects are asked to express their personal opinion answering to a questionnaire.

3.8 Some Marketed Anti Aging Products

NATURA BISSE
Diamond Extreme Anti Aging Bio Regenerative Extreme Cream.

PAYOT Benefice Soleil Anti-Aging Protective Cream SPF 30 UVA/UVB.

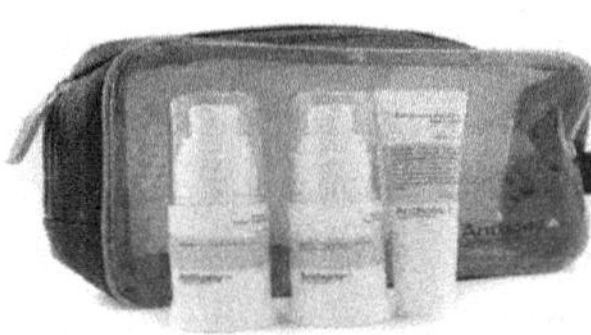

ANTHONY Logistics for men the Anti-Aging Starter Kit: Facial Treatment + Facial Serum + Eye Cream.

ORLANE B21 Anti-Aging Sun Cream SPF 30 for Face and Body

Revitol Anti Aging Solution

[Colour Fig. on page 398-399]

3.9 Conclusions

Solar energy in the form of UV and IR radiation and its effects on human skin have been extensively studied and currently are the best understood of all the extrinsic factors contributing to skin aging. Intrinsic, biologic aging can differ morphologically and pathophysiologically from extrinsic, environmentally induced aging of the skin. Many of these differences and changes recently have been associated with protein biochemical, cellular, and metabolic reactions involving various free radicals, oxidants, and reductants that are biochemically essential to the very existence of any aerobic biological system. The induction of many of these free radicals and reactive oxygen species has been attributed to the environment and its pollutants, which then affect cellular biochemical systems either favorably or unfavorably, depending on the intracellular redox homeostasis of oxidants and antioxidants.

If we study about the concentration of plasma DHEA-S, it is very low before puberty, but rapidly increases at puberty and thereafter decreases significantly, both age-dependently and linearly in males and females. The mechanism of action and the beneficial effects of DHEA have been clarified. Now the number of elderly people is increasing all over the world. Low concentrations of plasma DHEA-S accelerate the occurrence of such adult diseases as diabetes mellitus, atherosclerosis, dementia and osteoporosis. Therefore, the replacement of DHEA is important for the prevention of adult disease as an anti-aging steroid.

References

1. Zoe Diana Draelos. What is anti-aging? *Journal of Cosmetic Dermatology* 2007; 73–74.
2. Oliver P Kreyden. Antiaging – a scientific topic or just a social trend? *Journal of Cosmetic Dermatology*. 2005; 228–229.

3. Pie´rard GE. Aging across the life span: time to think again. *J Cosmet Dermatol* 2004; **3**:50–53.

4. Braverman ER. Ageprint for antiaging medicine. *J Eur Anti Aging Med* 2005; **1**:7–8.

5. Suresh IS. Rattan. Hormesis in aging. *Ageing Research Reviews* 2008; **7**:63–78.

6. Byung Pal Yu. Approaches to anti-aging intervention: the promises and the uncertainties. *Mechanisms of Ageing and Development.* 1999; **111**:73–87.

7. Trautinger F. Mechanisms of photodamage of the skin and its functional consequences for skin aging. *Clin Exp Dermatol* 2001; **26**:573–577.

8. Pie´rard GE. The quandary of climacteric skin aging. *Dermatology* 1996; **193**:273–274.

9. De Grey AD, Ames BN, Andersen JK, et al. Time to talk SENS: critiquing the immutability of human aging. *Ann NY Acad Sci* 2002; **959**:452–462.

10. Giacomoni PU, Rein G. Factors of skin aging share common mechanisms. *Biogerontology* 2001; **2**:219–229.

11. Kaya G, Saurat JH. Dermatoporosis: a chronic cutaneous insufficiency/fragility syndrome. Clinicopathological features, mechanisms, prevention, and potential treatments. *Dermatology* 2007; **215**:284–294.

12. Nikola Getoff. Anti-aging and aging factors in life. The role of free radicals. *Radiation Physics and Chemistry*. 2007; **76**:1577–1586

13. Rittie L, Fisher GJ. *Ageing Research Reviews*. 2002; **1**:705–720.

14. Anthony V. Benedetto DO. The Environment and Skin Aging. *Clinics in Dermatology*. 1998; **16**:129-139.

15. Rainer H. Straub, Maurizio Cutolo, Bettina Zietz, Ju¨rgen Scho¨lmerich. The process of aging changes the interplay of the immune, endocrine and nervous systems. *Mechanisms of Ageing and Development.* 2001; **122**:1591–1611.

16. Thomas E. Johnson. Genetic influences on aging. *Experimental Gerontology*, 1997; **32**:11-22.

17. Vijay K. Kapoor, Janhvi Dureja and Renu Chadha. Synthetic drugs with anti-ageing effects. *Drug Discovery Today*. 2009; **14**:899-904.

18. Mikhail V. Blagosklonny. An anti-aging drug today: from senescence-promoting genes to anti-aging pill. *Drug Discovery Today*. 2007; 12.

19. http://store.himalayahealthcare.com

20. http://revitolreviews.org

21. Ruiz MA, Clares B, Morales ME, Gallardo V. Evaluation of the anti-wrinkle efficacy of cosmetic formulations with an antiaging peptide. *Ars Pharm,* 2010; **50(4)**; 168-176.

22. www.JanMarini.com

CHAPTER 4

ANTIPERSPIRANTS AND DEODORANTS

Y. Madhusudan Rao, Shayeda, D. Sathish, S. Himabindu

Center for Biopharmaceutics and Pharmacokinetics, University College of Pharmaceutical Sciences, Kakatiya University, Warangal-506 009, Andhra Pradesh, India.

4.1 Introduction

Perspiration is one of the essential processes of the normal functioning of skin. Sweating is the body's natural process of cooling.[1] Antiperspirants and deodorants are among the most widely used products under the personal care sector. Antiperspirants are products which minimize the sweat secretion while deodorants mask the body odour. The art of making the body smell better was evident in the early civilizations of Babylon, Assyria, Persia, China, Greece, and Rome.[2]

4.1.1 Physiology of Sweat Glands and Composition of Sweat

The human axilla region contains eccrine, and apocrine sweat glands. Approximately 25,000 sweat glands/axilla can produce up to 12 g sweat/hour.[3,4]

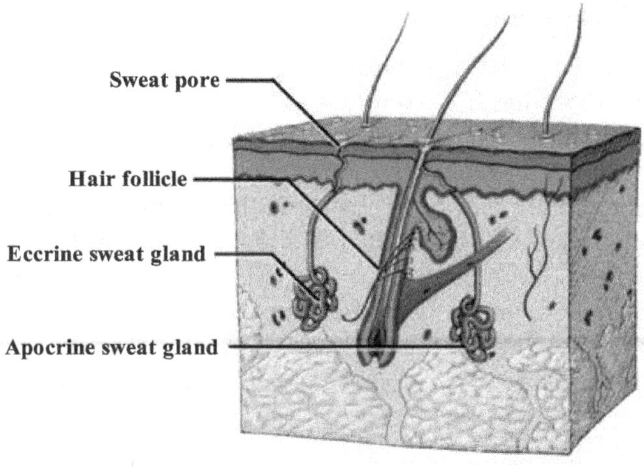

Fig. 4.1 Structure of sweat glands. [Colour Fig. on page 399]

Eccrine glands

These glands have sensory and excretory function which are stimulated by emotional and thermal stimuli.[5] They produce clear, colorless, and odorless liquid containing 98% to 99% water and 1% to 2% inorganic and organic compounds.[6] Inorganic components include NaCl and traces of K^+, Ca^{+2} , Mg^{+2} , Fe^{+3} and Cu^{+2} ions. Organic components include lactic acid, citric acid, formic acid, propionic acid, butyric acid, urea, and ammonia. These glands produce majority of sweat and are responsible for most of the underarm wetness. Antiperspirants are effective in reducing the amount of sweat produced only from eccrine glands. Eccrine sweat consists of water (99%), sodium chloride (0.7%), lactic acid (0.1%), ascorbic acid (0.04%), citric acid (0.04%), acetic acid (0.01%), propionic acid (0.006%), caprylic and caprionic acid (0.005%) and trace amounts of urea and uric acids.

Apocrine glands

These glands produce a milky, viscous fluid during puberty at specific regions of the body, especially the underarm pit.[7] Unlike eccrine glands, the openings of these glands are not at the skin surface but appear at the hair follicle. Skin bacteria decompose apocrine sweat, which is responsible for the characteristic malodour of human sweat. Apocrine sweat consists of water, proteins, carbohydrates, and ammonium salts.[8] Lipids, cholesterol, and steroids are also reported to be present in the apocrine sweat.[9]

4.1.2 Development of Antiperspirants and Deodorants

Ziryab invented under-arm deodorants in Al-Andalus in the 9th century.[10] In 1888, the first commercial deodorant, Mum, was developed and patented by a U.S. inventor in Philadelphia, Pennsylvania.[11] In the late 1940s, Edward Gelsthorpe developed an applicator based on the newly invented ball-point pen.[11] In 1952, their company began to market the product under the name Ban Roll-On.[11] The product was briefly withdrawn from the market in the U.S.[4] It is once again available at retailers in the U.S. under the brand Ban.[12] In the UK it is sold under the names Mum Solid and Mum Pump Spray.[11] Chattem acquired Ban deodorant brand in 1998[13] and subsequently sold it to Kao Corporation in 2000.[14]

Jules Montenier on January 28, 1941 patented the modern formulation of the antiperspirant.[15] This patent addressed the problem of the excessive acidity of aluminium chloride and its excessive irritation of the skin, by combining it with a soluble nitrile or a similar compound. This formulation was first found in "Stopette" deodorant spray, which Time Magazine called "the best-selling deodorant of the early 1950s".[16]

The first aerosol antiperspirant in the marketplace was Gillette's Right Guard[17], in the early 1960s.[18] Aerosols became more popular because of the ease of application without coming in contact with the underarm area.[17] By the late 1960s, half of all the antiperspirants sold in the U.S. were aerosols, and they continued to grow in all sales to 82% by the early 1970s. However, in the late 1970s the issues raised by the Food and Drug Administration (FDA) and the Environmental Protection Agency (EPA) had great impact on the popularity of these products. The FDA prohibited the use of the active ingredient, aluminium zirconium chemicals in aerosols, due to safety concerns over long term inhalation and the EPA limited the use of chlorofluorocarbon (CFC) propellants used in aerosols due to the fact that these gases can contribute to depletion of the ozone layer. As the popularity of aerosols slowly decreased, stick antiperspirants became more and more popular. Today, sticks are the most popular type of antiperspirant.[17]

4.2 Antiperspirants

An antiperspirant, is defined by the Department of Health and Human Services as “A drug product applied topically that reduces the production of perspiration (sweat) at that site”.[19]

Antiperspirants are also deodourants because of their ability to reduce perspiration that serves as a medium in the development of axillary odor, whereas, a deodorant product only reduces the body odour and does not reduce perspiration and hence it can only be labelled as a deodorant.

4.2.1 Antiperspirant's Action

The action of antiperspirant depends mostly on the type of active incorporated in the formulation (aluminum salts, nonionic agents, or ionic agents). The antiperspirants based on aluminum and/or aluminum zirconium salts act by the mechanical blockage of sweat glands by forming an occlusive plug of metal hydroxide in the eccrine duct[20], which prevent the eccrine secretions from reaching the skin surface in the axilla without significantly altering balance of the thermal regulatory system. Studies based on tape stripping experiments followed by analysis of transmission electron micrographs of an ACH-treated eccrine sweat gland duct show an obstructive amorphous material supporting the theory of a mechanical obstruction of sweat glands.[21,22]

These occlusive plugs can block the sweat duct for seven to 14 days depending on the rate of skin desquamation, consumer's hygiene regime, activity type, and quality of the product.[24] The FDA has included in the OTC Antiperspirant Final Monograph guidelines, the minimum standard for effectiveness at 20% sweat reduction to allow a product to be labeled as an antiperspirant.[25]

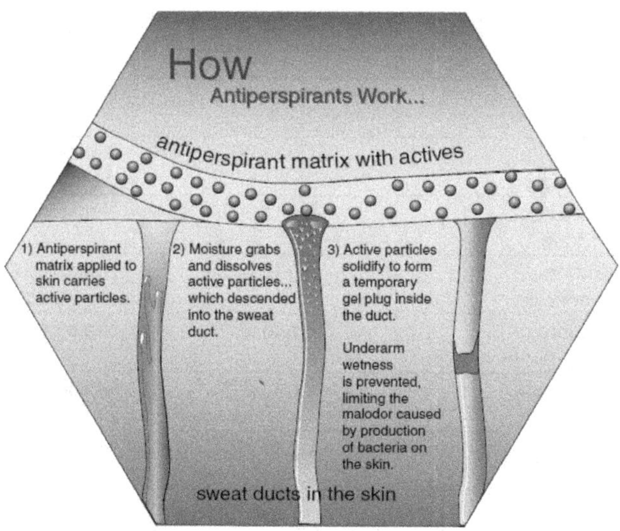

Fig. 4.2 Figure showing shallow plug formation in the sweat duct explaining the mechanism of action of current antiperspirant products.[23]

4.2.2 Formulation

Active ingredients

The final OTC antiperspirant monograph included the 18 approved active ingredients for use in antiperspirant products in the U.S. Table 4.1 shows some details of each of the approved ingredients, in which the approved active ingredient can be formulated. There are no specific active ingredient lists specified by the European Union (EU) or Japan.

Table 4.1 Antiperspirant Active Ingredients.

Active ingredient	Concentration	Dosage form
Aluminum chloride	Up to 15% (calculated on hexahydrate form)	Only aqueous solution (must be nonaerosol)
Aluminum chlorohydrate	Up to 25%	Aerosol or nonaerosol
Aluminum chlorohydrex polyethylene glycol	Up to 25%	Aerosol or nonaerosol
Aluminum chlorohydrex propylene glycol	Up to 25%	Aerosol or nonaerosol
Aluminum dichlorohydrate	Up to 25%	Aerosol or nonaerosol
Aluminum dichlorohydrex polyethylene glycol	Up to 25%	Aerosol or nonaerosol
Aluminum dichlorohydrex propylene glycol	Up to 25%	Aerosol or nonaerosol
Aluminum sesquichlorohydrate	Up to 25%	Aerosol or nonaerosol
Aluminum sesquichlorohydrex polyethylene glycol	Up to 25%	Aerosol or nonaerosol
Aluminum sesquichlorohydrex propylene glycol	Up to 25%	Aerosol or nonaerosol
Aluminum zirconium octachlorohydrate	Up to 20%	Nonaerosol
Aluminum zirconium octachlorohydrex gly	Up to 20%	Nonaerosol
Aluminum zirconium pentachlorohydrate	Up to 20%	Nonaerosol
Aluminum zirconium pentachlorohydrex gly	Up to 20%	Nonaerosol
Aluminum zirconium tetrachlorohydrate	Up to 20%	Nonaerosol
Aluminum zirconium tetrachlorohydrex gly	Up to 20%	Nonaerosol
Aluminum zirconium trichlorohydrate	Up to 20%	Nonaerosol
Aluminum zirconium trichlorohydrex gly	Up to 20%	Nonaerosol

Major antiperspirant marketers are currently producing products incorporating actives with enhanced effectiveness such as activated aluminium chlorohydrate and activated aluminium zirconium chlorohydrate. The activated antiperspirant salts are identical in chemical compositions to the conventional actives. 'Activated' or 'enhanced' species have distribution of the active molecular species, thereby resulting in significantly increased sweat reduction capabilities when compared to the standard or inactivated product.[26]

The ideal requirements when designing an antiperspirant formulation include

1. The formulation should minimize sweat production for longer duration
2. The product should be non-toxic and should not cause any irritation
3. There should be a good skin feel when using the product.
4. Suitable perfumes should be used (bold perfumes in antiperspirants for men and mostly pleasant perfumes in formulations for women).
5. The delivery system selected should keep the actives in solubilized form.

4.2.3 Regulatory Status

The regulatory status of antiperspirants is different in various regions of the world market place.

India

In India a well defined Drugs and Cosmetics Act (1940) operates the regulations of cosmetics under the authority of Central Drugs Standard Control Organization (CDSCO). In India an antiperspirant is categorized as an over-the-counter (OTC) drug product. The deodorant market in India is worth Rs 200 crore. On an average, deodorants sell at least 5% more than talcum powders in supermarkets. The success of deodorants in the urban market has encouraged the leading players in the sector to launch more deo-related products. The latent demand for antiperspirants and deodorants in India is not actual or historic sales. Nor is latent demand future sales. In fact, latent demand can be either lower or higher than actual sales if a market is inefficient (i.e., not representative of relatively competitive levels). In India we can find a large demand for deo-sprays and roll-ons rather than other formulations.

United States

In the United States an antiperspirant is an over-the-counter (OTC) drug product which is regulated by the Food and Drug Administration (FDA). In 1972 the FDA announced a proposed review of the safety, effectiveness, and labeling of all OTC drugs by an independent advisory panel. In 1978 the FDA announced that OTC antiperspirants are generally recognized as safe and effective and not misbranded. In 1982 the FDA issued a tentative final monograph for antiperspirants. In 1990 the FDA issued a rule that some antiperspirant ingredients are not generally recognized as safe and effective and are misbranded. In 2003 the FDA issued the final monograph for antiperspirant products and it became effective from December 2004 and did not address foot antiperspirancy claims. But the monograph did not identify any OTC antiperspirant products which are effective in reducing perspiration.[19]

European Union

In the Europe countries antiperspirants are considered to be cosmetic products which are regulated by European Cosmetic Directive, which defines cosmetic product as "any substance or preparation intended to come in contact with the various surface areas of the body (epidermis, hair, and capillaries, nails, lips, and external genital organs) or with the teeth and buccal mucosae, solely or principally for cleansing, perfuming, or protective purposes in order to maintain them in good condition, modify their appearance, and/or improve body odor, and/or protect or maintain them in good order".[27-30] The European Cosmetic Directive has several objectives, but the ultimate goal is to deliver safe products to the consumer.

Japan

In Japan antiperspirant products are regulated by Japan's Pharmaceutical Affairs Law (PAL). Antiperspirant products in Japan are regulated and classified as quasi-drugs. A quasi-drug is an article used only for certain purposes that are specifically designated by the Ministry of Health and Welfare (MHW). Antiperspirants are categorized according to the effects against body odor, perspiration odor, and suppression of perspiration.[23]

4.2.4 Delivery Systems and Application Forms for Antiperspirant Actives

Antiperspirant actives can be formulated in a variety of delivery systems like anhydrous suspensions, water- or hydroalcoholic-based solutions, and emulsions. Typical application forms for antiperspirants can be broadly classified into three categories: sticks, roll-ons and aerosols.

Deodorant/antiperspirant sticks

Sticks can be further classified into different classes like suspension sticks, gel sticks, and emulsion sticks.

Suspension sticks

The active ingredient in the form of a powder is suspended in a silicone oil phase and stearyl alcohol is usually used as the hardening agent. The molten mass crystallizes into a matrix of stearyl alcohol saturated with the silicone oil and suspended particles.[31,32] Quaternium-18 hectorite can reduce the settling of the actives. Cyclomethicones give the stick a dry, silky feel; non-volatile oils, like PPG-14 butylether, minimize white residues on the skin.[33]

Gel sticks

Various gelling agents employed in this kind of sticks include N-acyl amino acid amides (N-lauroyl-L-glutamic acid dibutylamide) and 12 hydroxyacid and dibenzylidene sorbitol [dibenzylaldehyde monosorbitol acetal, (DBMS A)]. These sticks turn clear after application to the skin (no-residue stick)[34], without leaving any white residue on skin.

Table 4.2 Suspension Stick.

Suspension Stick	Weight %
Stearyl alcohol	18-22
Cyclomethicone	52-56
PPG-14 butylether	1-3
Hydrogenated castor oil	0.5-3
Talc	1-3
Antiperspirant	18-22
Fragrance	0.5-2

Table 4.3 Gel Sticks.

Clear anhydrous gel sticks	Weight %
Dibenzylidene sorbitol	1-3
Dimethicone copolyol	1-3
Di-isopropyl sebacate	1-3
Glycine	0.5-2
Dipropyleneglycol	08-12
Propyleneglycol	31-35
Antiperspirant powder	48-52

Emulsion sticks

They can be either O/W emulsions or W/O emulsions. The O/W Emulsions are clear while W/O Emulsion Sticks are white in colour. In both the cases the actives are solubilized in water phase.

Table 4.4 W/O Emulsion Sticks.

W/O Emulsion Sticks	Weight %
Stearyl alcohol	17-21
Volatile silicone	24-28
Mineral oil	0.5-2
2-Methyl-2,4 pentandiol	1-3
Polyglycerol-4 isostearate	1-3
ACH solution (50%)	48-52

ACH, aluminum chlorohydrate

Antiperspirant roll-ons

Roll-on products give a nongreasy and nonoily feel in the axilla and spreadability of the contents is also good. They can be formulated into many categories such as aqueous solutions, alcoholic solutions, hydro alcoholic solutions, emulsions or suspensions and transparent roll on (micro emulsion gel).

Clear hydroalcoholic roll-on

The active ingredient is solubilized in water/alcohol system of and thickened with a water-soluble polymer like hydroxyethylcellulose. The inclusion of alcohol in the formula gives compared with the clear aqueous solution-based roll-ons, a fresh sensation in the axilla and facilitates drying of the product. Excellent antiperspirant efficacy is another benefit of hydroalcoholic roll-ons.

Emulsion roll-on

These can be either of O/W or W/O types. In both the types the actives are dissolved in aqueous phase. The O/W systems are added with ethoxylated surfactants, like PEG-40 stearate, to solubilize the oil phase. Compared to O/W roll-on formulations the W/O formulations are weaker in efficacy because the actives are encapsulated within the internal phase and the external oil phase often gives a sticky feeling. Emulsion roll-ons can also be formulated into W/S systems or O/W Micro-Emulsion Gel. In W/S formulations Silicone oils are used which give a better skin feel compared to the traditional oily components, like ester oils or triglycerides used in O/W roll-on formulations. O/W Micro-Emulsion Gels use the principle of phase inversion temperature (PIT) where a mixture of surfactants, oils, and water is heated from 60°C-90°C to give a W/O emulsion above the PIT. During cooling, the mixture shows phase inversion to give white or transparent O/W emulsions.[35]

Table 4.5 O/W Emulsion Roll-On.

O/W Emulsion Roll-On	Weight %
PEG-40 stearate	3-7
Cetyl alcohol	1-5
Mineral oil	1-3
Glycerin	0.5-3
Polysorbate-80	0.5-3
Mg-aluminum silicate	0.6-0.10
Antiperspirant active	18-22
Water	64-68

Table 4.6 Hydroalcoholic Roll-On.

Hydroalcoholic Roll-On	Weight %
Antiperspirant active	18-22
PPG-5 ceteth 20	0.5-3
Water	33-37
Ethanol	40-44
Hydroxyethylcellulose	0.3-0.7

In the above formula PPG-5 cetech 20 is a solubilizer, emollient, humectant for clear gels. It reduces the fabric staining in antiperspirants.

Suspension roll-on

In this type of systems powered antiperspirant active is suspended in cylomethicone. The roll-on can be formulated with or without ethanol. Quaternium-18 hectorite is used as a thickener which prevents settling of the suspended particles. This delivery system does not give a wet feeling after application and gets dried off easily. Actives like ZAG complexes give high efficacy to underarm products (Table 4.7).

Antiperspirant aerosols

Aerosols are the most popular delivery systems for antiperspirants for consumers who prefer a hygienic and easy-to-use application form. Typical ingredients for aerosols include isopropyl myristate, isopropyl palmitate, volatile silicone, dimethicone, silica, clays, propylene carbonate, and ethanol. Propellants include propane, butane, and isobutane (Table 4.8). As acidic aqueous ACH solutions lead to corrosion of the aerosol can, current aerosol antiperspirant products are formulated as water-free suspensions. The active is suspended as a powder in an oil phase like cyclomethicone or in a mixture of ester oils/cyclomethicone. Agglomeration of solid particles and settling of actives can be minimized by the usage of suspending agents like fumed silica (amorphous silicon dioxide) or clays (bentonite and hectorite). The clays form a weak gel in the presence of an oil phase that can be destroyed by shaking the aerosol can before usage. The gel structure is reformed on standing, thereby holding the active in suspension. Because the organoclays are agglomerated, shear is needed to deagglomerate the platelets, and a polar activator like propylene carbonate or ethanol is used to disperse them and induce the gelation of the oil phase.

The steps involved to prepare an aerosol product can be summarized in the following sequence[36]:

1. Preparing bentonite or hectorite clay with the emollient in the presence of the polar activator and shearing the mixture.
2. Adding the antiperspirant active until a uniform agglomeration-free suspension is obtained.
3. Filling the concentrate into the aerosol can and adding the propellant (pressure filling).

Efficacy studies of aerosols, including comparison with other drug delivery systems, have been reported in the literature.[37] ZAG complexes are not allowed to be used in aerosols.

Table 4.7 Suspension Roll-On.

Suspension Roll-On	Weight %
Volatile silicone	63-67
Quaternium-18 hectorite	11-15
Silica	0.3-0.7
Antiperspirant powder	18-22
Fragrance	0.5-3

Table 4.8 Antiperspirant Aerosol

Antiperspirant aerosol	Weight %
Volatile silicone	11-15
Quaternium-18 hectorite	0.6-1
Ethanol	0.6-1
Antiperspirant powder	08-12
Propellant (butane/propane)	73-77

Ref source for formulations[38]

4.2.5 Labeling Requirements for Antiperspirants

According to the antiperspirant monograph, labelling requirements for an antiperspirant drug product are as follows:

- A statement that the product be identified as an antiperspirant and describing the drug identity by its established name, if a drug is present.
- When describing "uses" the following phrases may be used: "decreases," "lessens," or reduces underarm: "dampness," "perspiration," "sweat," "sweating," or "wetness."
- Other language can be appended to the phrase if it is truthful and not a misleading statement describing an established use as follows: "decreases, lessens or reduces" underarm "dampness, perspiration, sweat, sweating or wetness due to stress."

For products that claim to reduce the sweat production to the minimum standard of 20% over a 24-hour period the label may state either "all day protection," "lasts all day," "lasts 24 hours," or "24-hour protection." For products that demonstrate extra effectiveness of above 20% sweat reduction the label may state "extra effective."

The product label must also contain the following items listed under "Warnings:"

"Do not use on broken skin"

"Stop use if rash or irritation occurs"

"Ask a doctor before use if you have kidney disease"

If the product is aerosolized:

"When using this product keep away from face and mouth to avoid breathing it" "Directions:"

"Apply to underarms only"

4.3 Deodorants

Deodorants are topically applied products designed to reduce underarm odour.

The armpit, also known as the axilla, is the home to four principal groups of bacteria, with staphylococcal or aerobic coryneform species acting as the dominant strain. The high moisture content and high pH value in the axillary region compared to other regions of the body provide a favorable environment for the development of this microflora. Microbial biotransformation of components of apocrine secretion, e.g., isovaleric acid and androstenone to the corresponding volatile metabolites including ammonia and short chain fatty acids, which are characteristically malodorous, is the main reason for axillary odor.

4.3.1 Strategies to Reduce Underarm Odor

Antiperspirant active-containing deodorants

Antiperspirant actives such as aluminum chlorohydrate or the Al–Zr complexes reduce the secretion of eccrine sweat thereby reducing the moisture necessary for the proliferation of axillary microflora. Aluminium salts decrease the pH value in the axillary region due to their acidic nature which plays a major role in bacterial growth inhibition.

Odor-masking deodorants

Perfumes are added to the deodorant formulations to mask the underarm odor. They are incorporated in the range of 0.2% to 1.5%. The final perception of the perfume varies among individuals and depends mainly on the specific underarm odor as the perfumes blend with the underarm odor and thereby mask it.[39] Attempts have also been made to neutralize the underarm odor by incorporating compounds such a sodium bicarbonate and zinc carbonate into deodorant formulations.[40-43]

Odor-quenching deodorants

Zinc salts of ricinoleic acid metal oxides such as the oxides of calcium, magnesium, and zinc have odor quenching activity. Ligand-exchange reactions of ricinoleic acid for odorous principles of sweat are probably the reason for the quenching properties of zinc ricinoleate[44], while the metal oxides act by forming the corresponding metal soaps.[45]

Antimicrobial active-containing deodorants

Usage of antimicrobials is the most widely used strategy to overcome underarm odor. This approach is based on the simple fact that destruction of bacteria causing the breakdown of underarm sweat into odorous principles, could help prevent underarm odor. Ethanol is probably one of the best-known actives for deodorization.[46] Addition of antimicrobials gives an added benefit to the formulation for a long-term deodorization.

Triclosan (2,4,40-trichloro-20-hydroxydiphenylether) is a broad-spectrum antimicrobial active against most Gram-positive and Gram-negative bacteria. Triclosan containing deodorant formulations have proven better deodorizing capability compared to the Triclosan-free formulations.[47]

Products containing glyceryl fatty acid esters have been successfully marketed as antimicrobial deodorants. Unlike triclosan, they have the advantage of higher biodegradability and selective bacterial action. When combined with farnesol and phenoxyethanol, glyceryl monolaurate showed synergistic effect against coryneform bacteria. Many Mono and oligoglyceryl fatty acid esters such as glyceryl monocaprylate, monocaprinate, monolaurate, and diglyceryl monocaprinate are shown to be effective deodorizers.[48-52] The fatty acid esters of sucrose like sucrose monostearate and sucrose monolaurate have also shown deodorizing properties due to their antimicrobial activity.

4.4 New Concepts for Controlling Underarm Odor

Chitosan

Chitosan has deodorizing properties which can be used in combination with aluminum salts.[53] Chitosan is derived from a naturally occurring polysaccharide, chitin. Deacetylation of the amino group in chitin leads to the production of slightly water-soluble chitosan.

Bacterial enzyme inhibitors

According to a patent filed in 1990, the enzyme amino acid (3-lyase) present in the underarm microflora, acts as a catalyst in the breakdown of apocrine sweat components resulting in malodour. Several classes of enzyme inhibitors such as derivatives of hydroxylamines, 3-substituted amino acids, cycloserine, and pyridoxal were identified that inhibit the bacterial enzyme and minimize the odor generation.[54] An alternatel approach is to provide an alternative substrate for the bacterial enzyme instead of sulphur-containing amino acid sequences of apocrine sweat. This approach leads to the generation of non-odorous ingredients, such as benzoic acid, or pleasant odor-generating substances, such as phenylacetic acid.[55]

Antiadhesives

This strategy is based upon the concept of preventing the underarm microflora from adhering to the skin surface. Proteins, oligosaccharide structures, lipids, and hydrophobic surfaces of the skin structure are involved in the adhesion of bacteria. Imitation of these adhesion motifs by saccharides such as oligosaccharides, polysaccharides, and glycoproteins minimize the adhesion of bacteria thereby reducing the underarm malodor. Recently, sucrose myristate and sucrose laurate have been discovered to have antiadherent property useful against underarm microflora.

4.5 Application forms for Deodorant Actives

Deodorant actives are delivered through different delivery systems such as creams, sticks, aerosols and pump sprays.

Deodorant creams

The current market share of deodorant creams is small compared to other forms. They are prepared by incorporating an antibacterial agent in a vanishing cream base. The deodorant cream absorbs the odorous material from the skin surface and the antimicrobials included prevent the further development of odor. These have the disadvantage of maintaining good sanitary state of the container as the product is applied with fingers and repeated usage may lead to the contamination of the product. However the cosmetic elegance of the cream, high efficacy, non-irritant, emollient effect which the cream imparts, stand on the positive side of this type of delivery systems.

Deodorant sticks

This type of delivery system was popular for many years. Deodorant sticks are mainly of two kinds, ethanol-based and the propylene glycol-based sticks.[56] Ethanol based sticks give a cooling sensation due to the evaporation of ethanol during application but this property can cause the problem of shrinkage of the stick. Propylene glycol-based sticks are more resistant to shrinkage. Sodium stearate at 6% to 8% is incorporated as a solidifying agent in deodorant sticks. Other variations of the sticks such as polymer gum bases and aqueous emulsion bases are also available.

Table 4.9 Deodorant Stick

Deodorant stick	Weight %
Water	14-18
Ethanol	73-77
Deodorizer	0.5-2
Sodium stearate	4-8
Fragrance	0.6-1.2

Deodorant aerosols

The aerosol type deodorant systems employ an antimicrobial active dissolved in an ethanol and/or propylene glycol carrier. If non-alcoholic system is used, a small amount of non-ionic wetting agent is added to disperse the perfume. Because of the anhydrous nature, deodorant sprays provide a dry skin feeling to the underarm skin.

Liquefied hydrocarbon propellant such as propane, butane, and isobutane are the most commonly used propellants. The amount of sprayable contents reaching the underarm skin surface varies from 20% to 60% and depends on several related parameters such as spray rate, distance from the skin surface, particle size, concentrate/propellant ratio and fragrance/deodorizer concentration. Polyethylene-spray-type containers are the most suitable for package of deodorant sprays. Labelling of the container should essentially include the flammability risks of volatile organic compounds used in the formulation.

Table 4.10 Deodorant Aerosol

Deodorant aerosol	Weight %
Alcohol	40-44
Laureth-4	0.3-0.7
Deodoriser	0.5-2
Fragrance	0.3-0.7
Isobutane	45-49
Propane	6-10

Deodorant pump sprays

The threat of ozone depletion posed by the propellants employed in the aerosol preparations led to the development of deodorant pump sprays. Though formulations which maximized the dryness of the product keeping stickiness and oilyness to the minimum were developed, these pump sprays could not completely replace the aerosol preparations as they do not approach the dryness of the aerosol spray.

Different types of pump sprays include:

Hydroalcoholic Pump Sprays

PIT-Emulsion Pump Sprays

Microemulsion Pump Sprays

Hydroalcoholic Pump Sprays incorporate a deodorizing active and a compatible perfume in a low viscous hydro alcoholic solution. To maintain the homogeneity of the solution solubilizer such as PEG-40 is added to the formulation. The hydroalcoholic systems have the disadvantage of causing irritation especially to the shaved axilla. To overcome this PIT-Emulsion Pump Sprays have been introduced which work on the principle of phase inversion temperature (PIT) technology. The droplet size of these systems ranges from 80 to 250 nm.

PIT emulsions are usually white or bluish-white products, in order to achieve transparency Microemulsion Pump Sprays were introduced. Completely transparent systems can be developed by maintaining the droplet size below 100 nm. The main advantage of Microemulsion Pump Sprays compared with classical microemulsions is the low surfactant concentration (< 10%).

Table 4.11 Deodorant Pump Spray

Pump spray	Weight %
Water	33-37
Alcohol	58-62
PEG-40 hyd. Castor oil	1-3
Deodorizer	1-3
Fragrance	0.2-0.6

4.6 Staining by Antiperspirants

Some times we cannot avoid staining of clothing by antiperspirants. Cotton and linen fabrics are highly susceptible to stain formation, while polyester, nylon and wool are less susceptible. If acid-sensitive dyes are used in clothing, they will change colour when it comes contact with an antiperspirant or an antiperspirant mixed with perspiration. Of course we can remove this type of stain by washing with a dilute solution of ammonia. Staining is also possible when deposit of aluminium salt combined with perspiration and body oils. When alkaline soap or laundry detergent contacts the fabric, an insoluble aluminium soap may form yellow stain which is also sticky. Removal of this stain is difficult if repeated ironing is done. Blueing agents (violet dyes) or coloured detergents may also combine with the aluminium salt to produce a blue or grey stain. The oily and waxy portions of an antiperspirant product residue are removed by dry-cleaning solvents, but we cannot remove the aluminium salts in the fabric. The iron content should be reduced in antiperspirant formulations which causes fabric staining and fragrance incompatibility.

Staining can be reduced by incorporating specific water soluble mild reducing agents including various sulphur or phosphorus compounds or stannous or titanous salts in to the composition of antiperspirants. Urea in concentrations of 5-10% will give good fabric protection with an aluminium salt. Glycine in concentrations of 3-10% will give satisfactory fabric protection and is somewhat more stable than urea.

4.7 Toxicology[57]

The effect of antiperspirants on health depends on the extent of usage and type of skin. For example only few people are allergic to aluminium and may experience contact dermatitis when exposed to deodorants containing aluminium salts. The skin may develop an allergic, axillary granuloma response when exposed to a deodorant containing zirconium. Similarly potassium alum is a weak irritant. For the people who are having sensitive skin, alcohol-free deodorants are available.

Aluminium neurotoxicity

Aluminium which is present in most of the antiperspirants, has been reported as a neurotoxin in very high doses. It adversely affects the blood-brain barrier, causes DNA damage at high doses. The Food and Drug Administration "acknowledges that small amounts of aluminum can be absorbed from the gastrointestinal tract and through the skin." An increased amount of aluminum is present in the brains of many Alzheimer's patients. A study indicated the use of aluminium-containing antiperspirants has been linked with the systemic accumulation of aluminium which increases the risk of Alzheimer's disease.

Breast cancer

A big rumour is there in the internet that antiperspirant use causes breast cancer. There are no published epidemiologic studies to support or refute this claim. According to the American Cancer Society (ACS), studies have not shown any direct link between parabens and any health problems, including breast cancer. According to the National Cancer Institute (NCI), there is no evidence linking the use of underarm antiperspirants or deodorants and the subsequent development of breast cancer. The cosmetics industry insists the paraben chemicals used as preservatives in underarm deodorants and other cosmetics, which are regulatory approved, are safe.

The journal The Breast Cancer Research proposed a link between breast cancer and the application of cosmetic chemicals including phthalates and aluminum salts in the underarm region, because of their oestrogenic and genotoxic properties, which provides an evidence-based hypothesis capable of further research.

Renal dysfunction

The people with renal dysfunction have to concentrate on the antiperspirants containing aluminium. The FDA warns that people with renal dysfunction may not be aware that the daily use of antiperspirant drug products containing aluminum may put them at a higher risk because of exposure to aluminum in the product. So according regulatory agencies, such type of persons should consult a doctor before using antiperspirants containing aluminum.

Hindustan Unilever Limited manufactures Clinical protection Anti-Perspirant Energizing Deodorant.

Nivea roll on for men

[Colour Fig. on page 399]

Oriflame India Refreshing Sensitive Deodorant Wipes for All Skin Types

Oriflame India Roll-on Anti-perspiring Deodorant with Lime and GingerExtracts

Hindustan uni lever Rexona deo

Adidas Body Care

[Colour Fig. on page 400]

4.8 Natural Deodorants

Natural deodorants are prepared based on vegetable enzymes, herbs or essential oils to neutralize or destroy odors. Natural ingredients which are having antibacterial properties are used in natural deodorants. Ingredients like lavender, mint, tea tree oil, sodium bicarbonate (baking soda) also work very well for destroying odors.

For example, Lavanila healthy deodorant contains Aloe Barbadensis Leaf Juice (Aloe Juice, Water), Propanediol (Corn Derived), Zea Mays (Corn) Starch, Sodium Stearate (Coconut Derived), Silica, Carrageenan (Seaweed Derived), Stearyl Behenate (Coconut Derived), Citrus Medica Limonum (Lemon Peel Oil), Inulin (Artichoke Derived), Saccharomyces Ferment, Alpha-Glucan Oligosaccharide (Sugar Derived), Yeast Beta Glucan, Lonicera Caprifolium (Honeysuckle) Flower Extract, Usnea Barbata (Lichen) Extract, Valeriana Officinalis Root Extract (Valerian), Hydrastis Canadensis (Goldenseal) Extract, Melaleuca Alternifolia (Tea Tree) Flower/Leaf/Stem Extract, Lycium Barbarum Fruit Extract (Goji Berry), Botanical Fragrance Blend.

4.8.1 Home made Antiperspirants[58]

To make 1 pint /570 ml of antiperspirant we have to use

225 ml purified water

225 ml rubbing alcohol

2 table spoons alum

3 table spoons rose water

Note: Rubbing alcohol (USP / BP) is prepared from a special denatured alcohol solution and contains approximately 70% by volume of pure, concentrated ethanol (ethyl alcohol) or isopropyl alcohol (isopropanol).

4.8.2 Home made Deodorant

To make 8 fl oz /225 ml

4 tea spoons alum

2 tea spoons baking soda

up to 225 ml rubbing alcohol

4.9 Environmental Impact of Conventional Deodorants

Showering washes our deodorants and antiperspirants down the drain, introducing known or suspected toxins into our nation's waterways. Octoxynol compounds, otherwise known as alkylphenol ethoxylates (APEs), are found in deodorants, antiperspirants, and bodies of water. These chemicals are slow to break down and have been shown to disrupt the endocrine systems of fish, birds, and mammals. The process of mining aluminum used in antiperspirants destroys the landscape, pollutes water, and consumes vast amounts of electricity.

Some manufacturers of natural deodorants are:

Aubrey Organics, Miessence, Earth Essentials, Maine*, Crystal Body, Jasön*, Pure and Natural, Weleda, Avalon Natural Products, Dessert Essence, Kiss My Face, Terra Natural, Burt's Bees

*Some products may contain proplyene glycol.

Some formulations of natural deodorants

Soapwalla's Deodorant Cream

[Colour Fig. on page 400]

Ingredients

Organic jojoba, sunflower, and rosehip seed oils; shea butter; a combination of all-natural and gluten-free vegetable clays and powders; aluminum-free sodium bicarbonate; organic vegan kosher glycerin; a combination of organic lavender, peppermint, sweet orange, bergamot and tea tree essential oils.

Lemongrass Rosemary Deodorant Spray (Natural)

[Colour Fig. on page 400]

Ingredients

Quadruple-distilled grain spirits, organic lemongrass essential oil, organic rosemary essential oil.

Spearmint and Tea Tree 'Pit Putty with Baking Soda

[Colour Fig. on page 400]

Ingredients

Organic arrowroot powder, organic coconut oil, aluminum-free baking soda, organic spearmint essential oil, organic tea tree essential oil

Lavera Body Spa

[Colour Fig. on page 400]

Ingredients

Lavera soft roll-on deodorant is aluminum and alcohol-free and will not clog pores or irritate the skin. Odor is absorbed naturally with pure plant extracts. Perspiration is minimized with natural bamboo and cotton fibers. Bamboo has proven antibacterial properties to help combat odor, and its soft, smooth composition makes it an ideal ingredient for sensitive skin. Natural essential oils provide a clean, fresh scent.

Calendula Blossom Natural Deodorant Spray

[Colour Fig. on page 401]

Ingredients

Deionized Water, Natural Grain Alcohol, Vegetable Glycerin, Calendula Oil, d-Alpha Tocopherol (Vitamin E), Camomile Oil, Arnica Extract, Rose Water, Calamine Powder, and a complex of Sandalwood Oil, Patchouli Oil, Jasmine Oil, Fir Oil, Vanilla Oil, Cedarwood Oil and Rose Oil.

Men's Stock Natural Dry Herbal Pine Deodorant

[Colour Fig. on page 401]

Ingredients

Alcohol denat., hamamelis virginiana (witch hazel) extract, arnica montana (arnica) extract, calamine, tocopherol acetate (vitamin E), calendula officinalis (calendula) oil, pinus sylvestris (pine) oil.

E Plus High C Roll-On Deodorant

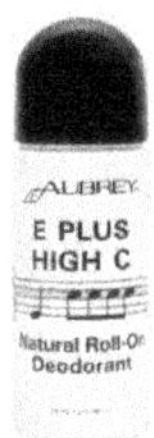

[Colour Fig. on page 401]

Ingredients

Rose Water, Coconut Fatty Acid Cream Base, Organic Aloe Vera, Natural Grain Alcohol, Calendula Oil, Vitamin E, Calamine Powder, Oils of Arnica Flower, Camomile, Sandalwood, Patchouli, Jasmine, Fir, Vanilla, Cedar wood and Rose.

4.10 Evaluation Procedures

The performance of aerosol antiperspirants is tested by antiperspirant efficacy, deodorant efficacy, staining potential and cosmetic acceptability.

Antiperspirant efficacy

Both *in vitro* and *in vivo* methods are available to measure antiperspirant efficacy. Qualitative measures include the use of indicators in conjunction with papers, pastes, films, and lacquers. One of the test involves the use of a contact indicator spot test which was based on a color reaction between pyrogallol and ferric hydroxide in the presence of water from sweat.

Quantitative measures include gravimetric or humidity sensing techniques with human volunteers. We cannot apply this method in animals, such as cats, mice, or rats, even though they have eccrine glands, they differ histologically from those of man. In humans gravimetric measurement of the total amount of perspiration secreted may be accomplished by the use of weighed pads or by the use of dessicant cups.

Factors affecting sweating rate

There are differences in the amount of sweat produced from right to left axilla, but that the ratio of these differences is consistent. Sweating is a cyclical process and is not proportional to the number of total glands. In the measurement of sweat, absorbent pads are more acceptable physiologically than cups. Other factors which affect sweating rate include: relative humidity, equilibrium of sweating rate, emotional or mental stimulation, position of the body during sweating, skin area being tested, skin temperature, conditioning to environment, sex differences, and metabolic rate.

Methods of evaluation[59]

Normal activity method

It utilizes normal environment conditions with 15-20 people. Before the start of any test, there is a 5 days period in which the panelists use no underarm products except a placebo soap. Test material is applied only to the left axilla, the right axilla serving as the control. For roll-on formulations, 1 g of product is applied with a soft brush. For aerosols, a 1-spray from a distance of 6 in. is applied uniformly to the axillary vault. After 5 minutes, to permit evaporation of any volatile materials, a preweighed moisture collection pad is applied. The panelists are then allowed to carryout normal activities for 4 hours. At the end of the 4-hour period, the absorbent pads are removed and placed in tared plastic ointment jars and weight of perspiration is determined by difference.

Controlled environment method

It utilizes thermally controlled environmental conditions with same number of panellists, 1 week day period in which the panelists use no underarm products. Controlled sweat collections are made on Monday and Tuesday of the test week. Post-treatment sweat collections are made on Wednesday, Thursday, and Friday. Test materials are assigned in such a way that samples are applied to the right axilla of half the panelists and to the left axilla of the remaining panelists. Axillae are rinsed with clear, warm water and dried just before each application. For aerosol products, the axillae are sprayed from the distance of 6 inches for 2 seconds. Sweating is induced by having the subject sit in a room maintained at 100°F ± 2°F and at a relative humidity of 35%. At the end, the remaining procedure is same as discussed above. For each individual, the per cent change in sweat rate is calculated as:

% change in sweat rate = 100 (1 - post-treatment ratio /avg control ratio)

Deodorant efficacy evaluation

Deodorant efficacy is evaluated by comparison of the effect of one treatment in one axilla versus a second treatment in the other axilla of the individuals in panel groups. Similar comparative methods may employ a crossover procedure. Axillary odor may be judged by the panel participants themselves, by trained judges, or both. Deodorant effect is determined at various intervals during the test, or at cessation to treatment. Evaluation may be made by estimating the degree of odor of both the axille and the under-garment at the side of contact. Odor judgment is based on arbitrary numerical scales. An odor scale of 1 (little or no odor) to 5 (strong or disagreeable odor) was used. The data from the test and control periods were subiected to Student's *t* test and were highly significant. Recent method is based on the development of chromatographic patterns of axillary odors.

Staining potential

Initially, formulations were tested for staining propensity by applying the product directly to the fabric. It was found that this was not a satisfactory procedure since it did not reflect actual use conditions and a comparative procedure was developed. In this procedure, a panel is used made up of 10 men and 10 women. Subjects are evaluated for stain propensity in each axilla using the following schedule. On day 1, a 3-sprays of the product is applied by a technician using a metronome for timing. The new T-shirt is then worn. Four hours later, the spraying procedure is repeated. 2 hours later, the T-shirts are collected and laundered. The same routine is then followed for 2 more days. At the end of the third day, the axillary areas of each T-shirt are evaluated for intensity of stain using a photovolt reflectometer equipped with tristimulus filters. Readings are taken using cach of the 3 filters and the staining value is calculated from the formula:

$$\frac{\text{amber - blue}}{\text{green} \times 10}$$

A value of 1 or higher indicates considerable fabric staining. There will be a considerable variations in stain potential of products, depending on product form and the type of suspending oils used.

Cosmetic acceptability

Cosmetic acceptability is important among all other properties of antiperspirants and deodorants. A product is cosmetically better when it goes on dry, without caking, and is gentle to both skin and clothing. The propellant, when optimized, can reduce coldness of the spray when applied to the skin. Cosmetic acceptability is evaluated by full scale market research procedures, along with laboratory procedures for individual properties.

Safety

Safety of antiperspirant formulations is important in terms of effect of the product on the skin and its aerosolized properties. Regular safety evaluation involves determination of acute oral and dermal toxicity, primary eye and skin irritation, acute and sub acute inhalation studies in rabbits and monkeys, and sensitization in guinea pigs and in humans. Aerosol antiperspirants are famous due to low potential inhalation hazards.

4.11 Conclusion

With few new ingredients being licensed for use in antiperspirants and deodorants, companies must rely on formulation advances for improved products. Future trends were identified as improved delivery systems, optimised antibacterial compounds and more effective fragrances. Delivery systems may be spray, gel, stick or roll-on; whichever is used, the white residue associated with aluminium salts is a problem to be overcome. Producing a clear product is the way most manufacturers have chosen to convince the consumer that their product is safe and invisible in use.

References

1. Miller J. *The H & R Book of Perfume*. London: Johnson, 1984.
2. Parisee AJ. Antiperspirants. In: Waggoner WC, ed. *Clinical Safety and Efficacy Testing of Cosmetics*. New York: Marcel Dekker, 1990:163-223.

3. Bielfeldt S, Frase T, Gassmiiller J. New sensitive method for assessment of antiperspirants with intraindividual comparison of eight formulations. *SOFW* 1997; **1237**:639–642.

4. Gebhardt W. Do cutaneous coryneform bacteria produce short-chain fatty acids *in vitro*? *Dermatologica* 1989; **178**:121–122.

5. Sato K, Kang WH, Saga K, et al. Biology of sweat glands and their disorders. I. Normal sweat gland function. *J Am Acad Dermatol* 1989; **20**:537–563.

6. Anonymous. Deodorants and antitranspirants. In: Harry RG, ed. *Harry's Cosmeticology*. Aylesbury: Leonhard Hill Books, 1973:251–275.

7. Barth JH, Kealey T. Androgen metabolism by isolated human axillary apocrine glands in hidradenitis suppurativa. *J Dermatol* 1991; **125**:304–308.

8. Klein RW. pH and perspiration. *Cosmet Toiletr* 1980; **95**:19–24.

9. Giovanniello R. Antiperspirants and deodorants. In: Williams DF, Schmitt WH, eds. *Chemistry and Technology of the Cosmetics and Toiletries Industry*. 2nd ed. London: Blackie Academic Professional, 1996:310–343.

10. Salma Khadra Jayyusi, Manuela Marin (1994). *The Legacy of Muslim Spain*. Brill Publishers. p. 117. ISBN 90-04-09599-3

11. Joey Green (2004). "The Apothecary: Elixiers, Remedies, and Tonics". *Joey Green's Incredible Country Store: Potions, Notions and Elixirs of the Past--and How to Make Them Today*(1 ed.). Rodale Books. pp. 356. ISBN 1-57954-848-2.

12. "Chattem acquires Ban deodorant brand". *Nashville Business Journal*. March 2, 1998.

13. "CHATTEM ACQUIRING BAN BRAND FOR $165 MILLION". *The New York Times*. February 24, 1998.

14. "CHATTEM AGREES TO SELL BAN DEODORANT LINE TO JERGENS". *The New York Times*. August 25, 2000.

15. US 2230084

16. Corporations: Scalping the Competition". Time magazine. July 12, 1963.

17. "Antiperspirant/Deodorant Stick". *eNotes*."Dial Agrees to Buy P&G Deodorant Brands". *Pierce Mattie Public Relations New York Blog*.

18. Federal Register, Antiperspirant Drug Products for Over-the-Counter Human Use. Final Monograph, Food and Drug Administration 21 CFR Parts 310, 350 and 369, U.S. Vol. 68. Rockville, Md: *Department of Health and Human Services,* 2003:34273–34293.

19. Quatrale RP. The mechanism of antiperspirant action. *Cosmet Toiletr* 1985; **100**:23–26.

20. Quatrale RP, Coble DW, Stoner KL, et al. The mechanism of antiperspirant action on aluminium salts II. Historical observations of human eccrine sweat glands inhibited by aluminum chlorohydrate. *J Soc Cosmet Chem* 1981; **32**:107–136.

21. Quatrale RP, Coble DW, Stoner KL, et al. Mechanism of antiperspirant action on aluminum salts III. Historical observations of human sweat glands inhibited by aluminum zirconium chlorohydrate glycine complex. *J Soc Cosmet Chem* 1981; **32**:195–221.

22. Zoe Diana Draelos, Cosmetic Formulation of Skin Care Products, Vol 30, P128.

23. Swaile DF. Variation in efficacy of commercial antiperspirant products based on differences in active composition and manufacturing method. In: 61st Annual Meeting of the American Academy of Dermatology. San Francisco, CA: *American Academy of Dermatology*, March 21–26, 2003:P337.

24. Tagami H. Claim Support in Japan: Legal Aspects. In: Elsner P, Merk HF, Maibach HI, eds. *Cosmetics: Controlled Efficacy Studies and Regulations*. Berlin: Springer, 1999:36–49.

25. Hilda Butler Poucher's Perfumes, *Cosmetics and Soaps*, 10th Edition P79.

26. Accessed May 2005 at http://sweathelp.org.

27. Lowe NJ, Glaser DA. Botulinum toxin type A in primary axillary hyperhidrosis. In: A 52-week, Multi-Center, Double-Blind, Randomized, Placebo-Controlled Trial; 62nd Annual Meeting of the American Academy of Dermatology, Feb. 6–11, 2004:P195.

28. Kowalski JW, Eadie N, Dagget S, et al. Validity and reliability of the Hyperhidrosis Disease Severity Scale (HDSS). In: 62nd Annual Meeting of the American Academy of Dermatology. Washington, DC: American Academy of Dermatology, Feb. 6–11, 2004:P195.

29. Masson, Ph. The Contribution of the European Cosmetic Directive Towards International Harmonization: Impact on the Evaluation of Safety and Efficacy. In: Elsner P, Merk HF, Maibach HI, eds. *Cosmetics: Controlled Efficacy Studies and Regulations*. Berlin: Springer, 1999:20–35.

30. Geria N. Formulation of stick antiperspirants and deodorants. *Cosmet Toiletr* 1984; **99**:55–66.

31. Geria N. Antiperspirant sticks. *Cosmet Toiletr* 1996; **111**:53–69.

32. Shevade M, Bianchini R, Lee R. Low residue antiperspirant solid stick composition. US patent No. 5531986.

33. Fox C. OTC products. *Cosmet Toiletr* 1996; **111**:53–69.

34. Schreiber J, Klier M, Wolf F, et al. Kosmetische oder dermatologische Gele auf der Basis von Mikroemulsionen. DE Patent 19 509 079.

35. Giovanniello R. Antiperspirants and deodorants. In: Williams DF, Schmitt WH, eds. *Chemistry and Technology of the Cosmetics and Toiletries Industry*. 2nd ed. London: Blackie Academic Professional, 1996:310–343.

36. Fondots DC. Antiperspirants, a look across the Atlantic. *Cosmet Toilet Manuf Worldwide* 1993; **108**:181–185.

37. Andre′ O. Barel, Marc Paye, Howard I. Maibach, *Handbook of Cosmetic Science and Technology* Third Edition, 2007:635-638.

38. Rastogi SC, Johansen JD, Frosch P, et al. Deodorants on the European market: quantitative chemical analysis of 21 fragrances. *Contact Dermatol* 1998; **38**:29–35.

39. Lamp JH. Sodium bicarbonate: an excellent deodorant. *J Invest Dermatol* 1946; **7**:131–133.

40. Berschied JR. Antiperspirant-deodorant cosmetic stick products containing active agent particles in organic matrix, which matched densities for homogeneous products. Patent No. WO 9413256.

41. Winston AE. Microporous alkali metal carbonate powder-comprises particles of average particle size of 0.1 to 50 microns, surface area of 5 to 20 sq.m/f, average pore size of 10 to 500 nm and total pore volume of 0.1 to 2 cc/g and is useful as lightweight deodorant ingredient. Patent No. WO 9424996.

42. Park AC. Propellant-free deodorant composition, for topical application—comprising sparingly water-soluble salts or oxide (s) of zinc or magnesium, water-absorbing cellulosic polymer and volatile silicone. Patent No. EP 471392 A.

43. Zekorn R. Zinc ricinoleate. *Cosmet Toilet* 1997; 112:37–40.

44. Kanda F, Yagi E, Fukuda M, et al. Quenching short chain fatty acids responsible for human body odors. *Cosmet Toilet* 1993; **108**:67–72.

45. Baxter PM, Reed JV. The evaluation of underarm deodorants. *Int J Cosmet Sci* 1983; **5**:85–95.

46. Cox AR. Efficacy of the antimicrobial agent triclosan in topical deodorant products. *J Soc Cosmet Chem* 1987; **38**:223–231.

47. Haustein UF, Herrmann J, Hoppe U, et al. Growth inhibition of coryneform bacteria by a mixture of three natural products: farnesol, glyceryl monolaurate, and phenoxyethanol: HGQ. *J Soc Cosmet Chem* 1993; **44**:211–220.

48. Klier M, Schneider G, Traupe B, et al. Desodorierende Wirkstoffkombinationen auf der Basis von Wollwachssauren und Monocarbonsauren. DE 4305889.2.

49. Klier M, Rockl M, Schneider G, et al. Deodorant active substance combinations made from wool grease acids and partial glycerides. EP 689418 Al.

50. Klier M, Rockl M, Traupe B, et al. Deodorizing combinations of agents based on a co-alkane dicarboxylic acid and fatty acid partial glycerides. EP 729345 Al.

51. Klier M, Traupe B, Wolf F. Deodorant agent compositions containing cx, co-alcanoic diacids, and mono-carboxylic esters of oligomer glycerols. EP 691125 Al.

52. Wachter R, Lehmann R, Panzer C. Desodorierende Zubereitungen. DE 19540296.

53. Lyon S, O'Neal C, van der Lee H, et al. Amino acid P-lyase enzyme inhibitors as deodorants. WO 9105541.

54. Laney J. O-Acyl serines as deodorants. WO 9507069.

55. Calogero AV. Antiperspirant and deodorant formulation. *Cosmet Toilet* 1992; **107**:63–69.

56. Deodorant From Wikipedia, the free encyclopedia.

57. www.makeyourown.net

58. Eric jungermann, Antiperspirants: New Trends in Formulation and Testing Technology, *J. Soc. Cosmet. Chem.*, 1974; **25**:621-638.

CHAPTER 5

SUNSCREENS

Y. Madhusudan Rao[1], T.Ashok[2], D.Sathish[1]

[1]Center for Biopharmaceutics and Pharmacokinetics, University College of Pharmaceutical Sciences, Kakatiya University, Warangal-506 009, Andhra Pradesh, India.

[2]Dr. Reddy's Laboratories, Hyderabad, Andhra Pradesh, India.

5.1 Introduction

The skin is essentially a functional interface between a living organism and its environment, reacting to various stimuli in that environment. Solar radiation or sunlight is a major component of the human environment. Exposure to sunlight is a major factor in the etiology of the progressive unwanted changes in the appearance of skin, i.e., photo-aging, and in the risk of skin cancers.[1-3] The evidence supportive of this view comes from epidemiology, clinical studies, and experimental studies in humans, laboratory animals, and *in vitro* systems. It is well established that acute exposure of unprotected skin to ultraviolet (UV) radiation in sunlight produces numerous physiological effects beyond the most obvious which is sunburn.[4] Since exposure to UV radiation in sunlight is associated with deleterious dermatological events, reducing solar UV exposure will diminish damage to the skin. The complete avoidance of solar UV is neither achievable nor entirely healthy. It is known that exposure to sunlight has health benefits including production of vitamin D.[5] As such, moderation seems prudent when considering the balance between the established damage and benefits of solar exposure. To this end, a "safe sun" strategy has been developed and promoted by healthcare professionals worldwide.[6-8] An important part of this "safe sun" strategy is the use of sunscreens.

Once the energy from UV is absorbed in to the skin, it may produce new chemical entities, e.g., 60, 40 DNA photoproducts, free radicals, etc., or dissipate the excess energy as heat or phosphorescence. This absorption and subsequent conversion of energy contribute to the processes involved in the etiology of skin cancer and photoaging. Preventing solar UV from interacting with skin chromophores is the primary function of sunscreens. To this end, sunscreen products are quite simple; they absorb/reflect/scatter UV radiation from sunlight before this energy can be absorbed by chromophores residing in the skin. As it turns out, sunscreen products are technically complex. Moreover, such products must be applied to be effective, and as with any other preventative measure, compliance is the key to achieve health benefits. Now a days consumers are giving preference to skin care cosmetics which contain ultraviolet (UV) filters as they know the effect of UV light exposure. According to an estimate in USA nonmelanoma skin cancer cases are exceeding more than a million per year.[9] Photoaging is responsible for 90% of the skin aging.[10] UV radiations can effect directly and indirectly. Former includes DNA effect and later includes effect on immune system of the skin. There are three recognized types of skin cancer: basal cell carcinoma, squamous carcinoma, and melanoma. The daily use of sunscreen shows very good effects like prevention of the formation of squamous cell carcinomas of the skin, actinic or precancerous keratosis, solar elastosis and immunosuppression.[11-16]

5.1.1 History

In the United States in 1928[17], benzyl salicylate and benzyl cinnamate, were first incorporated into a commercially available sunscreen emulsion. Later that in 1930s in Australia phenyl salicylate (Salol) was used.[18] In 1943 patent was filed on Para-aminobenzoic acid (PABA) which lead to further development of PABA derivatives. During World War II, U.S. military used red veterinary petrolatum (RVP) as UV filter which increased interest in sunscreen products. Most of the researchers have focused on the invention of sunscreens for the prevention of melanoma and photoaging which protects throughout the entire UVA range. The effectiveness of sunscreens was originally achieved by incorporation of soluble organic UV absorbers such as cinnamates and others into cosmetic formulations.

A sunscreen cosmetic could be defined as, "Any cosmetic product containing UV filters in its formulation in order to protect the skin from the solar deleterious UV-light, avoiding or minimizing the damage that this radiation might cause on human health."

Of the wavelengths of radiation which do reach the Earth's surface, ultraviolet has the highest energy, making it the most important in relation to sun exposure. Over the years, photobiologists have arbitrarily described different sub-regions of the UV spectrum each defined by a somewhat indistinct physiological activity. They are, in descending order of energy: far-UV radiation (100-200 nm), UVC (200-280 nm), UVB (280-320 nm) and UVA (320-400 nm).

The far-UV and UVC region

This is also called as germicidal UV region because this region has ability to kill single-cell organisms. The ozone layer can prevent the entry of far-UV and UVC on to earth, but unfortunately the layer becomes disappearing due to the changes in the environment.

The UVB region

As an aide-memoire, UVB is often simply identified as UV-4B' for burning. This is because it is the primary initiator of sunburn, contributing approximately 85% of summer sunburn reaction. However it is also responsible for the initiation of certain skin cancers, many photo-dermatoses, premature skin ageing and for the generation of the photo-protective pigment known as melanin which gives our skin its suntanned appearance. On a positive note, UVB is also responsible for synthesis of vitamin D in the skin.

The UVA region

UVA is often identified as UV-'A' for ageing. This is because its long-term effects on the dermal layers of human skin manifest themselves as visual wrinkling and ageing of the skin. However, UVA is also capable of generating both immediate skin pigmentation and delayed pigmentation, the latter being the tanning response. UVA also contributes approximately 15% of the sunburn reaction which occurs as a result of overexposure to summer sunshine. Many photo-dermatological skin conditions such as polymorphic light eruption (PLE), solar urticaria and chronic actinic dermatitis (CAD), occur as a direct result of exposure to UVA light, whilst several 'photo-active' substances can also produce abnormal skin reactions as a result of exposure to UVA light. Recent work indicates that UVA is also implicated in skin cancer.[19,20] The variations in energy of the different UV regions lead to the visualization of effects at different times. Immediate pigmentation due to UVA develops only after a few hours and thus may afford the skin some minimal initial protection. Reddening due to UVA, however, may not take place for up to 72 hours after exposure. UVB erythemal reactions develop after as little as 8 hours and may persist for 24 hours and longer. Tanning may or may not appear, depending on the skin type of the individual and his or her capacity for producing melanin. The severity of all responses to UV light depends upon the intensity and total dose of the sunlight received. This may be modified by latitude, altitude, season, time of day, cloud cover, atmospheric pollutants, etc. UVB will not penetrate window glass, UVA may do so and therefore exposure to UVA may continue even when indoors or whilst driving for example.

Another classification of UV light is also available i.e., UVR reaching the Earth's surface can be divided into UVB (290-320 nm) and UVA (320-400 nm). UVA can be further subdivided into UVA I (340-400 nm) or far UVA and UVA II (320-340 nm) or near UVA.

Table 5.1 UV and neighboring spectra.

Spectrum	Wavelengths (nm)
X-Ray	0.01-10
Vacuum UV	10-200
UVC	200-290
UVB	290-320
UVA	320-400
Visible	400-760

5.1.2 Function

Sunscreens are photochemical systems containing UV-filters which absorb/scatter/reflect solar UV to protect the skin from harmful radiation. There are 17 active sunscreen ingredients currently approved by the FDA (Table 5.1), compared with at least 34 in Australia and 28 in the European Union (EU). The usual concentration of UV filters in cosmetics is between 0.1 and 10%.

Table 5.2 Sunscreens approved by U.S. FDA

Sunscreen agent	Max. conc'n %	Range of protection (nm)
Inorganic		
Titanium dioxide	25	290-350
Zinc oxide	25	290-400
Organic UVB		
PABA	15	260-313
Padimate O (2-ethylhexyl 4-dimethylaminobenzoate)	8	290-315
Octinoxate (octyl methoxycinnamates)	7.5	280-310

Table 5.2 *Contd...*

Sunscreen agent	Max. conc'n %	Range of protection (nm)
Cinoxate	3	270-328
Octisalate (octyl salicylate)	5	260-310
Homosalate	15	290-315
Trolamine salicylate	12	269-320
Octylocrylene	10	287-323
Ensulizole (phenylbenzimidazole sulfonic acid)	4	290-340
Organic UVA		
Oxybenzone	6	270-350
Sulisobenzone	10	250-380
Dioxybenzone	3	206-380
Meradimate (menthyl anthranilate)	5	200-380
Avobenzone	3	310-400
Ecamsule (terephthalydene dicamphor sulfonic Acid)	10	295-390

Ref source 21 (as of Dec. 7, 2009)

So many unapproved sunscreen agents and non-pharmacological agents are used in many formulations which include

UVB

Octyl triazone (ethylhexyl triazone)

Enzacamene (methyl benzylidene camphor)

Amiloxate (isoamyl p-methoxycinnamate)

Broad spectrum (UVB/UVA)

Mexoryl XL (drometriazole trisiloxane)

Tinosorb S (bemotrizinol)

Tinosorb M (bisoctrizole)

UVAsorb HEB (diethylhexyl butamido triazone)

Neo Heliopan AP (bisdisulizole disodium)

Uvinul A Plus

Non-pharmacological agents

Topical antioxidants

DNA repair enzymes

Types of the skin and SPF

To make a clinically useful assessment of a person's genetic resistance to photodamage, six skin types were recognized, a simple classification based on the patient's response to two questions: 1. How easily do you burn after sun exposure? 2. How well do you tan? (Table 5.3).

Table 5.3 Types of the skin and SPF values[22]

Category	Skin Type	SPF
I	Always burns, never tans	15 >
II	Often Burns, some times tans easily	15
III	Some times Burns, Often tans (avg caucasian)	10-15
IV	Rarely Burns, Always tans (olive skin")	6-10
V	Moderately pigmented (brown skin)	4-6
VI	Heavily pigmented (black skin)	none

Sun protection factor (SPF)

The primary method of evaluating the efficacy of sunscreens historically has been through the measurement of the SPF.

Minimum erythemal dose (MED)

The minimal erythemal dose (MED) of UV radiation is the minimal dose that produces sunburn. Depending upon wavelength and intensity of the source of irradiation, an MED time (or dose) can vary from a few minutes (high-intensity UVB) to many hours (sunlightintensity UVA). The most widely accepted measure comparing the ability of various sunscreens to protect the skin from burning is the sun protection factor (SPF). The SPF is defined as a ratio: the minimum UV dose required to produce erythema in suncreen-protected skin, divided by the UV dose required to produce in unprotected skin.

SPF = MED of sunscreen protected skin /MED of unprotected skin.

$$SPF = \frac{\int_{280\,nm}^{400\,nm} E_\lambda S_\lambda \, d\lambda}{\int_{280\,nm}^{400\,nm} E_\lambda S_\lambda T_\lambda \, d\lambda}$$

Where,

E_λ: spectral irradiance of used light spectrum at wavelength λ;

S_λ: erythemal action spectrum at wavelength λ;

T_λ: measured sample transmittance at wavelength λ.

"When using a SPF of 15, a fair-skinned person who normally sunburns in 20 minutes of midday sun exposure may tolerate 15 times 20 minutes (300 minutes) without burning.'' However, that a doubling of the SPF does not imply a doubling of UV blockage, because an SPF of 15 blocks out 94% of UVB rays, and a SPF 30 filters out almost 97% of UVB rays. This correlation between SPF and degree of protection is part of the reason why the FDA has proposed to categorize SPF labels into low (SPF 2-15), medium (SPF 15-30), high (SPF 30-50), and highest (SPF 50+) categories. One source states that the reason for the grouping of all SPFs greater than 50 into one category is because the FDA believed that there was no data demonstrating the accuracy and reproducibility of specific SPF values over 50. The SPF does not provide information regarding the ability of sunscreens to withstand aqueous conditions, such as sweating and swimming. As a result of these inadequacies, the FDA has proposed methods to address these issues. Sunscreens with SPF greater than 15 may be meaningless, except for skin types I and II, patients with clinical photosensitivity disorders, under appliers and persons with added exposure risks due to elevation and reflectance.

Once the appropriate sunscreen type has been selected, one must ensure proper usage. The current FDA and ADA recommendation is an initial application of 2 mg/ cm^2 of body surface area, which, for a person weighing 70 kg, equates to 1 oz of sunscreen protectant. However, studies have shown that actual usage by individuals is significantly less, which can lead to significant clinical consequences. The sunscreen should be re-applied 15 to 20 minutes after first sun exposure with continued application every 2 hours of exposure, or after significant sweating or water exposure.

5.2 Products

The choice of a 'best' sunscreen depends upon skin type, exposure habits, medical needs and personal preferences. If we consider photoprotection, one should use a sufficiently substantive sunscreen with an SPF of at least 15. Even with these qualifications, there are dozens from which to choose. Some may prefer gels, other lotions. Price may be a factor.

The ideal properties of sun protection products include

(i) well tolerated;

(ii) cosmetically pleasant;

(iii) non-toxic;

(iv) equally effective against UVA and UVB;

(v) photostable;

(vi) water resistant;

(vii) with a high 'Sun Protection Factor'.

Based on the physical properties of the active agent (from a formulation point of view) UV filters can be classified into one of four groups[23]:

- Water soluble salts, e.g., ensulizole
- Oil soluble crystalline solids, e.g., avobenzone, and the benzophenones
- Polar oils, e.g., octinoxate, octisalate, homosalate, and octocrylene
- Insoluble powders/particulates, e.g., zinc oxide and titanium dioxide

If we use water soluble salts, we have to incorporate high polymer levels to achieve desired thickness of the product. Because they reduce the capability of most aqueous polymeric thickeners. So usage of high polymer makes the product feel sticky and heavy on the skin. Similarly Oil soluble crystalline solids need high levels of oily solvents/emollients to dissolve them and keep them from crystallizing in the product over time which make the product feel greasy and oily. Polar oils make the product feel greasy and oily, especially at high concentrations. Insoluble powders/particulates can make the product feel dry and draggy, and often can lead to an undesirable white appearance on the skin.[24-27]

Sunscreen lotions and creams are easily applied and may be the best choice for persons with dry skin. Sprays and aerosols are useful for hard to-reach areas or large body surface areas, and finally, sticks and waxes are a good choice for application to the face and around the eyes. Sunscreen often is worn only at times of recreation or during extreme sun exposure; however, it is estimated that more than half of the yearly UV radiation occurs in non-summer months, and even on cloudy days up to 80% of UV radiation is unfiltered through clouds. The proper choice of sunscreen, application method, and diligence of application are all important aspects of proper sunscreen usage.[28]

Vehicle type and application methods

Sunscreen vehicles often determine product efficacy. To maintain the photo-protective properties and photo-stability of its UV filters, a sunscreen vehicle must minimize interaction of inert and active ingredients. Vehicle type also determines sunscreen durability and water resistance. The FDA designates sunscreens with intact photo-protective properties after two 20 minutes exposures to water as ''water resistant.'' The term ''very water-resistant'' has replaced ''water proof'' and applies to sunscreens remaining effective after four 20 minutes periods of water immersion. But despite their label, even 'water resistant' sunscreens can exhibit a gradual loss in SPF with subsequent water immersions. Sunscreen vehicles include lotions/creams, waterbased gels, sticks, sprays, and cosmetics. Lotions and creams, consisting of either oil-in-water or water-in oil emulsions, permit the greatest diversity of formulations and are most commonly used. Gels are easily washed away by swimming and sweat, but are preferred by patients with oily skin or recurrent acne. Sticks are used for protecting small areas like the lips or nose. Sprays are convenient, but are often applied insufficiently. Sunscreen agents may also be found in hair care products, such as shampoos and artificial dyes, to protect against UV-induced color change and protein damage.

5.3 Regulatory Issues

India

In India, sunscreens are regulated by the Drugs and Cosmetics Act, under the category of cosmetics. But unlike the guidelines mentioned by the Food and Drug Administration (FDA) in the United States, India possess no separate regulations for sunscreen products available in the Indian market. Some Indian companies follow the US guidelines for ingredients and get their products tested in Germany.

United States

In the FDA monograph, the term ''sunscreen drugs'' is used to refer to sunscreen actives or ultraviolet (UV) filters. Currently there are two procedures for registering and obtaining FDA approval for sunscreen drugs: New Drug Application and the Time and Extent Application (TEA). The FDA introduced the TEA in 2002 as a faster and less costly alternative to a New Drug Application. To be considered for TEA, a minimum of 5 years of over-the-counter marketing of the product in the same country is required; data generated from that country can then be submitted to the FDA for consideration.[29]

New FDA sunscreen rules

FDA ruled that sunscreens can no longer claim they are "sunblocks." Since no sunscreen can block all of the sun's harmful rays, the FDA ruled, that term is patently misleading. Nor will it allow sunscreens to claim they are "sweatproof" or "waterproof" for the same reason. Sunscreens will be permitted to say they are "water resistant" but they must show immersion test data to support 40 minutes or 80 minutes protection to indicate just how long they'll be effective before a reapplication will be needed.

Similarly, the FDA will insist on some clarity about claims of "broad spectrum" protection. Only sunscreens that protect against both UVB and UVA rays will be permitted to bill themselves that way. And their SPF rating must be backed by test data that shows they offer protection that is proportional for UVA wavelengths, which has not been the case prior to this because SPF ratings were based solely on UVB testing. The FDA did not insist, as many consumer groups had advocated, on banning SPF claims greater than 50+ even though higher ratings may lead some users to conclude, mistakenly, that they are getting vastly more protection the higher up the scale they move and can therefore spend much longer in the sun without worry. As far as they go, the new FDA rules on sunscreens will help consumers to make better choices, especially those who haven't bothered to educate themselves about the key attributes and differences in sunscreen products. The FDA proposed an amendment on August 27, 2007 to update sunscreen-labeling regulations. The major points presented included limiting SPF labelling to 50+ for products with SPF values of 60 and above, addition of a 4-star UVA protection rating system, approval of new combinations of sunscreen ingredients, and improved usage directions placed on approved products.

Europe

In Europe, sunscreen products are considered to be cosmetics, which protect the skin from sunburn. European Union (EU) allows, some agents which are not available in the United States. EU included TiO_2 to their approved list. Zinc oxide (ZnO) is not included in this list which may be used in cosmetic products.[30]

Australia

In Australia Sunscreens are regulated as therapeutic goods. According to the Australian Standard SPF designations greater than 30 are not permitted (SPF 30 represents the maximum designation). Australian Approved Names (AAN) for approved active sunscreen ingredients are the same as FDA drug nomenclature with a few differences.

Other Countries

Most non–European countries follow the European directive. Other countries follow U.S. FDA with few exceptions or differences in the concentrations and variety of UV filters (31).

For people of darker skin color the risk of skin cancer is much lower than that of people of lighter skin color due to genetic differences in pigmentation of the skin. But for people of darker skin color, it is still very important to use a sunscreen to prevent, wrinkling, premature aging but a lower SPF sunscreen in ranges of 15 to 30 would do the job. For people traveling to regions closer to the equator, the ultraviolet rays of the sun become more harmful due to the closer distance between the sun and earth, hence, for people of darker skin color a higher SPF number sunscreen is recommended if traveling to equatorial countries.

5.4 Mechanism of Action

Sunscreens are of two types: chemical sunscreens which absorb UVR and physical sunscreens which reflect and/or scatter UVR. Chemical sunscreens enjoy much wider acceptance, being cosmetically invisible. Physical sunscreens are generally messy and opaque compounds, commonly containing one or more of the following: titanium dioxide, zinc oxide, talc, starch, ferric chloride, kaolin, or ichthammol. Usually, physical sunscreens resist water wash-off, and are consequently useful for commonly burned sites in lifeguards, surfers, and others. Patients with UVA and visible light photo-sensitivities also benefit from physical sunscreens. However, white opaque physical sunscreens (such as zinc oxide) require the addition of a pigmented light absorber (such as iron oxide) to adequately protect in the visible range.[32-34]

5.5 Individual UV Filters

To be considered as a potential UV screening agent a chemical entity must have the following attributes:

1. It must absorb UV light over a broad or specified part of the spectrum without any chemical breakdown.
2. It must possess suitable characteristics to allow it to be readily formulated into cosmetic vehicles and should be absorbed easily into the skin.
3. It must be resistant to removal by water or sweat.
4. It must not require too-frequent re-application to be effective.

5. It must be highly effective at low concentrations.
6. It must be non-toxic, non-irritant and non-sensitizing.

Sunscreen ingredients can be classified into two groups as discussed previously. One group considers the chemical structure and another consider absorption spectrum.[35,36]

Organic sunscreens

Organic UVB agents

Most of the organic sunscreen ingredients filter UVB, act by absorbing UVR and converting it to heat energy. PABA is the most potent UVB agent, whose ability to bind keratinocytes increases skin staining, but allows it to withstand water immersion and perspiration. Many reports of contact allergies to PABA exist, and it has therefore been largely replaced by less effective PABA derivatives, such as padimate O, which have better safety profiles and rarely stain skin. Padimate O is generally used in combination with other UV filters to increase overall SPF.

Cinnamates, including octinoxate and cinoxate, are currently the most popular UVB filters in the United States because they do not stain and rarely cause irritation. They are less potent than padimate O and have reduced water resistance, cinnamate-based sunscreens require frequent reapplication.

Salicylates, the weakest organic UVB agents, include octisalate, homosalate, and trolamine salicylate. These agents possess favorable safety profiles and are added to sunscreens in relatively high concentrations to augment UVB protection. Octisalate and homosalate are highly photostable agents used to reduce photodegradation of other active sunscreen ingredients. They are also hydrophobic and can serve as solvents for other sunscreen agents. In contrast, trolamine salicylate is water soluble and is often found in hair products.

Octocrylene is a weak UVB absorber. Although octocrylene improves photostability, it is costly and difficult to integrate into sunscreen products. Ensulizole is a water-soluble UVB filter, which provides a lighter, less oily consistency than most other sunscreen ingredients and is often found in daily moisturizers.

Organic UVA agents

Benzophenones provide broad-spectrum UVB and UVA protection. However, they are photolabile and their oxidation can interrupt the antioxidant system. The FDA has approved 3 benzophenones: oxybenzone, sulisobenzone, and dioxybenzone.

Oxybenzone is most commonly used, but has the highest incidence of photoallergic contact dermatitis. Meradimate is a weaker filter used to enhance UVA2 protection. Avobenzone (butyl methoxydibenzoyl-methane), a potent UVA filter, was the first FDAapproved organic agent to effectively filter UVA1. However, it is highly photolabile; 1 hour of sun exposure decreases its photoprotective properties by 50%to 60%. Avobenzone can also affect the stability of other active sunscreen ingredients. Helioplex stabilizing technology, patented by Neutrogena, combines avobenzone, oxybenzone, and diethylhexyl 2,6- naphthalate and is designed to prevent avobenzone photodegradation. Approved by the FDA in 2006, ecamsule (terephthalydene dicamphor sulfonic acid; Mexoryl SX; L'Oreal, Paris, France) is the newest broad-spectrum agent. Ecamsule has been shown to prevent or reduce UV-induced pigmentation, pyrimidine dimer formation, p53 protein accumulation, alteration of Langerhans cell density, and photodermatoses. In the United States, ecamsule is now exclusively found in Anthelios products, combined with avobenzone and octocrylene.

Broad-spectrum products

Most sunscreen agents provide protection in a particular UV range and offer insufficient photoprotection when used alone. Cinnamates and salicylates are often mixed with other UVB absorbers to augment SPF. Broad-spectrum (UVB/UVA) products are produced by combining filters with varying UV absorption spectra. For example, avobenzone, a superior UVA blocker, can be combined with homosalate and octisalate, UVB filters, to yield broad-spectrum coverage. Because of the increased photolability of benzophenones and avobenzone, octocrylene is often added to improve sunscreen photostability with these agents. Organic and inorganic filters may also act synergistically to increase SPF. Inorganic agents scatter UV light, increasing the photons' optical pathways and enhancing subsequent absorption by organic agents.

Inorganic agents

Inorganic sunscreen ingredients act by reflecting or scattering visible, UV and infrared radiation over a broad-spectrum. The major inorganic agents used today are zinc oxide and titanium dioxide, which are photostable and require a thick application to achieve adequate reflection. Zinc oxide offers better UVA protection, whereas titanium dioxide provides superior UVB protection and has a whiter tone because of its higher refractive index. The reddish hue of iron oxide, another physical blocker, is closer to natural skin color and is often added to sunscreens to mask the opacity of titanium dioxide and zinc oxide. Because of aesthetic concerns, inorganic agents were unpopular until recently, when particulate forms were introduced. Microsized titanium dioxide and zinc oxide (10-50 nm) decrease visible light scattering and improve cosmetic acceptability more than their 200 nm to 500 nm nonmicrosized, opaque forms. They can also absorb UVR, but the absorption range of the particulate form shifts toward shorter wavelengths, away from the UVA zone. Microfine particles also tend to aggregate, leading to decreased efficacy. To prevent this, they are coated with dimethicone or silica, thereby reducing free radical formation and increasing photostability. Because of their photostability, inorganic agents are preferred for children and sunscreen-allergic individuals. Inorganic, opaque sunscreens may also protect against visible light induced photosensitivity diseases.

Other agents in the sunscreen products

Waterproofing agents

An important requisite of any sunscreen product is that it should withstand water, either in the form of sweat, or from the sea or a swimming pool. During bathing the skin continues to be exposed to high levels of irradiation as UV light readily penetrates the water's surface. It is highly desirable therefore that the product is not easily washed off. Naturally one can and should re-apply the product after immersion, especially as it is likely to have been towelled off during drying, but this is often inconvenient or forgotten. Waterproofing characteristics should therefore be built into formulations.

There are official tests for standards of water resistance which involve an *in vivo* SPF measurement before and after immersion for a fixed period in water. If a product is to be described as water-resistant it should retain at least 50% of its SPF following moderate activity in water, or the SPF should remain within the same protection category of either minimal, moderate, extra, maximal or ultra protection depending on the test method used. Water resistance can be achieved in a number of ways. Oil-based formulations or stick formulations have inbuilt water repellency due to their nonaqueous nature. In these cases the product sits on the skin as an oily or waxy film which is not easy to dislodge. The majority of sun protection products, however, are emulsions which can contain very high levels of water. Waterin-oil emulsions are usually inherently water-resistant. The low levels of water present as the dispersed phase are readily lost on application to the skin to leave the continuous oil phase smoothly spread over the surface to give a waterrepellent film.

Water-in-oil emulsions though, are not very acceptable to the consumer because they often have a heavy, greasy feel. Oil-in-water systems are cosmetically more elegant and have a better skin feel. These also deposit an oily film on the skin once the high levels of water have evaporated but, by nature of their surfactant systems, they are easy to re-emulsify in the presence of water from a pool or the sea and consequently are easier to remove. An ideal system would be one which has the elegance of an oil-in-water emulsion but which, on application to the skin, rapidly loses water and inverts to a water-in-oil system. Thus a repellent oil film would be deposited on the skin surface. This can be achieved by a fine balance of surfactant ingredients or by the use of quick-breaking carbomer emulsiflers. The choice of sunscreen can also influence water resistance. It is claimed that PABA-type sunfilters are more resistant to wash-off than other organic sunscreens because they can penetrate deeper into the skin's layers.

As far as actual ingredients which impose water resistance are concerned, the most well known are the silicone oils. These materials are extremely resistant to water penetration, are eminently spreadable and form a continuous thin water-repellent film on the skin surface which is highly acceptable. The most widely used materials are dimethicone 350, cyclomethicone and dimethicone/trimethylsiloxysilicate which are all excellent waterproofing agents. More recently other polymeric film-formers have gained favour as waterproofing agents. Alkylated polyvinylpyrrolidones, which are closely related to the film-formers found in hairsprays, are also excellent for imparting water resistance to a formulation. As little as 1-2% will produce a repellent film which readily satisfies the legislatory tests, but these compounds require high levels of other suitable materials such as the emollient esters to ensure spreading and continuity of the film.

5.6 Formulations

Sunscreen products are available in various forms such as gels, sticks, oils or emulsions. Each form has a particular consumer acceptability, typical ingredient type and manufacturing process.

Emulsions

These are the most famous sunscreen formulations, because of formation of a uniform non-transparent film on the skin. Desired SPF can be obtained and they have the ability to penetrate the skin's horny layer to some degree. As other products they are oil-in-water, water-in-oil emulsions.

Table 5.4 sunscreen emulsion.

Ingredient	%w/w
Phase A (oil phase)	
Emollients	5-10
Actives	Drug level 0.05-0.2
Antioxidant	1-2
Emulsifier(primary) Emulsifier	1-2
(secondary)	0.5-2
Wax	0.5-5
Silicones	
Phase B (water phase)	Q.S
Deionized water	2-7
Humectant Preservative	0.05-1.0
Thickener	0.1-2
Emollient	0.5-2

Sunscreen lotion

Like other O/W cosmetic emulsions, sunscreen lotions have traditionally been emulsified with stearate or nonionic surfactants at 2% - 6%. Inherent to surfactant emulsification of UV absorbers is the propensity for the surfactants to remove the absorbers from the skin when contacted by water. Although the vast majority of sunscreen products in the market contain water-insoluble actives, the surfactants can re-emulsify the actives and cause wash-off, leaving the skin unprotected.

Formulators have countered this phenomenon by incorporating waxes or water resistant, film-forming polymers into their formulations. Such a polymer forms an effective barrier which prevents absorber wash-off, but it may produce negative aesthetic effects such as long rub-in times and a tacky or heavy feel on the skin.[37]

Table 5.5 Waterproof Sunscreen Lotion (SPF 8).

Ingredient	%w/w	Function
PART A		
Deionized Water	70-74	Diluent
Hydroxypropyl		
Methylcellulose(1.0% solution)	08-12	Aqueous Smoothing Aid
Quatemium 15	0.1-0.2	Preservative
Disodium EDTA	0.01-0.02	Chelating Agent

Table 5.5 *Contd...*

Ingredient	%w/w	Function
PART B		
Octyl Methoxy Cinnamate	05-09	UVB Absorber
Octyl Salicylate	01-05	UVB Absorber
Oxybenzone	01-03	UVA Absorber
C12-15 Alcohols Benzoate	02-06	Emollient/Solvent
Acrylates/C10-30		
Alkyl Acrylate Crosspolymer	0.15-0.35	Emulsifier
Carbomer	0.10-0.30	Thickener
Methyl Paraben	0.10-0.30	Preservative
Propyl Paraben	0.01-0.08	Preservative
PART C		
Triethanolamine (99%)	0.20-0.60	Neutralizing Agent

Preparation Procedure:

1. Combine Part A ingredients. Mix until homogeneous.
2. Combine first four Part B ingredients in a separate vessel. Mix until oxybenzone has been dissolved. Warming will hasten dissolution.
3. Disperse last four Part B ingredients in Part B vessel. Mix to break-up lumps.
4. With vigorous agitation, add Part B to Part A. Mix for 20-40 minutes or until a smooth, non-grainy dispersion is apparent. Add Part C (triethanolamine) and mix until a smooth, lustrous product is obtained.

Sunscreen gel stick

To overcome the disadvantages with gel like low SPF and low water resistance property, gel sticks are prepared. These are useful for direct application of sunscreens to a specific small area such as the nose, lips and forehead. The melting point of the stick and its performance on the skin depends on the selection of waxes.

Table 5.6 Sunscreen gel stick[38]

Ingredient	%w/w
Phase A	
Poly butane	31-35
Jojoba oil	26-30
Poly (C20-28 olefin)	20-24
Poly (C30-45 olefin)	7-11
Hydroxy stearic acid	1-3
Phase B	
Zinc oxide and Triethoxycaprylylsilane	3-7

Procedure:

1. Combine all ingredients in Phase A
2. Heat Phase A ingredients carefully until melted.
3. Mix until uniform.
4. Add Phase B with adequate mixing to obtain a complete dispersion.
5. Pour into containers.

   Expected SPF value would be 7-8

Table 5.7 Sunscreen gel stick[39].

Ingredient	%w/w
Mineral Oil	63-67
Octinoxate	5-9
Octisal	3-7
Diethylhexyl 2,6 Naphthalate	2-6
Glyceryl Isostearate (and) Caprylic/Capric Glycerides	14-18
Sodium Stearate	1-3

Procedure:

1. Combine the sodium stearate and glyceryl isostearate (and) caprylic/capric glycerides, mix well and heat till homogeneous.
2. In a separate vessel heat the mineral oil, diethylhexyl 2,6 naphthalate, octinoxate and octisal to the same temperature.
3. Add step 1 to step 2 and mix.
4. Cool to room temperature.

In our lab we have formulated and evaluated sunscreens. Here we are enclosing one of the formulation and method of preparation.

Formulation

Titanium dioxide	5	mg
Stearic acid	5	mg
Cetostearyl alcohol	3.75	mg
Liquid paraffin	5	mg
Propyl paraben	0.02	mg

Glycerol	5	mg
Methyl paraben	0.15	mg
Triethanolamine (99%)	0.625	mg
Distilled water up to	100	ml

Method of preparation

Stearic acid, cetostearyl alcohol, liquid paraffin, propyl paraben are heated to 70°C. A part of water, methyl paraben and triethanolamine are heated to 75°C and added to melted oil phase with stirring. To this dispersion of titanium dioxide, glycerol and remaining part of water are added. Stirring is continued to cool.

5.7 Marketed Products

There are several marketed sun screen products available, a few of them are given below.

L`Oreal India Pvt. Ltd.

Lakmé Ultra Matte Sun Protection Cream

Mary Kay Cosmetics Pvt. Ltd.

Blue Lizard Regular Suncream 30+

[Colour Fig. on page 401-402]

Most Dermatologist Recommended Sunscreen Brands

1. Neutrogena
2. Coppertone
3. Anthelios
4. Blue Lizard
5. SolBar
6. Aveeno
7. Oil of Olay
8. Vanicream
9. Bull Frog
10. Ombrelle

5.8 Role of Herbs as Sunscreen Agents

Sage extract

Sage belongs to mint family. It is famous for healing properties of its volatile oils. Sage decreases perspiration. So this is used in deodorant preparations. The sage essential oil consists of camphor, cineole, thujone and borneol. These put together are antimicrobial, which destroys or stops the growth of disease causing microorganisms, and antispasmodic, which relieves or prevents spasms. An antioxidant compound called a flavonoid and phenolic acids are present which also exhibits antimicrobial action.

Shea butter (*Butyrospermum parkii*)

Shea Butter is good for dry skin, sunburn, blemishes, cracked heels and skin, itchy skin, stretch marks, scars, chapped lips, eczema, diaper rash, hair moisturizer, burns, athlete's foot, insect bites and stings, arthritis, muscle fatigue, dry skin, scrapes, It is a very superior moisturizer with all natural vitamin A, an anti-inflammatory, a minor sunscreen agent (up to SPF 6), and it also reduces wrinkles.

Cinnabloc

Cinnabloc is a natural cinnamate, which derived from extracts of rhizomes of Spiked *Ginger lily* and *Greater galangal*. Cinnabloc protects the skin from harmful effects of UVA and UVB rays. Himalaya company has received US patent for discovering Cinnobloc and successfully using it as an effective sunscreen agent.

Chamomile

Chamomile is an annual plant of the sunflower family Asteraceae. Chamomile contains phenolic derivatives, which have an antiseptic and healing quality, which is most helpful in relieving skin congestion. These soften the skin, making it an effective ingredient in any anti-aging cosmetic product. The alpha-bisabolol in the oil promotes granulation and tissue regeneration. The flavonoids as well as the lipophilic (sesquiterpenes) compounds found in camomile oil help to reduce capillary fragility, which in turn helps to strengthen the skin. The vasoconstrictor properties again help to reduce redness of the skin, which is due to enlarged capillaries. Chamomile is important ingredient in most of the natural sunscreen products.

Aloe vera

Aloe vera is a species of succulent plants that belong to the lily family, Liliaceae. There are around 250 species of *Aloe vera* plants world over. Skin and *Aloe vera* are very much connected nowadays *Aloe vera* has many benefits. It is used as a cooling agent, when ingested it increases immunity, relieves digestive tract trouble and soothes the body. In spite of all these benefits *Aloe vera* is widely used in treating skin-related problems. *Aloe vera* is used in many sun protection lotions. Owing to *Aloe vera*'s cooling property, it is widely used to treat sun burns and sun-related skin conditions. *Aloe vera* 'the burn plant' is a multi-healer. Owing to its anti-inflammatory, anti-fungal, healing and cooling properties it is a very useful natural element to treat our skin. *Aloe vera* also contains a rich source of amino acids, vitamins A, C, F, B, niacin and traces of Vitamin B_{12}.

Other herbs used in sunscreen products include green tea , calendula, sesame, olive, coconut and peanut oils, extract of helichrysum, carrot-seed essential oil etc.

Natural sunscreens in the market

Sunblock SPF30 with Chamomile extract

[Colour Fig. on page 402]

Ingredients

Polyester, special emulsifying cream basis, titanium dioxide, glycerine, vitamin E, B_5 and C, propylene glycol, sunscreen agent- 2-octyl dodecanol, idopropynyl butylcarbamate and deionized water.

Sensitive SPF 20 Lotion

[Colour Fig. on page 402]

Ingredients

Aqua (water), *Aloe barbadensis* (*Aloe vera* gel), *Sesamum indicum* (Sesame oil), titanium dioxide, mica, zinc oxide, magnesium aluminium silicate, cetearyl glucoside, glycerin, parfum (essential oils), aluminum hydroxide, stearic acid, *Helianthus annuus* (Sunflower seed oil), *Echinacea pallida* (Echinacea extract), hydrolyzed silk, silica, xanthan gum, esculin, citric acid, sodium citrate, tocopherol, limonene, linalool, beta carotene.

Lotus herbals safe sun

[Colour Fig. on page 402]

Ingredients

Berry extracts, octyle methoxy cinnamate, menthyl anthranilate and titanium dioxide.

5.9 Homemade Sunscreen Lotion

Avocado oil, sesame oil and shea butter contain a low SPF sunscreen. However, they have limited VA/UVB-filtering ability and we should not use them as our only skin protection. For a natural sunscreen with a higher SPF, use a commercial sunscreen with titanium dioxide. To keep homemade sunscreen from spoiling, use only clean utensils for preparation and storage. Store lotions in the refrigerator, where they will keep for about 3-4 weeks. To achieve maximum protection, apply sunscreen to dry skin 30 minutes before exposure.

Natural protection cream recipe

- 3 tbsp. unrefined sesame oil
- 1 tbsp. unrefined avocado oil
- 1 tbsp. unrefined jojoba oil
- 1 tbsp. walnut or almond oil
- 1 tbsp. shea butter
- 2 tbsp. cocoa butter
- 1 tsp. beeswax
- 1 tsp. soy-lecithin liquid
- 2 tbsp. *Aloe vera* gel
- 2 tbsp. rose or lavender water
- 1/2 tsp. borax powder
- 20 drops carrot-seed essential oil
- 3-5 drops coconut fragrance oil (optional)

1. Melt the first 4 oils, butters and beeswax in a double boiler over medium heat until just melted. Add the soy-lecithin, and stir to blend. Remove from heat.
2. In a small saucepan, gently warm the *Aloe vera* gel and rose or lavender water, and stir in borax powder until dissolved. Remove from heat.
3. When the oil and water mixtures are still warm to the touch and about the same temperature, set the small saucepan into a bowl of ice. Drizzle in the oil mixture while mixing rapidly with a small whisk; a cream will quickly form.
4. Add carrot-seed essential oil and coconut fragrance oil, if desired; blend thoroughly.

NOTE: avoid using citrus oils, such as bergamont, orange, lemon or lime. They may cause unpleasant skin reactions when exposed to the sun. They also reduce a sunscreen's effectiveness.

For after-sun relief

- To help cool and moisturize sunburned skin, apply a thin coat of yogurt or *Aloe vera* gel to reddened areas.
- Spray pure lavender water or hydrosol freely on sun-damaged skin to keep skin hydrated, prevent peeling and promote the regeneration of cells.
- Add 2-3 drops of lavender oil to 1 tsp. of a carrier oil, such as sweet almond oil, and massage into affected area. Or apply diluted St. John's wort oil.[40]

5.10 Evaluation of Sunscreens

Sunscreen products formulated with the sunscreen materials at allowed or appropriate amounts must be tested for performance. A number of *in vitro* performance tests have been developed and advocated.

Initially testing of sunscreen compounds is most easily accomplished by spectrophotometric methods. The same method may be used for control purposes to assay the ultraviolet absorbed content of sunscreen preparation. The spectrophotometric methods can give, however, only is crudest approximation of the efficacy of sunscreen formulation. Testing on human skin, only currently accepted *in vivo* test for evaluation of sunscreen preparations.

In vitro tests

Spectrophotometric evaluation

Measurement would be much easier if the skin contained a photocell the protective agent were a clear solution in a cuvette and the sun were the light of a spectrophotometer.[41]

Dilution method (Solution method)

This method involves determination of the absorption characteristic of dilute solutions of a known weight of sunscreening agents in an ultraviolet transparent solvent such as isopropyl alcohol, methanol etc. This method is not suitable for the sunscreen preparations containing ingredients such as titanium dioxide and zinc oxide, because such ingredients are not soluble in solvents suitable for spectral analysis.[42]

Thin film technique

Method 1: This method measures the ultraviolet absorbing capacity of a thin film of sunscreen on quartz glass. Substances tested are rubbed on to one side of a quartz cuvette as thinly as possible. A clean cuvette serves as a control. A major limitation is the difficulty in producing a layer of equal thickness by digital application of the various products. The thinner the layer of substance the less it absorbs.[43]

Method 2: This method involves the examination of absorption or transmission data derived from thin film sandwiches of ingredients (or) products between quartz plate.[42]

Neither of these *in vitro* test systems is able to predict the efficacy of sunscreen ingredients accurately in product design to prevent sunburn. Both methods ignore skin surface phenomena as well as skin-vehicle interactions, important considerations in sunscreen testing. Such spectrophotometer evaluations of sunscreens will provide valuable guidelines; nevertheless; positive results will not guarantee the effectiveness of a preparation in practical application. Wiskesman and Zinnerman list nine factors that may be responsible for differences between effectiveness expected according to physical measurements:

1. The film thickness may fluctuate within wide range in addition to composition and method of application. It also depends on temperature.
2. The absorption capacity may be lost through chemical modifications of the sunscreen under the influence of the UV rays.
3. After evaporation of the solvent, the sunscreen may crystallize, which would inactivate it.

4. With emulsified products, changes in the emulsion pattern on the skin may reduce the effectiveness of the preparation.
5. The sunscreens may diffuse into the skin.
6. Mixture with skin secretion changes the composition of the sunscreen film and may alter its effectiveness.
7. Evaporation of solvent may cause the protective film to become brittle and cracked.
8. Perspiration or water may wash off water-soluble preparation.
9. The preparation may act as irritant or sensitizer and thus accelerate rather than prevents erythema.[44]

Sun exposure method using Sodium Nitroprusside solution for physical sunscreens

Sodium nitroprusside in aqueous solution is photosensitive. In sunlight it undergoes degradation to yield Prussian blue and nitric oxide (NO). Spectrophotometric measurements have often been used to determine the stability of sodium nitroprusside with most emphasis on increase in the absorbance at 390-395 nm with degradation.[45]

We have done this method in our lab by following procedure.

0.05% w/w solution of sodium nitroprusside in distilled water is prepared. 40 ml of this solution is placed into petri plate whose sides are covered with tape. Then top of the petri plates are covered with membrane. Three sets of these petri plates in triplicate, one set without preparation (membrane covered), second set protected with preparation without sunscreen (base) and third set protected with sunscreen preparation are used. One petri plate containing sodium nitroprusside solution is also used for direct exposure. 2 gm of preparation is spread over the membrane as uniform layer as possible with gloved finger. These are exposed to sunlight. At specific intervals, 5 ml of samples are collected and with same volume of Sodium Nitroprusside solution is added. The collected samples are measured Spectrophotometrically at 395 nm and absorbances are noted for all the samples.

Artificial transpore membrane method

This method relies on a spectral measuring device and an artificial transpore membrane. By comparing transmission of UV light through the membrane with and without a sunscreen, a transmission protection factor can be established at different wavelengths throughout the UVB and UVA range. The test is cheap and convenient laboratory surrogate for *in vivo* testing but it has not yet been fully validated and cannot be used for product that are alcohol-based (or) oil-based.[46]

Hairless mouse studies

This *in vitro* test was described by R.M. Sayre et al. In this method male and female Skh-1 and Skh-2 strain hairless mice, 5-6 weeks old were sacrificed by cervical dislocation and the skin removed from the dorsal area of the body. After immersion in 60°C water for 30 seconds, the epidermis was removed intact from the dermal layers by careful blunt dissection following the method of Blank. The epidermal layer was then floated onto a quartz plate and the excess moisture carefully removed. Forward scattering scans were run from 400 to 250 nm in the Beckman Acta-MVI recording spectrophotometer fitted with a diffuse reflectance sphere. Additional 2 mm UG-5 filters were used in both the sample and the reference beams to remove visible fluroescence from the epidermis and from some of the sunscreen formulae tested.

For each piece of epidermis examined, the first measurement obtained was a forward scattering scan of the unprotected epidermis. The carrier plate with the epidermis was then removed from the reflectance sphere and the epidermal area measured. The sunscreen to be tested was applied at a density of 2 mg/cm^2 or 2 μl/cm^2 and the forward scattering scan repeated for the epidermis with its applied product. To determine the absorption of the sunscreen product alone, the absorption of the untreated mouse epidermis was subtracted from the values for the product-treated epidermis point by point at 5 nm intervals.[47,48]

Isolated human epidermis method

Use of human epidermis may be better method instead of an artificial membrane. Diffey, B.L. used human epidermis, isolated by the method described Christophers and Kligmens technique. Epidermis could be obtained by raising suction blisters from surgical biopsy specimens or even from cadaveric skin and would obviate the need for human or animal experimentation.[49]

In vivo testing methods

In vivo animal testing methods

The animal models such as hairless mouse[50] and guinea pigs[51] were used as substitute for human subjects for determining the SPF value. Curtis A. Cole et al. developed a new simple and inexpensive method for evaluation of efficacy and safety of sunscreen product.[52] These animal models are useful to test product effectiveness during developmental stages of sunscreen formulation.

In vivo human testing

Despite the development of animal *in vivo* and *in vitro* testing procedures, human clinical testing remains the accepted method for determining the SPF values of sunscreen products. The standard tests vary from country to country but are all similar. They are based on exposure to the sun of more usually, to lamps that give carefully controlled amounts of radiation of very specific wavelengths. The thickness of the applied film and lamps specified in sunscreen testing vary from country to country. The US and Europe differ significantly. Australia has separate standards. The differences exist between the US and Europe are listed in Table 5.8.

Table 5.8 Comparison of American and German Sunscreen Testing Standards.

	US (FDA)[a]	German (DIN)[b]
Light source	**Filtered xenon arc (continuous emission spectrum in UVB region)** Sunlight	Osram Vitalux (300 W) (mercury vapor line spectrum) Sunlight testing not addressed
Application rate	**2 mg/cm²**	1.50 ± 0.15 mg/cm²
UV dose increments	**25%**	40%
Calculation of SPF	**Arithmetic mean**	Geometric mean
Standard reference	**8% homosalate** SPF 4.1 ± 0.8	2.7% p-methoxy-2-ethyl-hexyl cinnamate SPF 3.7 ± 0.3

[a]Proposed OTC standard method 8/25/78.

[b]Approved standard method DIN norm 67501 (1985).

Source ref from[53]

In its 1978 monograph on sunscreens, the FDA proposed specific procedures for testing the efficacy of these products as well as guidelines for interpreting the test results.

1. ***Selecting test subjects***

   Twenty fair skinned healthy volunteers with skin type I, II and III with no history of abnormal responses to sunlight such as phototoxic or photo-allergic reactions should be selected. Finally the skin on the back of each potential panelist should be examined for sunburn, suntan, scars (or) other conditions that might influence the test results. Each subject must be informed about the nature of the procedure and any potential hazards and must provide written consent to participate in the test.

2. ***Selecting irradiation source***

   The FDA allows the use of either natural sunlight or a solar simulator. However, while natural sunlight might seem like the best choice, investigators have generally encountered numerous difficulties. In particular, the intensity of ultraviolet radiation in natural sunlight varies. Time of day, season, altitude, latitude, cloudiness, and air pollution can all affect the amount of ultraviolet light reaching the subject. And since it would be difficult or impossible to control these factors, the preferred method of irradiation for sunscreen tests is a solar simulator, but it has some limitations:

   1. The test period is usually less than half an hour, where as in practice radiation last for several hours, slow chemical modifications or slow penetration of the substance into the skin would therefore not become apparent test but might play an important part in practice.
   2. The light of even the best ultraviolet lamp does not equal solar radiation. The intensity of shortwave rays (280 - 320 nm) in proportion to the total intensity of radiation is much higher for lamps than for the sun.

3. ***Determining the MED of the test subjects***

   To determine the MED, each panelist receives five timed exposure on the untreated, unprotected skin of the back. The exposure sites are usually at least 1 cm wide if a solar simulator is used, or 10 cm wide if the irradiation source is natural sunlight. Each exposure lasts 25% longer than the previous one. About 24 hours after these exposures have been completed, the test sites on all panelists are examined for erythema. Ideally, there should be at least one site that shows no erythema and a progression of greater and greater erythema at the sites with longer exposure times. The site was the smallest perceptible erythema (faint redness with distinct edges) is selected as the MED for that individual. This is referred to as the preliminary MED.

4. *Testing sunscreen efficacy*

The test sites should be located between the waist and the shoulder blades, parallel with the waist and are usually outlined by grids or templates of opaque materials such as medical tape. The test material and control of 2 mg or 2 μl of sunscreen for each 1 cm^2 of skin is carefully spread to ensure complete, uniform coverage at the test site. The skin is then allowed to dry at least 15 minutes before the next step begins. These sites are irradiated similar way as in the preliminary MED determination. About 16-24 hours after irradiation, each test site is examined for erythema. In our lab we have perfomed this test with slight modifications. In the study the unprotected test sites of 5 x 10 cm wide on the back of each volunteer were exposed to sunlight in increasing exposure times of 30, 40, 50 and 60 minutes for unprotected test site and of 200 minutes for the test site protected by applying 2 mg of sunscreen preparation per sq.cm area of test site. This is carried out during the time in between 10.00 am and 2.00 pm. After 16 hours, the exposed sites were examined for minimal perceptible erythema (Figure 5.1).

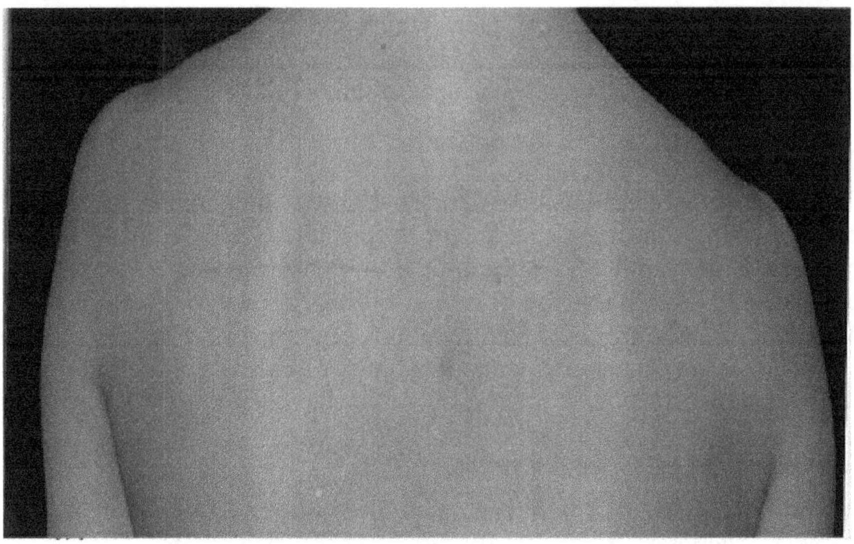

Fig. 5.1 photograph showing Erythema produced after exposure to sunlight.

[Colour Fig. on page 402]

5. ***Interpreting the test results***

   To determine the SPF of the sunscreen being tested, the MED of the treated area and the MED of the most recent test of unprotected skin (confirmed MED) must be obtained for each test site. The SPF ratings for each panelist are then calculated by dividing the MED of the treated area by the confirmed MED of untreated area. The overall SPF of the product is determined by calculating the arithmetic mean of the individual SPF ratings of the entire panel.

Evaluation of UVA protection

The SPF number on sunscreen product tells us practically nothing about the UVA protection. Since UVA rays have lower energy than UVB it would take an inordinately long time to generate an erythemal reaction to UVA radiation. Therefore concept of MED cannot be applied as a test for protection against UVA. Exposure of volunteers to UVA light with and without sunscreens, is not practical in view of the time necessary to produce erythema with UVA light alone.Various alternative methods have therefore been developed to evaluate UVA Protection. E.g., photosensitization of volunteers with a chemical such as Psoralens[54], use of patients with chronic actinic dermatitis[55], use of animal models[56] or use of an *in vitro* system. An important factor in any test of UVA screening is the bandwidth of UVA filter, which cover entire UVA radiation. Misleading protection factors may infact be obtained, if the action spectra of the sensitized skin and normal skin are not similar.

Systemic sunscreens

Oral photo-protection has been largely disappointing. While the value of effective oral sunscreens would be tremendous, development of such products is in its infancy. Only three oral photo-protectants are seriously utilized, and even then for only a handful of specific photosensitivity disorders. These are beta carotene for erythropoietic protoporphyria; chloroquine for lupus erythematosus; and psoralens for polymorphous light eruption.[22]

Side effects of topical sunscreens

All major groups of sunscreens can cause contact and/or photo-contact allergic reactions. While PABA is most often implicated, there are increasing numbers of reports that implicate other sunscreening agents as well, roughly paralleling the increasing use of these alternative agents. Interestingly, persons allergic to PABA are not necessarily allergic to less sensitizing PABA esters.

There are mixed reports regarding the penetration and systemic effects of microfine inorganic agents. An Australian government review concluded that nanosized zinc oxide and titanium dioxide remain on the skin surface without penetrating the stratum corneum. Studies have also demonstrated that nanosized titanium dioxide can pass through cell membranes and impair function of human dermal fibroblast cultures. Polymer-coating these particles may prevent cell membrane adhesion, thereby preserving cell function. Microfine zinc oxide and titanium dioxide can induce neural stem cell apoptosis, although this toxic effect may be more dose dependent than size dependent. Some organic sunscreen agents, including oxybenzone and octinoxate, have been detected in plasma and urine after 4 days of whole-body topical application. The concentrations used in this study were the maximum allowed in the EU, 10%, whereas the maximum approved concentrations in the U.S. for oxybenzone and octinoxate are 6% and 7.5%, respectively. But considering toxicity risk of systemic absorption of sunscreen ingredients, testing appropriate filter concentrations and commercial sunscreen formulations will be helpful, particularly in children and pregnant women.

Combination products containing sunscreen ingredients and n,n-diethyl-meta-toluamide (DEET), an insect repellent, are now readily available. Concurrent administration of DEET and oxybenzone may increase absorption of both agents and reduce SPF. While sunscreen should be reapplied at least every 2 hours, DEET should be applied sparingly and infrequently. Several sunscreen agents have been found to have estrogenic effects.[21]

Sunscreens suppress vitamin D_3 synthesis in the skin. This has led to concern regarding the promotion of rickets, especially in the elderly who typically ingest less milk and other vitamin D fortified products. An interesting study of submariners unexposed to sun showed that they were unable to maintain adequate levels of vitamin D on a typical diet that was not supplemented.[22]

Miscellaneous side effects of sunscreens include yellow staining of clothing by PABA, due to its photooxidation by UVR to a colored compound. This is not generally seen with PABA esters. Since PABA esters are less staining, as well as less allergenic, they have largely replaced unsubstituted PABA in more modern sunscreen formulations.

5.11 Conclusions

Efficient sunscreens have been developed during the past few years. Dermatologists and cosmetic industries have to educate their patients or consumers on how to use (quantity, re application) and how to choose a good sunscreen product based on skin type and SPF. They also have to educate their patients or consumers not only to wear a sunscreen when they are outdoors for an extended period of time during the summer months, but every day because repeated mini exposures account for 80% of the total exposure over a lifetime.

Researchers have to focus on the development of high SPF-broad spectrum (with UVA and UVB absorbers) and photostable sunscreens. Now the trend of herbal products is running successfully. Natural herbs are less toxic when compare with synthetic sunscreens, so many people are showing interest to choose sunscreen products with herbal ingredients.

References

1. Goldsmith L, Koh HK, Bewerse B, et al. Proceedings from the national conference to develop anational skin cancer agenda. American Academy of Dermatology and Centers for Disease Control and Prevention, April 8-10, 1995. *J Am Acad Dermatol* 1996; **34**:822–823.

2. Robinson JK, Amonette R, Wyatt SW, Bewerse BA, Bergfeld WF, Farris PK. Executive summary of the national "sun safety: protecting our future" conference: American Academy of Dermatology and Centers for Disease Control and Prevention. New York, May 1 and 2, 1997. *J Am Acad Dermatol* 1998; **38**:774–780.

3. Lim HW, Cooper K. The health impact of solar radiation and prevention strategies: report of the environment council, American Academy of Dermatology. *J Am Acad Dermatol* 1999; **41**:81–99.

4. IchihashiM,UedaM,Budiyanto A, et al. UV-induced skin damage. *Toxicology* 2003; **189**:21–39.

5. Holick MF. Sunlight and vitamin D for bone health and prevention of autoimmune diseases, cancers, and cardiovascular disease. *Am J Clin Nutr* 2004; **80**:1678S–1688S.

6. Grant-Petersson J, Dietrich AJ, Sox CH, Winchell CW, Stevens MM. Promoting sun protection in elementary schools and child care settings: the SunSafe Project. *J Sch Health* 1999; **69**:100–106.

7. Geller AC, Cantor M, Miller DR, et al. The Environmental Protection Agency's National SunWise School Program: sun protection education in U.S. schools (1999–2000). *J Am Acad Dermatol* 2002; **46**:683–689.

8. Meves A, Repacholi MH, Rehfuess EA. Promoting safe and effective sun protection strategies. *J Am Acad Dermatol* 2003; **49**:1203–1204.

9. Weinstock MA. Death from skin cancer among the elderly: epidemiological patterns. *Arch Dermatol* 1997; **133**:1207–1209.

10. Yaar M, Gilchrest BA. Aging versus photoaging: postulated mechanisms and effectors. *J Invest Dermatol Symp Proc* 1998; **3**:47–51.

11. Naylor MF, Farmer KC. The case for sunscreens: a review of their use in preventing actinic damage and neoplasia. *Arch Dermatol* 1997; **133**:1146–1154.

12. Gurish MF, Roberts LK, Krueger GG, et al. The effect of various sunscreen agents on skin damage and the induction of tumor susceptibility in mice subjected to ultraviolet irradiation. *J Invest Dermatol* 1975; **65**:543–546.

13. Thompson SC, Jolley D, Marks R. Reduction of solar keratoses by regular sunscreen use. *N Engl J Med* 1993; **329**:1147–1151.

14. Boyd AS, Naylor M, Cameron GS, et al. The effects of chronic sunscreen use on the histologic changes of dermatoheliosis. *J Am Acad Dermatol* 1995; **33**:941–946.

15. Roberts LK, Beasley DG. Commercial sunscreen lotions prevent ultraviolet-radiation–induced immune suppression of contact hypersensitivity. *J Invest Dermatol* 1995; **105**:339–344.

16. Stiller MJ, Bartolone J, Stern R, Smith S, Kollias N, Gillies R, Drake LA. Topical 8% glycolic acid and 8% L-lactic acid creams for the treatment of photodamaged skin: a double-blind vehicle-controlled clinical trial. *Arch Dermatol* 1996; **132**:631–636.

17. Shaath NA. Evolution of modern sunscreen chemicals. In: Lowe NJ, Shaath NA, Pathak MA, eds. *Sunscreens: Development, Evaluation, and Regulatory Aspects*. 2nd ed. New York: Marcel Dekker, 1997:3–31.

18. Rebut R. The sunscreen industry in Europe: past, present, and future. In: Lowe NJ, Shaath NA, eds. *Sunscreens: Development, Evaluation, and Regulatory Aspects.* New York: Marcel Dekker, 1990:161–178.

19. Peak, MJ. and Peak, J.G. Solar-ultraviolet-induced damage to DNA. *Photodermatol* 1989; **6**, 1-15.

20. Setlow, R.B. and Woodhead, A.D. (1994) Temporal changes in the incidence of malignant melanoma: explanation from action spectra. *Mutation Res.*, **307,** 365-374.

21. Divya R. Sambandan, BA, Desiree Ratner. Sunscreens: An overview and update. *J Am Acad Dermatol* 2011;**64**:748-58.

22. LEE A. Kaplan. Suntan, sunburn, and sun protection. *Journal of Wilderness Medicine* 1992; **3**:173-196.

23. Tanner PR. Sunscreen product formulation. *Dermatol Clin* 2006; **24**:53–62.

24. Comarow A. Should you pay $75 to block the sun? For most of us, a regular t-shirt is enough US News World Rep 1999; 127:59.

25. Nichols K, Desai N, Lebwohl MG. Effective sunscreen ingredients and cutaneous irritation in patients with rosacea. *Cutis* 1998; **61**:344–346.

26. Journe F, Marguery MC, Rakotondrazafy J, El Sayed F, Bazex J. Sunscreen sensitization: a 5-year study. *Acta Derm Venereol* 1999; **79**:211–213.

27. Stenberg C, Larko O. Sunscreen application and its importance for the sun protection factor. *Arch Dermatol* 1985; **121**:1400–1402.

28. John C. Koshy, Safa E. Sharabi, David Jerkins, Joshua Cox, BA, Sarah P. Cronin, BS, & Larry H. Hollier, Sunscreens: Evolving Aspects of Sun Protection. *Journal of Pediatric Health Care* 2010; **24(5)**: 343-346.

29. Camile L. Hexsel, Scott D. Bangert, Adelaide A. Hebert and Henry W. Lim. Current sunscreen issues: 2007 Food and Drug Administration sunscreen labelling recommendations and combination sunscreen/insect repellent products. *J Am Acad Dermatol* 2008; **59(2)**: 316-323.

30. Diffey BL, Tanner PR, Matts PJ, et al. *In vitro* assessment of the broad spectrum ultravioletprotection of sunscreen products. *J Am Acad Dermatol* 2000; **43**:1024–1035.

31. Steinberg DC. Regulations of sunscreens worldwide. In: Shaath NA, ed. *Sunscreens: Regulation and Commercial Development.* 3rd. ed. Boca Raton: Taylor and Francis, 2005: 173–198.

32. Shaath NA. On the theory of ultraviolet absorption by sunscreen chemicals. *J Soc Cosmet Chem* 1987; **82**:193.

33. Sayre RM, Killias N, Roberts RL, et al. Physical sunscreens. *J Soc Cosmet Chem* 1990; **41**:103–109.

34. Wenninger JA, McEwen GN Jr., eds. *International cosmetic ingredient dictionary and handbook.* 12th ed. Washington: The Cosmetic, Toiletry, and Fragrance Association, 2008.

35. André O. Barel, Marc Paye, Howard I. Maibach. *Handbook of Cosmetic Science and Technology*, 3rd, 2009; 314.

36. Rigel DS, Friedman RJ, Dzubow L, Bystryn JC, Reintgen D, Marks R, eds. *Cancer of the Skin*. Philadelphia: W.B. Saunders, 2005.

37. Lubrizol TECHNICAL DATA SHEET, TDS-232, Edition: October 15, 2007.

38. www.igicares.com

39. http://www.global-seven.com

40. http://www.suite101.com/article.cfm/herbal_lore

41. Karson J. Master, Robert M. Sayre, Mark Allen Everett. New Evaluation Techniques for Sunscreens. *Journal of the Society of Cosmetic Chemists*, Vol. 17, No. 10, 581-594.

42. Kreps SI, Goldemberg RL. *Cosmetics: Science and Technology*, vol I, Wiley, New York, 1972; 278.

43. Guinter kahn MD, George wilcox. Comparison of *in vitro* and *in vivo* Sunscreen Testing Methods. *J Soc Cosmetic Chemists* 1969; **20**:807-824.

44. Stephan Jellinek Joseph. *Formulation and function of* cosmetics. Wiley, New York, 1970; 323-350.

45. Richard. Sodium nitroprusside. *Analytical profiles of drug substances*, vol 6, Academic press, New York, 1977, 498-499.

46. Diffey BL, Robson J. A new substrate to measure sunscreen protection factors throughout the ultraviolet spectrum. *J Soc Cosmetic Chemists*, 1989; **40**: 127-133.

47. Robert M, Sayre, Agin PP, Gordon J, Edward M, A comparison of *in vivo* and *in vitro* testing of sunscreening formulas, *Photochemistry and Photobiology*, 1979; **29**: 559-566.

48. Sayre RM, Agin PP, Desrochers DL, Marlowe E. Sunscreen testing methods: *In vitro* prediction of effectiveness. *J Soc Cosmetic Chemists*. 1974; **25**: 639-644.

49. Albert MK, Enno C. Preparation of isolated sheets of human stratum corneum. *Archieves in Dermatology*. 1963; **40**: 127-132.

50. Hanna wolska MD, Andrzej L, MD, Francis NM. The Hairless Mouse as an Experimental Model for Evaluating the Effectiveness of Sunscreen Preparation. *J Soc Cosmetic Chemists*. 1974; **25**: 639-644.

51. Minoru F, Satoru A, Mieko Y, Keisuke N, Saburo O. New method for evaluating the effectiveness of sunscreen product. *J Soc Cosmetic Chemists*. 1982, **33**: 9-18.

52. Curtis A. Cole, P. Donald Forbes and Karen Ludwigsen, *Photodermatol*, 1989; **6**, 131.

53. US FDA, sunscreen drug products for over the counter human use:federal register, 1978, **43**: 38206-38269.

54. Kaidbey KH, Kligman AM, Laboratory methods for appraising the efficacy of sunsereens. *J Soc Cosmetic Chemists* 1978; **29**: 525-36.

55. Diffey BL, Farr PM. Sunscreen protection against UVB, UVA and blue light. *British Journal of Dermatology,* 1991; **124**:258–263.

56. Chew S, Leo D, Harber LC, Animal model for evaluation of topical photoprotection against UV Aradiation. *The Journal of Investigative Dermatology*, 1987, **89**: 410-414.

CHAPTER 6

HAIR DYES

Y. Madhusudan Rao, D. Sathish

Center for Biopharmaceutics and Pharmacokinetics, University College of Pharmaceutical Sciences, Kakatiya University, Warangal-506 009, Andhra Pradesh, India.

6.1 Introduction

6.1.1 Human Hair

Hair is often the first thing people notice, so it is important that our hair reflects our inner health and beauty. Just like our skin, our hair signifies our state of health, and will shine more when we take proper care of it. By taking care of our hair, it will give more confidence. Our hair is formed inside hair bulbs on our head. While hair contains water, lipids, traces of mineral elements and melanin, keratin is the main ingredient. The number of bulbs on an average person's head at birth is between 100 and 140 thousand. Our hair bulbs provide our hairs with the nutrients it needs to grow, reaching an average growth rate of 0.3 mm a day (1 cm per month). Hair grows more quickly in summer than in winter, and more slowly at night than during the day.

Figure 6.1.a shows a schematic of a human hair fiber with its various layers of cellular structure. Hair fibers (about 50–100 μm in diameter) consist of the cuticle and cortex, and in some cases medulla in the central region. All are composed of dead cells which are mainly filled with keratin protein. Table 6.1 displays a summary of the chemical species of hair. Depending on its moisture content, human hair consists of approximately 65-95% keratin proteins, and the remaining constituents are water, lipids (structural and free), pigment, and trace elements. Proteins are made up of long chains of various mixtures of some 20 or 50 amino acids. Each chain takes up a helical or coiled form. Among numerous amino acids in human hair, cystine is one of the most important amino acids. Every cystine unit contains two cysteine amino acids in different chains which lie near to each other and are linked together by two sulphur atoms, forming a very strong bond known as a disulfide linkage. In addition to disulfide bonds, hair is also rich in peptide bonds, and the abundant CO- and NH-groups present give rise to hydrogen bonds between groups of neighboring chain molecules. The distinct cystine content of various cellular structures of human hair results in a significant effect on their physical properties. A high cystine content corresponds to rich disulfide cross-links, leading to high mechanical properties. The species responsible for color in hair is the pigment melanin, which is located in the cortex of the hair in granular form. An average head contains over 100,000 hair follicles, which are the cavities in the skin surface from which hair fibers grow. Each follicle grows about 20 new hair fibers in a lifetime. Each fiber grows for several years until it falls out and is replaced by a new fiber. Hair typically grows at a rate on the order of 10 mm/month.[1]

Hair coloring is currently a globally accepted fashion phenomenon. From the young generation with playful attitude towards hair coloring to the older generation who hide their gray hair, hair coloring products have been consumed by both men and women. Hair colouring habits change in different parts of world. In Western countries bleaching of hair to light yellow to snow white is popular and liked. Blond hair is a fashion in those countries. In Asian and Eastern countries dyeing is popular to brown, black and yellowish tints. In India colouring to get jet black colour is most popular.

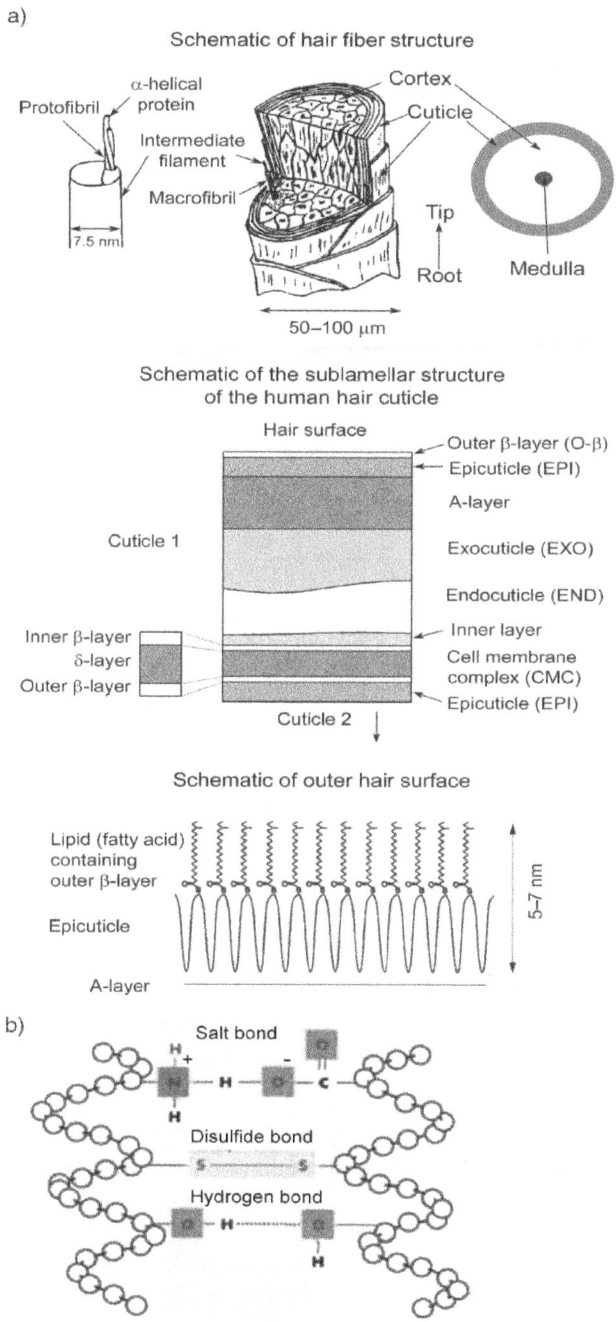

Fig. 6.1 (a) Schematic of hair fiber structure and cuticle sublamellar structure and **(b)** various bonds within hair cellular structure[1].

Table 6.1 Summary of chemical species present in human hair.

Keratin protein	65–95%
(Amino acids)	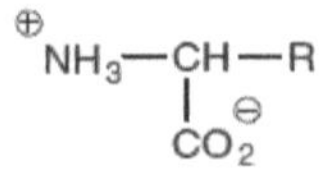 (R: functional group)
Cystine	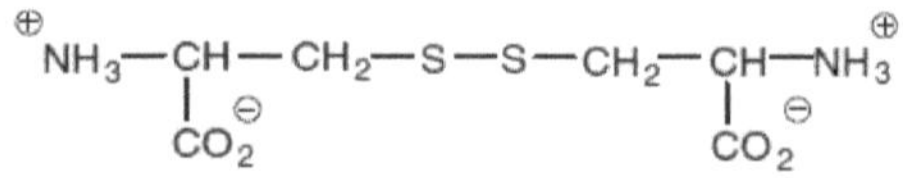
Lipids	Structural and free
18-Methyl eicosanoic acid (18-MEA)	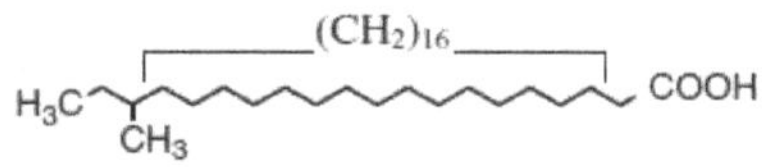
Water	Up to 30%
Pigment and trace elements	Melanin

6.1.2 Do or Dye

All hair dyes in the market consists of a developer (hydrogen peroxide) and an alkalizing ingredient ("Hair Coloring"). An alkaline or basic peroxide environment can be created by combining the hair color, alkalizing ingredient and developer. The peroxide enters the cortex and breaks down the melanin replacing it with new color. The cuticle of the hair is the outermost layer. It is composed of a transparent, scale-like single layer of overlapping cells. The function of these overlapping, shingle-like scales is to protect the cortex. Hair dye is absorbed into the shingles when dye is applied on the hair strands. The absorption depends on the size of the color molecules. Based on the duration of the color stay and size of the color molecule hair dyes can be classified into five groups which include temporary, semipermanent, demipermanent, permanent, and bleach ("Hair Coloring"). Infact Bleaching involves removal of the existing color which is subtraction rather than addition.

Over 3000 years henna and indigo have been used to color hair. Now the era of hair color is running successfully due to modern synthetic organic chemistry. In 1863 Hoffman noticed that a brown-black color was produced when paraphenylenediamine was oxidized. But due to the lack of communication the first commercial brand of hair color[1,2] was introduced in the market in 1907 by the scientist Eugene Schueller who was chemist and the founder of L'Oreal, one of the top leader in the world in hair coloring technology. Initially hair dye was used in the salon only, but the first home-use hair dye was introduced in 1950.

Hair pigment

Hair color is mostly the result of pigments: chemical compounds that reflect certain wavelengths of visible light. Hair pigment comprises less than 3% of the fiber mass of hair. There are three pigments (eumelanins, pheomelanins, and oxymelanins) found in human hair. Eumelanin has an oval or elliptical shape, which gives color to brown or black hair and is dark pigment. The higher the concentration of Eumelanin the darker the hair. It contains high amounts of 5,6-dihydroxyindole with lesser amounts of 5,6-dihydroxyindole-2-carboxylic acid. Pheomelanin produces the color in blonde or red hair. The higher the concentration of phaeomelanin, the lighter the hair. Unlike eumelanin, pheomelanin is smaller, partly oval and has a rod shape (10-12% sulphur and 1,4-benzothiazinylalanine) contains fewer sulphur atoms than pheomelanin. White hair contains no melanin at all and gray hair contains only a few melanin granules. A lesser pigment oxymelanin is yellow or reddish in color and probably represents bleached eumelanin pigment arising from partial oxidative cleavage of 5,6-dihydroxyindole units. It doesn't contain sulphur. To reproduce a natural hair color, hair dyes attempt to mimic these pigments.

6.2 Types of Hair Dyes

Hair coloring products are usually categorized by the length of time the coloring imparted to the hair survives shampooing.

Table 6.2 Types of hair dye.

Type of Hair dye	Chemical reaction	End result	Duration of effect	Advantages	Disadvantages
Gradual	Deposition of metal salts	Gradual brown hair darkening	Requires continuous application	Inexpensive, easy to apply	Cannot be combined with other chemical hair processing
Temporary	Acid textile dyes	Blending of hair tones	One shampoo exposure	Short-lived, inexpensive	May rub off on clothing or run with water exposure
Semipermanent: vegetable	Henna with metal salts	Reddish hues to hair	4–6 shampoo exposures	Low incidence of allergenicity	Leave hair somewhat harsh
Semipermanent: textile	Textile dyes	Tone hair, minimally cover gray	4–6 shampoo exposures	Add color highlights	Short-lived color
Demipermanent	Deeper penetrating textile dyes	Tone hair, minimally cover gray	10–12 shampoo exposures	Longer-lasting with no obvious hair grow-out	Cannot completely cover gray
Permanent	Oxidation/ reduction reaction	Darken hair color, cover gray	Permanent	Excellent coverage of gray hair	Color is permanent
One-step bleaching	Oxidation/ reduction reaction	Lighten hair color, cover gray	Permanent	Achieve light blond hair shades	Damaging to hair
Two-step bleaching	Oxidative alkaline Reaction	Dramatically lighten hair color, cover gray	Permanent	Achieve dramatic hair color lightening	Very damaging to hair

Ref source from[3]

6.2.1 Gradual Hair Dyes

Gradual hair dyes are alsocalled as metallic or progressive hair dyes which require repeated application for gradual darkening of the hair shaft. For example Grecian Plus Gradual Haircolor Foam 5 oz (142 g) gradually restores lost color to graying hair thickens, conditions, fresh, clean scent, easy-to-use foam, works for any color hair, restores lost color to gray hair, gradually. Day by day, Grecian Plus gradually replaces gray with natural-looking color. We can stop anytime and leave a little gray, or keep going until all the gray is gone.

Grecian Plus Gradual Haircolor Foam 5 oz (142 g). [Colour Fig. on page 403]

We cannot control the final color with gradual dye. But these are popular because of low cost and self application at home. Gradual dye contains water-soluble metal salts. These are sometimes also are called as color restorers and Progressive hair dyes. These salts will deposit on the hair shaft in the form of oxides, suboxides, and sulphides. The metals used are lead, silver, copper, bismuth, nickel, iron and manganese. The problem with these dyes is that the hair must grow out before other dyeing or waving is used. If gradual dye is mixed with other dyes, the metal present in the gradual dye can breakdown hydrogen peroxide which ruptures the hair shaft. As the gradual dye requires continuous application, is not suitable for men who cut their hair frequently.

6.2.2 Temporary Hair Dyes

As the name itself indicates it is removed at the first shampoo only. In hair dyes market it occupies only 3%. The durability may be increased by exposing hair to heat. But the disadvantages include staining of clothes when it gets wet and the particle size is too large to penetrate through the cuticle. But the main advantage is it will not damage the hair shaft and the persons who are allergic to paraphenylenediamine can use these dyes. Most of the people prefer these to get blue, green, red, or purple hair for special occasions like dramas. It is also famous to create platinum hair. Several types of temporary dyes are available like liquid, mousse, and gel. Liquid temporary dyes are also referred to as 'hair rinses' as they are frequently applied in the shower following shampooing. We can remove the excess dye by rinsing. Temporary coloring formulation is achieved by a mixture of color additives, surfactant and acid or alkali. Cationic basic dyes are often used in the formulations. Several different kinds of dyes are used for one formulation to achieve the desired hair color.

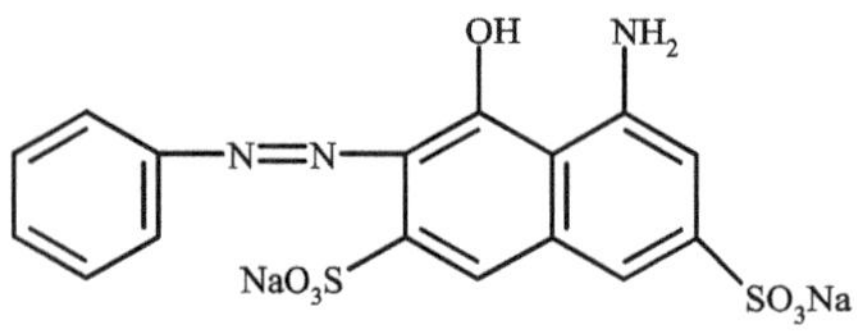

D & C red No. 33

Acid Fuchsine

(Disodium 5-amino-4-hydroxy-3-(phenylazo) -naphthalene-2,7-disulfonate)

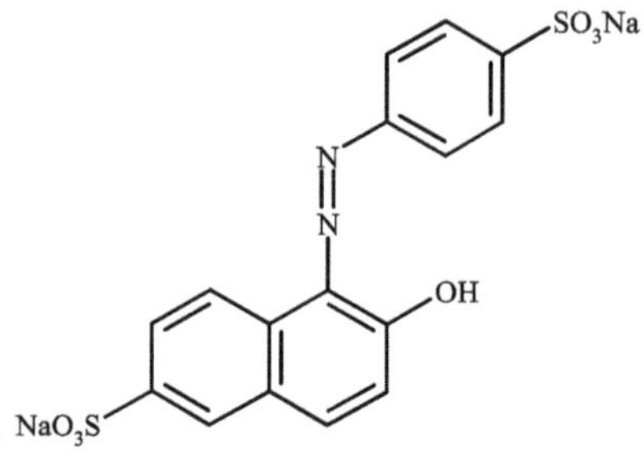

FD & C yellow No. 6

Sunset Yellow

(Disodium 6-hydroxy-5-[(4-sulfophenyl) azo]-2-naphthalenesulfononate)

Fig. 6.2 Example of cationic basic dyes used in temporary hair coloring products[2].

Table 6.3 Sample temporary hair coloring product ingredient[2].

Ingredient	Weight % of ingredient for desired hair cool		
	Brown	**Red**	**White**
Nonoxynol-9	1.0	1.0	1.0
Hydroxyethylcellulose (HHR)	0.7	0.7	0.7
Cetylrimmonium chloride	0.6	0.6	0.6
Neodol 91-2.5	0.5	0.5	0.5
Citric acid trihydrate	0.5	-	0.5
Trisodium phosphate	-	0.3	-
Direct black 51	0.05	0.01	-
Acid violet 43	0.04	0.03	-

Table 6.3 *Contd...*

Ingredient	Weight % of ingredient for desired hair cool		
	Brown	Red	White
Acid orange 24	0.04	0.02	-
External D & C Violet 2	-	-	0.03
D&C Red 33	-	-	0.01
FD&C Yellow 6	-	-	0.005
FD&C Yellow 10	-	-	0.005
Water	96.54	96.79	96.65

6.2.3 Semipermanent

This class of dyes, initially designed exclusively for gray-hair coverage, has progressively grown in importance as the formulation changes extended the color palette and improved the durability of the imparted color. To remove semipermanent dyes 4-6 shampooings are required as weak polar and Van der Waals attractive forces are involved. To obtain the desired shade, 10-12 dyes are mixed and they produce tone-on-tone coloring rather than producing more color changes, so their role is actually in toning rather than dyeing hair. So semipermanent dyes are known as 'on shade.' Semi-permanent hair coloring product does not require any peroxide or mixing. The formulation consists of solvents, surfactants, amides, fragrances, and acid or alkali. The solvents most commonly used are water and glycols or glycol derivatives and the purpose of the acid or alkali is to adjust the pH. The types of dyes used are neutral aromatic amine, nitro aromatic amine, or anthraquinone derivatives. The dyes can be classified as mono-, di-, or trinuclear (ring) dyes. Studies have shown that small mononuclear hair dyes has a higher rate of rinsing out. Larger dyes are able to reach more hindered position in the hair shaft and therefore the hair color lasts longer.

The famous and historical example for vegetable dye is henna which was used in Egypt 4000 years ago. Henna is botanically called as *Lawsonia alba.* Still most of the people are using to get orange-red color to hair or to mask white hair. It also acts as a conditioner. Henna comes under the category of semi-permanent dye because minimal cuticle penetration occurs allowing removal of the dye in 4-6 shampooings. Another famous one is black walnut shells. Now a days synthetic henna products are in the market to replace natural one. The main disadvantage of natural henna is that it leaves the hair stiff and brittle after repeated applications. The chemical responsible for this action is Lawsone and is nearly 100 times effective. Henna can be mixed with, indigo, tea, amla, bhringraj etc., to get desired shades.

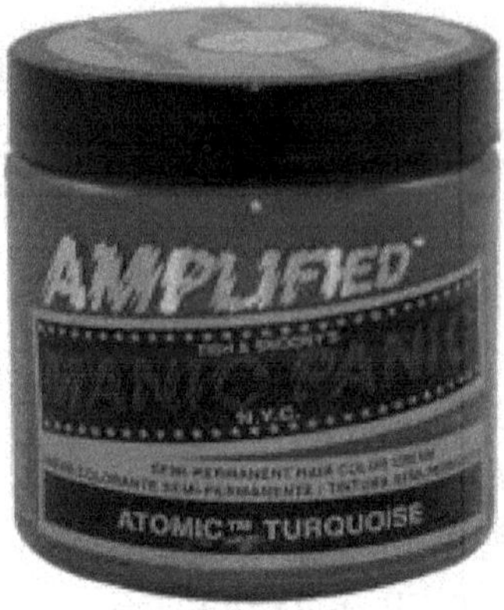

Manic Panic Amplified Semi-Permanent Hair Color Cream.
[Colour Fig. on page 403]

Herbal Hair Color and Henna hair color dye. [Colour Fig. on page 403]

Table 6.4 Sample semi-permanent hair coloring product ingredients*.

Ingredient	Weight % of ingredient for desired hair cool		
	Light brown	**Dark brown**	**Red-auburn**
Cocodiethanolamide	10.0	10.0	10.0
Sodium dodecyl benzene sulfonate (52%)	4.0	4.0	4.0
Neodol 91-2.5	6.0	6.0	6.0
Sodium lauryl sulphate	2.5	2.5	2.5
2-nitro-*p*-phenylenediamine	0.4	0.4	0.4
HC Red No. 3	0.2	0.2	-
HC Yellow No. 2	0.2	0.2	0.2
HC Blue No.2	-	0.1	-
Water	76.7	76.6	76.9

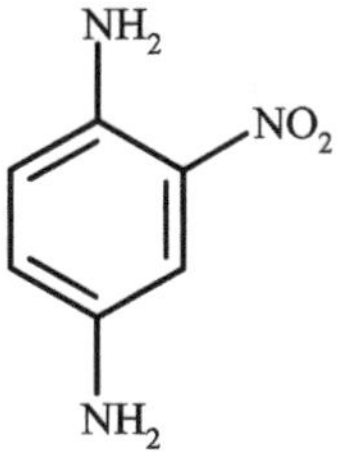

2-Nitro-p-phenylene diamine (red)

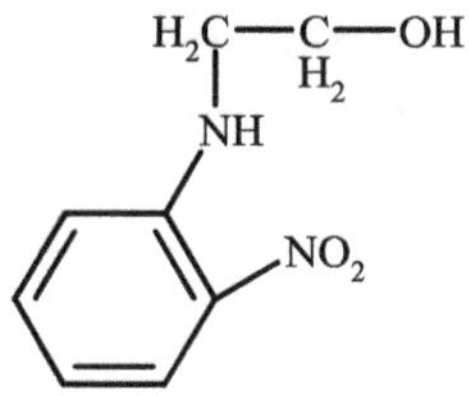

HC yellow No. 2

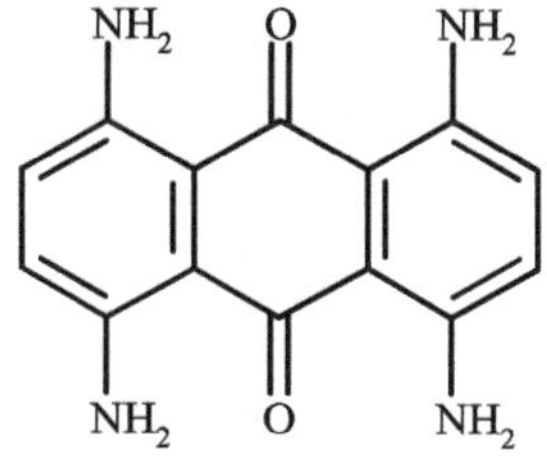

Disperse blue 1

Fig. 6.3 Example of semi-permanent dyes[2].

6.2.4 Permanent and Demi-permanent Hair Color

Permanent hair coloring product is formulated with two different components of precursor-coupler base and oxidizing base. The precursor-coupler base consists of surfactants, alkaline, reducing agent, precursors, couplers, and water (Table 5). The oxidizing base consists of an oxidizing agent (e.g. peroxide), stabilizer for the peroxide, and surfactants (Table 6.6). Since the peroxide is unstable in alkaline solution, the precursor-coupler base and the oxidizing base have to be formulated separately for product storage. Surfactants are used to help dissolve the precursors and couplers, to assist in spreading the dye evenly over the hair, and to thicken the product so it does not drip easily while applying the product.[4] Alkaline is required to facilitate the oxidation reaction, and the reducing agent to inhibit oxidation of precursors by air. The surfactant in the oxidizing base works as a thickener by the surfactants precipitating on dilution when the two components are mixed together, resulting in a much thicker mixture .[5]

Table 6.5 Ingredients for various hair dyes.

Ingredient	Weight % of ingredient for desired hair cool			
	Dark brown	Light brown	Red	Balck
Dodecyl benzene Sulfonate (50%)	14.0	14.0	14.0	14.0
Cocodiethanolamide	9.0	9.0	9.0	9.0
Neodol 91-2.5	6.0	6.0	6.0	6.0
Ammonium hydroxide	6.0	6.0	6.0	6.0
Sodium sulphite	0.3	0.3	0.3	0.3
p-Phenylenediamine	0.4	-	-	0.4
o-Aminophenol	0.3	0.4	-	0.2
p-Aminophenol	-	0.4	0.4	-
4-Methyl-5-aminophenol	-	-	0.4	-
m-Aminophenol	-	-	-	0.2
Water	64.0	63.9	63.9	63.9

Dyes for permanent coloring are achieved by an oxidation reaction of a dye precursor followed by a reaction with a dye coupler. Schematic reaction of an oxidation dye is shown in Figure 6.4.

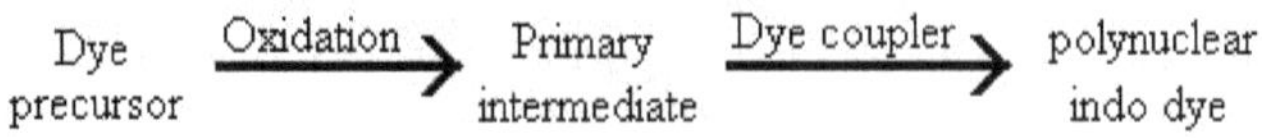

Fig. 6.4 Schematic reaction of oxidative hair dyeing reaction.

Table 6.6 Sample Oxidizer base ingredients.

Ingredient	Weight %
Hydrogen peroxide (30%)	50.0
Dodecyl benzene sulfonate (50%)	33.0
Phosphoric acid	1.0
Water	16.0

The oxidation reagents used generally are hydrogen peroxide and ammonium hydroxide, and the primary intermediates are usually *ortho-* or *para*-substituted amino aromatic compounds. Dye couplers are electron-rich aromatic phenols or amines. Figure 6.5 and 6.6 shows some sample dye precursors and dye couplers, respectively. Combination of different dye precursors and dye couplers gives different coloring affect.

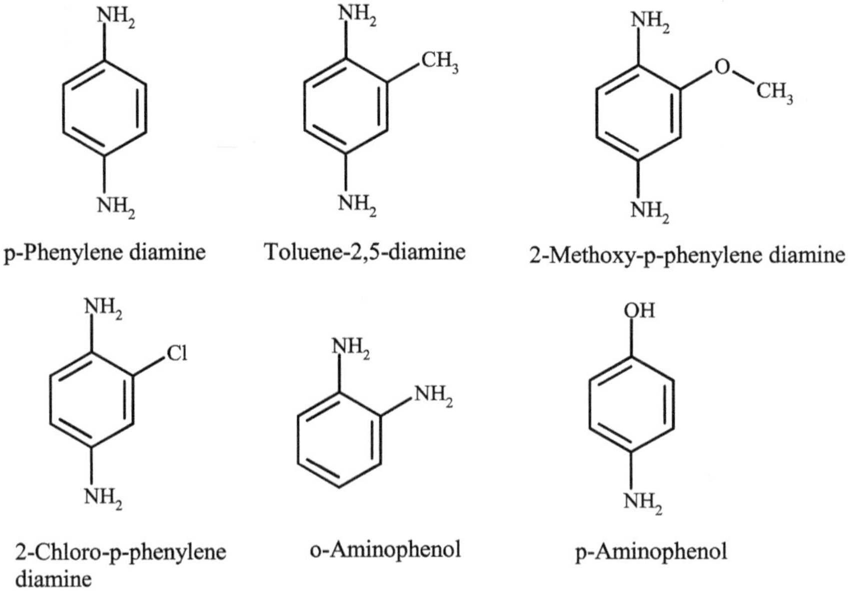

Fig. 6.5 Examples for dye precursors.

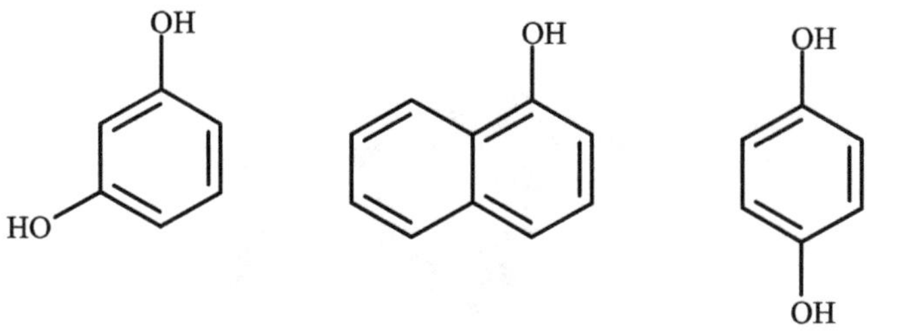

Resorcinol 1-N aphtol Hydroquinone

Fig. 6.6 Examples for dye couplers.

Demi-permanent hair dyes are similar to the permanent hair dyes in terms of oxidative dyes but resembles the lasting properties of a semi-permanent hair color. The peroxide amount is less so it causes less damage to the hair.

Wella Color Charm Demi-Permanent Hair Color # 4/0 Medium Natural 60 ml. [Colour Fig. on page 403]

Profession by Indola. [Colour Fig. on page 403]

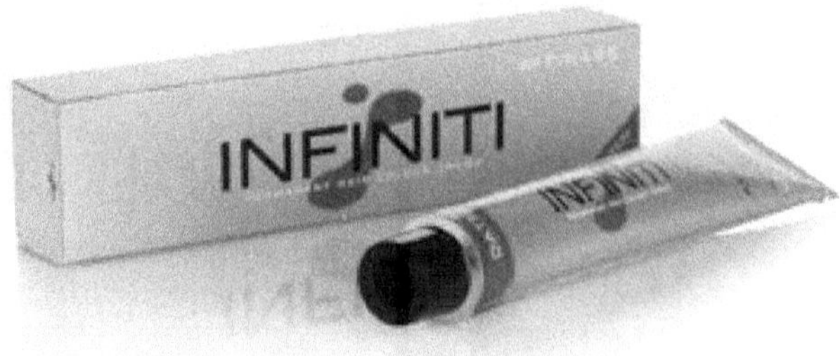

Infiniti Permanent Hair Colour Creme by Affinage. [Colour Fig. on page 404]

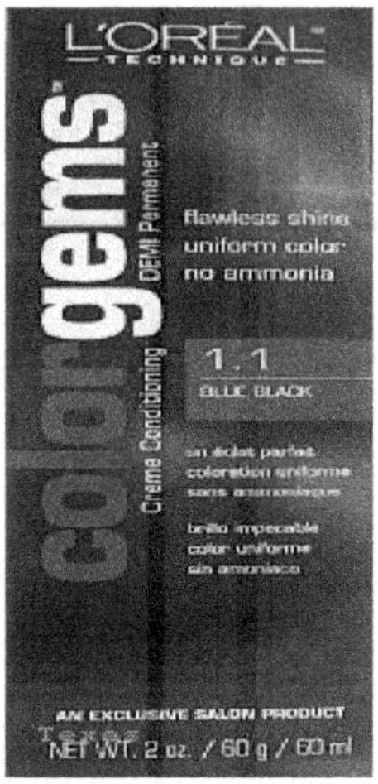

Color Gems Creme Conditioning DEMI Permanent. [Colour Fig. on page 404]

6.3 Coloring Techniques

Single process

It is a simple method of using coating or penetrating tints on all of the hair, while using one of the above mentioned color types: temporary, semi permanent or permanent colors, to achieve a solid color look. While following this process we have to consider the type of hair whether it is never colored hair or previously colored hair.

Double process

It is a time consuming method of using two-step coloring. It requires a professional hairdresser. Either a single process all over the hair on virgin hair or just the re-growth area on an already processed hair using the lightener (also called bleach usually mixed with 20 vol. Peroxide), then applies the toner (usually mixed with 5-10 vol. Peroxide).

High-lights

It is a time consuming method which creates a "natural look". This technique is to enhance or change hair color less dramatically then single or double process. For reflection of hair, a colorist may use a permanent tint, hi-lift tint or a lightener. It is usually applied in between foils for toning down or covering the gray hair.

Low-lights

Low lights may be applied with the techniques mentioned above. They are usually used for toning down an over lightened hair, growing out the hi-lighted hair, etc. In case of semi-permanent dyes, they are small enough to enter the hair shaft and can easily leave the hair shaft as the hair is washed (Figure 6.7). The color of the hair is a result of the diffusion of dyes into the hair shaft.

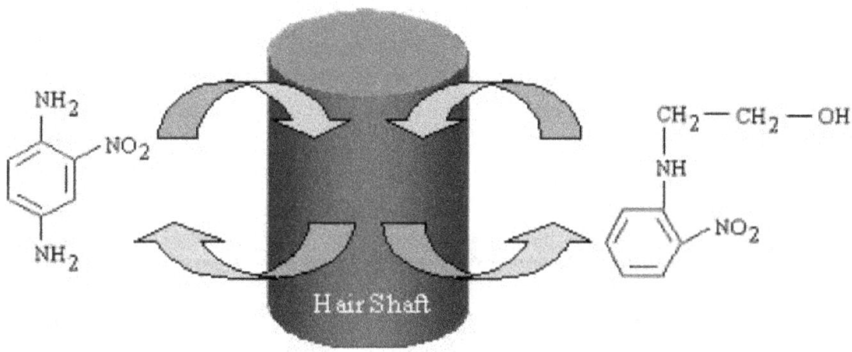

Fig. 6.7 Semi-permanent dyes are small enough to enter and exit the hair shaft. As the hair is being washed, the dye leaves the hair shaft as the hair returns to its original color[8]. [Colour Fig. on page 404]

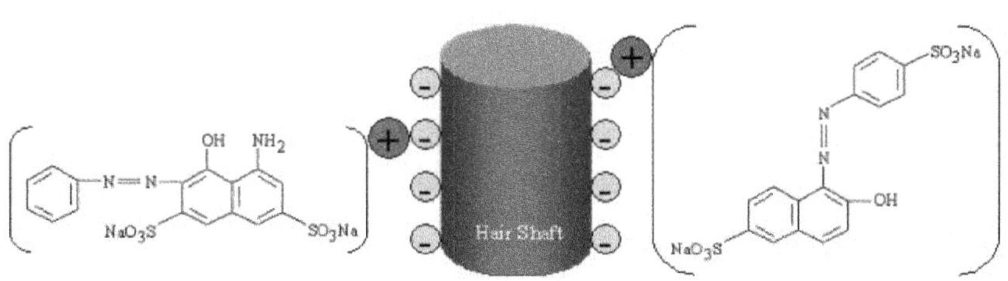

Fig. 6.8 Schematic of the cationic basic dye attracted to the surface of the hair shaft. After a few wash, the dye will leave the hair surface[6-8].
[Colour Fig. on page 404]

The cationic dyes used in temporary coloring are too large of a molecule to enter the hair shaft. Instead, the molecules stick onto the hair shaft as a result of the net negative charge on the hair surface (Figure 6.8). Since the temporary dyes stick to the surface of the hair, it is easily removed by one to three washes. However, if the hair has been chemically treated (e.g. permanent hair coloring) prior to the application of the temporary dye, the hair becomes more porous and allows the dye to penetrate into the hair shaft, resulting in the hair color to last longer.

6.4 Special Focus on Natural Hair Colorants

In comparison to natural hair dyes, synthetic hair dyes are reported to cause skin and other skin related diseases. The manufacturing process is hazardous to health of the people involved in the process and its applications leads to environmental pollution and also causes potential side effects to the consumers of the product. The fear of side effects from the synthetic dyes has limited its use by health conscious customers throughout the world and has to overcome various regulatory barriers before it reaches its destination. (Table 6.7 gives list of banned substances in hair dyes). A dye can generally be described as a colored substance that has an affinity to the fiber, fur or hair. The dye is generally applied as aqueous solution, and may require a mordant to improve the fastness of the dye on the fiber, fur or hair. Natural dyes also referred as mordant dyes.

Different mordant will give different hue color with the same dye. A mordant is thus an agent which allows a reaction to occur between the dye and the fiber, hair or fur. From ancient days various materials from plants like Henna, Chamomile, Indigo, etc. are used to dye the grey hair to get natural black colour.

But instead of getting black colour people get red to copper colour. Loss of colour in hair is due to varied reasons like genetic influence, effect of environmental factors, use of alcoholic preparations, etc. Though permanent synthetic hair dyes are available in varied colour and ranges retain natural lustre, they have the chief disadvantage of producing hypersensitive reactions in some individuals. Some hair dyes marketed as natural dye, contain 1-3% of phenylenediamine which is a synthetic hair dye and stain the skin and clothes during use. So formulation of a product containing only plant product is essential, which is safe for use and does not have the problems of staining skin during use and hypersensitive reactions. In our lab we developed a product to get natural black colour using combination of different plant materials.

The leaves of henna, indigo, brahmi, tea and bhringraj, fruits of amla, shoe flowers, and cinnamon bark were collected from different places and dried in shade. They were made into powders and used for the preparation of hair colorants. The human hair was collected from barber shops and temples from which white hairs were separated and used for the studies.

6.4.1 Preliminary Preparation of Natural Hair Colorants

Case study: Y Madhusudan Rao*, Shayeda and P Sujatha. Formulation and evaluation of commonly used natural hair colorants. *Natural Product Radiance*, Vol. 7(1), 2008, pp.45-48

One gram each of henna, indigo, amla, bhringraj, hibiscus, brahmi, catechu, cinnamon and tea powder was taken separately and added 200 mg (20%) of urea in each sample. A smooth paste was made with water separately. The pastes were kept aside for 1 hour for imbibitions. The hair was kept in the above pastes for 1 hour and then washed with water and observed for its colouring.

Selection of suitable combination with henna

1 gm of henna was mixed with same proportion of indigo, tea, amla, bhringraj and 20% urea and water was added to that in order to make a smooth paste. The paste was kept aside for 1 hour for imbibition. The hair was kept in above paste for 1 hour. After that it was washed with water and observed for its colouring.

Selection of suitable combination of henna and indigo

Henna was mixed with indigo in different ratios from 1:1 to 1:5, mixed with water to make smooth paste and processed similarly as above to observe colouring.

Effect of pH on the selected combination on henna and indigo

1:3 Ratios of henna and indigo were selected because it produced altered colour and effect of pH was studied. To the paste of above ratio, dilute ammonia solution was added in order to obtain the pH of 6, 7, 8, 9. Further process was same for observing its effect.

Effect of successive application of selected combination of henna and indigo

1:3 Ratios of henna and indigo were selected and to that successive application of paste was studied. The henna and indigo paste was applied 2 to 4 times and washed repeatedly with shampoo and observed for its colouring.

Effect of modifying agents over hair colorants

1 gm of henna and 3 gm of indigo powders were weighed and taken in a dish; 20% of urea and 1% of ferric chloride were added and made into paste. The paste was kept for 1 hour. Similarly, preparations containing 3 and 6% of ferric chloride were also prepared. The above pastes were applied to the white hair, waited for 1 hour. The hair colour was observed under microscope after washing with water. Similarly, same concentrations of copper sulphate were also prepared and observed.

Comparative evaluation of the formulation with marketed brands

For comparison with the prepared paste with 1:1 henna and indigo with 20% of urea prepared paste two marketed herbal hair colorants [containing para phenylenediamine (PPD) in their formulation]. The above three pastes were applied to the hair, waited for 1 hour and observed after washing.

Sensitivity test

Primary irritation testing

This test was conducted on two albino rabbits to detect the potential primary irritants present in the developed formulation. The animal ethical committee approval was also taken. It was ascertained that the animals did not have any skin sensitization or irritation history. The right side of back of each rabbit was clipped with sharp blade, which was sterilized previously. The henna and indigo was applied on the lightly scarified skin of the right side and the left side of the rabbit's back and the areas were covered with closed patches. The covered patches were kept in position for 24 hours. The applied areas were examined at intervals of 4 hours for assessment of changes on the skin associated with irritation.

Predictive sensitivity testing

The ascertainment of the irritant and sensitizing potential of formulation is prophetic or predictive sensitivity testing. Under this test the ingredients of the formulation and the formulation as a whole were tested for their irritation and sensitivity.[12] This testing was conducted on 8 female volunteers hence, human ethical committee approval was obtained The formulation was applied to 1 cm^2 area of the cotton gauze. The gauze was backed with adhesive tape in order to hold it in position. Then 8 female volunteers were asked to apply this patch to the inner surface of forearm. The purpose of selection of this site for application was to enable the volunteer to readily remove the patch if any irritation is encountered. The volunteers were asked to remove patch immediately, if they feel itching or burning. Further they asked to keep the patch site dry, avoid rubbing or scratching test site. The patch was kept in position for 24 hours. After 24 hours, the patch was removed. The test site was observed up to 40 minutes from the time of removal. This time interval is necessary so that the skin may recover from the effects of pressure of certain patch test substances. Among these dyes henna and indigo produced good coloration because henna gives an orange-red colour and indigo gives an intense violet colour. By using these two powders a suitable brown colour can be developed. The other plants did not produce the desired coloration to the hair.

It can be concluded from the investigation that by changing the proportion of henna and indigo a suitable brown colour could be obtained for hair. A pH of 7 was best for penetration of hair colorant. Repeated application of the henna and indigo product gives an increase in the colour intensity. Addition of ferric chloride enhance the colour retaining property. It was observed that when indigo leaves are subjected to ageing give more colour intensity. No influence of ageing was observed in colour intensity with henna powder. Advantage of this natural hair colorant is that it does not cause any irritation. Staining of nails or fingers is not seen while preparing the hair colorant formulation or paste which is the main problem with marketed products. At the same time the colour does not stick to the clothes which come into contact with the product. Hence it is a suitable natural hair colorant and can be recommended for further studies and use.[9]

Table 6.7 List of 179 substances banned for use in hair dye products (Updated: February 2010).

Ref. No. Annex II to CD	Chemical Name / INCI - Name	CAS No.
289	Lead acetate	301-04-2
363	o-Phenylenediamine	95-54-5
364	2,4-Diaminotoluene	95-80-7
376	1-Methoxy-2,4-diaminobenzen	615-05-4
377	1-Methoxy-2,5-diaminobenzene	5307-02-8
380	Basic Violet 3	548-62-9
383	2-Amino-4-nitrophenol	99-57-0
384	2-Amino-5-nitrophenol	121-88-0
386	CI 42640	1694-09-3
387	Acid Yellow 36	587-98-4
388	Basic Violet 1	8004-87-3
398	CI 45170, CI 45170:1	81-88-9; 509-34-2
406	4-Ethoxy-2,4-diaminobenzene	5862-77-1
407	1-beta-Hydroxyethyl-2,4-diaminobenzene	14572-93-1
408	Catechol	120-80-9
409	Pyrogallic acid	87-66-1
412	4-Amino-2-nitrophenol	119-34-6
413	1-Methyl-2,6-diaminobenzen	823-40-5
700	Disperse Blue 1	2475-45-8
1055	Disperse Yellow 3	2832-40-8
1188	Basic Green 4	569-64-2
1204	m-Phenylenediamine	108-45-2
1212	6-Methoxy-2,3-pyridinediamine HCl	94166-62-8
1213	2,3-Naphthalenediol	92-44-4
1214	2,4-Diaminodiphenylamine	136-17-4
1215	2,6-Bis(2-hydroxyethoxy)-3,5-pyridinediamine HCl	117907-42-3
1216	2-Methoxymethyl-p-aminophenol HCl	29785-47-5 (HCl)
1217	4,5-Diamino-1-methylpyrazole HCl; sulfate	21616-59-1 HCl
1218	4,5-Diamino-1-((4-chlorophenyl)methyl)-1H-pyrazole sulfate	163183-00-4
1219	4-Chloro-2-aminophenol	95-85-2
1220	4-Hydroxyindole	2380-94-1
1221	4-Methoxytoluene-2,5-diamine HCl	56496-88-9
1222	5-Amino-4-fluoro-2-methylphenol sulfate	163183-01-5
1223	N,N-Diethyl m-aminophenol	91-68-9
1224	N,N-Dimethyl-2,6-pyridinediamine HCl	-
1225	N-cyclopentyl-m-aminophenol	104903-49-3
1226	N-Methoxyethyl-p-phenylenediamine HCl	72584-59-9
1227	2,4-Diamino-5-methylphenetol HCl	113715-25-6
1228	1,7-Naphthalenediol	575-38-2
1229	3,4-Diaminobenzoic acid	619-05-6
1230	2-Aminomethyl-p-aminophenol HCL	135043-65-1; 79352-72-0
1231	Solvent Red 1	1229-55-6
1232	Acid Orange 24	1320-07-6
1233	Acid Red 73	5413-75-2
1234	PEG-3,2',2'-di-p-Phenylenediamine	144644-13-3
1235	6-Nitro-o-Toluidine	570-24-1
1236	HC Yellow No 11	73388-54-2

Table 6.7 *Contd...*

1237	HC Orange No 3	81612-54-6
1238	HC Green No 1	52136-25-1
1239	HC Red No 8 and its salts	97404-14-3; 13556-29-1
1240	Tetrahydro-6-nitroquinoxaline and its salts	158006-54-3; 41959-35-7
1241	Disperse Red 15, except as impurity in Disperse Violet 1	116-85-8
1242	4-amino-3-fluorophenol	399-95-1
1244	1-Methyl-2,4,5-trihydroxybenzene and its salts	1124-09-0
1245	2,6-Dihydroxy-4-methylpyridine and its salts	4664-16-8
1246	5-Hydroxy-1,4-benzodioxane and its salts	10288-36-5
1247	3,4-Methylenedioxyphenol and its salts	533-31-3
1248	3,4-Methylenedioxyaniline and its salts	14268-66-7
1249	Hydroxypyridinone and its salts	822-89-9
1250	3-Nitro-4-aminophenoxyethanol and its salts	50982-74-6
1251	2-methoxy-4-nitrophenol (4-Nitroguaiacol) and its salts	3251-56-7
1252	C.I. Acid Black 131 and its salts	12219-01-1
1253	1,3,5-Trihydroxybenzene (Phloroglucinol) and its salts	108-73-6
1254	1,2,4-Benzenetriacetate and its salts	613-03-6
1255	Ethanol, 2,2'-iminobis-, reaction products with epichlorohydrin and 2-nitro-1,4-benzenediamine (HC Blue No. 5) and its salts	68478-64-8; 158571-58-5
1256	N-Methyl-1,4-diaminoanthraquinone, reaction products with epichlorohydrin and monoethanolamine (HC Blue No. 4) and its salts	158571-57-4
1257	4-Aminobenzenesulfonic acid and its salts	121-57-3
1258	3,3'-(Sulfonylbis(2-nitro-4,1-phenylene)imino)bis(6-(phenylamino)) benzenesulfonic acid and its salts	
1259	3(or5)-((4-(Benzylmethylamino)phenyl)azo)-1,2-(or1,4)-dimethyl-1H-1,2,4-triazolium and its salts	
1260	2,2'-((3-Chloro-4-((2,6-dichloro-4-nitrophenyl)azo)phenyl)imino)bisethanol (Disperse Brown 1) and its salts	23355-64-8
1261	Benzothiazolium, 2-[[4-[ethyl(2-hydroxyethyl)amino]phenyl]azo]-6-methoxy-3-methyl- and its salts	
1262	2-[(4-Chloro-2-nitrophenyl)azo]-N-(2-methoxyphenyl)-3-oxobutanamide (Pigment Yellow 73) and its salts	13515-40-7
1263	2,2'-[(3,3'-Dichloro[1,1'-biphenyl]-4,4'-diyl)bis(azo)]bis[3-oxo-N-phenylbutanamide] (Pigment Yellow 12) and its salts	6358-85-6
1264	2,2'-(1,2-Ethenediyl)bis[5-((4-ethoxyphenyl)azo]benzenesulfonic acid) and its salts	
1265	2,3-Dihydro-2,2-dimethyl-6-[(4-(phenylazo)-1-naphthalenyl)azo]-1H-pyrimidine (Solvent Black 3) and its salts	4197-25-5
1266	3(or5)-[[4-[(7-amino-1-hydroxy-3-sulphonato-2-naphthyl)azo]-1-naphthyl]azo]salicylic acid and its salts	
1267	2-Naphthalenesulfonic acid, 7-(benzoylamino)-4-hydroxy-3-[[4-[(4-sulfophenyl)azo]phenyl]azo]- and its salts	
1268	(μ-((7,7'-Iminobis(4-hydroxy-3-((2-hydroxy-5-(N-methylsulphamoyl)phenyl)azo)naphthalene-2-sulphonato))(6-)))dicuprate(2-) and its salts	
1269	3-[(4-(Acetylamino)phenyl)azo]-4-hydroxy-7-[[[[5-hydroxy-6-(phenylazo)-7-sulfo-2-naphthalenyl]amino]carbonyl]amino]-2-naphthalenesulfonic acid and its salts	
1270	2-Naphthalenesulfonic acid, 7,7'-(carbonyldiimino)bis(4-hydroxy-3-[[2-sulfo-4-[(4-sulfophenyl)azo]phenyl]azo]-, and its salts	25188-41-4
1271	Ethanaminium, N-(4-[bis[4-(diethylamino)phenyl]methylene]-2,5-cyclohexadien-1-ylidene)-N-ethyl- and its salts	

Table 6.7 *Contd...*

1272	3H-Indolium, 2-[[(4-methoxyphenyl)methylhydrazono]methyl]-1,3,3-trimethyl- and its salts	
1273	3H-Indolium, 2-(2-((2,4-dimethoxyphenyl)amino)ethenyl)-1,3,3-trimethyl- and its salts	
1274	Nigrosine spirit soluble (Solvent Black 5)	11099-03-9
1275	Phenoxazin-5-ium, 3,7-bis(diethylamino)-, and its salts	47367-75-9
1276	Benzo[a]phenoxazin-7-ium, 9-(dimethylamino)-, and its salts	
1277	6-Amino-2-(2,4-dimethylphenyl)-1H-benz[de]isoquinoline-1,3(2H)-dione (Solvent Yellow 44) and its salts	2478-20-8
1278	1-Amino-4-[[4-[(dimethylamino)methyl]phenyl]amino]anthraquinone and its salts	12217-43-5
1279	Laccaic Acid (CI Natural Red 25) and its salts	60687-93-6
1280	Benzenesulfonic acid, 5-[(2,4-dinitrophenyl)amino]-2-(phenylamino)-, and its salts	15347-52-1
1281	4-[(4-Nitrophenyl)azo]aniline (Disperse Orange 3) and its salts	730-40-5
1282	4-Nitro-m-phenylenediamine and its salts	5131-58-8
1283	1-Amino-4-(methylamino)-9,10-anthracenedione (Disperse Violet 4) and its salts	1220-94-6
1284	N-Methyl-3-nitro-p-phenylenediamine and its salts	2973-21-9
1285	N1-(2-Hydroxyethyl)-4-nitro-o-phenylenediamine (HC Yellow No. 5) and its salts	56932-44-6
1286	N1-(Tris(hydroxymethyl))methyl-4-nitro-1,2-phenylenediamine (HC Yellow No. 3) and its salts	56932-45-7
1287	2-Nitro-N-hydroxyethyl-p-anisidine and its salts	57524-53-5
1288	N,N'-Dimethyl-N-Hydroxyethyl-3-nitro-p-phenylenediamine and its salts	10228-03-2
1289	3-(N-Methyl-N-(4-methylamino-3-nitrophenyl)amino)propane-1,2-diol and its salts	93633-79-5
1290	4-Ethylamino-3-nitrobenzoic acid (N-Ethyl-3-Nitro PABA) and its salts	2788-74-1
1291	(8-[(4-Amino-2-nitrophenyl)azo]-7-hydroxy-2-naphthyl)trimethylammonium and its salts, except Basic Red 118 (CAS 71134-97-9) as impurity in Basic Brown 17	
1292	5-((4-(Dimethylamino)phenyl)azo)-1,4-dimethyl-1H-1,2,4-triazolium and its salts	
1293	m-Phenylenediamine, 4-(phenylazo)-, and its salts	495-54-5
1294	1,3-Benzenediamine, 4-methyl-6-(phenylazo)- and its salts	
1295	2,7-Naphthalenedisulfonic acid, 5-(acetylamino)-4-hydroxy-3-((2-methylphenyl)azo)- and its salts	
1296	4,4'-[(4-Methyl-1,3-phenylene)bis(azo)]bis[6-methyl-1,3-benzenediamine] (Basic Brown 4) and its salts	4482-25-1
1297	Benzenaminium, 3-[[4-[[diamino(phenylazo)phenyl]azo]-2-methylphenyl]azo]-N,N,N-trimethyl- and its salts	
1298	Benzenaminium, 3-[[4-[[diamino(phenylazo)phenyl]azo]-1-naphthalenyl]azo]-N,N,N-trimethyl- and its salts	
1299	Ethanaminium, N-[4-[(4-(diethylamino)phenyl)phenylmethylene]-2,5-cyclohexadien-1-ylidene]-N-ethyl- and its salts	
1300	9,10-Anthracenedione, 1-[(2-hydroxyethyl)amino]-4-(methylamino)- and its derivatives and salts	86722-66-9
1301	1,4-Diamino-2-methoxy-9,10-anthracenedione (Disperse Red 11) and its salts	2872-48-2
1302	1,4-Dihydroxy-5,8-bis[(2-hydroxyethyl)amino]anthraquinone (Disperse Blue 7) and its salts	3179-90-6
1303	1-[(3-Aminopropyl)amino]-4-(methylamino)anthraquinone and its salts	
1304	N-[6-[(2-Chloro-4-hydroxyphenyl)imino]-4-methoxy-3-oxo-1,4-cyclohexadien-1-yl]acetamide (HC Yellow No. 8) and its salts	66612-11-1

Table 6.7 *Contd...*

1305	[6-[[3-Chloro-4-(methylamino)phenyl]imino]-4-methyl-3-oxocyclohexa-1,4-dien-1-yl]urea (HC Red No. 9) and its salts	56330-88-2
1306	Phenothiazin-5-ium, 3,7-bis(dimethylamino)- and its salts	
1307	4,6-Bis(2-Hydroxyethoxy)-m-Phenylenediamine and its salts	
1308	5-Amino-2,6-Dimethoxy-3-Hydroxypyridine and its salts	104333-03-1
1309	4,4'-Diaminodiphenylamine and its salts	537-65-5
1310	4-Diethylamino-o-toluidine and its salts	148-71-0
1311	N,N-Diethyl-p-phenylenediamine and its salts	93-05-0
1312	N,N-Dimethyl-p-phenylenediamine and its salts	99-98-9
1313	Toluene-3,4-Diamine and its salts	496-72-0
1314	2,4-Diamino-5-methylphenoxyethanol and its salts	141614-05-3
1315	6-Amino-o-cresol and its salts	17672-22-9
1316	Hydroxyethylaminomethyl-p-aminophenol and its salts	110952-46-0
1317	2-Amino-3-nitrophenol and its salts	603-85-0
1318	2-Chloro-5-nitro-N-hydroxyethyl-p-phenylenediamine and its salts	50610-28-1
1319	2-Nitro-p-phenylenediamine and its salts	5307-14-2
1320	Hydroxyethyl-2,6-dinitro-p-anisidine and its salts	122252-11-3
1321	6-Nitro-2,5-pyridinediamine and its salts	69825-83-8
1322	Phenazinium, 3,7-diamino-2,8-dimethyl-5-phenyl- and its salts	
1323	3-Hydroxy-4-[(2-hydroxynaphthyl)azo]-7-nitronaphthalene-1-sulphonic acid and its salts	16279-54-2
1324	3-[(2-nitro-4-(trifluoromethyl)phenyl)amino]propane-1,2-diol (HC Yellow No. 6) and its salts	104333-00-8
1325	2-[(4-chloro-2-nitrophenyl)amino]ethanol (HC Yellow No. 12) and its salts	59320-13-7
1326	3-[[4-[(2-Hydroxyethyl)Methylamino]-2-Nitrophenyl]Amino]-1,2-Propanediol and its salts	173994-75-7
1327	3-[[4-[Ethyl(2-Hydroxyethyl)Amino]-2-Nitrophenyl]Amino]-1,2-Propanediol and its salts	114087-41-1
1328	Ethanaminium, N-[4-[[4-(diethylamino)phenyl][4-(ethylamino)-1-naphthalenyl]methylene]-2,5-cyclohexadien-1-ylidene]-N-ethyl- and its salts	
1329	4-[(4-Aminophenyl)(4-iminocyclohexa-2,5-dien-1-ylidene)methyl]-o-toluidine (CAS 3248-93-9; EINECS 221-832-2) and its hydrochloride salt (Basic Violet 14; CI 42510) (CAS 632-99-5; EINECS 211-189-6)	
1330	4-(2,4-Dihydroxyphenylazo)benzenesulphonic acid (CAS 2050-34-2; EINECS 218-087-0) and its sodium salt (Acid Orange 6; CI 14270) (CAS 547-57-9; EINECS 208-924-8)	
1331	3-Hydroxy-4-(phenylazo)-2-naphthoic acid (CAS 27757-79-5; EINECS 248-638-0) and its calcium salt (Pigment Red 64:1; CI 15800) (CAS 6371-76-2; EINECS 228-899-7)	
1332	2-(6-Hydroxy-3-oxo-(3H)-xanthen-9-yl)benzoic acid; Fluorescein (CAS 2321-07-5; EINECS 219-031-8) and its disodium salt (Acid yellow 73 sodium salt; CI 45350) (CAS 518-47-8; EINECS 208-253-0)	
1333	4',5'-Dibromo-3',6'-dihydroxyspiro[isobenzofuran-1(3H),9'-[9H]xanthene]-3-one; 4',5'-Dibromofluorescein; (Solvent Red 72) (CAS 596-03-2; EINECS 209-876-0) and its disodium salt (CI 45370) (CAS 4372-02-5; EINECS 224-468-2)	
1334	2-(3,6-Dihydroxy-2,4,5,7-tetrabromoxanthen-9-yl)-benzoic acid; Fluorescein, 2',4',5',7'-tetrabromo-; (Solvent Red 43) (CAS 15086-94-9; EINECS 239-138-3), its disodium salt (Acid Red 87; CI 45380) (CAS 17372-87-1; EINECS 241-409-6) and its aluminium salt (Pigment Red 90:1 Aluminium lake) (CAS 15876-39-8; EINECS 240-005-7)	
1335	Xanthylium, 9-(2-carboxyphenyl)-3-(2-methylphenyl)amino)-6-((2-methyl-4-sulfophenyl)amino)-, inner salt (CAS 10213-95-3); and its sodium salt (Acid Violet 9; CI 45190) (CAS 6252-76-2; EINECS 228-377-9)	
1336	3',6'-Dihydroxy-4',5'-diiodospiro(isobenzofuran-1(3H),9'-[9H]xanthene)-3-one; (Solvent Red 73) (CAS 38577-97-8; EINECS 254-010-7) and its sodium salt (Acid Red 95; CI 45425) (CAS 33239-19-9; EINECS 251-419-2)	

Table 6.7 *Contd...*

1337	2',4',5',7'-Tetraiodofluorescein (CAS 15905-32-5; EINECS 240-046-0), its disodium salt (Acid Red 51; CI 45430) (CAS 16423-68-0; EINECS 240-474-8) and its aluminium salt (Pigment Red 172 Aluminium lake)(CAS 12227-78-0; EINECS 235-440-4)
1338	1-Hydroxy-2,4-diaminobenzene (2,4-Diaminophenol) (CAS 95-86-3; EINECS 202-459-4) and its dihydrochloride salt (2,4-Diaminophenol HCl) (CAS 137-09-7; EINECS 205-279-4)
1339	1,4-Dihydroxybenzene (Hydroquinone) (CAS 123-31-9; EINECS 204-617-8)
1340	[4-[[4-anilino-1-naphthyl][4-(dimethylamino)phenyl]methylene]cyclohexa-2,5-dien-1-ylidene]dimethylammonium chloride (Basic Blue 26; CI 44045) (CAS 2580-56-5; EINECS 219-943-6)
1341	Disodium 3-[(2,4-dimethyl-5-sulphonatophenyl)azo]-4-hydroxynaphthalene-1-sulphonate (Ponceau SX; CI 14700) (CAS 4548-53-2; EINECS 224-909-9)
1342	Trisodium tris[5,6-dihydro-5-(hydroxyimino)-6-oxonaphthalene-2-sulphonato(2-)-N5,O6]ferrate(3-) (Acid Green 1; CI 10020) (CAS 19381-50-1; EINECS 243-010-2)
1343	4-(Phenylazo)resorcinol (Solvent Orange 1; CI 11920) (CAS 2051-85-6; EINECS 218-131-9) and its salts
1344	4-[(4-Ethoxyphenyl)azo]naphthol (Solvent Red 3; CI 12010) (CAS 6535-42-8; EINECS 229-439-8) and its salts
1345	1-[(2-Chloro-4-nitrophenyl)azo]-2-naphthol (Pigment Red 4; CI 12085) (CAS 2814-77-9; EINECS 220-562-2) and its salts
1346	3-Hydroxy-N-(o-tolyl)-4-[(2,4,5-trichlorophenyl)azo]naphthalene-2-carboxamide (Pigment Red 112; CI 12370) (CAS 6535-46-2; EINECS 229-440-3) and its salts
1347	N-(5-Chloro-2,4-dimethoxyphenyl)-4-[[5-[(diethylamino)sulphonyl]-2-methoxyphenyl]azo]-3-hydroxynaphthalene-2-carboxamide (Pigment Red 5; CI 12490) (CAS 6410-41-9; EINECS 229-107-2) and its salts
1348	Disodium 4-[(5-chloro-4-methyl-2-sulphonatophenyl)azo]-3-hydroxy-2-naphthoate (Pigment Red 48; CI 15865) (CAS 3564-21-4; EINECS 222-642-2)
1349	Calcium 3-hydroxy-4-[(1-sulphonato-2-naphthyl)azo]-2-naphthoate (Pigment Red 63:1; CI 15880) (CAS 6417-83-0; EINECS 229-142-3)
1350	Trisodium 3-hydroxy-4-(4'-sulphonatonaphthylazo)naphthalene-2,7-disulphonate (Acid Red 27; CI 16185) (CAS 915-67-3; EINECS 213-022-2)
1351	2,2'-[(3,3'-Dichloro[1,1'-biphenyl]-4,4'-diyl)bis(azo)]bis[N-(2,4-dimethylphenyl)-3-oxobutyramide] (Pigment Yellow 13; CI 21100) (CAS 5102-83-0; EINECS 225-822-9)
1352	2,2'-[Cyclohexylidenebis[(2-methyl-4,1-phenylene)azo]]bis[4-cyclohexylphenol] (Solvent Yellow 29; CI 21230) (CAS 6706-82-7; EINECS 229-754-0)
1353	1-((4-Phenylazo)phenylazo)-2-naphthol (Solvent Red 23; CI 26100) (CAS 85-86-9; EINECS 201-638-4)
1354	Tetrasodium 6-amino-4-hydroxy-3-[[7-sulphonato-4-[(4-sulphonatophenyl)azo]-1-naphthyl]azo]naphthalene-2,7-disulphonate (Food Black 2; CI 27755) (CAS 2118-39-0; EINECS 218-326-9)
1355	Ethanaminium, N-(4-((4-(diethylamino)phenyl)(2,4-disulfophenyl)methylene)-2,5-cyclohexadien-1-ylidene)-N-ethyl-, hydroxide, inner salt, sodium salt (Acid Blue 1; CI 42045) (CAS 129-17-9; EINECS 204-934-1)
1356	Ethanaminium, N-(4-((4-(diethylamino)phenyl)(5-hydroxy-2,4-disulfophenyl)methylene)-2,5-cyclohexadien-1-ylidene)-N-ethyl-, hydroxide, inner salt, calcium salt (2:1) (Acid Blue 3; CI 42051) (CAS 3536-49-0; EINECS 222-573-8)
1357	Benzenemethanaminium, N-ethyl-N-(4-((4-(ethyl((3-sulfophenyl)methyl)amino)phenyl)(4-hydroxy-2-sulfophenyl)methylene)-2,5-cyclohexadien-1-ylidene)-3-sulfo-, hydroxide, inner salt, disodium salt (Fast Green FCF; CI 42053) (CAS 2353-45-9; EINECS 219-091-5)
1358	1,3-Isobenzofurandione, reaction products with methylquinoline and quinoline (Solvent Yellow 33; CI 47000) (CAS 8003-22-3; EINECS 232-318-2)
1359	Nigrosine (CI 50420) (CAS 8005-03-6)
1360	8,18-Dichloro-5,15-diethyl-5,15-dihydrodiindolo[3,2-b:3',2'-m]triphenodioxazine (Pigment Violet 23; CI 51319) (CAS 6358-30-1; EINECS 228-767-9)
1361	1,2-Dihydroxyanthraquinone (Pigment Red 83; CI 58000) (CAS 72-48-0; EINECS 200-782-5)
1362	Trisodium 8-hydroxypyrene-1,3,6-trisulphonate (Solvent Green 7; CI 59040) (CAS 6358-69-6; EINECS 228-783-6)
1363	1-Hydroxy-4-(p-toluidino)anthraquinone (Solvent Violet 13; CI 60725) (CAS 81-48-1; EINECS 201-353-5),

Table 6.7 *Contd...*

1364	1,4-bis(p-Tolylamino)anthraquinone (Solvent Green 3; CI 61565) (CAS 128-80-3; EINECS 204-909-5)
1365	6-Chloro-2-(6-chloro-4-methyl-3-oxobenzo[b]thien-2(3H)-ylidene)-4-methylbenzo[b]thiophene-3(2H)-one (VAT Red 1; CI 73360) (CAS 2379-74-0; EINECS 219-163-6)
1366	5,12-Dihydroquino[2,3-b]acridine-7,14-dione (Pigment Violet 19; CI 73900) (CAS 1047-16-1; EINECS 213-879-2)
1367	(29H,31H-Phthalocyaninato(2-)-N29,N30,N31,N32)copper (Pigment Blue 15; CI 74160) (CAS 147-14-8; EINECS 205-685-1)
1368	Disodium [29H,31H-phthalocyaninedisulphonato(4-)-N29,N30,N31,N32]cuprate(2-) (Direct Blue 86; CI 74180) (CAS 1330-38-7; EINECS 215-537-8)
1369	Polychloro copper phthalocyanine (Pigment Green 7; CI 74260) (CAS 1328-53-6; EINECS 215-524-7)

6.5 Hair Dye Poisoning

Hair dye ingestion is an uncommon form of poisoning in the west, however, in some parts of the world such as East Africa and Indian Sub-continent it is not uncommon. The main component of hair dye causing toxicity is Paraphenylenediamine (PPD). This compound has been found to cause angioneurotic edema, rhabdomyolysis and acute renal failure.[10]

6.5.1 Hair Dyes and Cancer Risk

There is an association between occupational exposure to hair dyes and incidence of cancers. Permanent oxidant hair dyes are consisted of many chemical components including *ortho*-phenylenediamines. Hair dyes contain many chemical components. Severin et al.[11] showed 2,4-diaminotoluene induced DNAdamage. Studies demonstrated that *o*-phenylenediamine derivatives, 2,4-diaminoanisole[12] and nitro-2-aminophenols [13] induced oxidative DNA damage.

6.6 Occupational Exposures of Hairdressers and Barbers and Personal use of Hair Colourants[14]

6.6.1 Professional use of Hair Colourants

Bladder cancer

The cohort studies indicated an increased risk for cancer of the urinary bladder among male hairdressers, but not among female hairdressers. In a large Scandinavian cohort of hairdressers, barbers, beauticians and other related workers identified in the 1970 census and followed-up for 20 years, there was a significant 50% increase in risk for bladder cancer in men and a non-significant 10% decrease in risk in women. Allowance for smoking was generally not possible, although results for lung cancer suggest that higher exposure to tobacco in hairdressers could not totally account for the bladder cancer excess.

More than 20 case control studies were available for evaluation. Most of these, including three of the larger studies, reported increased risks in the range of 1.3-1.7 in male hairdressers. A pooled analysis of 11 studies conducted in six European countries found no significant increase in risk among male or female hairdressers. Overall, risks appeared generally lower for women than for men. The number of exposed subjects was generally small, and did not allow a reliable assessment of the risk by duration and period of exposure.

In view of the consistent yet modest increase in risk reported in studies of hairdressers and barbers, especially men, and in the absence of solid data on the relation between duration and period of exposure, the Working Group concluded that there was limited evidence of an increased risk for bladder cancer in hairdressers.

Haematological malignancies

With regards to cancers of the haematological system, the heterogeneity in the diseases included and the differences in the classification used often hampered comparison between the results of different studies. Although one cohort study of barbers among male US veterans and an Italian case–control study reported significant increases in risk for multiple myeloma based on only few exposed cases, these results were not replicated in other studies. In the large Scandinavian cohort, no excess was found in either sex for multiple myeloma or for other haematological malignancies.

Breast cancer

Many studies on breast cancer, including the largest case-control and cohort studies, did not show any increased risk for breast cancer associated with professional use of hair colourants.

Childhood cancers

One cohort study and five case–control studies investigated the risk for childhood cancers in the offspring of hairdressers and barbers. Although some positive associations were reported, an overall evaluation is difficult because of the different sites and/or histologies investigated in various studies and the problems in the identification of the relevant period of exposure (before or around conception, or during pregnancy).

Other sites

Ovarian cancer

A modest increase in risk for ovarian cancer was reported in two cohorts of US cosmetologists and Scandinavian hairdressers, which was significant only in the latter study. The excess in risk appeared stronger in or limited to women exposed in earlier periods. No case–control study was available for evaluation. The lack of adjustment for potential confounders, especially reproductive history and oral contraceptive use, does not allow confounding to be ruled out.

Lung cancer

Small increases in lung cancer risk of the order of 20–40% were found in most cohort studies, which did not, however, adequately adjust for smoking. A higher prevalence of smokers among hairdressers than in the general population was reported in Scandinavia and the USA. No informative case–control study was available for evaluation. The Working Group concluded that tobacco smoking cannot be excluded as a likely cause of the modest excess in lung cancer observed in hairdressers.

6.6.2 Personal use of Hair Colourants

The Working Group revised and evaluated the epidemiological evidence of an association between cancer at several sites and personal use of hair dyes.

Bladder cancer

Several studies with contradictory results have been published. Increased risks for bladder cancer were reported in two studies in the USA, while no association was found in three larger studies, two from the USA and one from Spain. These recent studies had similar characteristics in design and methodology. One study from the USA suggested an increased risk for bladder cancer among users of hair colourants, in particular among those who exclusively used permanent hair dyes. Further, this study showed that exclusive use of permanent dyes among subjects with slow acetylation (NAT2 genotype) or among CYP1A2 slow metabolizers was associated with an increased risk for bladder cancer. The other studies did not confirm these results. In the Spanish study, there was no indication of an increased risk for bladder cancer associated with the NAT2 genotype, but there was a non-significant association with NAT1*10. The available cohort studies were largely negative for bladder cancer. The available meta-analyses did not show an association. The Working Group considered that the available evidence for cancer of the bladder was overall inadequate.

Haematological malignancies

The results for this tumour type were difficult to interpret: many different malignancies are involved, and many of the studies do not provide analyses for the different disease entities. Historically, the results have been inconsistent in identifying an increased risk. While cohort studies were largely negative for haematological malignancies, the results of case–control studies varied greatly. In those that showed an increased risk, the increase tended to be moderate. A recent pooled analysis was evaluated with particular interest because it was a large study evaluating hair-dye exposure in relation to single lymphoma entities including case–control data derived from Canada, the USA and six countries in Europe. The study showed an overall increased risk of 1.1 among women who were regular users, and of 1.3 among those women who had started regular hair-dye use before 1980. The risk was consistently elevated for follicular lymphoma and chronic lymphocytic leukaemia, but not for other types. For these lymphoma subtypes, the risk did not vary by intensity, years of use or type of exposure, remaining generally of the order 1.2–1.4. When the period of first use was considered, the increased risk for chronic lymphocytic leukaemia was mainly observed among those who started use before 1980, with a statistically significant increase in risk among those reporting use for more than 20 years. For follicular lymphoma, increased risks were observed throughout the two study periods. Overall, the Working Group considered this evidence to be inadequate.

Breast cancer

For breast cancer the Working Group considered the evidence as inadequate based on several studies, none of which except one showed an association.

Childhood cancers

For childhood cancers, the studies evaluated dealt with childhood brain tumours and Wilms tumours. The Working Group discussed in depth the potential biases and study limitations that could explain some of the increased risks observed for some brain tumours, and considered that some of the reported associations could not be simply explained by recall bias, as mothers may not have known about this hypothesis at the time of the studies. The Working Group considered that the evidence presented in the studies was inadequate.

Other sites

Only a few studies were available to the Working Group, and no evaluation was made.

When the researchers analyzed the risks of several specific non-Hodgkin lymphoma (NHL) subtypes, they found that hair dye users had increased risks of both follicular lymphoma and chronic lymphocytic leukemia/small lymphocytic lymphoma.[15] For the most part, the increases were limited to women who began using hair dye before 1980, although an increased risk of follicular lymphoma was observed among women who began using dark-colored dyes after 1980. Although these results are consistent with the idea that earlier hair dyes were more carcinogenic, it is also possible that the absence of increased risk for hair dye users who began using dyes after 1980 reflects lower cumulative exposure levels or insufficient time since first exposure for any increase in risk to become apparent.

Studies of the association between personal hair dye use and the risk of leukemia have had conflicting results. For example, one case-control study examined hair dye use among 769 patients with adult acute leukemia and 623 people without leukemia in the United States and Canada.[16] It found that the risks of acute leukemia were higher among users of earlier formulations of both permanent and nonpermanent (i.e., semipermanent and temporary) dyes than among those who had not used dyes, although the increases were not statistically significant. No risk increases were seen among users of more recent dye formulations. Risk was greatest among those who had used permanent dyes for longer durations (15 or more years). However, a case-control study in Italy found no association between use of permanent hair dye overall and risk of leukemia, although users of black permanent dyes, but not of other color dyes, did have an increased risk. This study, however, did not collect information on the timing or frequency of hair dye use.[17]

Research on personal hair dye use and risks of bladder and breast cancer has produced conflicting results. Data from multiple studies have been pooled as a way of analyzing the risks of these cancers among hair dye users. An analysis of pooled data from 12 studies of bladder cancer and hair dye use published between 1977 and 2006 found no evidence that personal use of hair dyes is associated with increased risk of bladder cancer[18], this study does not support an association between hair dye use and bladder cancer.

Researchers who reviewed data from 14 studies of female breast cancer and hair dye use published between 1977 and 2002 found that dye users had no increase in the risk of breast cancer compared with nonusers.[19]

Research on hair dye use and the risks of other cancers is more limited. Although some studies have shown associations between hair dye use and risk of developing or dying from specific cancers, these associations have not been seen in other studies. Because of differences in study design, it has not been possible to pool the results of studies of most cancers.

Further carcinogenic studies on the components of hair dyes are needed to prevent cancer among people exposed to hair dyes, occupationally and personally.

6.7 Hair-Color Safety and Regulatory Issues

Because of the allergenic potential of some of the materials used in hair dyes (primarily p-phenylenediamine, or PPD), hair colorants in the United States display on the label as a legal requirement a warning, plus instructions for a 24-hour patch test with the precursors and hydrogen peroxide mixed in the same manner as in use. As required by Section 601(a) of the Federal Food, Drugs and Cosmetics Act, the warnings reads as follows:

"This product contains ingredients which may cause skin irritation on certain individuals and a preliminary test according to accompanying directions should be made. This product must not be used for dyeing the eyebrows or eyelashes; to do so may cause blindness".

It should be noted that allergic contact dermatitis to hair dyes appears to be far less common today than decades ago. It has been suggested that PPD, although a strong sensitizer, is not likely to produce skin sensitization because of the short contact time with skin and rapid reaction of PPD with the oxidizing agent and couplers. Concerns as to the possible carcinogenicity of some hair ingredients arose in 1975 when these were reported to be mutagenic for bacteria in bioassays. Presently, it is not clear how significant a risk this poses to users of hair dyes. Because hair dyes have been in common use for over 50 years, epidemiological studies on cancer rates in occupationally exposed groups or the users of hair dyes are of particular value. So far, the results of most of these suggest that hair dyes do not pose a carcinogenic risk.

6.8 Home Made Organic Hair Dyes

If we want achieve our desired hair colour and retain ability to control the intensity of the shade, we should use chemical free and organic hair dye to colour our hair. There is no completely organic hair dye on the market today, but we can make our own organic hair dye at home.

Lighteners

By using the following tips we can lighten our hair organically. The duration of process depends on the darkness of the hair. More dark hair takes more time.

- Mix 1 cup organic lemon juice and 3 cups Chamomile tea. Massage into hair and expose the hair to sun for some time. We can repeat this for fast result.
- Mix up mashed organic Rhubarb with 4 oz organic pineapple juice. Let the mixture soak into our hair and expose the hair to sun for some time.
- Mix 3/4 cup honey with $1^1/_2$ cups organic plain yogurt to damp hair. Massage into our hair and wrap head in saran wrap, after 6-8 hours rinse it.
- Mix 4 tablespoons Cinnamon with 8 oz yogurt. Massage into hair and let it soak in for 30 minutes.

Darkeners

By using the following tips we can darken our hair organically.

- Half cup of dry organic Sage is boiled with 2 cups of water. Strain and massage into hair. Leave it for 40 minuets and rinse.
- One third cup of walnut shells, 3 black tea bags are mixed with $2^1/_2$ cups of water and boil. Strain and massage into hair. Leave in until next shampoo.
- Make a strong tea from black tea leaves and cherry bark and continue the boiling until it gets dark. Massage into clean hair and leave in until next shampoo.
- We can repeat the above tip for coffee and leave it black and allow it to cool. Massage into hair and let sit for 15 minutes. Rinse hair with warm water.[20]

6.9 Conclusion

In reviewing the various substances used for dyeing the hair, one is forced to recognise that, inspite of the very real utility of a number of preparations, the ideal hair dye has yet to be discovered. However, most of the technologies of permanent hair dyes are based on an approach of 150 years using PPD, a chemical that produces tones and dark brown when exposed to air. Concerns about the health safety of common use of PPD and other ingredients in hair dyes, and the demand for methods to dye it more convenient; have led to a boom in research on new dyes and alternative technologies.

Scientists are making progress toward those goals. For example, between future hair coloring techniques include dyes or pigments composed of nanometer-sized particles that penetrate into the hair and be trapped in it more effectively, providing a more durable color. They are also developing substances that stimulate specific genes that produce melanin, the pigment that gives color to hair. These substances promise to produce a wider range of more natural looking colors, from blonde to dark brown and black, with better prospects of obtaining more natural and less likely to arise concerns about toxicity.

References

1. Bhushan B, *Biophysics of Human Hair*, Biological and Medical Physics, Biomedical Engineering, Springer-Verlag Berlin Heidelberg 2010.
2. Robbins, Clarence R.; *Chemical and Physical Behavior of Human Hair, 3rd Edition*; Springer-Verlag New York, Inc.; 1994.
3. Zoe Diana Draelos, Hair Care-*An Illustrated Dermatologic Handbook* 2005; 103-104.
4. Corbett J. Hair coloring processes. *Cosmet Toilet* 1991; **106**:53–7.
5. Arakindakshan MI, Persad S, Haberman HF, Kurian CJ. A comparative study of the physical and chemical properties of melanins isolated from human black and red hair. *J Invest Dermatol* 1983; **80**:202–6.
6. Casperson S. Men's hair coloring: a review of current technology. *Cosmet Toilet* 1994; **109:** 83-7.
7. Cesarini JP. Hair melanin and hair colour. In: Orfanos CE, Happle R, eds. *Hair and hair diseases.* Berlin: Springer-Verlag, 1990:166–97.

8. Vardy DA, Marcus B, Gilead L *et al.* A look at gray hair. *J Geriatric Dermatol* 1993; **1**:22–7.

9. Madhusudan Rao Y, Shayeda and P Sujatha. Formulation and evaluation of commonly used natural hair colorants *Natural Product Radiance*, Vol. 7(1), 2008, pp.45-48.

10. Bhargava P, Matthew P. Case Report. JAPI, Vol. 55, 2007, 871-872.

11. Severin I, Jondeau A, Dahbi L, Chagnon MC, 2,4-Diaminotoluene (2,4-DAT)-induced DNA damage, DNA repair and micronucleus formation in the human hepatoma cell line HepG2, Toxicology 213 (2005) 138–146.

12. Chen F, Murata M, Hiraku Y, Yamashita N, Oikawa S, Kawanishi S, DNA damage induced by *m*-phenylenediamine and its derivative in the presence of copper ion, Free Radic. Res. 29 (1998) 197–205.

13. Chen F, Murata M, Hiraku Y, Yamashita N, Oikawa S, Kawanishi S, Metal-mediated oxidative DNA damage induced by nitro-2-aminophenols, Cancer Lett. 126 (1998) 67-74.

14. WORLD HEALTH ORGANIZATION INTERNATIONAL AGENCY FOR RESEARCH ON CANCER (IARC) IARC Monographs on the Evaluation of Carcinogenic Risks to Humans. Volume 57, 642-645.

15. Zhang Y, de Sanjose S, Bracci PM, et al. Personal use of hair dye and the risk of certain subtypes of non-Hodgkin lymphoma. *American Journal of Epidemiology* 2008; **167(11)**:1321–1331.

16. Rauscher GH, Shore D, Sandler DP. Hair dye use and risk of adult acute leukemia. *American Journal of Epidemiology* 2004; **160(1)**:19–25.

17. Miligi L, Costantini AS, Benvenuti A, et al. Personal use of hair dyes and hematolymphopoietic malignancies. *Archives of Environmental and Occupational Health* 2005; **60(5)**:249–256.

18. Kelsh MA, Alexander DD, Kalmes RM, Buffler PA. Personal use of hair dyes and risk of bladder cancer: A meta-analysis of epidemiologic data. *Cancer Causes and Control* 2008; **19(6)**:549–558.

19. Takkouche B, Etminan M, Montes-Martinez A. Personal use of hair dyes and risk of cancer: A meta-analysis. *Journal of the American Medical Association* 2005; **293(20)**:2516–2525.

20. http://www.organichairdye.org/make-organic-hair-dye-at-home/.

CHAPTER 7

PSORIASIS

P.K. Lakshmi and Ch. Saroja

Professor & Head, Department of Pharmaceutics, G. Pulla Reddy College of Pharmacy, Mehdipatnam, Hyderabad-28.

7.1 Introduction

Psoriasis is a common dermatosis, causing hyper proliferation of epidermal cells of skin affecting 1-3% of the population. It is found worldwide and varies among different ethnic groups. According to many reports, the prevalence is from 0-11.8%. These surveys have been done by many methods like clinic based, population based, examination based or questionnaire based. The highest prevalence is seen in Norway followed by Denmark and USA. The prevalence in Africa varies depending on geographic location, being lowest in West Africa. Psoriasis is less prevalent in China and Japan than in Europe, and is entirely absent in natives of the Andean region of South America. Incidence of psoriasis is low in Asians. Psoriasis found equally in males and females.[1-5]

The incidence of psoriasis in children increased from 29.6% per 100,000 in 1970 through 1974 to 62.7 per 100,000 in 1995 through 1999. Chronic plaque psoriasis was the most common type (73.7%) of psoriasis in children, and the most commonly involved sites were the extremities (59.9%) and the scalp (46.8%).[6]

7.2 Etiology and Pathophysiology

Psoriasis is an auto immune disorder associated various etiological factors. The literature study reveals that intestinal pathology is the strong etiological factor for psoriasis. Researches hypothesize that intestinal permeability is the primary factor for pathogenesis. Various factors produce thinning of jejunum and duodenum of intestinal walls which allows toxic material to leak in to the system. This finds the way in to the skin circulation causing plaques of psoriasis. Michalleson et al found that highly increased tryptase positive mast cells in the duodenal stroma could also be the reason for psoriasis.[7-10]

It is seen in patients of joint involvement, in the absence of serum rheumatoid factor, present psoriasis about 10-30%. The most common form of psoriasis being chronic plaque psoriasis (CPP), which, as the name implies, is often persistent with a gradual onset. Guttate psoriasis (GT) is seen with children and young adults. The clinical manifestations are acute eruption on the trunk and limp, usually resolve in three months. In some patients GT can progress to CPP. The other types of psoriasis are erthrodermic with the clinical manifestations of spreading lesions on the whole of skin surface and pustular psoriasis with a manifestation on the palms and soles.

Comorbid conditions are another reason for etiology and pathophysioloy of psoriasis. Conditions like diabetes, obesity, heart problems could be one of the reasons associated for psoriasis. The other factors such as dietary habits, nutritional status, genetic factors also influencing one. Coexistence of psoriasis and kidney disease was found in many literatures.[11-14]

Recently it has been found that psoriasis has been related to auto immune function. In psoriasis T cell become activated and skin cells gets hyper proliferated. The specific trigger for T cell is unknown. Various allergens are known to trigger immune system making the immune system deranged. Diet also plays a major role in modifying immune system. Treatment with low protein diet found to have better effect against psoriasis. Certain food like carbonated beverages, tomatoes also aggravates psoriasis.

Peptidoglycon, a major cell wall component of Gram-positive bacteria found to be present in psoriasis patients. Since peptidoglycon is one of the T-cell stimulator which is the commonest etiology of psoriasis.[15,16]

Genetics plays a major role in etiology and pathophysiology of psoriasis. There is a familial pattern in 30% of cases. Although the pathogenesis of psoriasis has not been fully elucidated, an immunologic–

genetic relationship is likely. Cutaneous and systemic over expression of various proinflammatory cytokines (TNF, interleukins, interferon-gamma) has been demonstrated in psoriatic patients. The majority of authors observed increased plasma TNF levels in active psoriatic patients, a decrease in TNF cytokine levels after successful anti-psoriatic treatment using different methods, including PUVA, UVB plus topical corticosteroids and dithranol, were observed.[17]

Psoriasis is the outcome of an inappropriate immunocyte-based activation event, together with a defect in keratinocytes, whose combination results in the full psoriatic phenotype.

The newer studies state that effect on immune system causing hyper proliferation of epidermis leading to pathogenesis in psoriasis. Intrinsic defects in cytokine and growth factor signaling in keratinocytes may be responsible for their hyper proliferation and differentiation to T-cell derived signals. Other skin resident cells such as fibroblasts, mast cells, and endothelial cells also contribute to psoriasis pathogenesis by expressing molecules involved in T-cell recruitment and activation.[18,19]

Emotions and stress has been found to have role in pathogenesis of psoriasis. Therefore, relaxation and other psychotherapeutic modalities can diminish or reverse psychosomatic effects through their ability to alter the activity of the autonomic nervous system; in this manner they may play a very important role in the treatment of psoriasis.[20,21]

Genetic susceptibility

↓

Environmental factors (emotions, drugs stress)

↓

Inflammation, Keratinocyte dysfunction, vascular dysfunction

↓

Clinical psoriasis

Drugs can exacerbate psoriasis. Drugs like, lithium, beta blockers, antimalarials are found to exacerbate psoriasis. NSAIDS such as indomethacin, withdrawal of corticosteroids also found to exacerbate. Pustular psoriasis was reported with atenolol. Cardiovascular drugs like digoxin, clonidine, amiodarone, some neuroleptics, antiepiletics, antidepressants, diuretics, sulphonamides and antibiotics such as penicillin, amoxicillin, ampicillin, colony stimulating factor and anti hyperlipedemics etc, can either cause or exacerbate psoriasis.. The exact causes of exacerbation or causative reasons were not known.[22-32]

Table 7.1 Typical patterns of psoriasis.

Chronic plaque psoriasis:	Large flat patches (plaques) covered in scale, most often on elbows, knees and lower back
Flexural psoriasis:	Smooth well-defined patches in body folds
Scalp psoriasis:	One or more scaly plaques in the scalp
Acute guttate psoriasis:	Numerous and often widespread small patches
Sebopsoriasis:	Overlap of seborrhoeic dermatitis and psoriasis, affecting scalp, face, ears and chest
Palmoplantar psoriasis:	Several patterns of psoriasis on the palms and soles
Nail psoriasis	Pitting, onycholysis, yellowing and ridging
Koebnerised psoriasis:	Psoriasis arising in healing wounds or scars
	Photosensitive psoriasis: psoriasis affecting sun-exposed skin
Pustular psoriasis	Generalised or localised to palms and soles
Erythrodermic psoriasis:	Severe psoriasis affecting the entire skin surface
Psoriatic arthritis	Joint disease related to psoriasis

7.3 Evaluation of Psoriasis

Accurate assessment of severity of psoriasis is utmost important aspect in clinical prognosis of psoriasis. There are various evaluation methods used to evaluate the severity of psoriasis. The Psoriasis Area and Severity Index (PASI), Psoriasis Global Assessment (PGA) and Lattice system global assessment (LGA).

The PASI involves the assessment over the head, trunk, upper and lower extremities of erythema, infiltration, desquamation and body surface area involvement. PGA involves assessment by physician on 7 point scale from clear to severe. The LGA involves assessment on 8 point scale from clear to very severe. PASI final score will not reveal any conclusiveness to physician and PGA gives little guidance to investigators. Hence LGA is developed to overcome deficiencies of other evaluation. This method clearly defines the method of rating and clinical description of the result provided.[33-36]

7.4 Current Conventional Therapeutic Approaches

The current therapeutic approaches in the treatment includes, successful treatment of each case by case, evidence based medicine, empirical therapy, pathogenesis related established treatment and novel drug delivery system targeting skin.

Until recently, the mainstays of topical therapy have been corticosteroids, tars, anthralins and keratolytics. Recently, however, vitamin D analogs, a new anthralin preparation and topical retinoids have expanded physicians' therapeutic armamentarium. These new topical therapies offer increased hope and convenience to the large patient population with psoriasis. Although it is rarely life-threatening, psoriasis can cause significant morbidity, social embarrassment, financial cost and disruption in patients' lives. While patients with extensive and severe disease may require potent oral therapy, less severe psoriasis is typically treated with topical medications.

7.5 Conventional Systemic Therapy[37,38,39]

Most of the FDA approved systemic therapies available for the treatment of psoriasis lead to relapse of the disease on discontinuation of drug thereby limiting their use as suppressive agents rather than curative alternatives. Also approved systemic therapies are often associated with short term and long term side effects. For example, Cyclosporine is known to cause nephrotoxicity on prolonged use limiting its use to no more than a year. Its use for more than 2 years is known to increase the risk of malignancy especially of nonmelanoma skin cancers. Methotrexate, a dihydrofolate inhibitor often prescribed for treatment of psoriasis due to its potential action on rapidly dividing T-lymphocyets is known to cause immunosuppression in the patient. Acitretin, an oral retinoid with unclear mechanism of action probably acts on retinoid receptors of keratinocyte nucleus and hence has less influence on unbalanced immune processes in psoriasis. Acitretin is known to cause side effects like hepatotoxicity, calcification of tendons, serum lipid alterations, and most notably teratogenicity thus limiting its use in pregnant women. PUVA therapy is another approved therapy option. But its inconvenient treatment regimen consisting of 2-3 times a week for several such weeks in physician's office makes it less sought out option among patients.

Due to lack of selective action of above mentioned agents on immune system, newer agents such synthesized proteins like alefacept, efalizumab, etanercept, and infliximab that would selectively target the immune components involved in the development of psoriasis are being investigated for the treatment of moderate to severe psoriasis and are described in detail elsewhere in this chapter. Table 7.2 summarizes marketed formulations available for systemic psoriasis treatment.

Table 7.2 Marketed formulations of Systemic agents used in psoriasis.

Drug	Brand names	Form / strength	Manufacturer
Sulfasalazine	Iwata, Saaz DR, Saaz-DS DR-, Salazar enteric-coated, Salazopyrin, Sazo-EN enteric-coated	Tab of 500/ 1000mg	Cadila (Vibra), IPCA Cadila HC,Wallace
Methotrexate	Alltrex, biotrexate, caditrex, dermatrex, folitrax, hi-trex, imutrex, merex, methocel	Tab 2.5 mg Vial 15mg, 50 mg	Miracalus, Biochem, Cadila (Oncocare), East West, IPCA, VHB (Cytocare), Cipla, Intas, Celon (Vivilon)
Cyclosporine	Cyclophil me, graftin, cyrin, imusporin, panimun bioral	Cap: 25, 50, 100mg, softgel 25/50, 100mg soln: 100 mg x 1 mL x 50ml,	Biocon, Ranbaxy,(Super speciality), Claris Dabur, Cipla, Panacea

Table 7.2 *Contd...*

Drug	Brand names	Form / strength	Manufacturer
Acitretin	Aceret, acetec ,acitrin	Cap 10,25mg	Glenmark (Gracewell), Dr. Reddy's, IPCA
Infliximab	Remicade	Vial 10 mg	fulford india ltd
Leflunomide	Arava, cleft , lefno lefra lefumide, lisifen rumalef	Tab, 10, 20mg	Aventis Pasteur, Ranbaxy (Consumer HC) IPCA, Torrent (Prima) Cipla Cadila (Vibra) Zydus (Synovia)
Thioguanine	Thionine	Tab 40 mg	Chandra Bhagat Pharma
Azathioprine	Azathioprine, azap ,azimune azoprine azoran imuran imuzat thiopress	Tab 25, 50 mg	Alkem (Cytomed) Chandra Bhagat Pharma Sun (Inca) VHB (Critical Care) RPG LS GSK Elder United Biotech Troikaa Zydus (Biogen)
Tacrolimus	Crolim olmis pangraf tacrograf seegraf tacromus tacrotec tacsant vingraf	Cap 0.5, 1 mg, 5 mg	Ranbaxy (Super speciality) Unichem Micro (Foresee), Panacea, Biocon, Zydus, Cadila, United Biotech, Sandoz, Emcure
Hydroxyurea	Cytodrox, hondrea, hydran, urdox	500 mg	Cipla, alkem (cytomed), chandra bhagat (maxicare), cadila-h

7.6 Topical Therapy

7.6.1 Corticosteroid Therapy

Corticosteroid therapy is most widely prescribed treatment. These are available in low, medium, high, and ultra-high potency. The steroid with the lowest effective potency should be used, particularly on the face skin and folds. More potent steroids are usually required for palms and soles. Lotions and gels are commonly used on the scalp. Steroids are safe when used for short term treatments. Once daily application is better than twice daily.

Adverse effects include, atrophy, striae (particularly in intertriginous areas), telangiectasia, rosacea, perioral dermatitis, glaucoma, cataracts, contact sensitization (to the steroid itself as well as to the base and preservatives), tachyphylaxis (lack of effect with continued use), flare upon discontinuation, adrenal suppression (> 50 mg of ultra high potency steroids/wk should not be used).[40-42]

7.6.2 Keratolytics

Commonly used keratolytic agent is salicylic acid. It is usually prescribed in concentrations between 2% and 10% and should not be applied extensively on the body, especially in children, because it can induce salicylism. Stronger concentrations of keratolytics (20% salicylic acid) can be applied for about two weeks to remove the thick scale to enable other topical therapies to better penetrate the skin. Urea-containing preparations and alpha-hydroxy acids, such as glycolic and lactic acids, are also effective keratolytics.[40,41]

7.6.3 Anthralin

Anthralin (dithranol), a derivative of anthracene is widely used in the treatment of psoriasis and is available as creams, ointments and paste under various brands namely Dithrocream, Zithranol-RR, Micanol, Psorlin, Dritho-Scalp, Anthraforte, Anthranol, Anthrascalp, Psoriatec. The precise mechanism of action of anthralin is not clearly known but its anti proliferative and anti inflammatory properties in psoriatic skin is well demonstrated. Since anthralin can penetrate psoriatic skin effectively (within 30min) when compared to normal skin, weaker concentrations (0.1-0.5%) are applied overnight whereas concentrations in the range of 1-2% are applied for between 30 minutes and 1 hour.

However patients using anthralin products are suggested through boxed warnings in the product label to use protective dressing like gloves due to its ability to "stain" hair, skin, nails, clothing and bedding often permanently. Also anthralin can cause severe irritation to the skin hence contact to normal skin should be avoided by applying petroleum jelly to the normal skin during usage of anthralin products.[42,43]

7.6.4 Coal Tar

Coal tar is one of the oldest treatment options available for treatment of mild to moderate psoriasis. However after the development of biologics, tar is not recommended as first line of treatment for severe cases. But due the availability of coal tar in over-the-counter (OTC) forms, patients tend to choose it for the treatment of psoriasis limited to several well-defined areas such as plaque psoriasis. Coal tar like anthralin acts by exerting anti proliferative and anti inflammatory action. Coal tar is available in the form of ointments, creams or shampoos in concentrations ranging 0.5% to 5%. The main limitations of coal tar products are its odor, irritation and staining potential, redness of skin. Use of protective clothing can avoid staining problems; applying tar products atop of moisturized skin can reduce irritation and applying sunscreen will reduce the sensitivity of skin to develop sun burns following coal tar application. Some studies show that coal tar in high concentrations may cause cancer but it is proven that usual concentration range (0.5-5%) is usually safe. The National Psoriasis Foundation recommends that anyone using coal tar recognize the signs of skin cancer and report any suspicious lesions to their dermatologist or visit http://www.psoriasis.org/treatment/psoriasis/topicals/tar.php. However, USFDA has not found any problems among persons using tar products.[44-46]

7.6.5 Vitamin D Analogs

Hypocalcemia can cause various forms of psoriasis especially it can cause pustular psoriasis. Calcipotriene, a topical vitamin D analog, applied twice daily, is generally well tolerated, although the face and groin areas should be avoided since it may cause irritant dermatitis. Like corticosteroids, calcipotriene can be considered a first-line agent and is available as an ointment, cream or solution. Use of calcipotriene should be discontinued when a woman becomes pregnant.[46-49]

7.6.6 Retinoids

Systemic retinoids have been used for the treatment of recalcitrant, severe psoriasis. Oral retinoids, such as etretinate, are associated with several adverse effects, such as teratogenicity, serum lipid and transaminase elevations, mucocutaneous toxicity, skeletal changes and hair loss. Topical retinoids were developed to avoid many of these systemic side effects.

Clinical studies have demonstrated the efficacy of both 0.05% and 0.1% tazarotene gel. The gel formulation is suitable for the treatment of scalp psoriasis. Unlike calcipotriene, tazarotene can be used to treat psoriasis of the face. Local skin irritation and pruritis are frequent side effects of tazarotene, and care must be used to ensure that the medicine is applied only to lesional skin. Since tazarotene may be teratogenic, women of child-bearing age should be warned of the potential fetal risk and should use adequate birth-control measures.[50,51]

Topical methotrexate novel drug delivery system, available in the form of topical gel is reported in literatures and available in India. It is used in the treatment of localized psoriasis with lessthan 25% of the affected body surface area.[52,53]

Table 7.3 Advantages and disadvantages of topical Agents for the treatment of psoriasis.

Drug	Advantages	Disadvantages	Other information
Corticosteroids	Easy to use, rapid onset	Tachyphylaxis, atrophy, telangiectasia and adrenal suppression possible	Can be used in combination with calcipotriene or tazarotene
Calcipotriene	Well-tolerated	Expensive, may cause skin irritation	Potential for hypercalcemia with excessive use
Anthralin	Once-daily administration, well-tolerated	May stain and/or cause skin irritation	Microencapsulated form may be less staining and irritating
Tars	Effective with UV light therapy	May cause skin staining, folliculitis, contact allergy; malodorous	Commonly used for psoriasis of the scalp
Tazarotene	-	Expensive, may be teratogenic; irritating to uninvolved skin	First topical retinoid indicated by the FDA for treatment of psoriasis

Table 7.4 Topical drugs used in the treatment of psoriasis[54-55].

1.Topical corticosteroids	Drugs	Trade name	Manufaturer name
iii. Highest potency corticosteroids (class II and class I) Examples:	Amcinonide Betamethasone Dipropionate Clobetasol Propionate Desoximetasone Diflorasone Diacetate Fluocinonide Halcinonide Halobetasol Propionate	Amcinonide: Topical As 0.1% cream/lotion/oint: Apply 2-3 times/day. Clobetasol propionate TOPINATE® Micro Gratia, 0.05 % w/w x 15g Flucinonide: Topical As 0.05% cream/gel/lotion/oint/scalp application: Apply 1-4 times/day. Diflorasone Diacetate DIFLORATE®) Halocinonide (CORTILATE®): Topical As 0.1% oint/cream/lotionHalobetasol Propionate (HALOBETA®) : 0.05 % w/v x 20g	Intermed,Cosme HC Unichem Micro Gratia Laborate (Multicure) Dr. Reddy's
ii. Moderate potency corticosteroids (classes III, IV, and V) Examples:	Betamethasone dipropionate Betamethasone valerate Desoximetasone Diflorasone Diacetate Fluocinolone Acetonide Flurandrenolide Fluticasone	Betamethasone : ABC DERM cream, ALCODERM cream, DIPROVATE cream	Cipla. Fulford, Emcure

Table 7.4 *Contd...*

	Propionate Hydrocortisone butyrate Hydrocortisone valerate Mometasone Furoate Prednicarbate Triamcinolone Acetonide		
i. Lower potency topical corticosteroids (class VI and VII)	Alclometasone dipropionate Betamethasone valerate Desonide Fluocinolone Acetonide Hydrocortisone Triamcinolone Acetonide	Desonide:DESOWEN cream: desonide. DESOWEN lotion: desonide. 0.05 % w/w x 10g Fluocinolone Acetonide(FLUCIN®)-0.025 % w/w x 1 g x 15g Hydrocortisone (CORT-H®):1 % w/w x 1's Triamcinolone Acetonide :(CORTRIMA:0.1 % x 15g	Galderma Agio, Micro Labs, Ranbaxy Cipla Neon Labs Nulife,Wyeth
Other topical agents for the treatment of psoriasis Examples:	Calcipotriene/Betamethasone Dipropionate Calcipotriene sCalcitriol Salicylic Acid Tazarotene Coal Tar Anthralin	Heximar-b, daivobet Daivonex,heximar, psotriol Sorvate Oint Available in combination A-ret-tz, Tazotop, Zorotene Castor-ct, cotar, exorex, protar, protar Scytera™ (coal tar) Foam 2% for the treatment of chronic psoriasis	Shalaks,Win medicare Win Medicare, Shalaks, Sysmed Glenmark Shalaks,Sun, Elder Ranbaxy, Brawn, Percos Promius Pharma

7.7 Various Therapies used in the Treatment of Psoriasis[56]

7.7.1 Immunotherapy for Psoriasis

Psoriasis was initially viewed only as a disease of epidermal keratinocyte hyper-proliferation with cutaneous inflammation as a secondary feature. But the discovery that cyclosporine, which is generally used as an immunosuppressant in patients with psoriatic arthritis, led to rapid resolution of the psoriatic skin lesions due to its T-cell specificity hinted the involvement of immunogenic component in pathogenesis of disease. Psoriasis is hence categorized as a Th1-cytokine-mediated autoimmune disease because psoriatic plaques were found to be infiltrated with Th1 cytokines, such as interferon-γ, interleukin-2, and interleukin-12.[57,58] Disease initiation is suggested to be mediated through Antigen presenting cells (APCs) like dendritic cells (DCs) and macrophages (MAC) presenting foreign antigens or self-antigens to T-lymphocytes and there by activating them and the activated T-cells differentiate into inflammatory IFN- γ-producing Th1 cells and IL-17- producing Th17 cells leading to proliferation of keratinocytes and endothelia, though self antigens that may be responsible for the disease development are not yet identified. One of these antigens may be a self-peptide cross-reactive to streptococci because streptococcal infections precede psoriasis in more than 90% of patients with type I psoriasis. It is postulated that invasion of tissues by such activated T-lymphocytes from the periphery is essential for the development and maintenance of psoriasis plaques. It is now firmly established that the two receptors, LFA-1 and CLA (cutaneous lymphocyte antigen), are expressed on most T-cells infiltrating psoriatic plaques. Such broader understanding of pathogenesis of psoriasis gave way to the development of novel targeted therapy options like immunotherapy.

Immunotherapy for the treatment of psoriasis hence involves various approaches targeted to the immune components involved in disease progression. Silencing of mast cells, interrupting the interaction between Th1/Th17 cells and pro-inflammatory macrophages/dermal DCs, and the deviation of Th1/Th17 responses into Th2 responses, cytokine modulating and TNF antagonists are the principle approaches.

Considering the involvement of Th1/Th17 in development of psoriasis, either deviation of Th1/Th17 into Th2 cells or blocking of IL-12/IL-23 with monoclonal antibodies should control the autoimmune diseases and may result in long-term protection.[59] Hence restoring the Th1:Th2 ratio to unity in psoriasis by systemic administration of a Th2 cytokine is considered as rational approach and such an approach using interleukin-10 has proved beneficial.[60] Other cytokines-interleukins 4 and 11 are also under investigation for this indication.

The interaction between antigen-presenting cells (APCs), T cells and endothelial cells (ECs) is involved decisively in the pathophysiology of psoriasis.

(a) The interaction between APCs and T-cells can be inhibited by a blockade of antigen presentation and/or costimulation.

(b) After adhesion to ECs, activated T-cells migrate into the skin, the target organ. Thus, inhibition of this adhesion is another attractive therapeutic possibility.

Activated immune cells (including APCs, T-cells and ECs) produce excessive quantities of pro-inflammatory mediators and type-1 cytokines, such as tumor necrosis factor α, interleukin-2 (IL-2), interferon γ and IL-12, which trigger the inflammatory reaction further and are, therefore, also of pathophysiological significance. In contrast to this, the anti-inflammatory type-2 cytokines are formed in insufficient amounts. The ratio of pro-inflammatory to anti-inflammatory and type-1 to type-2 cytokines determines the presence or absence of the psoriatic inflammation.

Thus, neutralization or antagonization of the proinflammatory and type-1 cytokines, or replacement with anti-inflammatory and type-2 cytokines represents further new therapeutic possibilities.

These approaches may be categorized broadly as either T-cell targeting or cytokine modulating. T cell targeting therapies involving inhibition of T-cell activation include use of antibodies to the T-cell receptor CD254 and inhibition of co-stimulatory molecules that mediate binding between antigen-presenting cell and T-cells.

7.7.1.1 Blockade of interactions between APC- T-cells/ T-cells- EC

Activation of T-cells which is the main reason for disease progression is triggered not only by activation of T-cell receptors but also requires co-stimulation. Hence blockade of co-stimulation represents a effective target for the therapy. Thus, LFA-3TIP blocks the leukocyte functional antigen (LFA)-3–CD2 interaction; cytotoxic-T-lymphocyte-associated antigen (CTLA)-4 fusion protein blocks the interaction of CD80 and CD86 (B7 molecules) with CD28; anti-CD80 mAb blocks the CD80–CD28 interaction; and anti-CD11a mAb blocks the interaction of LFA-1 with intercellular adhesion molecules (ICAMs). All these agents demonstrated good tolerability and anti psoriatic effects in clinical trials. For instance, LFA-3TIP showed > 50% improvement after eight weeks of treatment in more than half of the 24 patients. CTLA4-Ig on intravenous administration showed a dose-dependent improvement of > 50%, in 46% of the patients, in an open Phase I/II study.[61-62] Phase II trials with an anti-CD80 mAb given as intravenous infusion for four times over a 3- to 6-week period in a group of 35 patients showed a considerable improvement of skin lesions in 40% of patients leading to a reduction of > 50% in the PASI (A. Gottlieb et al., unpublished). The humanized anti-CD11a mAb which acts by inhibiting the interaction of CD11a (LFA-1) with various ICAM (intercellular adhesion molecules, which are often expressed on activated endothelial cells and antigen presenting cells) when infused once in 31 patients lead to inhibition of both the APC–T-cell interaction and the adhesion of T cells to and/or their subsequent activation by endothelial cells and hence migration to target organ, the skin.[63]

7.7.1.2 T-cell targeting by using antibodies

Earlier antibodies used were of murine in origin which led to development of tolerability problems and production of neutralizing antibodies. These unwanted effects are now overcome by using humanized monoclonal antibodies like hu1124, efaluzimab, which are directed to the CD11a component of lymphocyte-function-associated antigen-1 (LFA-1). Kim Papp and colleagues[64] reported that intravenous administration of these antibodies once weekly for 8 weeks produced significant improvement in moderate or severe psoriasis in 25% (19/75) of patients without any side effects and without any significant reduction in the number of circulating lymphocytes.

7.7.1.3 IL-2 Diptheria toxin Vs CD5 MAb

IL-2DT directly kills cells bearing IL-2-receptor, whereas anti-CD25 mAb acts specifically on the IL-2–IL-2-receptor interaction without leading to depletion of T-cells. IL-2 and IL-15 (often over expressed in psoriatic lesions) have two receptor chains (β chain) in common, and hence might be another interesting target for the therapy of psoriasis.

The fusion protein concept can be explained by alefacept, a fusion protein of IgG1 and LFA-3 and the complex formed by cytotoxic T-lymphocyte-associated antigen 4 and an immunoglobulin (CTLA4-Ig). Alefacept inhibits T-cell activation by blocking the binding of LFA-3 to CD2 and selectively reduces the number of circulating memory effector CD45RO+ T-cells by apoptosis mediated by natural killer cells. Charles Ellis and Gerald Krueger[65] reported more than 75% clinical improvement in 32% (31/97) of patients with moderate or severe psoriasis when alefacept was given intravenously once a week for 12 weeks. In an open-label study,[66] the fusion protein CTLA4-Ig, which blocks binding of CTLA4 receptors (CD28/CD152) to the receptor B7 on antigen-presenting cells, also produced improvement in psoriasis.

7.7.1.4 Cytokine modulation

The other approach cytokine modulation, acts either directly by blocking pro-inflammatory cytokines such as tumour necrosis factor-γ (TNF-γ) or indirectly by switching the cytokine profile within plaques of psoriasis.

Infliximab, a monoclonal antibody against TNF-γ, licensed for therapy of patients with Crohn's disease who commonly develop psoriasis compared to healthy individuals was found to cure the disease completely in 73% of patients after three intravenous infusions given over 6 weeks.[67,68]

Etanercept[69], a recombinant human soluble receptor for TNF-γ, was found to produce a 75% reduction in clinical severity of disease in 26% of patients and hence was less effective compared to Infliximab.

Other anticytokines under study for the treatment of psoriasis include anti-interleukin-8 and anti-interferon-γ.

7.7.1.5 TNF antagonists

TNF antagonists act by potent neutralization of the effector cytokine produced by mast cells, macrophages/dermal DCs, and T-cells and probably by deletion of immune cells, such as macrophages/dermal DCs and T-cells, because these cells may express TNF on their cell surface.

Neutralization of interferone-γ a proinflammatory type-1 cytokine, which is often over-expressed in psoriasis and maintaining a balance between type-1 (interferone-γ) and type-2 cytokines (IL-4) by deviating over expressed type-1 cytokine pathway to type-2 cytokine pathway are important approaches in regulating the disease progression.

IL-4: Due to its ability to act as auto inducer, IL-4 is recently tested for the therapy of psoriasis. When a group of 22 patients were given various doses of injections of IL-4 over six weeks, side-effects were observed only after the highest dosage. Among twenty patients who have completed the study, PASI of 18 patients fell by 60-80% within the six-week period indicating that IL might serve as a novel target.

IL-10: IL-10 exerts its anti inflammatory properties by inhibition of antigen presentation, decreased production of pro-inflammatory mediators (e.g. TNF-α), increased production of anti-inflammatory mediators. IL-10 therapy led to a decrease in the level of cutaneous IL-8 and an increase in IL-4 expression indicating a shift to type 2 cytokine pathways. These findings were corroborated by good clinical efficacy (PASI reduction by 50-60%) achieved after 6-7 weeks of subcutaneous injections, daily or three times a week in two Phase II clinical studies.

IL-11: *In vitro*, IL-11 reduces the production of TNF-α, IL-1β and IL-12, and in various animal models, it alleviates inflammatory activity. In a recent open Phase I/II study, psoriasis patients were treated with recombinant IL-11; 12 patients were given daily subcutaneous injections for a period of eight weeks. In seven of the 12 patients, anti-psoriatic effects were observed, with the PASI falling by 20-80%. The response to therapy was accompanied by a reduction in the intralesional expression of the genes encoding IFN-γ, IL-8, IL-12, TNF-α, IL-1β and CD8.[70]

Table 7.5 Immunotherapy: Biological agents used in the treatment of psoriasis[71,72].

Mechanism	Immunoagents	Selected Biological agents mechanism	Administration route
Action on the function of antigen-presenting cells	CTLA-4 (BMS 188667) • LFA-3TIP (Amevive/Alefacept) • Anti-CD80 antibodies (IDEC 114) • Calcitriols (Rocaltrol) • Fumaric acid esters (Fumaderm)	Alfacept: Binds to CD2 on T cells blocking costimulation and inducing T cell apoptosis	Intra muscular
T-cell inhibitors	• Macrolides [FK506 (Tacrolimus), SDZASM981 (Pimecrolimus) and sirolimus (Rapamycin)] • Anti-CD2 antibodies [MEDI507 (Siplizumab)] • Anti-CD3 antibodies (OKT3, HuM291) • Anti-CD4 antibodies (BB14) • Mycophenolate mofetil (CellCept) • IL-2-coupled diphtheria toxin (DAB398IL-2) • Anti-CD25 antibodies (Basiliximab, Dalizumab)	Tacrolimus inhibits T-lymphocyte activation by first binding to an intracellular protein, FKBP-12. A complex of tacrolimus-FKBP-12, calcium, calmodulin, and calcineurin is then formed and the phosphatase activity of calcineurin is inhibited. This effect has been shown to prevent the dephosphorylation and translocation of nuclear factor of activated T-cells (NF-AT), a nuclear component thought to initiate gene transcription for the formation of lymphokines (such as interleukin-2, gamma interferon). Tacrolimus also inhibits the transcription.	Topical

Table 7.5 *Contd...*

Mechanism	Immunoagents	Selected Biological agents mechanism	Administration route
		for genes which encode IL-3, IL-4, IL-5, GM-CSF, and TNF-α, all of which are involved in the early stages of T-cell activation. Additionally, tacrolimus has been shown to inhibit the release of pre-formed mediators from skin mast cells and basophils, and to down regulate the expression of FcεRI on Langerhans cells	
Inhibitors of adhesion	Anti-CD11a antibodies [hu1124 (Efalizumab)] • Anti-CD6 antibodies (ior-t1)	Efalizumab :Blocks binding of T cells to ICAMs on antigen-presenting cells, endothelial cells and activated keratinocytes	Subcutaneous
Inhibitors of pro-inflammatory cytokine/mediator action	Anti-IL-8 antibodies (ABX-IL8) • Anti-TNF-̧(antibodies (Infliximab) • Soluble TNF-̧(receptors [Etanercept (Enbrel)] • LTB4-receptor antagonist (VLM 295) • Anti-IFN-©antibodies	Etanercept :Binds to and nactivates soluble TNF-a and TNF-b Infliximab :Binds to and inhibits soluble and membrane-bound TNF-a	Subcutaneous Intravenous
Administration of anti-inflammatory cytokines	• IL-4, • IL-10,• IL-11 Anti-IL-12/IL-23	Anti-IL-12/IL-23: Binds to the p40 chain shared by IL-12 and IL-23 preventing its binding to the IL-12 receptor b1 chain	Subcutaneous

Table 7.6 Biological agents used in the treatment of psoriasis.

Type of therapis	Biological agents	Details
Reduction of the number of pathogenic T cells	• Amevive (LFA3TIP). • denileukin diftitox	• ONTAK (denileukin diftitox) -The pathogenic T cells in psoriasis lesions are activated T cells that express the IL-2 receptor (CD25).2 DAB389-IL-2 is a fusion toxin composed of the amino acid sequences for diphtheria toxin conjugated to the sequences for IL-2. The high affinity IL-2 receptor on activated T cells binds DAB389-IL2, which mediates selective cell death
Inhibition of T cell activation and migration	• Raptiva (Efaluzimab, anti-CD11a). • CTLA4Ig • IDEC-114 • Siplizumab • Zenapax • Simulect • OKTcdr4a • SDZ ASM 981.	• CTLA4Ig is a chimeric fusion protein that binds to CD80 (B7-1) and CD86 (B7-2) on antigen-presenting cells (APCs) and prevents their costimulatory interaction with CD28 on T cells, thus blocking their activation. IDEC-114 is a primatized monoclonal antibody that binds to the high affinity B7-1 (CD80). the manufacturer decided on September 6, 2002, to no longer pursue a psoriasis indication. • .Siplizumab, a humanized monoclonal antibody directed against CD2, prevents the CD2-LFA3 costimulatory signal • Zenapax (Daclizumab, anti-CD25) is a humanized antibody to the _ subunit (CD25) of the IL-2 receptor that blocks normal IL-2 binding to this receptor. • Simulect (Basiliximab) is a chimeric human/mouse antibody directed against the IL-2 receptor that has been used in combination with cyclosporine to treat severe recalcitrant psoriasis.

Table 7.6 *Contd...*

Type of therapis	Biological agents	Details
		• OKTcdr4a (IMUCLONE), a humanized anti-CD4 IgG4 monoclonal antibody, has been used in 1 pilot, multicenter, multiple-dose, placebocontrolled study in the treatment of moderate-tosevere psoriasis. • SDZ ASM 981, a novel ascomycin macrolactam derivative, inhibits the proliferation of T cells after antigen-specific or nonspecific stimulation. It is a specific inhibitor of the production of proinflammatory cytokines from T cells and mast cells and appears in initial studies to be highly effective in psoriasis
Immune modulation	• Recombinant human IL-10 (Tenovil). • Oprelvekin. • PVAC • Psoraxine • Peptide T.	• IL-10 administration shifts cytokine profiles to a TH-2 pattern (increasing IL-4, IL-5, and IL-10). IL-10 may decrease the rate of relapse and prolong disease-free intervals in patients with psoriasis Oprelvekin (recombinant humanized IL-11) modulates macrophages and type-1 Tlymphocyte function in cell culture and shows anti-inflammatory activity in animal models • PVAC is heat-killed, delipidated *Mycobacteriumvaccae* suspension that is given intradermally into nonlesional skin. The mechanism of action behindthis therapy is thought to be an increase in TH-2 typecytokines. Psoraxine, a vaccine originally developed to induce resistance against leishmaniasis, Marked decreases in PASI scores were noticed in vaccinated patients with psoriasis.

Table 7.6 *Contd...*

Type of therapis	Biological agents	Details
		Peptide T, an octapeptide from the V2 region of gp120 of HIV, has immune modulating effects and has improved psoriasis in several small series.
Blocking activity of inflammatory cytokines	• Enbrel (etanercept). • Remicaide (infliximab). • ABX-IL8 • SMART anti-INF-_.	Tumor necrosis factor inhibition tips the balance of cytokines toward an antiinflammatory environment. ABX-IL8 is a fully humanized IgG2 monoclonal antibody directed against IL-8. Keratinocyte- derived IL-8 is involved in attracting lymphocytes and neutrophils into the skin SMART anti-INF-_, a humanized monoclonal antibody that binds and inactivates the proinflammatory cytokine INF-_
Non specific therapies	Tazoretene Targretin Liarozole	• Tazarotene is a retinoid agonist specific for the retinoic acid receptor- _ More favorable safety profile compare to acitrtin. • Targretin (bexarotene) is specific for the retinoid X receptor. Trials for psoriasis involving oral and topical formulations are currently in progress • Liarozole, an inhibitor of the cytochrome P450 pathway, and thereby 4-hydroxylation of retinoic acid, has improved plaque psoriasis
Antiangiogenesis	Extracts of shark cartilage prepared with homogenization and ultrafiltration to derive the active agent (AE-941). Topical AE-941 found to have beneficial effect in psoriasis, most likely from antiangiogenic and antiinflammatory properties	
Photo-dynamic therapy	Photodynamic therapy relies on the use of lightsensitive molecules called photosensitizers coupled with the appropriate wavelength of light, causing photoactivation and the formation of singlet oxygen. Singlet oxygen accumulation produces peroxidative reactions, leading to cell damage and death. Benzoporphyrin derivative (verteporfin), a second generation porphyrin, has been shown to be efficacious in psorais	
Apheresis	Patient whole blood is circulated through an extracorporeal filter column that selectively removes activated granulocytes and monocytes and modulates adhesion molecules and complement activity.	

Table 7.7 FDA approved biologics[73].

Amevive (alefacept)	Given by an intramuscular injection once per week for 12 weeks Additional 12-week treatment cycles might be necessary or recommended	FDA-approved for treating psoriasis	Blood tests required every two weeks during treatment to monitor immune cell counts
Enbrel (etanercept)	Patients give themselves an injection once or twice a week Taken continuously to maintain results May reduce the progression of joint damage	FDA-approved for treating psoriasis, psoriatic arthritis, rheumatoid arthritis, juvenile rheumatoid arthritis and ankylosing spondylitis	Occasional blood tests are recommended
Humira (adalimumab)	Individuals give themselves an injection usually every other week Patients should be screened for latent (hidden) tuberculosis (TB) before taking Humira May reduce the progression of joint damage	FDA-approved for treating psoriasis, psoriatic arthritis, ankylosing spondylitis and rheumatoid arthritis	Occasional blood tests are recommended
Remicade	Given by three infusions in a doctor's	FDA-approved for psoriasis,	Blood tests are recommended on

Table 7.7 *Contd...*

(infliximab)	office during the first six weeks of treatment Later infusions repeated every eight weeks Patients should be screened for latent (hidden) tuberculosis (TB) before taking infliximab May reduce the progression of joint damage	psoriatic arthritis, rheumatoid arthritis, ulcerative colitis, ankylosing spondylitis and Crohn's disease	a regular basis
Simponi (golimumab)	Patients give themselves an injection one time per month Patients should be screened for latent (hidden) tuberculosis (TB) before taking May reduce the progression of joint damage	FDA-approved for psoriatic arthritis, rheumatoid arthritis and ankylosing spondylitis	Blood tests are recommended on a regular basis
Stelara (ustekinumab)	After two initial doses at weeks 0 and 4, patients receive an injection by a health care provider once every 12 weeks Patients should be screened for latent (hidden) tuberculosis (TB) before taking Stelara	FDA-approved for plaque psoriasis	Occasional blood tests are recommended

7.7.2 Laser Therapy

Laser therapy for the treatment of psoriasis can be exploited in cases where the disease is resistant to conventional treatment options like topical corticosteroids and vitamin D3 analogues or systemic therapies or light based therapies such as PUVA or narrowband UVB. Laser therapy can also be used as an adjunct therapy when diseased area is "difficult-to-reach" such as gluteal crease or cosmetically sensitive areas like scalp.

Excimer laser and pulsed dye laser are the two laser based therapy options available for psoriasis treatment. The mechanism by which laser treats the disease is by preventing the replication of epidermal cells there by preventing spread of psoriatic plaques and by inducing localized suppression of immune function which in turn will alleviate the inflammation associated with psoriasis.

Excimer laser

The Excimer laser specifically emits light at a 308 nm wavelength that falls within ultraviolet region. Hence excimer laser treatment, yielded similar clinical results as that of NB-UVB treatment. The excimer laser can target select areas of the skin affected by mild to moderate psoriasis. Individual response to the treatment varies. It can take an average of four to 10 sessions to see results, depending on the particular case of psoriasis. It is recommended that patients receive two treatments per week, with a minimum of 48 hours between treatments. There is not yet enough long-term data to indicate how long the improvement will last following a course of laser therapy. The Excimer laser is recently approved by the Food and Drug Administration (FDA) for treating chronic, localized psoriasis. The two brands currently on the market are the Xtrac and the Xtrac velocity.[74-79]

Pulsed lasers generally emit laser light of high-energy in ultra short pulse durations with relatively long intervening time periods between each pulse. A 585 nm pulsed dye laser (PDL) (E.g., PhotoGenica V) with pulse durations ranging from 450 millisec to 40 millisec, prevents T-cell binding to microvasculature supplying the psoriatic area by selectively targeting abnormal dermal vasculature in psoriatic plaques and a better response has been noted especially in truncal plaques compared with those on the extremities. Treatment consists of 15 to 30 minutes sessions every three weeks. For patients who respond, it normally takes about four to six sessions to clear the target lesion. The most common side effect is bruising after treatment, for up to 10 days. There is a small risk of scarring.[80-82]

In a comparative study between excimer and pulsed dye lasers in the treatment of psoriasis in 22 patients, 13 patients were responsive to the excimer system, two patients to PDL irradiation, and 7 patients responded equally to both.[83]

In spite of advantages that PDL requires fewer treatments and is associated with fewer side effects, excimer laser was found to be effective than PDL in many patients with psoriasis. However the PDL therapy might be useful in excimer-laser-resistant cases as few of the patients studied responded only to the PDL but not excimer laser.

Also PDL treatment can be used as an adjunctive to topical calcipotriol, salicylic acid, or both to obtain enhanced therapy benefits.

7.7.3 Herbal

Due to long term treatment course and debilitating nature of psoriasis, patients often switch to complementary and alternative medicine in addition to standard therapies. Herbal remedy is an important CAM modality used by patients apart from other approaches like special diets and dietary supplements.

Laser treatment options like ultraviolet [UV] B or psoralen plus UVA therapy are often time-consuming and use of drugs for treatment like methotrexate, acitretin, cyclosporine on chronic use lead to organ toxicity with chronic use.[84] Immunotherapy with infliximab, etanercept, adalimumab, efalizumab, and alefacept are immunosuppressive and hence could increase the risk of infections and malignancies with long-term use, and are limited by their high cost.[85,86] Despite the advent of multiple systemic therapy and topical therapy options for severe psoriasis, many patients with this disease are unable to achieve effective long-term control.[87,88]

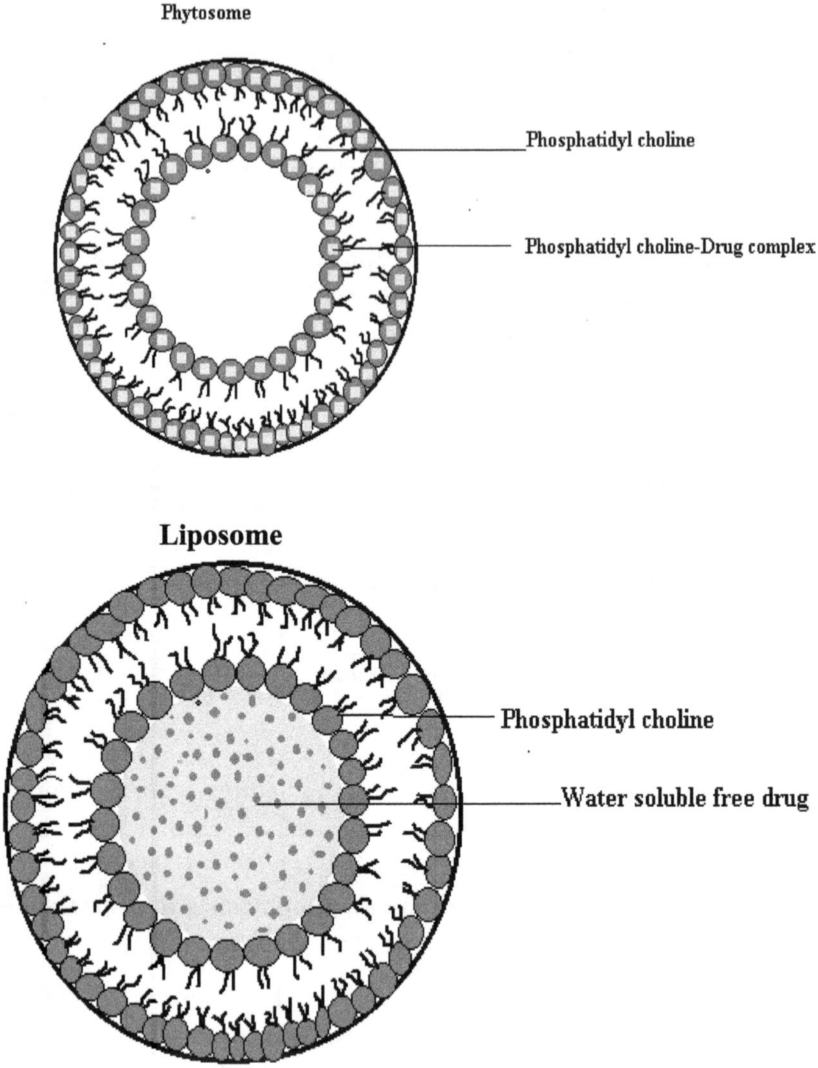

Fig. 7.1 Difference between liposome and phytosome (Redrawn from reference 89).

7.7.3.1 *Aloe vera* (90)

Aloe vera has analgesic, anti allergic, anti pruritic, wound healing, and anti-inflammatory properties. In a placebo -controlled, double-blind study of aloe vera in 60 patients with slight to moderate psoriasis (PASI score

4.8-16 .7) conducted by Syed et al.[91], group treated with aloe vera showed a mean decrease in PASI score from 9.7 to 2.2 versus a decrease of 8.9 to 8.2 among placebo treated patients with no reported adverse effects. Aloe vera formulated as a hydrophilic cream (0.5%), was applied for 4 weeks, thrice daily. Positive response was defined as a ‘‘progressive reduction of lesions, desquamation, decreased erythema, infiltration and lower PAS I score.’’

In another randomized, double- blind, placebo controlled study (right/left comparison study) conducted by Paulsen et al.[92], a score sum of erythema, infiltration, and desquamation (modified local PASI score) decreased in 72.5% of aloe vera treated patients versus 82.5% of placebo treated patients (P = 0.0197). Aloe vera was given in gel form for 4 weeks, twice daily to 41 patients. However this study reported a side effect of dryness, stinging, soreness, and erythema.

7.7.3.2 *Mahonia aquifolium*

Mahonia aquifolium commonly known as barberry or Oregon grape contains berberine, an isoquinoline alkaloid as an active compound and is known for its anti inflammatory, anti neoplastic, and anti bacterial properties. The compound has demonstrated efficacy in several open label studies for psoriasis treatment. For instance, in a double- blind, placebo controlled, multicenter trial (6 sites in the United States and Canada) conducted by Bernstein et al.[18], Relie´va , a product containing 10% *M. aquifolium*) lead to PASI score of 3.93 in herb treated patients compared to 6.85 in the placebo group. The compound was applied topically twice daily to a target plaque for 12 weeks.[93]

7.7.3.3 *Oleum horwathiensis*

Oleum horwathiensis is a combination of active extracts of Achilleae herb a (yarrow), *Allium sativum* (garlic), Calendulaeflos (calendula), *Taraxaci radix* (dandelion root), Urticafolium (stinging nettle), and *Veronica officinalis* (common gypsyweed). The extract was dissolved in soft paraffin and was used In a double- blind, placebo-controlled trial by Lassus and Forsstro¨m[19], where in out of 50 patients treated topically with oleum horwathiensis or placebo for 12 weeks, 42 patients have completed the study and it was reported that the mean overall symptom severity score for pruritus, erythema, and induration was lower in the oleum horwathiensis group, compared with placebo, at all time points. But no “significant difference” between both the groups was observed at any time point.[94]

7.7.3.4 *Indigo naturalis*

Indigo naturalis, widely used as a remedy in ancient Chinese medicine, is obtained as a dark blue powder from plants such as *Baphicacavthus cusia, Polygonum tinctorium, Isatis indigotica* and *Indigofera tinctoria.* The anti psoriatic effect of *Indigo naturalis* is hypothesized due to controlling the hyperproliferation and/or abnormal differentiation of epidermal keratinocytes leading to decrease in epidermal thickness and elongated rete ridges for psoriatic lesions. This effect of Indigo naturalis was studied by Lin et al., in skin samples of six patients using techniques like immune histo chemical staining for the expression of proliferating cell nuclear antigen (PCNA) and involucrin. In this study, indigo naturalis ointment (a mixture of indigo naturalis powder and vehicle in a 1:10 ratio) or vehicle was applied only on psoriatic lesions of patients for 8 weeks. Tissue sections from the patients were immunostained with anti-human PCNA and involucrin antibodies followed by labeled streptavidin-biotin (LSAB) immunohistochemical method (Dakocytomation). There was a decrease in PCNA and increase in involucrin in psoriatic lesions after *Indigo naturalis* treatment. Additionally, cultured actively proliferating keratinocytes were utilized to study the gene expressions of PCNA and involucrin. Indigo naturalis extracts were added in increasing doses (10 to 500 mg/ml) to cultured keratinocytes which on analysis by real-time R T-PCR, western blot ting and indirect immunofluorescent labeling demonstrated a decrease in the number of cultured keratinocytes and a dose proportional G0 /G1 arrest probably catalyzed by major components of Indigo naturalis, indirubin and indigo. However PCNA down regulation and increase in involucrin were found to be modulated only by indirubin.[95]

In the case of *Wrightia tinctoria*, a clinical study had shown its usefulness to treat psoriasis.[96]

7.7.3.5 *Oral curcumin*

Curcumin or curcuminoids, important constituents of Curcuma longa have demonstrated the inhibitory effect on immunological factors like nuclear factor kappa B14-18 and downstream, inflammatory gene products such as Th-1 type cytokines (i.e., tumor necrosis factor-a , interferon-g) critical to the pathophysiology of psoriasis in various *in vitro* and animal studies.[97-100]

The efficacy of curcumin in the treatment of psoriasis has been further tested in a phase II, open-label, and Simon's two-stage trial where in a 4.5 g/day of oral curcuminoid C3 complex (highest dose of oral curcumin) was administered to patients with plaque psoriasis. End points included improvement in Physicians Global Assessment score, Psoriasis Area and Severity Index score, and safety end points throughout the study. The intention-to-treat analysis response rate was 16.7% (95% confidence interval: 2%, 48%) and both responders achieved a Psoriasis Area and Severity Index 75 score. Since curcumin doses up to 8 g/day for up to 12 months were reported to be well tolerated in human beings, further studies can be conducted with higher doses.[101] Also administration of higher doses of curcumin alone or curcumin in combination with absorption enhancers may enhance the bioavailability of curcumin. Liposomal formulations of curcumin with improved bioavailability are now being developed and may be considered for future trials[102]. Topical formulations for curcumin were developed with minimum success as curcumin stains the skin yellow and therefore compromise patient compliance.

7.7.3.6 *Anthralin*

Anthralin is an antipsoriatic agent that is derived from chrysarobin, a substance found in the Brazilian tree *Andira araroba*. Yet to decipher mechanism of action, anthralin is known to decrease inflammation and cellular proliferation in psoriasis and increase cellular differentiation. No known systemic side effects are reported for this compound but the only draw back with anthralin is that it leaves a brownish-purplish stain on skin and clothing, and often causes local irritation.

In a study conducted by Yamamoto et al.[103] to evaluate the efficacy of topical anthralin on nail psoriasis, where in twenty patients suffering from cutaneous psoriasis with nail involvement were instructed to apply for 5 months, anthralin (0.4%-2.0%) daily and wash it off after a 30 minute period, 60% of patients demonstrated ''fair'' or ''little'' improvement, while 20% showed no response. Anthralin was found to be effective in patients with onycholysis and subungual hyperkeratosis than those with pitting. The reason stated was the inability of anthralin to penetrate into the nail matrix which is the source of pitting. The treatment was followed by the application of 10% triethanolamine to prevent staining by the formulation.

7.7.4 Phototherapy

Phototherapy[104] is the exposure to non-ionizing radiation for therapeutic use. It may arise as a result of exposure to natural light, UVB or UVA radiation, or a combination of both. It is a therapeutic technique employing a photosensitizing chemical substance, followed by electromagnetic non-ionizing radiation. Treatment involves exposing the skin to an artificial UVB light source for a set length of time on a regular schedule. This treatment is administered in a medical setting or at home. In practice, it is typically administered using psoralen (as the photosensitizer) and long-length ultraviolet radiation (UVA). UV light in its many forms offers highly-effective treatment for most psoriasis patients. It should be pursued under doctor supervision, with careful attention to minimizing its risks, particularly avoiding burns and limiting total dose over time as much as possible. But UV light is likely to continue to be a promising option for certain populations, including children, pregnant women, and people who have other health conditions that block them from using some of the pills and injections that psoriasis patients use.

Psoriatic patients are 'different' from normal people in that while normal people avoid exposure to UV light , psoriatics (people with psoriasis) tend to expose their skin to UV light which is essential for the treatment. However it exposes the disease to the world leading to the unwelcoming attention. UVA chambers have proven to be a boon for psoriatic patients in this context.

Vertical UVA chambers enable the entire cutaneous area to be irradiated uniformly and in the appropriate dosage. The lamps employed have a half-life of about 1000 hours, and their emission spectrum has a maximum peak of about 360 nm. Constant therapeutic effect can be achieved by gradually increasing the UVA dose, taking into account the patient photo-type 3, 6, 7 and the determination of the minimal phototoxic dose.

Short-term side effects include erythema, pruritus, pigmentation, and, occasionally, a high phototoxicity. In addition, good ocular protection against the effects of the Sun or other sources of radiation is required on the days on which treatment is administrated. Long-term effects induced by UVA radiation include photoaging, carcinogenetic effects, immunosuppression, and cataracts.

The most commonly employed, both orally and topically, are 5-methoxypsoralen, or 5-MOP; 8-methoxypsoralen, or 8-MOP; and trioxsalen, or TMP.

Psoralen + UVA (PUVA)

UVA and UVB are the non-ionizing radiations present in natural sunlight effective for the treatment of psoriasis.

UVA unlike UVB is ineffective alone for the treatment of psoriasis and should be used in conjunction with light sensitizing medication such as psoralen which can be applied topically or taken orally. Often called PUVA, this process is proven to be most effective for the treatment of stable plaque psoriasis, guttate psoriasis, and psoriasis of the palms and soles. However PUVA is associated with side effects like redness of skin, itching and nausea which are often alleviated with certain remedies. Nausea can be prevented by including ginger in the diet while taking oral psoralen. Antihistamines, capsaicin related products and oatmeal products provide relief from PUVA associated itching.

Simple exposure to UVB light of 310 nm band range is proven to be effective for the treatment of psoriasis. Though UVB exposure does not require supplementation with photosensitizing agents, the effectiveness of treatment can be increased by using other topical treatments such as anthralin, coal tar, and vitamin A and D derivatives, or systemic treatments such as methotrexate and soriatane.[105]

7.7.5 Surgical Treatment

Though wide variety of options are available for the treatment of psoriasis, the outcome from such regimen has been only short term and relapse of the disease incase of discontinuation or withdrawal of therapy is commonly observed among patients. Hence attempts have been made to explore surgery as a treatment option when other treatment methods are found to be ineffective.

Sogaard et al.,[106] of Arhus Municipal Hospital, Denmark have demonstrated in a study on patients with plaque psoriasis, the effectiveness of excision of the superficial skin layers as an effective and easy alternative to medical treatment. All the patients were subjected to dermatome shaving of psoriasis affected skin. The wound resulting from the operation procedure was treated by taking a skin graft from some other site (which acts as donor site) of same person. Patients were followed up to 3 to 36 months during which in 17 patients grafted area healed completely developing normal skin free from psoriasis. Minor recurrences were observed along the margin of shaven area in 7 patients and in 1 patient further shaving resulted in a recurrence free skin area.

7.8 Novel Drug Delivery Systems for Psoriasis Therapy

Psoriasis, a rarely life threatening disease by its nature is commonly treated by using creams and ointments by topical route among others. The barrier effect of stratum corneum offers several challenges for the availability of drugs from conventional topical formulations like lotions and creams.

Challenges in the topical drug delivery

- Variability in the barrier effect of different areas of same person and inter individual variability
- Irritation potential and toxicity of drug
- Susceptibility to first pass metabolism in skin
- Inadequate knowledge on technology to localize or increase the drug penetration
- Variability in the capacity of skin turn over and metabolism
- Lack of proper definition of bioequivalence criteria

Advances topical drug delivery has opened doors for several other alternatives in fact superior topical delivery systems with better biodistribution properties for local delivery of active agents thereby avoiding unnecessary exposure of other organs to xenobiotics, thereby avoiding toxic side effects and alleviating symptoms of psoriasis. Hence novel drug delivery systems like liposomes, niosomes, nanoparticles are being widely investigated for improving the penetration ability of "difficult to penetrate" novel macrolides like tacrolimus, pimecrolimus[107] and many other agents as discussed in Table 7.8.

Lipid Vesicles

Lipid vesicles like liposomes, niosomes and ethosomes[108] are advantageously exploited for topical delivery of anti psoriatic agents for the following reasons:

(i) Organic solvents used in lipid vesicular systems promote solubilization of lipophilic actives like corticosteroids

(ii) Lipid vesicular systems may either form a thin lipid film on the surface of the skin, or increase total lipid content of the skin thus preventing water loss from the skin and promoting partitioning of drug into the lipid domain of skin thus forming depot resulting in higher epidermal and dermal drug concentrations.

(iii) Lipid vesicles enhance the permeation of drug molecules across the skin due to penetration enhancing activity of phospholipid molecules or nonionic ether surfactants thereby leading to higher localized drug concentrations;

Liposomes and niosomes

Liposomes are vesicular systems containing one or more concentric lipid bilayers enclosing aqueous compartment. Liposomes enhance the penetration of drug as shown in the Figure 7.2, by either fusing with the lipids of skin, by acting as penetration enhancers disrupting the stratum corneum barrier or by increasing partitioning of hydrophilic drug into lipid layers of skin. Liposomes are widely exploited for the topical delivery of anti psoriatic drugs like dyphylline which is a CAMP phosophodiesterase inhibitor.[109] Also corticosteroids like triamcinolone acetonide[110]; hydrocortisone, betamethasone dipropionate were formulated as liposomes for topical delivery.

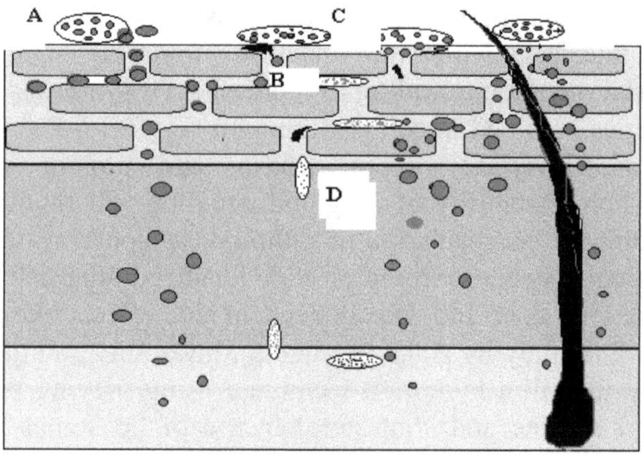

A- Free drug mechanism
B.Penetration enhancing process of liposomal components
C.Vesicle adsorption and/or fusion with Stratum corneum
D.Vesicle penetration into or into through the intact skin

Fig. 7.2 Possible mechanism of liposome through skin[111].
[Colour Fig. on page 405]

Niosomes are non ionic surfactant vesicles and fusion of such vesicles on the surface of the skin when applied might lead to the establishment of large concentration gradients across the skin due to increase in skin residence time of drug and reducing the systemic absorption.[112] Also niosomes reduce transepidermal water loss, replenish skin lipids there by imparting smoothness to the skin thus promoting drug penetration. Non ionic surfactant vesicles are made up from single chain surfactant molecules such as polyoxyethylene alkyl ethers, polyoxyethylene alkyl esters, diacyl glycerides or saccharose diesters, often in combination with cholesterol. Niosomes overcome certain limitations associated with liposomes like chemical instability and variable purity of phospholipids.

In an *in vivo* study conducted by Korting et al. in ten patients with atopic eczema and ten patients with psoriasis vulgaris,[113] the efficacy of betamethasone diproprionate encapsulated in liposomes was compared with cream formulation of same drug. The liposomes were prepared from egg lecithin and were incorporated in a polyacrylate gel. Liposomal formulation was found to exert higher anti-inflammatory action compared to cream and no anti-proliferative effect was observed.

Dithranol is one of important agents used for therapy of psoriasis. Dithranol interfers with the electron transport chain of inner mitochondrial membrane leading to reduced ATP synthesis[114] and inhibit many enzymes involved in cell proliferation (E.g., G-6-P dehydrogenase, ornithine decarboxylase, lipooxygenase, and protein kinase C[115]). However, photo instability of drug and irritating and staining properties of drug prompted encapsulation of dithranol in liposomes and niosomes as such vesicular systems would provide localized drug delivery there by reducing the total dose and dose dependent side effects like irritation and staining. In this study by Aagarwaal et al., liposomes and niosomes were prepared by thin film hydration technique using varying proportions of phosphatidyl choline and cholesterol incase of liposomes and Span 60 and cholesterol incase of niosomes keeping amount of charge inducer, dicetyl phosphate (imparts negative charge to vesicles and thus prevent aggregation) constant and the effectiveness of vesicular formulations was compared with cream formulation of same drug. Entrapment efficiency was found to increase from 2.0 mg/120 mg to 2.2 mg/ 140 mg to 3.0 mg/150 mg of total lipids on increasing cholesterol concentration while keeping DTH and PC concentrations constant. Authors attributed this increase in the entrapment efficiency to the anti-leak properties of cholesterol in the bilayer membranes, which in turn allow enhanced drug level in liposomes. Highest entrapment efficiency was obtained at equimolar ratios of cholesterol and phosphotidyl choline for liposomes.

Incase of niosomes, increasing Span 60 at constant levels of drug and cholesterol increased the amount of drug entrapped from 1.54 mg/174 mg to 1.86 mg/210 mg of total lipids. This is attributed to the increased solubility of drug in the lipophilic environment. However equimolar ratio of span 60 and cholesterol resulted in a decrease in drug loading and increasing amounts of cholesterol was found to damage the vesicular bilayer leading to drug leakage. The *in vitro* permeation study using mouse abdominal skin shows significantly enhanced permeation with vesicles as indicated by flux of dithranol from liposomes (23.13 mcg/cm^2/hour) and niosomes (7.78 mcgg/cm^2/hour) as compared with the cream base (4.10 g/ cm^2/hour).[116]

Ethosomes

Ethosomes are ethanolic liposomes comprising of about 45% alcohol. It is postulated that increased penetration enhancement effect by ethosomes is due to fluidization of ethosomal lipids with lipids of stratum corneum.

Dubey et al.,[117] prepared ethosomes of a hydrosoluble, anti-psoriatic and anti cancer drug methotrexate. Methotrexate (MTX) selectively inhibits DNA synthesis in psoriatic epidermal cells, thus decreasing mitotic activity. Topical administration of methotrexate would be advantageous in that several side effects associated with oral route (E.g., low bioavailability, interindividual variability, GI side effects like nausea and vomiting) are eliminated. Ethosomes prepared by mechanical dispersion were compared with conventional liposomes. Highest entrapment efficiency (68.71 ± 1.4%) was obtained for ethosomal formulations containing 3% phospholipid content and 45% ethanol. The greater entrapment of MT X in ethosomes (68.71 ± 1 .4%) as compared to conventional liposomes (53.1 ± 3.2%) might be due to the greater retentivity of MTX in ethanol present in ethosomal core. Optimal nanometric size range was obtained for the same formulation and was found to be (143 ± 16 nm). MTX loaded ethosomal carriers also provided an enhanced transdermal flux of 57.2 ± 4.34 μg/cm^2/hour and decreased lag time of 0.9 h across human cadaver skin. Skin permeation profile of the developed formulation further assessed by confocal laser scanning microscopy (CLSM) revealed an enhanced permeation of Rhodamine Red (RR) loaded formulations to the deeper layers of the skin (170 μm).

Topical photodynamic therapy (PDT) with 5-aminolevulinic acid (ALA) (a second-generation photosensitizer) is a safe and effective treatment option for psoriasis.[118] PDT acts by modulating cellular functions leading to induction of transcription factors (especially AP-1 and NF-κB) but not cellular death. PDT is a composite technique which basically requires three elements: a photosensitizer, light irradiation, and singlet oxygen. ALA is a form of prodrug, which release the photosensitizer component, protoporphyrin IX (PpIX), *in vivo* after the exogenous application of ALA. But ALA being hydrophilic exhibit poor skin penetration. To overcome this limitation, Yi-Ping Fang et al., formulated ALA as ethosomes using phosphatidylethanolamine as carrier by thin film hydration method to examine the penetration efficacy and observed a 5-26 fold increase in cumulative drug amounts in the healthy as well as psoriatic murine skin model compared to aqueous solution of ALA. CLSM technique have given additional clarification that the intensity of photosensitizer increased by 3.64-fold in psoriatic murine skin compared to aqueous solution of ALA.[119]

Transferosomes

Transferosomes[120] are ultra deformable, elastic liquid state vesicles comprising phospholipid and an edge activator which is usually a single chain surfactant molecule that destabilizes the lipid bilayers of the vesicles and increases their deformability by lowering the interfacial tension. This feature enable the transferosomes to squeeze through intercellular junctions. Transferosomes overcome the barrier resistance offered by skin to transport of actives as they open intercellular junctions and are capable of adjusting themselves to the confining channels through which they carry the drug to site of action.

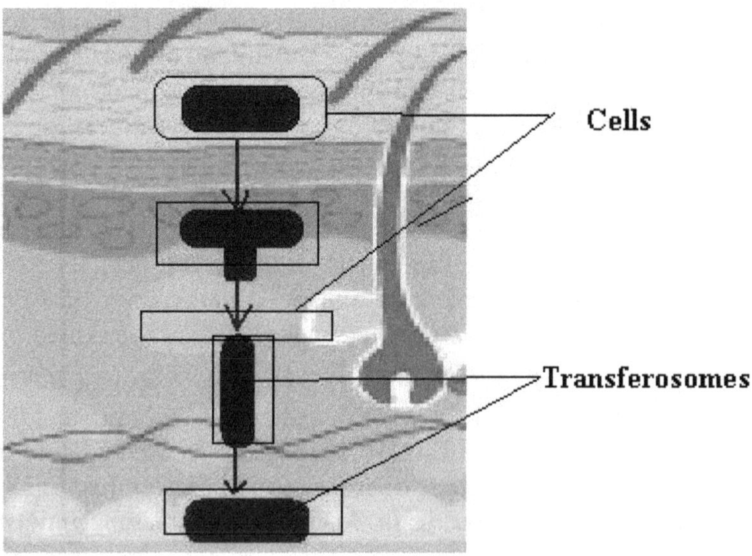

Fig. 7.3 Mechanism of permeation of transferosome through skin[111].

[Colour Fig. on page 405]

Gregor Cevc et al.,[121,122] studied the anti inflammatory activity which is proportional to site of action permeation of triamcinolone-acetonide formulated as transferosomes using polysorbate and soy phosphatidyl choline. Cream or lotion of the same drug was taken as reference. Trasferosomes resulted in high degree of drug localisation, thereby prolonging the duration of action over cream or lotion. The dose required to exert anti inflammatory effect through transferosomes was found to reduce by ten fold when compared to conventional cream or lotion.

Nanogel

Nanogels employ cross linked colloidal particles of 100 nm to 1 μm size responsive to various stimuli like change in temperature, ionic strength, and pH and hence potential as novel delivery systems. Nanogels can be produced from monomers like styrene, methyl methacrylate, divinylbenzene and thermo responsive N-isopropylacrylamide (NIPAM) monomer. The idea of drug delivery via nanogels have emerged from the concept that certain polymers (Eg: N-isopropylacrylamide) undergo swelling followed by volume collapse depending on the environment which they are in. Below lower critical solution temperature, polymer coils randomly due to salvation of linear polymer chain leading to hydrogen bond formation between solvent and amide side chain of polymer and subsequent swelling. As the temperature exceeds lower critical solution temperature, hydrogen bonds dissociate expelling the interior water and on macro scale when the polymer is cross linked by a cross linker this phenomenon appears as "volume collapse" and the corresponding temperature is known as volume phase transition temperature (VPTT). Hence nanogels absorb drug molecules during swelling phase and deliver during collapse phase.

Since topical therapy was proven to be effective and has its share of advantages for treatment of psoriasis, nanogels are being widely researched for delivery of anti-psoriatic agents.

Gillian et al.,[123] examined the penetration efficacy of methotrexate (MTX) loaded into polyNIPAM-co-BA nanogel in the presence of pH regulator sodium carbonate through heat-separated epidermal membranes *in vitro*, silastic membrane and ex vivo porcine skin in terms of reduction in the levels of key inflammatory mediator, prostaglandin E2 (PGE2) on assaying the skin models. Addition of saturated aqueous sodium carbonate lead to an increase in MTX flux from 1.4 ± 0.3 ng $cm^{-2}h^{-1}$ to 3.1 ± 0.22 ng $cm^{-2}h^{-1}$ ($p < 0.05$). Half saturated solution gave the same results. It was observed that nanogel demonstrated 7% de-swelling at

25°C-37°C. No permeation was observed across silastic membrane. PGE2 levels were reduced by 33% for MTX-nanogel but by 57% when MTX-nanogel was supplemented with saturated aqueous Na_2CO_3 ($p < 0.01$). Inclusion of sodium carbonate in the formulation presumably increased the solubility of released drug during gel collapse thereby increasing the concentration gradient and hence the flux.

Priya et al.,[124] examined the additive effect of nanospheres dispersed in hydrophilic gels along with penetration enhancers like azone on the permeation of lipophilic actives into the skin and their localization in skin layers using diclofenac sodium to optimize gel formulation variables and fluorescent nile red for *in vitro* and *in vivo* skin distribution studies as model compounds so that this type of nanogels can be fabricated for the delivery of drugs for the treatment of cancers, psoriasis and other skin diseases. Tyrosine nanospheres were dispersed in hydrophilic polymers like carbopol and HPMC. Nanopsheres dispersed in 1% w/v HPMC gave gel with desired rheological properties that is free from cellular toxicity or tissue irritation. *In vitro* permeation studies in human cadaver skin revealed a 1.4 and 1.8 fold increase in the deposition of Nile Red in upper and lower epidermis respectively, was observed with nanospheres dispersed in gel when compared to aqueous nanosphere formulation. *In vivo* studies also showed a 1.4 fold increase in permeation of nile red from naosphere gel compared to its aqueous counterpart through porcine stratum corneum/epidermis. An additional 1.4 fold has been achieved by using azone in the nanosphere gel formulation.

Tretinoin is associated with skin irritation and has low water solubility and is unstable in the presence of air, light and heat despite its potential in treating skin disorders including psoriasis. Sagar et al., explored solid lipid nanogel of tretinoin using microemulsion technique and compared it with marketed product in terms of skin irritancy, skin tolerance, occlusivity and drug release. Results have shown that sln nanogel performed better than marketed product. Entrapment efficiency of about 46% was achieved with novel lipid carriers like highly purified grade stearine fractions derived from natural lipids (MK St and KFSt). Also a mean particle size < 100 nm has been achieved with novel SLN gels.[125]

The potential of tretinoin nanocapsules embedded in carbopol hydrogels as a delivery system was investigated in a study. Polycaprolactone based tretinoin nanocapsules were prepared by interfacial deposition of preformed polymer. Nanocapsules embedded in carbopol hydrogel were evaluated for spreadability, skin localization and stability in comparision with marketed cream formulation, VITANOL-A.

The hydrogel demonstrated non Newtonian behavior which is desirable in terms of restricting the flow of preparation when applied and also superior spreadability compared to marketed product. Also nanogels demonstrated lower photodegradation compared to nanosuspensions of tretinoin and the marketed cream. Lag time with nano encapsulation was found to increase by two folds indicating retention of drug for longer time on the skin surface.[126]

Microemulsion

Microemulsions are thermodynamically stable, transparent colloidal dispersions of oil and water which are stabilized by surfactants and co-surfactants and are characterized by spontaneous formation without requiring energy input. The drug delivery potential and solubilization potential of microemulsions make them attractive colloidal carrier systems for highly lipophilic drugs.

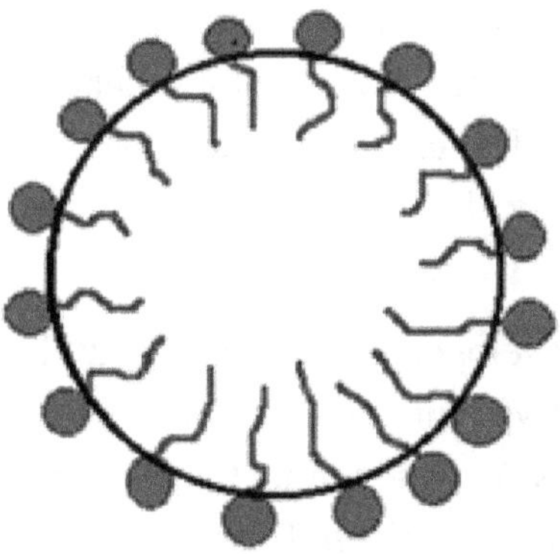

(a)

(b)

Fig 7.4 Cross-section of (a) nanoemulsion and (b) biopolymeric nanoparticle.[127]

[Colour Fig. on page 406]

Goebel et al.,[128] investigated the potential of microemulsion carrier systems for the topical delivery of immunosuppressant drug, tacrolimus compared to approved tacrolimus ointment, Protopic. Tacrolimus being highly lipophilic is not an amenable drug candidate for topical delivery. Hence the authors attempted to formulate a hydrophilic carrier with high solubilization potential an attribute possessed by oil in water microemulsion. Microemulsions were prepared using skin tolerable surfactants like lecithin and alkylpolyglucosides (APG), a group of biodegradable, non-ionic and non-ethoxylated surfactants. As cosufactants, 1,2-alkanediols (1,2-Pentylene glycol) were incorporated due to their influence on curvature and fluidity of interface which in turn would reduce the interfacial tension. Dibutyl adipate (Cetiol B) constituted the lipophilic phase. Results from *ex vivo* skin permeation studies revealed that about 20.95 ± 12.03% of tacrolimus (sum of the amount found in the dermis and acceptor compartment) was bioavailable from microemulsion formulations after incubation for 1000 minute whereas marketed topical ointment of tacrolimus used as control gave only concentration of 6.41 ± 0.57%.

Baroli et al.,[129] developed a novel microemulsion for 8-methoxsalen (8-MOP), a photoactive furocumarin derivative used for psoralen plus long wavelength UVA irradiation to overcome several limitations associated with the active moiety. Topical administration of psoralen for psoriatic treatment leads to hyper pigmentation and a phototoxic response. Also psoralen has poor oral bioavailability due to its low water solubility and first pass metabolism. All these factors necessitate development of topical formulations with good clinical efficacy and lower toxic effects. Microemulsions were prepared using water, isopropyl myristate, Tween 80: Span 80:1,2-Octanediol (3:1:1.2 w/w) as surfactant and co-surfactant mixture. *In vitro* permeation studies revealed a 1.9-4.5 fold increase in the 8-MOP total penetration through the skin compared to penetration enhancer like isopropyl myristate. Also the prepared microemulsions were found to achieve a 1.5-4.5 fold increase in the skin accumulation of 8-MOP.

Microneedle roller for psoriasis therapy

Microneedles[130] are micron sized sharp projections fabricated onto the polymer patch to affect the drug absorption via skin. The projections of the microneedle when pressed against skin, puncture small holes through the skin through which drug permeates and thus enhance the passage of drugs through the skin. However, due to inherent limitations with microneedles like the difficulty in application of microneedle to large surface area of skin led to the development of polymer microneedle rollers which are much easier to apply to large skin areas by just rolling them during which microneedle will puncture holes into the skin many times.

Metal microneedles; microneedles prepared by etching or press work; polymer microneedles produced by micro embossing process are few of the microneedle variants. Metal microneedle rollers conventionally prepared with stainless steel, were developed for multiple use purposes, and had the limitation of difficulty in cleaning them after each use.

Current design of polymer microneedles is based on fabrication of individual rows of microneedles followed by their assembly into two-dimensional arrays. The process involves UV crosslinking of needle material, hot embossing of general purpose polymer and hand assembly of microneedle arrays on a roller.

Park et al., fabricated a new polymer microneedle roller through one step process using a replicated polymer film to provide a simple way to increase skin permeability. The novel process involves micromolding a master structure generated by inclined rotational UV lithography and mounting the replicate film with PLA microneedles and CMC microneedles onto a cylindrical roller. Drug delivery through PLA microneedles proceeded via two step process which includes piercing holes in the skin followed by application of a topical formulation like naoparticles that delivers the drug through holes made in the skin. Whereas CMC microneedles delivered the drug by instant local surface erosion immediately after the insertion of microneedles into the skin.

The amount of drug administered into the skin is determined by the number of holes, which can be controlled by the microneedle roller design and the number of times it is rolled on the skin, as well as the drug concentration, formulation and other factors.

Only a small application force was found to be sufficient to pierce hole into skin as in the novel design microneedles were pressed sequentially into the skin row by row than pressing all at once as is the case with microneedle patch and hence promote entry and lateral diffusion of a small molecule and polymeric nanoparticles. Drug delivery through polymeric microneedle rollers can be exploited for the treatment of diseases involving large areas of skin like psoriasis as these microneedle rollers allow the application of drugs to such wider skin areas. Only limitation observed with the novel roller design is partial mechanical failure of needles at the boundary of the roller due to angle of force applied. Hence geometry of microneedle determining mechanical strength of needle is a factor to be considered during fabrication.

Solid lipid naoparticles

Delivery of drugs through barrier skin layer, stratum corneum is often promoted by the use of penetration enhancers. Due to safety concerns and poor performance of penetration enhancing systems at low concentration levels, alternative systems like micro and naodispersions like solid lipid nanoparticles (SLN) and nanostructured lipid carriers (NLC) are now being studied extensively.

Solid lipid nanoparticles[131] and NLCs are dispersions of lipid cores containing dissolved or dispersed drug with their surface embedded with surfactant molecules. One feature that distinguishes SLNs from NLCs is that the former is made of lipids solid at room temperature whereas the latter comprises of both solid and liquid lipids. NLCs are mainly designed to increase the room for drug incorporation which is created by asymmetric structures of lipid mixture. Solid lipids such as glycerol behenate (Compritol® 888 ATO), glycerol palmitostearate (Precirol® ATO 5), or the wax cetyl palmitate have been used as lipid carriers. Nanolipid carriers being able to promote lipid exchange between lipids of the skin and the particulate carriers enhance the drug permeability through skin. Having such potential to penetrate skin, lipid nanocarriers offer a new treatment option for skin diseases like psoriasis.

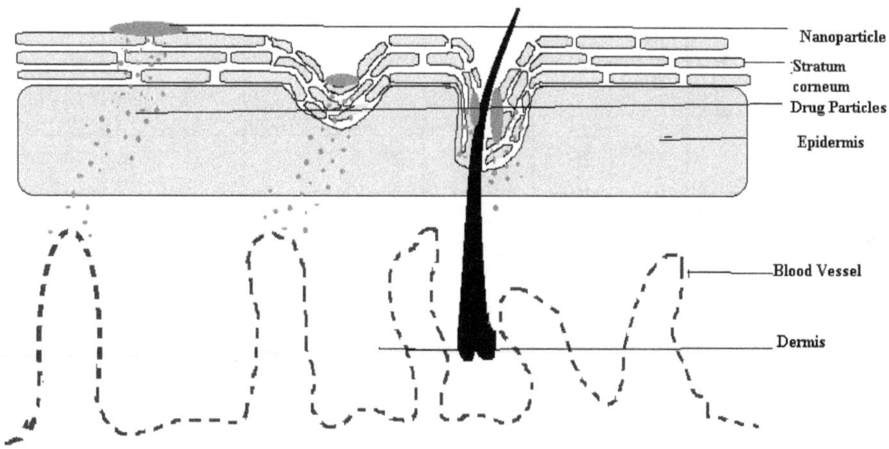

Fig. 7.5 Topical nanoparticle delivery through skin.[127]
[Colour Fig. on page 406]

Tacrolimus[132] an antipsoriatic drug has been formulated as modified nanolipid carriers (MNLC) and their gel forms with glyceryl trimyristate as lipid and propylene glycol monocaprylate as lipophilic solubilizer. MNLCs were prepared by hot homogenization method. Further MNLCs were incorporated into gels by using carbopol 980 as gelling agent. The developed formulation was found to be superior in terms of drug loading, stability, invitro release and biodistribution when compared to SLN formulation or marketed product, Protopic. Inclusion of solubilizer was found to increase the entrapment efficiency of the drug upto 96.66% due to formation of imperfect lipid structures offering more space for drug accommodation. Increased stability of MNLC was attributed to reduction in the amount of total lipid concentration which could otherwise lead to gelation of the system. T-MNLC-enriched gels showed significantly superior skin penetration and localized skin bio distribution as revealed by localized radioactivity in the skin during gamma scintigraphy studies in albino rats. Draize primary skin irritation test on albino rabbits showed significantly lower skin irritation potential of tacrolimus MNLCs (T-MNLC) compared to reference. Also T-MNLC gel showed better invitro release profile compared to marketed product.

Table 7.8 Various colloidal carriers used as topical drug delivery system in the treatment of Psoriasis[133-145]

Formulations	Drug	Application of colloidal carrier	Method of preparation	/*In vitro*/Animal/human volunteer/patient study	Reference
Niosomes	Methotrexate	Improved transdermal penetration	Thin layer hydration and sonication	human volunteer/patient study	133-135
Niosomes	Urea	Improved transdermal penetration	Tansmembrane pH gradient method	human volunteer/patient study	136
Niosomes	Methotrexate & urea combination	Improved transdermal penetration	Thin layer hydration and sonication ,Tansmembrane pH gradient method	human volunteer/patient study	137
Liposomes incorporated in polyacrylate gel	Betamethasone dipropionate	Higher anti-inflammatory action compared to cream and no anti-proliferative effect was observed.	Liposomes in polyacrylate gel	human volunteer/patient study	113
Niosomes and liposomes	Dithranol	Improvement in photostability and reduction of irritating and staining properties of drug	Thin film hydration technique	*In vitro* permeation study	116
Niosomes and liposomes	Urea	Improved penetration	Lipid hydration method	Patient study	138

Table 7.8 *Contd...*

Formulations	Drug	Application of colloidal carrier	Method of preparation	/*In vitro*/Animal/human volunteer/patient study	Reference
Transferosomes	Triamcinolone acetonide	Drug localization and dose reduction compared to conventional cream or lotion	Solvent dispersion	*In vivo* biodistribution study	121, 122
Ethosomes	Methotrexate	Improved transdermal penetration & to avoid systemic side effects	Mechanical dispersion method	*In vitro* permeation study	117
Ethosomes	5aminolevulinic acid (ALA)	Improvement in penetration of hydrophilic ALA	Thin film hydration	*In vitro* permeation study	119
Liposomal gel	Temoporfin	Improve the stability of drug containing hydrogels	Hydrophilic gel	Stability studies	139
Lipid coated microparticles	Coal tar	To overcome skin irritation and staining in scalp psoriasis	Lipid coated microparicles by condendation	Animal study (antipsoriatic activity in mouse tail model of psoriasis.	140
Solid lipid nano particles	Methotrexate	Improved transdermal penetration & to avoid systemic side effects	hot microemulsion congealing technique	Patient study	141
Gel	Methotrexate/ azone	Improved transdermal penetration and to avoid systemic side effects	Hydrophilic gel	Patient study	142

Table 7.8 *Contd...*

Formulations	Drug	Application of colloidal carrier	Method of preparation	/*In vitro*/Animal/human volunteer/patient study	Reference
Gel	Methotrexate	Improved transdermal penetration & to avoid systemic side effects	Hydrophilic gel	Patient study	143
Nanogel	Tretinoin	Improved stability and skin tolerance with reduced irritation potential	Microemulsion technique	*In vivo* study in rabbits	125
Solid lipid nanoparticles	Tacrolimus	Iimprovement in drug loading, stability, invitro release and biodistribution	Hot homogenization followed by incorporation into gel	Biodistribution study albino rats and skin irritation study in rabbits	132
Microemulsion	Tacrolimus	Improvement in solubility of highly lipophilic drug for topical delivery	Microemulsion	*Ex vivo* skin permeation study	128
Microemulsion	8methoxsalen	Improvement in bioavailability and reduction in hyperpigmentation potential and phototoxic response of drug	Microemulsion	*In vitro* permeation studies	129
Iontophoresis	Methotrexate	Improvement in skin penetration of drug	Hydrogels	*In vitro* study	144
Solution	Methotrexate	Transdermal penetration	50% propylene glycol mixture	*In vitro* study	145

Nail delivery

Nail psoriasis is common in 80% of patients who suffer from skin psoriasis. However 1-5% of patients may not experience an overt skin disease. Nail psoriasis can lead to pitting of nail plates, fragile nails that tend to crumble easily or onycholysis (separation of the nail plate from the nail bed, which may be focal or distal), subungual hyperkeratosis and splinter haemorrhages depending upon whether the area effected is nail matrix or nail bed respectively. Psoriasis of nail folds results in inflamed and swollen nail folds a condition termed as paronychia leading to ridging of the nail plate. Nail psoriasis is a condition that requires chronic treatment that should be strictly maintained as relapse is common. Current treatment options available for nail psoriasis are corticosteroid injections into nail folds; oral therapy with agents such as, methotrexate, etretinate, and cyclosporine. However limitations associated with current treatment options like pain on injection, systemic adverse reactions to oral therapy, alternative mechanisms for the delivery of actives is being investigated and nail delivery has been widely studied in particular.

Drug has to cross barriers like keratinized nail plate (which has low permeability to drug molecules) for it to permeate through nail bed and nail matrix. Drug permeation can be assisted by removing a part of this barrier. This can be done by physical and chemical means.

Physical methods

Clinical studies of Lauharanta et al.[146] and Kobayashi et al.[147] have shown that filing dorsal nail plate (which is practically possible compared to ventral plate) there by removing part of nail plate was found to promote drug permeation after application of formulation.

Chemical methods

Chemical methods i.e. use of penetration enhancers target and destabilize the keratin by breaking down disulphide, peptide, hydrogen and polar bonds there by damage the integrity of barrier layer. Chemical agents can be broadly classified under two categories:

(i) ***Softening agents:*** urea and salicylic acid, which soften nail plates

(ii) ***Keratolyticc agents:*** sulfhydryl compounds such as cysteine which cleave the disulphide linkages of nail proteins and destabilize the keratin structure.

Softening agents

Nail plate is comparable to a concentrated hydrogel that permeates molecules.[148] Softening agents act by hydrating and softening the nail plate there by reducing the density of nail plate hydrogel creating large pores that would promote diffusion of the drug molecules.

Ex vivo experiments[147] showed enhanced permeation of antifungal, bifonazole, from a bifonazole/urea ointment through infected (onychomycoses) human toenails and a change in the morphology of fungal cells was also observed after 5 days of treatment (application of the ointment on the dorsal nail surface while the corneocyte layers disintegrated due to the urea.

However softening agents alone were not found to be effective as nail penetration enhancers as reported in several studies. Penetration of antifungal agents like miconazole, ketoconazole and itraconazole) into nails was not enhanced when urea was used at 40% in the formulation or when nails were soaked in 20% w/ v salicylic acid solution for 10 days prior to permeation studies.[148] Also the penetration of 5-FU was found to be reduced when urea and sodium salicylate were included in the formulations inspite of increased swelling of nail plate[149].

Keratolytic agents

Compound containing sulfhydryl groups (e.g., acetylcysteine, cysteine, mercaptoethanol) were found to be more effective as nail penetration enhancers when compared to softeners as the sulfhydryl groups in these compounds reduce the disulfide bonds in the nail proteins and destabilize the keratin network thereby permeating drug molecules. Acetyl cysteine alone or in combination with softening agents like urea enhanced the permeation of antifungals like itraconazole.[150] Urea unfolds the keratin structure thus promoting cleavage of disulfide bonds by acetyl cysteine. Drug penetration was found to increase linearly with increase in the amount of acetyl cysteine.

In a left-right study design, acetylcysteine promoted the penetration of oxiconazole into the middle layer of nail from 1% w/v oxiconazole lotion (with or without acetylcysteine, 15% w/v) applied to ring and middle fingers of healthy volunteers, twice daily for 6 weeks.[151] Residence time in the middle layer was increased from 4.2 to 5.5 weeks in the presence of acetylcysteine.

Papain an endopeptidase enzyme containing highly reactive sulfhydryl group has shown promising results as penetration agent. Papain increased the flux of antimycotic agents, miconazole nitrate, ketoconazole nitrate and itraconazole nitrate in decreasing order through the nail plates pre soaked in a phosphate buffer containing papain (15% w/v) for 1 day, followed by soaking in salicylic acid solution (20% w/v) for 10 days. The decreasing order of flux for miconazole nitrate, ketoconazole nitrate and itraconazole nitrate through nail plates is in accordance with the increasing molecular weight of the actives.

Nail lacquer-drug delivery systems

Nail lacquer drug delivery systems incorporate drug within the nail lacquers commonly used in nail paints. Conventional nail lacquers generally consist of solvents; film forming polymers, resins to increase film adhesion to nail plate; plasticisers to confer flexibility and durability to the film formed and to increase the viscosity of preparation which makes it "applicable". Such a system when applied to the nail plate, forms a water insoluble film (containing drug dissolved or dispersed in a monolithic matrix) adhering to the nail plate due to the evaporation of organic solvent. The drug is then slowly released from the film due to the concentration gradient between original lacquer preparation taken on to the applicator and lacquer film formed after solvent evaporation. Drug concentration in the latter being greater than former, promotes drug diffusion and penetration into the nail plate and the nail bed. Also the film formed on the nail plate hyperhydrates the upper nail layers by exerting shielding effect to water loss from nail surface.

Formulation factors influencing drug delivery through nail:

- Molecular size of drug
- Partition coefficient of drug
- Solubility of the drug in the polymer film
- Solubility of drug in the nail
- Diffusion coefficient of drug in the polymer film
- Diffusion coefficient of drug in the nail plate
- Drug content in the film

Clinical studies demonstrating efficacy of drug containing nail lacquers

Ciclopirox at concentrations above the inhibitory and fungicidal concentrations of most pathogens was found to penetrate all the layers of the toe nail after repeated applications as by Bohn and Kraemer.[152]

In two double-blind, vehicle-controlled multicentre studies conducted by Gupta et al.[153] to evaluate the efficacy of cicloprox in onychomycosis caused by dermatophytes, ciclopirox nail lacquer 8% was found to give a higher mycologic cure rate compared to placebo when the lacquer was applied daily for 48 weeks.

Lauharanta[146] evaluated the effectiveness of 2% concentration of amorolfine against 5% amorolfine concentration in the treatment of onychomycosis in a double-blind, randomized study. The lacquer was applied once a week for up to 6 months. The response among the patients for 2% amorolfine Vs 5% amorolfine was 12% cure, 55% improvement in the nail, 33% failure Vs 38% cure, 32% improvement and 30% failure. Increasing the frequency of application from once weekly to twice weekly gave improved response that was statistically insignificant.[155]

In another double blind placebo controlled study, Baran and Tosti[156] reported improved therapeutic response on increasing the duration of treatment with clobetasol-17-propionate nail lacquer system for the topical treatment of nail psoriasis.

Table 7.9 Nail drug delivery system.

S.No	Marketed nail drug delivery system	Manufacturer	Approval date	Formulation	Dosage and Administration
1	Loceryl®	Galderma	1992	Clear, colourless liquid and contains the antifungal **amorolfine (5%)**, Eudragit RL 100, glycerol triacetate, butyl acetate, ethyl acetate and ethanol.	Applied 1 – 2 times weekly to infected nail plates for up to 6 months (fingernails) and 9 – 12 months for toe nails
2	Penlac®	SANOFI AVENTIS US	1999	Clear, colourless liquid, it contains the antifungal agent **ciclopirox (8%)**, ethyl acetate, isopropanol and butylmonoester of poly (methyl vinyl ether/maleic acid).	Applied once daily, for up to 48 weeks. The film is removed every 7 days, with alcohol before re-application of the lacquer.

Codrug approach

Codrug or mutual prodrug refers to combination of two or more drugs wherein drugs as active groups (rather than inactive groups as in prodrug approach) are directly or indirectly (e.g., a cleavable spacer) bonded together by a covalent linkage. Codrug approach is gaining increasing popularity as codrugs were found to provide improved absorption rate when compared to individual drugs or prodrugs and due to ease with which they can be transported to the target site of action. However the resulting codrug should be stable in gastrointestinal conditions at the same time should be hydrolysable to give the individual drug moieties. Carrier in codrug should be biologically active, nontoxic, nonantigenic, and chemically stable and should have adequate loading capacity and should not accumulate in the body.

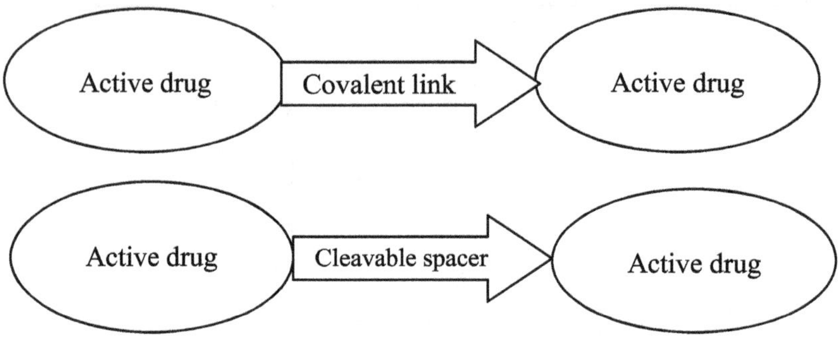

Fig 7.6 Codrug approach.

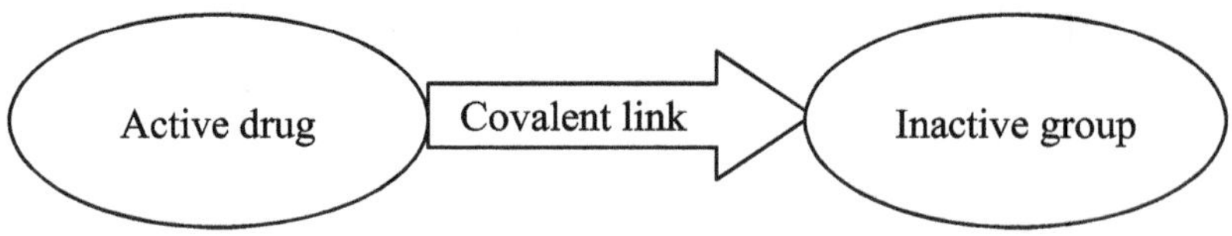

Fig 7.7 Prodrug approach.

In the treatment of psoriasis, codrug concept has been exploited by Ben-Shabat et al.[157] The authors have prepared codrug of linolenic acid and calcipotriol by condensing linolenic acid (18:3n -3 PUFA) or γ-linolenic acid (18:3n-6 PUFA) with calcipotriol. The resulting acyl ester codrug resulted in better penetration followed by formation of more dermally active drug through transesterification and ester hydrolysis of the penetrating esters to new bioforms/isomers.[158]

Prodrugs used in psoriasis treatment

A Prodrug is a pharmacologically inactive compound which upon enzymatic cleavage or chemical transformation *in vivo*, yields a pharmacologically active compound.

Mycophenolate mofetil

Mycophenolate mofetil (MMF)[159] is the prodrug of mycophenolic acid (MPA), a medication used to treat psoriasis in the 1970s until side effects and the concern of carcinogenesis led to its discontinuation. The prodrug, MMF, emerged decades later in the transplant field. Dermatologists have since used MMF off-label to treat various inflammatory skin conditions, with most research concentrating on its use in psoriasis, autoimmune blistering disorders, dermatitis, and connective tissue disorders. The appeal of MMF is predicated upon its lymphocyte specificity and consequent decreased toxicity profile. These attributes may make it a preferable treatment option. Its use in the field of dermatology is currently limited by a lack of randomized controlled trials, potential unknown side effects, and cost of treatment.

Tazarotene

Tazarotene[160] is a pro-drug of the more water soluble tazarotenic acid. Tazarotene is a topical, receptor-selective retinoid vitamin A analog used to manage stable plaque psoriasis, acne vulgaris. Parent drug, tazarotenic acid does not interconvert to any other retinoids that could potentially activate other retinoid receptors. In psoriasis, tazarotene normalizes keratinocyte differentiation, reverses keratinocyte hyperproliferation and has anti-inflammatory effects. Tazarotene is efficacious as monotherapy, but is more commonly used in combination with phototherapy or with a topical corticosteroid in order to enhance efficacy and tolerability.

In October 2001, the US FDA approved Tazorac® cream 0.1% (tazarotene, Allergan) for the treatment of acne vulgaris. Since 1997, Tazorac® gel (0.05% and 0.1%) has been available for the treatment of stable plaque psoriasis and the 0.1% gel is also indicated for the treatment of mild-to-moderately severe facial acne vulgaris. Tazorac® cream (0.05% and 0.1%) was approved by the US FDA in 2000 for the treatment of plaque psoriasis.

5-Fluorouracil (5FU) prodrugs

5-FU an antipsoriatic drug is usually administered by intravenous route. However 85% of injected dose is deactivated by dihydropyrimidine dehydrogenase (DPD) and hence in patients with higher DPD activity, 5-FU treatment results in low bioavailability and in patients with low DPD activity it would lead to 5-FU toxicity. Hence administration of 5-FU prodrugs to overcome these limitations is being explored. The 5-FU prodrugs that have been found to be useful for treatment of psoriasis in humans are capecitabine (N^4-pentyloxycarbonyl-5′-deoxy-5-fuorocytidine), 5-fluoro-pyrimidinone (5-FP), TS-1 (S-1, ftorafur), FdUMP, 1-(2′-oxopropyl)-5-FU, and alkyl-carbonyl-5-FU. The preferred 5-FU prodrug for use in psoriasis therapy is capecitabine.

Capecitabine[161] is a prodrug of the antimetabolite 5-FU, crosses the gastrointestinal barrier intact, and is rapidly and almost completely absorbed. Unlike 5-FU, capecitabine can be given orally thus making hospitalization required for 5-FU IV therapy unnecessary. This increases patient compliance as patients are exempted from bearing pain due to intravenous injections. Since such prodrugs can be taken orally, risk of local infection and/or thrombophlebitis due to intravenous catheterization is minimized. Capecitabine can be given effectively by non-pulse and pulse dosing. For non-pulse dosing used in the treatment of psoriasis, the effective amount of capecitabine is between 100 and 2500 milligrams per square meter of body surface area per day.[162] Pulse dosing refers to the administration of drug doses in "pulses" or "intervals" wherein first dose administered is allowed to clear from patient's body before next dose is given. In case of pulsed dosing regimen for capecitabine, an amount of capecitabine in between 100 and 5000 milligrams per square meter of body surface area is given orally daily for one week followed by an interval of drug free one week period and this one week cycle is repeated. The amount of drug given, duration of drug administration and duration of drug free period are usually individualized for patients to minimize the occurrence of adverse events.

Capecitabine itself causes a skin disease known as hand-foot syndrome which involves erythema, pain and ulceration, surprisingly is found effective in the treatment of psoriasis.

PUFA prodrugs

Lipophilic prodrugs of actives by deriveatizing with fatty acids for the topical treatment of psoriasis are being explored. For topical therapy in particular, the resulting prodrugs should increase the skin permeability after which the prodrug should be liable for enzymatic cleavage releasing active drug. So far short chain saturated carboxylic acids are used as derivatizing agents in developing prodrugs. Extensive studies are still to be done on the use of long chain polyunsaturated fatty acids (PUFA) which are widely used in the treatment of psoriasis are still to done though long chain saturated fatty acids (palmitate, stearate) have demonstrated their ability as lipophilic prodrugs with penetration enhancing properties.

Advantages:

1. PUFA prodrugs are more lipophilic than parent compounds thereby enhancing their penetration and hence bioavailability.
2. PUFA like γ-linolenic acid (GLA) themselves are known to exert anti inflammatory, anticancer and cardiovascular effects.

Acidic drugs like theophylline can be linked to PUFA. Theophylline[163] can be directly attached to PUFA by N-acyl derivatives. Theophylline, an anti asthmatic can also be used in the treatment of psoriasis due to its proven anti-inflammatory property (acts by elevating cAMP levels). However due to its short half life and narrow therapeutic range, it is associated with limitations like repeated administration of drug and toxic drug levels in plasma. Hence theophylline is administered topically to overcome these limitations.

7.9 Investigational Drugs of Psoriasis

Most of the psoriasis therapy revolves around drugs which are used to suppress immunity to treat this autoimmune disorder. These therapies are nonspecific. The future of posriasis therapies lies in use of biological agents and the development is focused on T lymphocyte and its cytokines. The mode of action of biologics have been categorized as that

- reduce the number of pathogenic T cells;
- inhibit T-cell activation and migration;
- act as immune modifiers; and
- block the activity of inflammatory cytokines.

There are other therapies aimed at antiangiogenesis and nuclear hormone receptors.

Table 7.10 The other investigational drugs in pipeline[164].

Condition	Intervention	Phase
Psoriasis Parapsoriasis	Drug: Infliximab	Phase III
Nail Psoriasis Plaque Psoriasis	Drug: etanercept	Phase IV
Plaque Psoriasis Psoriasis Vulgaris	Drug: Taclonex Ointment and Hydrogel Patch Drug: Taclonex Ointment	Phase IV
Psoriasis	NCT00096928	Phase IV
Psoriasis	Drug: acitretin	Phase IV
Psoriasis	Drug: apremilast	Phase II
Psoriasis	Drug: etanercept / placebo Drug: placebo / etanercept	Phase IV
Psoriasis	Device: NB-UVB Drug: Etanerept Drug: Etanercept	Phase IV
Psoriasis Parapsoriasis	Drug: Infliximab	Phase III
Psoriasis	Drug: Imiquimod Drug: Clobetasol (glucosteroid) Device: Excimer laser (UVB light) treatment	-
A Pilot Study of Topical Antiflammin-2 for Psoriasis	NCT00001371	-
Atopic Dermatitis Psoriasis	Drug: Vitamin D3 Drug: Placebo	Phase II
Psoriasis	Drug: Ciclosporin 0.5% (Formulation 01B) Drug: Ciclosporin 1.5% (Formulation 02B) Drug: 0.1% betamethasone Drug: 0.005% calcipotriol Drug: Formulation 00B	Phase I Phase II
Psoriasis Vulgaris	Drug: LEO90100 cutaneous spray, ointment Drug: Daivobet®/Taclonex® ointment Drug: LEO 90100 cutaneous spray, ointment, vehicle with betamethasone dipropionate Drug: LEO 90100 cutaneous spray, ointment, vehicle Drug: Daivobet® ointment	Phase II

Table 7.10 *Contd...*

Condition	Intervention	Phase
Psoriasis Vulgaris	Drug: Combination of clobetasol propionate plus calcipotriol ointment, clobetasol propionate ointment, calcipotriol ointment, and the ointment vehicle	Phase I
Psoriasis	Drug: Chondroitin sulphate	Phase IV
Psoriasis	Biological: infliximab	Phase III
Psoriasis	Drug: Aminopterin	Phase I
Psoriasis	Biological: adalimumab	Phase II Phase III
Psoriasis	Drug: Etanercept	Phase III
Psoriasis	Drug: adalimumab	Phase III
Psoriasis	Drug: Methotrexate and Etanercept Drug: Etanercept ONLY	Phase III
Psoriasis	Drug: Etanercept	Phase IV
Psoriasis	Drug: Transitioning patients from cyclosporine to alefacept	Phase II
Psoriasis	Biological: ENBREL (entanercept)	Phase IV
Psoriasis	Drug: efalizumab Drug: placebo	Phase IV
Psoriasis	Biological: Humira (adalimumab)	Phase III
Psoriasis	Drug: Tacrolimus Cream	Phase III
Psoriasis	Drug: Raptiva (efalizumab)	Phase III
Psoriasis	Drug: Infliximab	Phase III
Psoriasis	Drug: Etanercept	Phase III
Psoriasis	Drug: Etanercept plus tacrolimus	Phase II
Psoriasis	Drug: Mechanism of action of alefacept	Phase II
Psoriasis	Drug: Talarozole	Phase II
Psoriasis	Drug: adalimumab Drug: MTX Drug: placebo adalimumab, placebo MTX	Phase III

7.10 Regulatory Aspects Anti-Psoriatic Drugs

In the present era, application of translational research in skin diseases are widening and integration of humanized xenotransplantation disease models with experimental clinical studies are focused. Many of the auto immune diodres can be evaluated in these models. These models can be useful in understanding visible disease, detailed histological, cellular and genomic features for investigational analysis.[165,166]

Many of the pharmacological *in vivo* models for skin diseases are not a true representation of cellular and molecular level of human skin diseases. But xenotransplantation of normal or affected skin from patients has the advantage of tissue from human containing relevant biological materials for investigation. Xenotransplatation models have been used very widely in psoriasis for the discovery new molecules in treatment of psoriasis. The human psoriasis xenograft SCID mouse model[167] split skin or full thicknessskin biopsies of chronic plaque stage psoriasis are transplanted on to SCID mouse. These graft survives and maintain the psoriatic phenotype for six to eight weeks. This time would be ideal time for testing the test molecule. Histologicl studies would reveal the antipsoriatic effect.

Correlation between anti-psoriatic mouse model and clinical efficacy of drugs like calcipotriol, 1a,25-dihydroxycholecalciferol, dexamethasone, clobetasol propionate, betamethasone dipropionate, cyclosporine A, efalizumab, infliximab are well documentated. Regulatory authorities permit experimental clinical studies without extensive preclinical package in psoriasis. A new microdosing technique has been in to practice without traditional preclinical package. The patients can be involved in testing of new molecules (FDA guidance (FDA guidance on exploratory, investigational new drug application [49] and the position paper 'Nonclinical Safety Studies to support Clinical Trials with a Single Microdose' published by the European Medicines Agency.[168] The purpose of this guideline is to determine the pharmacokinetic properties of the new drugs up on systemic administration but at a level that it should not produce any pharmacological or toxic adverse effects. The same principle is extended to dermatological drugs. Microdosing of the new drug molecule can be applied to localized area in the skin to achieve required pharmacological effect. This can be tested *in vitro* for penetration and induction of systemic side effects. Regulatory authorities endorse this type of studies and this studies would provide an important tool in drug discovery process in dermatology.[169]

Formulation of noveldrug delivery sytems like nanoparticles for skin possess lot of toxicity issues. Repeated trauma from nanoparticles could lead to squamous metaplasia dysplasia and neoplasia of epithelial linings. Diseases like psoriasis can cause skin more permeable.skin care products are aimed for treating damaged or diseased skin and often they contain penetration enhancers. To date, manufacturers have not published the degree or depth of penetration of nanomaterials in their products. Hence any novel drug delivery system should approach in the development of toxicity free formulations rather than focusing only on penetration and treatment temporarily without analyzing the long term effects.[170,171]

The future of dermatological drugs lies in application of biomarkers in humanized xenotransplantation models and experimental clinical studies in the context of translational research will improve experimental disease models. These models will be more predictive to the clinical outcome rather than traditional studies and thereby reduce cost for more comprehensive preclinical safety testing and efficacy trials and reduce the failure rate due to lack of efficacy for the benefit of patients and society.

7.11 Conclusion

Psoriasis though a common auto immune skin disorder draws its attention which necessitates treatment as the disease can affect various parts of body i.e. from scalps to palm and soles. Also considering the co morbid conditions like kidney disease and diabetes and the social stigma to be faced by patient that in turn will have an influence his/her psychological state, there is an urgent need to treat psoriasis. Increasing awareness of psoriasis treatment among patients can be realized by case studies of patients switching to complementary alternative treatment options like phototherapy, herbal treatment, laser, surgical methods in addition to conventional medicines.

Current therapy options include delivery of active agents via systemic and topical routes. Patients often experience serious side effects associated with actives delivered through systemic route or in the form of conventional creams and lotions. Development of effective agents which can completely “cure” rather than “suppress” the disease and effective delivery of available antipsoriatic drugs are the challenges lying ahead to be met for the successful management of psoriasis. Recent developments in drug discovery and drug delivery have to some extent met these challenges. Protein based molecules like alefacept, efalizumab, etanercept, and infliximab are synthesized to act selectively on components of immune system so that there is no excessive immune suppression. Novel drug delivery systems like lipid vesicles, nanoparticles, novel gels, micremulsions, iontophoretic techniques, nail drug delivery have resulted in successful encapsulation of several effective but difficult to permeate, unstable and irritable drugs surpassing all the limitations. Also several agents are being screened for their effectiveness in psoriasis treatment and are in clinical trials and this is a positive sign for the development of more effective molecules with less side effects.

References

1. Johann E. Gudjonsson, James T. Elder, *Psoriasis: Epidemiology Clinics in Dermatology* 2007; **25**: 535–546.
2. Shao CG, Zhang GW, Wang GC. Distribution of psoriasis in China: anationwide screening. *Proc Chin Acad Med Sci Peking Union Med Coll* 1987; **2**:59-65.
3. Braathen LR, Botten G, Bjerkedal T. Prevalence of psoriasis in Norway. *Acta Derm Venereol Suppl (Stockh)* 1989;**142**:5-8.
4. Kavli G, Forde OH, Arnesen E, Stenvold SE. Psoriasis: familial predisposition and environmental factors. *Br Med J (Clin Res Ed)* 1985;**291**:999-1000.
5. Gelfand JM, Stern RS, Nijsten T, et al. The prevalence of psoriasis in African Americans: results from a population-based study. *J Am Acad Dermatol* **2005**;52:23-6.
6. Megha M. Tollefson, Cynthia S. Crowson, Marian T. McEvoy, and Hilal Maradit Kremers,, Incidence of psoriasis in children: A population-based Study, *J am acad dermatol* 06 2010.
7. David l. Mcmillin, , douglas g. Richards, eric a. Mein,, and carl d. Nelson, Systemic aspects of psoriasis: an integrative Model based on intestinal etiology *Integrative medicine*, vol. 2, nos. 2/3, pp. 1999:105–113,.
8. Landsford FD. Psoriasis. In: McGarey W, editor. *Physicians reference notebook.* Virginia Beach, VA: A.R.E. Press; 1983. p. 303–11.
9. Mein E. *Keys to health.* New York: Harper & Row, 1989.
10. Michaelsson G, Kraaz W, Hagforsen E, Pihl-Lundin I, Loof L. Psoriasis patients have highly increased numbers of tryptase-positive mast cells in the duodenal stroma. *Br J Dermatol* 1997; **136**:866–70.
11. Henseler T, Christophers E. Disease concomitance in psoriasis. *J Am Acad Dermatol* 1995;**32**:982–6.

12. Anderson PC. Dialysis treatment of psoriasis. *Arch Dermatol* 1981;**117**:67–8.

13. Kramer P, Brunner FP, Brynger H, et al. Dialysis treatment and psoriasis in Europe. *Clin Nephrol* 1982;**18**:62–8.

14. Pagano J. *Healing psoriasis: The natural alternative.* Englewood Cliffs, NJ: The Pagano Organization; 1991.

15. Barbara S. Baker, Anne Powles1 and Lionel Fry, Peptidoglycan: a major aetiological factor for psoriasis?, *TRENDS in Immunology* Vol.27, 2006: No.12 Available online 12 October.

16. Simelyte, E. et al. Role of peptidoglycan subtypes in the pathogenesis of bacterial cell wall arthritis. *Ann. Rheum. Dis.* 2003;**62**:976–982

17. Aldona T. Pietrzak ,, Anna Zalewska , Grażyna Chodorowska , Dorota Krasowska , Anna Michalak-Stoma ,Piotr Nockowski, Paweł Osemlak , Tomasz Paszkowski, Jacek M. Roliński. Cytokines and anticytokines in psoriasis, *Clinica Chimica Acta* 2008; **39**:47–21

18. Psoriasis—recent advances in understanding its pathogenesis and treatment Gerald Krueger, MD and Charles N. Ellis, MD, Salt Lake City, Utah, and Ann Arbor, Michigan, *J Am Acad Dermatol* 2005;**53**:S94-100.

19. The role of cytokines in the psoriatic inflammation, Alexander Kapp, *Journal of Dermarological Science*, 1993; **5**:I33- 142.

20. Alan S. Boyd, MD, and Alan Menter, MD Dallas, Texas, Erythrodermic psoriasis ,Precipitating factors, course, and prognosis in 50 patients, *J am acad dermatol* 1989;**21**:985-91.

21. Susan A. Winchell, M.D., and Royce A. Watts, Relaxation therapies in the treatment of psoriasis and possible pathophysiologic mechanisms, *J am acad dermatol* 1988;**18**:101-4.

22. Drugs in exacerbation of psoriasis, Elizabeth A. Abel, Linda M. DiCicco, Elaine K. Orenberg, ,Jorma E. Fraki, and Eugene M. Farber, *J am acad dermatol* 1986;**15**:1007-1022.

23. Kaur S, Kumar B, Kaur I, Sharma BK: Psoriasis as side effect of [3-adrenergic blocking agent--proprano-Iol. *Indian Heart J* 1983;**35**:181-183.

24. Ridley CM: Skin reactions to beta-blockers. *Br Med J*, 1974;**4**:229.

25. Gawkrodger D J, Beveridge GW: Psoriasiform reaction,to atenolol. *Clin Exp Dermatol* 1984;**9**:92-94,.

26. Hu CH, Miller CM, Peppercorn R, Farber EM: Generalized pustular psoriasis provoked by propranolol., *Arch Dermatol* 1985;**121**:1326-1327.

27. Baker H: The influence of chloroquine and related drugs,on psoriasis and keratoderma blenorrhagicum. *Br J Dermatol*, 1966;**78**:161-166.

28. Harwell WB: Quinidine-induced psoriasis. *J am acaddermatot.* 1983; **9**:278. (Letter to Editor.)

29. Goette DK, Odom RB: Adverse effect of corticosteroids.*Cuffs* 1979; **23**:477-487.

30. Ellis CN, Fallon JD, Heezen JL, Voorhees JJ: Topical indomethacin exacerbates lesions of psoriasis. *J Invest Dermatol* 1983;**80**:362. (Abst.)

31. Wilkin J: Exacerbation of psoriasis during clonidine, therapy. *Arch Dermatol* 1981;**117**:4. (Letter to Editor.)

32. Nikolai tsankov,Jana kazandjieva, Kossara drenovska, Drugs in Exacerbation and Provocation of Psoriasis *Clinics in Dermatology* Y 1998;**16**:333–351.

33. Ellen L. Smith, Stephanie H. Pincus, Lynne Donovan, and Michael F. Holick, A novel approach for of psoriasis the evaluation and treatment Oral or topical use of 1,25-dihydroxyvitarnin D3 can be a safe and effective therapy for psoriasis, *J am acad dermatol* 1988;**19**:516-28.

34. Christopher S. Carlin, Steven R. Feldman, James G. Krueger, Alan Menter, and Gerald G. Krueger, A 50% reduction in the Psoriasis Area and Severity Index (PASI 50) is a clinically significant endpoint in the assessment of psoriasis, *J Am Acad Dermatol* 2004;**50**:859-66.

35. S. Priya Sivanesan, Shilpa Gattu, BS,c Judith Hong, Arianne Chavez-Frazier, Grace D. Bandow, Farah Malick, Greg Kricorian, and John Koo, Randomized, double-blind, placebo-controlled evaluation of the efficacy of oral psoralen plus ultraviolet A for the treatment of plaque-type psoriasis using the Psoriasis Area Severity

Index score (improvement of 75% or greater) at 12 weeks. *J Am Acad Dermatol* 2009; **61**:793-8.

36. Evaluating psoriasis with Psoriasis Area and Severity Index, Psoriasis Global Assessment, and Lattice System Physician's Global Assessment Richard G. Langley, and Charles N. Ellis, *J Am Acad Dermatol* 2004;**51**:563-9.

37. Warren RB, Griffiths CEM. Systemic therapies for psoriasis: methotrexate, retinoids, and cyclosporine. *Clinics in dermatology*. 2008;**26(5)**:438-47.

38. wohl M, Ali S. Treatment of psoriasis. Part 2. Systemic therapies. *Journal of the American Academy of Dermatology*. 2001;**45(5)**:649-61.

39. Sobell JM, Hallas SJ, editors. Systemic therapies for psoriasis: understanding current and newly emerging therapies 2003: Elsevier.

40. Camp RD, Psoriasis. In: Rook A, Wilkinson DS, Ebling FJ, Textbook of dermatology. 5th ed. Oxford: Blackwell Scientific, 1992; 1391-458.

41. Weinstein GD, Van Scott EJ. Autoradiographic analysis of turnover times of normal and psoriatic epidermis. *J Invest Dermatol*, 1965; **45**:257-62.

42. Marsden JR, Coburn PR, Marks J, Shuster S. Measurement of the response of psoriasis to short-term application of anthralin. *Br J Dermatol*, 1983; **109**: 209-18.

43. Lowe NJ, Ashton RE, Koudsi H, Verschoore M, Schaefer H. Anthralin for psoriasis: short-contact anthralin therapy compared with topical steroid and conventional anthralin. *J Am Acad Dermatol*, 1984; **10**:69-72

44. Dodd WA. Tars: their role in the treatment of psoriasis. *Dermatol Clin,* 1993; **11**:131-5.

45. Botson SH, Stenton SC, Simpson NB. Acute severe bronchoconstriction precipitated by coal tar bandages. *Clin Exp Dermatol*, 1995; **20**:58-9.

46. Pion IA, Koening KL, Lim HW. Is dermatologic usage of coal tar carcinogenic? A review of the literature. *Dermatol Surg*, 1995; **21**:227-31.

47. Kirsner RS, Federman D. Treatment of psoriasis: role of calcipotriene. *Am. Fam. Physician,* 1995; **52**: 237-40.

48. Lebwohl M. Topical application of calcipotriene and corticosteroids: combination regimens. *J Am Acad Dermatol,* 1997; **37(3 Pt 2)**:S55-8.

49. Fogh K, Kragballe K. Vitamin D3 analogues. *Clin Dermatol*, 1997; **15**:705-13.

50. Weinstein GD, Krueger GG, Lowe NJ, Duvic M, Friedman DJ, Jegasothy BV, et al. Tazarotene gel, a new retinoid, for topical therapy of psoriasis: vehicle-controlled study of safety, efficacy, and duration of therapeutic effect. *J Am Acad Dermatol*, 1997; **37**:85-92.

51. Marks R. Early clinical development of tazarotene. *Br J Dermatol* 1996; **135 (suppl 49)** :26-31.

52. Gerald D, Weinstein MD, Jerry L McCullough, Elise Olsen, Topical methotrexate therapy for psoriasis. *Arch Dermatol*, 1989; **125**: 229-230.

53. Ravi Kumar BC, Inderjeet Kaur, Bhusan Kumar, Topical methotrexate therapy in palmoplantar psoriasis. Indian Journal of Dermatology, *Venerology and Leprology,* 1999; **65(.6)**: 270-272

54. http://www.thomsonhc.com/ accessed on 6th august 2011

55. http://www.cimsasia.com/

56. Bayliffe AI, Brigandi RA, Wilkins HJ, Levick MP. Emerging therapeutic targets in psoriasis. *Curr Opin Pharmacol.* 2004;**4(3)**:306-10.

57. Schlaak JF, Buslau M, Jochum W, Hermann E, Girndt M, Gallati H, et al. T cells involved in psoriasis vulgaris belong to the Th1 subset. *J Invest Dermatol*. 1994;**102(2)**:145-9.

58. Yawalkar N, Karlen S, Hunger R, Brand CU, Braathen LR. Expression of interleukin-12 is increased in psoriatic skin. *J Invest Dermatol.* 1998;**111(6)**:1053-7.

59. Racke MK, Bonomo A, Scott DE, Cannella B, Levine A, Raine CS, et al. Cytokine-induced immune deviation as a therapy for inflammatory autoimmune disease. *The Journal of experimental medicine.* 1994;**180(5):**1961.

60. Asadullah K, Docke WD, Ebeling M, Friedrich M, Belbe G, Audring H, et al. Interleukin 10 treatment of psoriasis: clinical results of a phase 2 trial. *Arch Dermatol.* 1999;**135(2)**:187-92.

61. Abrams JR, Lebwohl MG, Guzzo CA, Jegasothy BV, Goldfarb MT, Goffe BS, et al. CTLA4Ig-mediated blockade of T-cell costimulation in patients with psoriasis vulgaris. *J Clin Invest.* 1999;**103**:1243-52.

62. Abrams JR, Kelley SL, Hayes E, Kikuchi T, Brown MJ, Kang S, et al. Blockade of T lymphocyte costimulation with cytotoxic T lymphocyte–associated antigen 4–immunoglobulin (CTLA4Ig) reverses the cellular pathology of psoriatic plaques, including the activation of keratinocytes, dendritic cells, and endothelial cells. *J. Exp. Med.* 2000;**192(5)**:681-694.

63. Krueger J, Gottlieb A, Miller B, Dedrick R, Garovoy M, Walicke P. Anti-CD11a treatment for psoriasis concurrently increases circulating T-cells and decreases plaque T-cells, consistent with inhibition of cutaneous T-cell trafficking. *J. Invest. Dermatol.* 2000;**115(2)**:333.

64. Papp K, Bissonnette R, Krueger JG, Carey W, Gratton D, Gulliver WP, et al. The treatment of moderate to severe psoriasis with a new anti-CD11a monoclonal antibody. *J Am Acad Dermatol.* 2001;**45(5)**:665-74.

65. Ellis CN, Krueger GG. Treatment of chronic plaque psoriasis by selective targeting of memory effector T lymphocytes. *N Engl J Med.* 2001;**345(4)**:248-55.

66. Abrams JR, Kelley SL, Hayes E, Kikuchi T, Brown MJ, Kang S, et al. Blockade of T lymphocyte costimulation with cytotoxic T lymphocyte–associated antigen 4–immunoglobulin (CTLA4Ig) reverses the cellular pathology of psoriatic plaques, including the activation of keratinocytes, dendritic cells, and endothelial cells. *J. Exp. Med.* 2000;**192(5)**:861-94.

67. Oh CJ, Das KM, Gottlieb AB. Treatment with anti-tumor necrosis factor a (TNF-a) monoclonal antibody dramatically decreases the clinical activity of psoriasis lesions. *J Am Acad Dermatol.* 2000; **42(5)**:829-30.

68. Chaudhari U, Romano P, Mulcahy L, Dooley L, Baker D, Gottlieb A. Efficacy and safety of infliximab monotherapy for plaque-type psoriasis: a randomised trial. *The Lancet.* 2001; **357(9271)**:1842-7.

69. Mease PJ, Goffe BS, Metz J, VanderStoep A, Finck B, Burge DJ. Etanercept in the treatment of psoriatic arthritis and psoriasis: a randomised trial. *The Lancet.* 2000; **356(9227)**:385-90.

70. Trepicchio WL, Ozawa M, Walters IB, Kikuchi T, Gilleaudeau P, Bliss JL, et al. Interleukin-11 therapy selectively downregulates type I cytokine proinflammatory pathways in psoriasis lesions. *J Clin Invest.* 1999; **104(11)**:1527-37.

71. Baker BS, Fry L. Immunotargeting: A biological approach to the treatment of psoriasis. Drug Discovery Today: *Therapeutic Strategies.* 2007; **4(3)**:201-7.

72. www.dailymed.nlm.nih.gov/

73. www.usfda.gov/, www.micromedex.com)

74. Taneja A, Trehan M, Taylor CR. 308-nm excimer laser for the treatment of psoriasis: induration-based dosimetry. Arch Dermatol. 2003;139(6):759-64.

75. Trehan M, Taylor CR. High-dose 308-nm excimer laser for the treatment of psoriasis. *J Am Acad Dermatol.* 2002; **46(5)**:732-7.

76. Tournas JA, Lowe NJ, Yamauchi PS. Laser and novel light source treatments for psoriasis. *Lasers Surg Med.* 2004; **35(3)**:165-73.

77. Gattu S, Rashid R, Wu J. 308 nm excimer laser in psoriasis vulgaris, scalp psoriasis, and palmoplantar psoriasis. *J Eur Acad Dermatol Ve-nereol.* 2009; **23(1)**:36-41.

78. Rodewald EJ, Housman TS, Mellen BG, Feldman SR. Follow up survey of 308 nm laser treatment of psoriasis. *Lasers Surg Med.* 2002; **31(3)**:202-6.

79. Taylor CR, Racette AL. A 308 nm excimer laser for the treatment of scalp psoriasis. *Lasers Surg Med.* 2004; **34(2)**:136-40.

80. Ros AM, Garden JM, Bakus AD, Hedblad MA. Psoriasis response to the pulsed dye laser. *Lasers Surg Med.* 1996; **19(3)**:331-5.

81. Zelickson BD, Mehregan DA, Wendelschfer-Crabb G, Ruppman D, Cook A, O'Connell P, et al. Clinical and histologic evaluation of psoriatic plaques treated with a flashlamp pulsed dye laser. *J Am Acad Dermatol.* 1996; **35(1)**:64-8.

82. Reiko N, Keiko K, Akimichi M. Efficacy of the 585 nm pulsed dye laser for treatment of psoriasis. *Jpn J Dermatol* 2006:**116**:449-54.

83. Taibjee S, Cheung S. Controlled study of excimer and pulsed dye lasers in the treatment of psoriasis. *Br J Dermatol.* 2005; **153(5)**:960-6.

84. Gelfand JM, Weinstein R, Porter SB, Neimann AL, Berlin JA, Margolis DJ. Prevalence and treatment of psoriasis in the United Kingdom: a population-based study. *Arch Dermatol.* 2005; **141(12)**:1537-41.

85. Kurd SK, Richardson SK, Gelfand JM. Update on the epidemiology and systemic treatment of psoriasis. *Exp Rev Clin Immunol.* 2007; **3(2)**:171-85.

86. Greaves M, Weinstein G. Treatment of psoriasis. *N Engl J Med.* 1995; **332(9)**:581-8.

87. Stern RS, Nijsten T, Feldman SR, Margolis DJ, Rolstad T, editors. Psoriasis is common, carries a substantial burden even when not extensive, and is associated with widespread treatment dissatisfaction. *J Investig Dermatol Symp Proc* 2004; **9**:136-9.

88. Gelfand JM. Long-term treatment for severe psoriasis: we're halfway there, with a long way to go. *Arch Dermatol.* 2007; **143(9)**:1191-3.

89. Saraf S. Applications of novel drug delivery system for herbal formulations. *Fitoterapia.* 2010; **81(7)**:680-9.

90. Vogler B, Ernst E. Aloe vera: a systematic review of its clinical effectiveness. *The British Journal of General Practice.* 1999; **49(447)**:823.

91. Syed TA, Ahmad SA, Holt AH, Ahmad SH, Afzal M. Management of psoriasis with Aloe vera extract in a hydrophilic cream: a placebo controlled, double blind study*. *Trop Med Int Health.* 1996; **1(4)**:505-9.

92. Paulsen E, Korsholm L, Brandrup F. A double blind, placebo controlled study of a commercial Aloe vera gel in the treatment of slight to moderate psoriasis vulgaris. *J Eur Acad Dermatol Venereol.* 2005;**19(3)**:326-31.

93. Bernstein S, Donsky H, Gulliver W, Hamilton D, Nobel S, Norman R. Treatment of mild to moderate psoriasis with Relieva, a Mahonia aquifolium extract-a double-blind, placebo-controlled study. *Am J Ther.* 2006; **13(2)**:121-6.

94. Lassus A, Forsström S. A double-blind study comparing oleum horwathiensis with placebo in the treatment of psoriasis. *J Int Med Res.* 1991; **19(2)**:137-46.

95. Lin YK, Leu YL, Yang SH, Chen HW, Wang CT, Pang JHS. Anti-psoriatic effects of indigo naturalis on the proliferation and differentiation of keratinocytes with indirubin as the active component. *Journal of dermatological science.* 2009; **54(3)**:168-74.

96. Mutheeswaran S, Pandikumar P, Chellappandian M, Ignacimuthu S. Documentation and quantitative analysis of the local knowledge on medicinal plants among traditional Siddha healers in Virudhunagar District of Tamil Nadu, India. *J. Ethnopharmacol.* 2011.doi:10.1016/j.jep.2011.06.003

97. Chan MMY. Inhibition of tumor necrosis factor by curcumin, a phytochemical. *Biochem Pharmacol.* 1995; **49(11)**:1551-6.

98. Jang MK, Sohn DH, Ryu JH. A curcuminoid and sesquiterpenes as inhibitors of macrophage TNF-release from Curcuma zedoaria. *Planta Med.* 2001; **67**:550-2.

99. Matsuda H, Tewtrakul S, Morikawa T, Nakamura A, Yoshikawa M. Anti-allergic principles from Thai zedoary: structural requirements of curcuminoids for inhibition of degranulation and effect on the release of TNF-[alpha] and IL-4 in RBL-2H3 cells. *Bioorg Med Chem.* 2004; **12(22)**:5891-8.

100. Gulcubuk A, Altunatmaz K, Sonmez K, Haktanir Yatkin D, Uzun H, Gurel A, et al. Effects of Curcumin on Tumour Necrosis Factor and Interleukin 6 in the Late Phase of Experimental Acute Pancreatitis. *J Vet Med A Physiol Pathol Clin Med.* 2006; **53(1)**:49-54.

101. Lao C, Ruffin M, Normolle D, Heath D, Murray S, Bailey J, et al. Dose escalation of a curcuminoid formulation. *BMC Complement Altern Med.* 2006; **6(1)**:10.

102. Huang MT, Ma W, Lu YP, Chang RL, Fisher C, Manchand PS, et al. Effects of curcumin, demethoxycurcumin, bisdemethoxycurcumin and tetrahydrocurcumin on 12-O-tetradecanoylphorbol-13-acetateinduced tumor promotion. *Carcinogenesis.* 1995; **16(10)**:2493-7.

103. Yamamoto T, Katayama I, Nishioka K. Topical anthralin therapy for refractory nail psoriasis. *J Dermatol.* 1998; **25(4)**:231-3.

104. Ledo E, Ledo A. Phototherapy, photochemotherapy, and photodynamic therapy: unapproved uses or indications. *Clinics in dermatology*. 2000; **18(1)**:77-86.

105. UVB Phototherapy" (php). National Psoriasis Foundation, USA. Archived from the original on 2007-06-22. http://web.archive.org/web/20070622180124/http://www.psoriasis.org/treatment/psoriasis/phototherapy/uvb.php. Retrieved 2007-09-23.)

106. Kiil J, Sogaard H. Surgical treatment of psoriasis. *The Lancet.* 1985;**326(8445)**:16-8.

107. Asadullah K, Volk HD, Sterry W. Novel immunotherapies for psoriasis. *TRENDS in Immunology*. 2002; **23(1)**:47-53.

108. Schreier H, Bouwstra J. Liposomes and niosomes as topical drug carriers: dermal and transdermal drug delivery. *J Control Release.* 1994; **30(1)**:1-15.

109. Touitou E, Shaco Ezra N, Dayan N, Jushynski M, Rafaeloff R, Azoury R. Dyphylline liposomes for delivery to the skin. *J. Pharm. Sci.* 1992; **81(2)**:131-4.

110. Mezei M, Gulasekharam V. Liposomes—a selective drug delivery system for the topical route of administration: gel dosage form. *J. Pharm. Pharmacol.* 1982;**34(7)**:473-4.

111. El Maghraby G, Barry B, Williams A. Liposomes and skin: From drug delivery to model membranes. *Eur J Pharm Sci.* 2008; **34(4-5)**:203-22.

112. Hofland HEJ, van der Geest R, Bodde HE, Junginger HE, Bouwstra JA. Estradiol permeation from nonionic surfactant vesicles through human stratum corneum *in vitro*. *Pharm. Res.* 1994;**11(5)**:659-64.

113. Korting H, Zienicke H, Schäfer-Korting M, Braun-Falco O. Liposome encapsulation improves efficacy of betamethasone dipropionate in atopic eczema but not in psoriasis vulgaris. *Eur J Clin Pharmacol.* 1990;**39(4)**:349-51.

114. Mahrle G, Bonnekoh B, Wevers A, Hegemann L. Anthralin: how does it act and are there more favourable derivatives?. *Acta Derm. Venerol. Suppl.* (Stockh.). 1994;**186**:83.

115. Reichert U, Jacques Y, Grangeret M, Schmidt R. Antirespiratory and antiproliferative activity of anthralin in cultured human keratinocytes. *J Invest Dermatol.* 1985; **84(2)**:130-4.

116. Agarwal R, Katare O, Vyas S. Preparation and *in vitro* evaluation of liposomal/niosomal delivery systems for antipsoriatic drug dithranol. *Int J Pharm.* 2001; **228(1-2)**:43-52.

117. Dubey V, Mishra D, Dutta T, Nahar M, Saraf D, Jain N. Dermal and transdermal delivery of an anti-psoriatic agent via ethanolic liposomes. *J Control Release.* 2007;**123(2)**:148-54.

118. Klein A, Babilas P, Karrer S, Landthaler M, Szeimies RM. Photodynamic therapy in dermatology–an update 2008. *J. Dtsch. Dermatol. Ges.* 2008; **6(10)**:839-45.

119. Fang YP, Huang YB, Wu PC, Tsai YH. Topical delivery of 5-aminolevulinic acid-encapsulated ethosomes in a hyperproliferative skin animal model using the CLSM technique to evaluate the penetration behavior. *Eur J Pharm Biopharm.* 2009; **73(3)**:391-8.

120. Geusens B, Strobbe T, Bracke S, Dynoodt P, Sanders N, Gele MV, et al. Lipid-mediated gene delivery to the skin. *Eur J Pharm Sci.* 2011; **43**:199-211.

121. Cevc G, Blume G. Biological activity and characteristics of triamcinolone-acetonide formulated with the self-regulating drug carriers, Transfersomes®. Biochimica et al. Biophysica Acta (BBA)-*Biomembranes.* 2003;**1614(2)**:156-64.

122. Cevc G, Blume G, Schätzlein A, Gebauer D, Paul A. The skin: a pathway for systemic treatment with patches and lipid-based agent carriers. *Adv. Drug Deliv. Rev.* 1996; **18(3)**:349-78.

123. Singka GSL, Samah NA, Zulfakar MH, Yurdasiper A, Heard CM. Enhanced topical delivery and anti-inflammatory activity of methotrexate from an activated nanogel. *Eur J Pharm Biopharm.* 2010; **76(2)**:275-81.

124. Batheja P, Sheihet L, Kohn J, Singer AJ, Michniak-Kohn B. Topical drug delivery by a polymeric nanosphere gel: Formulation optimization and *in vitro* and *in vivo* skin distribution studies. *J Control Release.* 2010; **149**:159-67

125. Mandawgade SD, Patravale VB. Development of SLNs from natural lipids: application to topical delivery of tretinoin. *Int J Pharm.* 2008; **363(1-2)**:132-8.

126. Ourique AF, Melero A, Silva CB, Schaefer UF, Pohlmann AR, Guterres SS, et al. Improved photostability and reduced skin permeation of tretinoin: Development of a semisolid nanomedicine. *Eur. J. Pharm . Biopharm.* 2011. doi: 10.1016/j.e jpb.2011.0 3.008

127. Prow TW, Grice JE, Lin LL, Faye R, Butler M, Becker W, et al. Nanoparticles and microparticles for skin drug delivery. *Adv. Drug Deliv. Rev.* 2011: **63**; 63:470–91.

128. Goebel ASB, Neubert RHH, Wohlrab J. Dermal targeting of tacrolimus using colloidal carrier systems. *Int J Pharm.* 2010; 159-168.

129. Baroli B, Lopez-Quintela MA, Delgado-Charro MB, Fadda AM, Blanco-Méndez J. Microemulsions for topical delivery of 8-methoxsalen. *J Control Release.* 2000; **69(1)**:209-18.

130. Park JH, Choi SO, Seo S, Choy YB, Prausnitz MR. A microneedle roller for transdermal drug delivery. *Eur J Pharm Biopharm.* 2010; **76(2)**:282-9.

131. Schäfer-Korting M, Mehnert W, Korting HC. Lipid nanoparticles for improved topical application of drugs for skin diseases. *Adv. Drug Deliv. Rev.* 2007; **59(6)**:427-43.

132. Pople PV, Singh KK. Development and evaluation of colloidal modified nanolipid carrier: Application to topical delivery of tacrolimus. *Eur . J. Pharm. Biopharm.* 2011.doi: 10.1 016/j.ejpb.20 11.02.0 16

Ref from NDDS table add:

133. Lakshmi P, Devi GS, Bhaskaran S, Sacchidanand S. Niosomal methotrexate gel in the treatment of localized psoriasis: Phase I and phase II studies. *Indian J Dermatol Venereol Leprol.* 2007; **73(3)**:157-61.

134. Lakshmi PK, Gayathri Devi S, Sacchidananda S, Shyamala Bhaskaran. Topical novel drug delivery system for the treatment of localized psoriasis. *Pharma Review* 2006; **4(23)**:73-80.

135. Lakshmi P, Devi S, Bhaskaran S, Sacchidananda S. Meenakshi: Clinical Management Of Psoriasis Using 0.25% Niosomal

Methotrexate Gel: A Placebo Controlled Double Blind Study. *The Internet Journal of Dermatology*. 2005; **3(1)**.

136. Lakshmi P, Bhaskaran S. PHASE II STUDY OF TOPICAL NIOSOMAL UREA GEL-AN ADJUVANT IN THE TREATMENT OF PSORIASIS. *International Journal of Pharmaceutical Sciences Review and Research*. 2011; **7(1)**:1-7.

137. Lakshmi PK, Gayathri Devi S, Sacchidananda S, Shyamala Bhaskaran, Topical niosomal methotrexate and urea combination in the treatment of psoriasis. *Acta Pharmaceutica Turcica*. 2004; **46**: 28-29.

138. Mazda F, Özer AY, Ercan MT, Hýncal AA. Preparation, characterization, *in vitro* and *in vivo* studies on urea liposomes and niosomes. *STP Pharma Sci.*, 1997; **7**: 205-214.

139. Dragicevic-Curic N, Winter S, Krajisnik D, Stupar M, Milic J, Graefe S, et al. Stability evaluation of temoporfin-loaded liposomal gels for topical application. *J Liposome Res*. 2010; **20(1)**:38-48.

140. Bhatia A, Singh B, Amarji B, Negi P, Shukla A, Katare OP. Novel stain free lecithinized coal tar formulation for psoriasis. *Int J Dermatol*. 2011.doi: 10.1111/j.1365-4632.2011.04913.x

141. Kalariya M, Padhi B, Chougule M, Misra A. Methotrexate loaded solid lipid nanoparticles for topical treatment of psoriasis: formulation and clinical implications. *Drug Del Tech*. 2004; **4**:65-71.

142. Sutton L, Swinehart JM, Cato A, Kaplan AS. A clinical study to determine the efficacy and safety of 1% methotrexate/Azone®(MAZ) gel applied topically once daily in patients with psoriasis vulgaris. *Int.J.of dermatol*. 2001; **40(7)**:464-7.

143. Syed TA, Hadi SM, Qureshi ZA, Nordstrom CG, Ali SM. Management of psoriasis vulgaris with methotrexate 0.25% in a hydrophilic gel: a placebo-controlled, double-blind study. *Journal of Cutaneous Medicine and Surgery: Incorporating Medical and Surgical Dermatology*. 2001; **5(4)**:299-302.

144. Alvarez-Figueroa M, Blanco-Mendez J. Transdermal delivery of methotrexate: iontophoretic delivery from hydrogels and passive delivery from microemulsions. *Int J Pharm*. 2001; **215(1-2)**:57-65.

145. Vaidyanathan R, Chaubal M, Vasavada R. Effect of pH and solubility on *in vitro* skin penetration of methotrexate from a 50% v/v propylene glycol-water vehicle._*Int J Pharm.* 1985; **25(1)**:85-93.

146. Lauharanta J. Comparative efficacy and safety of amorolfine nail lacquer 2% versus 5% once weekly. *Clin. Exp. Dermatol.* 1992;**17**:41-3

147. Kobayashi Y, Miyamoto M, Sugibayashi K, MORIMOTO Y. Drug permeation through the three layers of the human nail plate. *J. Pharm. Pharmacol.* 1999; **51(3)**:271-8..

148. Walters K, Flynn G. Permeability characteristics of the human nail plate. *Int. J. Cosmet. Sci.* 1983; **5(6)**:231-46.

149. Fritsch H, Stettendorf S, Hegemann L. Ultrastructural changes in onychomycosis during the treatment with bifonazole/urea ointment. *Dermatology.* 1992;**185(1)**:32-6.

150. Quintanar-Guerrero D, Ganem-Quintanar A, Tapia-Olguin P, Kalia YN, Buri P. The effect of keratolytic agents on the permeability of three imidazole antimycotic drugs through the human nail. *Drug Dev. Ind. Pharm.* 1998; **24(7)**:685-90.

151. Sun, Y., Liu, J.C., Wang, J.C.T., De Doncker, P., 1999. Nail penetration. Focus ontopical delivery of antifungal drugs for onychomycosis treatment. In: Bronaugh, R.L., Maibach, H.I. (Eds.), Percutaneous Absorption. *Drugs –Cosmetics – Mechanisms – Methodology*, 3rd Ed. Marcel Dekker Inc, New York, pp. 759 – 787.

152. Van Hoogdalem E, Van den Hoven W, Terpstra I, Van Zijtveld J, Verschoor J, Visser J. Nail penetration of the antifungal agent oxiconazole after repeated topical application in healthy volunteers, and the effect of acetylcysteine. *Eur. J. Pharm. Sci..* 1997;**5(3)**:119-27.

153. Bohn M, Kraemer KT. Dermatopharmacology of ciclopirox nail lacquer topical solution 8% in the treatment of onychomycosis. *J. Am. Acad. Dermatol.* 2000; **43(4)**:S57-S69.

154. Gupta AK, Fleckman P, Baran R. Ciclopirox nail lacquer topical solution 8% in the treatment of toenail onychomycosis. *J. Am. Acad. Dermatol.* 2000; **43(4)**:S70-S80.

155. Reinel D, Clarke C. Comparative efficacy and safety of amorolfine nail lacquer 5% in onychomycosis, once weekly versus twice weekly. *Clin. Exp. Dermatol.* 1992;**17**:44-9.

156. Baran R, Tosti A. Topical treatment of nail psoriasis with a new corticoid-containing nail lacquer formulation. *J. Dermatol. Treat.* 1999;**10(3)**:201-4.

157. Ben-Shabat S, Benisty R, Wormser U, Sintov AC. Vitamin D 3–Based Conjugates for Topical Treatment of Psoriasis: Synthesis, Antiproliferative Activity, and Cutaneous Penetration Studies. *Pharm. Res.* 2005; **22(1)**:50-7.

158. Das N, Dhanawat M, Dash B, Nagarwal R, Shrivastava S. Codrug: An efficient approach for drug optimization. *Eur J Pharm Sci* 2010; **41**: 571–88.

159. Orvis AK, Wesson SK, Breza Jr TS, Church AA, Mitchell CL, Watkins SW. Mycophenolate mofetil in dermatology. *J Am Acad Dermatol.* 2009; **60(2)**:183-99.

160. Guenther L. Topical tazarotene therapy for psoriasis, acne vulgaris, and photoaging. *Skin Therapy Lett.* 2002; **7(3)**:1-4.

161. Mayer EJ, Hamman RF, Gay EC, Lezotte DC, Savitz DA, Klingensmith GJ. Reduced risk of IDDM among breast-fed children. The Colorado IDDM Registry. *Diabetes.* 1988; **37(12)**:1625.

162. Cardozo TJ, Pui JC. Method of orally treating inflammatory skin conditions with prodrugs of 5-fluorouracil. Google Patents; 2006.

163. Burke M, Redden PR, Douglas JA, Dick A, Horrobin DF. *In vitro* hydrolysis of novel gamma-linolenoyloxyalkyl derivatives of theophylline._*Int J Pharm.* 1997;**157(1)**:81-91.

164. Cather JC, Abramovits W. Investigational therapies for psoriasis* 1. *Journal of the American Academy of Dermatology.* 2003; **49(2)**:133-8.

165. Petersen TK, Sørensen P. Translational dermatology in drug discovery: perspectives for integrating humanized xenograft models and experimental clinical studies. *Drug Discov Today Biosilico.* 2008;**13(5-6)**:240-6.

166. Boehncke WH. The Psoriasis SCID Mouse Model: A Tool for Drug Discovery? Animal models of T cell-mediated skin diseases. *Ernst Schering Res. Found. Workshop* 2005:213-34.

167. Svensson, L. et al. (2007) Evaluation of the psoriasis xenograft SCID mouse model for screening of novel compounds after topical delivery. *Inflam. Res.* 56, S436–S437

168. U.S. Department of Health and Human Services, Food and Drug Administration, Center for Drug Evaluation and Research (CDER) (2006) Guidance for Industry, Investigators, and Reviewers. Exploratory IND Studies. Pharmacology/Toxicology1–13)

169. A new microdosing technique (Committee for medicinal products for human use (CHMP) and European Medicines Agency (2004). Position paper on non-clinical safety studies to support clinical trials with a single microdose. 1–4.)

170. Nasir A. Nanotechnology and dermatology: Part II—risks of nanotechnology. *Clinics in Dermatology.* 2010; **28(5)**:581-8.

171. Walters KA. Penetration enhancers and their use in transdermal, therapeutic systems. In: Hadgraft J, Guy RH, editors. *Transdermal drug delivery: developmental issues and research initiatives.* New York:, Marcel Dekker; 1989. p. 197-246.

CHAPTER 8

LEUCODERMA AND ITS TREATMENT

Y. Madhusudan Rao, Shayeda and P. Renuka

Centre for Biopharmaceutics and Pharmacokinetics, University College of Pharmaceutical Sciences, Kakatiya University, Warangal-506009, A.P.

8.1 Introduction

Leucoderma/vitiligo occurs naturally with the depigmentation in which skin loses natural color gradually. It has many symptoms over all body from head to feet with white patches and white small dots. They start appearing on the skin and diverse parts of the body all of a sudden. And victims are very worried to observe changing their condition with white spots. White patches on skin are more common in sun-exposed areas, including the hands, feet, arms, face, and lips. The hair that grows on vitiligo affected areas turns white sometimes. It is a circumstance in which white patches develop on the skin. The whole body can be affected ever and most of the people having vitiligo may have white patches on vast area in very initial stage. Generally vitiligo appears in one of three patterns. The focal pattern is more common in which depigmentation is limited to one or a few areas of the body. However there is no way to foresee vitiligo if it will increase. The disorder is on the whole progressive with the time when these white spots will extend to other areas of the body. Vitiligo extends slowly may be over long years in some cases while in most of the cases it extends speedily. A few people have also stated that supplementary depigmentation is subsequent to the substantial period. People of all age levels may be carrier of vitiligo and every body part might be affected in any time at any age. To get rid of vitiligo, People still believe on the herbal treatments. It is the most popular and satisfactory treatment way adopted anywhere in the world. Vitiligo generally called white spots illness as well or leucoderma.

8.2 Pigmentation in Skin

Pigmentation means the process of skin which is responsible for the coloration of skin. It is also related to the mechanism of skin regarding absorption of heat coming from sunlight. It protects our body from hazardous rays of UVB light which interact with our body. UVB light is a big source of skin cancer. Skin color is the one of the most important factor to guess overall health condition of a person.

Melanocytes

Melanocytes are special skin cell which are responsible for pigmentation process of skin.

Melanin

A natural substance produced by pigmentation producing cells melanocytes which is responsible for natural skin and hair color. It is the melanin which deficiency or excess in skin causes different types of skin problem. Albinism and vitiligo occurs due to the deficiency of melanin in skin. Abnormalities in the function in the production of melanin by melanocytes cause different pigmentation problems in skin. Melanin has a special quality to absorb UV (ultraviolet) radiation from sun.

Hyperpigmentation

It occurs when the production of melanin substance increase from normal level. Normally dark spots or blotches on skin occur due to the hyper pigmentation. It may be observed that after long exposure to sun skin complexion become more darker. This happens due to the excessive of melanin spot.

Depigmentation

It is also called hypopigmentation. When some light spots appear in skin as compare to its surrounding, normally white patches in skin appear due the depigmentation in skin. It occurs when the amount of melanin decrease from a certain level in a particular part of the body. Most common depigmentation problem of the skin is vitiligo. About 50 million people on the globe are suffering from this skin condition.

Ultraviolet radiation

Special pigment material melanin has a quality to absorb UVB radiation. Though UV light therapy is also used for the treatment of many diseases. Rapid increase in using sunscreens in last few years is due to the UV rays. There is a close relation between sunlight and skin care. Premature aging and skin cancer are two main conditions due to sun light. Sun light is composed of different type of rays. These are differentiated from each other on the basis of their wave length. Most malicious rays present in sunlight are UVB light and UVA radiation. Both these damage genome and but in different ways, UVB damage DNA directly whereas UVA indirectly

UVB light

These rays poses wave length ranger from 280 nm to 315 nm. Due to the shorter wavelength these have higher frequency and highly energetic rays. These are the tanning radiations of sun.

It does not penetrate deeper into skin and affect epidermis (outer layer of skin).

When UVB light penetrate into skin it turns into energy. This is the reason that it causes tanning and when sun light contain sufficient amount of UVB light it causes burning in skin.

UVB treatment

UVB light is not only hazardous to health but use in several medical therapies for the cure of different disease and conditions. It is specially used for the treatment of chronic skin conditions like vitiligo, psoriasis and eczema etc. Vitiligo is a loss of pigmentation of skin. In treatment of vitiligo UVB treatment is used to enhance the pigmentation of skin. In psoriasis growth and die cycle time of skin cells decreases to about 6 days. These dead cells instead of leaving skin, stuck up the skin surface. And an inflammation developed in skin. UVB is an effective treatment of skin and slow down the rapid growth of skin cells.

UVA light

It is less hazardous as compared to UVB rays. Lies between wave length ranges 315 nm to 400 nm. Its strength in sunlight no longer remains variable. It causes brownish shade of skin when exposed to UVA light.

PUVA treatment

PUVA treatment is rapidly being popular for many skin diseases. In this mode of treatment first affected skin is sensitized and then exposed to UVA radiations.

8.3 Disorders of Pigmentation

Vitiligo

Vitiligo is a specific, common often inheritable, acquired disorder characterized by well-circumscribed milky white cutaneous macules devoid of identifiable melanocytes. It has a prevalence of approximately 1% and mostly individuals younger than 20 years old are affected. Four different theories have been implicated in the pathogenesis of the disease: the autoimmune, the neuronal, the self-destructive, and the combination of the former. Five different clinical patterns have been recognized: the generalized, the acrofacial, the focal, the segmental, and the universal. The disease has a variable course. Usually, it is slowly progressive but occasionally a rapid depigmentation can be noted. Because spontaneous repigmentation is observed in a small percentage (only 10-20%) and because the disease can be quite distressing, particularly in dark-skinned individuals, many patients seek medical advice.

There are many therapeutic modalities available, but the estimated effectiveness is low. The choice of therapy depends on the age of the patient, the clinical pattern of the disease (type, severity, activity), the psychologic impact, and the risk-to-benefit ratio of prolonged therapy. If the patient is not motivated enough, then reassurance is all that is needed. Advice concerning the use of camouflage and sunscreen with a sun protection factor of 15 or greater (for both UVB and UVA) should be given to every patient. Self-tanning preparations containing dihydroxy-acetone in concentration ranging from 2.5-10% but usually from 3-5% are valuable. Lawson found in the henna plant and juglone a walnut derivative that also stains the skin, although both lack skin substantivety and in addition discolor clothing. If medical action is undertaken, then the primary goal of therapy is to restore melanocytes to the skin. If the disease is so widespread that repigmentation is not possible, then the optimum outcome should be a cosmetically acceptable appearance. From all the treatments available, the widely accepted ones include topical corticosteroids, phototherapy, and chemical depigmentation.

8.4 Historical Aspects and Definition of Vitiligo

8.4.1 Ancient Views

Around 1500 BCE patchy skin diseases were determined which is now called as Vitiligo. In ancient days two types of skin diseases were determined, one of them is interpreted as Leprosy and another is Vitiligo which shows lack of pigmentation only[2,3]. It is said that skin disorders were indicated much earlier in the Chinese literature, but their description was rather vague until around 600 CE, when Dohi wrote of "Pin-yiian-hon-lun," which From tlrr Dcpwtrnmt cf Dermatology, University of Graz, Graz, Austria.

Vitiligo in contemporary dermatology

Today, vitiligo is defined as the prototype of hypomelanotic disorders[4]. It is a disease that occurs idiopathically and that is acquired in most cases. Clinically, it shows circumscribed leucoderma that may arise at any age, but it usually appears before the age of 30 years. Approximately 1% of the world population is believed to be afflicted. Variable penetrant autosomal dominant inheritance has been suggested, because familial incidence is common. Few or many white macules appear on exposed areas such as the dorsal aspects of the hands, and the face and neck. Facial lesions are commonly located around the eyes and mouth. Body folds-axilla and groin-may also be initial sites. The patches show a tendency to enlarge in the course of time." Microscopically, vitiligo features absence ot melanocytes and melanin within the epidermis and an increased cellularity in dermal layers. Characteristic histochemical and ultrastructural changes can be obser;red. The physical disfigurement caused by vitiliginous lesions often leads to social embarrassement. It is a major sociopsychological problem in arcar where dark skin predominates.

8.4.2 Nomenclature

The term "vitiligo" was used by a Roman Physician Celsus in the first century CE. There are some differences in the opinion between lexicographers and dermatologists for naming the term "vitiligo". According to some people it looks like white glistening of the flesh of calves (vituli) may have given rise to the generic term "vitiligo". Others suggest that it looks like patches in a calves fur, so it may be derived from "vitelius", the Latin word for "calf". Some people believe that it is derived from a lattin word "vitium" which represents a blemishing fault. Instead of settling the confusion it even adds to it: "Vitiligo a kind of lepros or cutaneous eruption consisting of spots, sometimes black, sometimes white, called morphea, alphus, melas, leuce; also in general a cutaneous eruption[6].

8.4.3 Vitiligo in the 19th Century

At the end of the 19th century, vitiligo was defined as a pigmentary dystrophy. Louis Brocq (1856-1928) termed the lack of pigmentation in vitiliginous lesions combined with an increase of pigmentation in the lesions' periphery "dyschromy"[7]. So many people described histopathological features of vitiligo, among them Moritz Kaposi (1837-1902) said that in vitiligo color change occurs due to the lack of pigment granules in deep rete cells in the skin and an increase of pigmentation can be found in the surrounding lesions. In the end of the century different approaches were proposed for the treatment of vitiligo. Ernest Besnier (1831-1909) recommended subcutaneous injection of pilocarpine and saline or bromoiodic baths. Different mixtures containing croton oil, iodine, sublimate, and naphtol have been used topically without convincing therapeutic results[8].

8.5 Vitiligo and Analogous Changes in the Pigmentation of the Skin

The amount of pigment in the skin forms one of the greatest and certainly the most striking of the differences between the various races of man. Even as to the origin and situation of the pigment there are at present some differences of opinion. There are certainly many pigment granules embedded in the columnar epithelial cells which form the basal layer of the epidermis, and in these the granules occur mainly at the margin of the cells. Some masses of pigment also exist in the lymph spaces which are situated between the epithelial cells and here they form branching figures in the centre of which sometimes a nucleus or a leucocyte can be seen. From the shape and situation of these groups of pigment granules it is not improbable that they are really special pigment cells, comparable with the chromatophores seen in the skin of frogs. In the very dark races the pigment is not confined to the basal layer of the epidermis, but it is also to be found in and between the cells of the prickle cell layer and the other strata as far as the transitional layer, and it is important to remember that in the derma also pigmented cells are to be found. The tint of the skin in the white races is due mainly to the color of the superficial fat and blood-vessels, modified slightly by the epidermal pigment, and the essential color of the epidermis itself. In dark races the greater amount of pigment in the epidermis and the pigment present in the derma hide the color of the fat and blood-vessels. The amount of pigment varies not only in different races but also greatly in different individuals of the same race, and even in different portions of the skin of the same person. Further, in one and the same portion of skin the degree of pigmentation may vary greatly from time to time. The most potent agent in increasing the pigment is to be found in the rays of the sun, especially in summer. The amount of increase may be great in those who tan easily, but if the exposure has not been too long the increase may completely disappear when the person is removed to a cooler climate or the season changes. In this country none of the browning of the summer survives more than a very few weeks of autumn. We have no reason to think that this increase of pigment is in any way different in nature from the normal pigmentation of the skin; it is a pure increase in quantity of the pigment in the normal situation. These vast differences in color may occur in those who are in perfect health and therefore we are justified in calling them physiological. Still, it is of interest to note that for the most part these changes are in the direction of an increase of pigmentation and not in its diminution.

Loss of pigment of the skin may occur from many causes: it may follow an injury or an inflammation; it may occur in the anesthetic variety of leprosy; it may result from the retrocession of a psoriatic patch; and it is not at all rare as a sequela of a secondary syphilitic eruption, and this last is sometimes called syphilitic leucoderma. Occasionally both in white and colored races pigment may be wholly absent from the skin. In these albinos there is generally nothing betokening any failure of general health, and apart from the interference with vision these persons suffer nothing from the absence of pigment.

Leucoderma may occur at any age, though the middle period of life is that at which it is most commonly met with and from 20 to 40 years of age it is most frequently seen. It has been observed as early as the fourth year and it also seen to commence in advanced old age. It is not very rare but it is probably much more frequent than statistics would suggest. *Hebra* met with it six times in 3000 cases that is, once in 500 and Dr. H. Radcliffe Crocker's experience is much to the same effect. Erasmus Wilson saw it once in 400 cases; others have seen it less frequently; McCall Anderson met with it only once in 2500 cases. There are certainly many cases which never apply for treatment-either the amount of whitening is slight or the affected parts are completely covered by the clothes. The two sexes are fairly equally affected, though in Levi's statistics there were three times as many men affected as women; but there must have been some special cause for this unusual predominance in his cases, for no one else has met with it.

The disease is certainly more commonly seen in the colored races. This is partly to be ascribed to the fact that it is more easily recognizable in those who are naturally dark than in the fair, for the loss of pigment must be the more recognizable the more pigment there is to lose. But this probably does not explain the whole of the apparent greater frequency in colored races, for no small proportion of the most marked cases seen in this country have acquired the disease in warm climates. Especially tropical climates have a definite etiological importance. Even India exposure to the sun seems to assist in the production of leucoderma, but this may be in part due to the fact that on a darkened skin unpigmented spots will be more readily seen. When many patients suffering from any disease are carefully examined leucoderma is often found to be present, unknown to the patients themselves; therefore, it must be obvious that statistics based on dermatological clinics cannot be depended.

Leucoderma begins by the appearance of small round white spots. These steadily increase in size and by growth and coalescence large white patches of irregular shape are formed. They have a very definite, clearly defined margin, and this is always convex towards the unaffected skin. This convexity shows in itself that the white area is the abnormal portion and that it is invading the surrounding skin. This is important in diagnosis, for the patients themselves often imagine that the white skin is the healthy portion and they ask for treatment of the darker skin. The patches are, white; it is the whiteness of an albino, it is an absolutely dull whiteness, not unpleasing in itself but contrasting unpleasantly with the surrounding pigmented area. Any hairs on the affected part nearly always lose their coloring matter and occasionally the hair may fall, but this is quite exceptional. The surface is absolutely unaltered in level; it is not in the least raised above or sunk below the level of the surrounding skin and its sensibility is never affected in the slightest degree. The change is merely a change of color and nothing more. In certain cases each whitened area is surrounded by a zone of deeper pigmentation; this is certainly not always present and Mr. Jonathan Hutchinson denies its existence; he maintains that the apparent darkening is merely an effect of the striking contrast between the normal and the depigmented part. He claims that if the whitened areas be covered by pieces of brown paper no marginal increase of pigmentation will be visible, and that this is so sometimes some suggest that an increase of pigment everywhere precedes the loss of Pigment even at the commencement.

An important character of leucoderma is the symmetry of the affection. Sometimes it amounts to little more than a tendency to symmetry, but often the symmetrical distribution is extremely well-marked, so that for each patch on one side of the body there is an exactly corresponding patch on the other. In some there is no attempt at symmetrical distribution and the disease may even be unilateral. The general tendency of each patch is to spread at the margin, and thus large white areas may be produced which are very striking when the patient belongs to a dark race. Occasionally it happens that the depigmentation is so very extensive that a darkly colored person, such as a negro, may become almost white. Occasionally some retrocession will occur and complete recovery is possible though far from common.

8.6 Etiology

The symmetrical distribution of the disease; secondly, the concurrence of the leucoderma with pathological conditions of the nervous system; and thirdly, the existence of degenerative changes in the peripheral nerves in cases of the disease and its characters. There is a very wide spread idea in dermatology that the symmetrical distribution of an eruption is an indication, or at least a suggestion, of its nervous origin, but this idea rests on a very small foundation. It is said it must be nervous in origin. Symmetry of distribution is in no way a sign of a connection with the nervous system. The custom of ascribing to a nervous origin the symmetrical eruptions is chiefly due to the idea that the affected areas correspond to the areas of distribution of certain nerves.

There is nothing that can really be called an inflammation, nothing that is really atrophic, we have merely a single change, loss of pigment. Therefore the problem is as much simplified as possible. Now there is certainly one disease of the skin as to the nervous origin of which there can be no dispute and that is herpes zoster, for there is no doubt as to the existence in typical cases of this disease of inflammation in the ganglion on the posterior nerve root. Now this disease, undoubtedly due to a nervous lesion, is remarkable in that it only affects one side of the body; it is true that on intensely rare occasions cases have been recorded in which a herpes zoster; was bilateral, but none will deny that these bilateral easel are very exceptional and do not occur more than once in ten thousand times. Therefore it is clear that a skin lesion affects both sides of the body. In itself no evidence in favor of its being nervous in origin, and in fact, so far as we may judge from herpes zoster, it is evidence against it.

Third possibility is if leucoderma areas do not correspond either to nerve root areas or the areas of distribution of individual nerves, can it be that they represent the areas of supply of minute peripheral branches. Here, again, a careful comparison of leucodermic patches will show that there is no such correspondence. A white patch may begin on the border line between two nerve areas and it will spread indifferently in all directions, showing that neither in its origin nor in its mode of spreading does the patch bear any relation to the distribution of the cutaneous nerves. The second reason which has been advanced for considering that leucoderma is nervous in its origin is its association with other manifestations of nervous disease. Many of the patients are said to be neurotic; Lebran even says that he considers that the presence of leucoderma is always a reason for looking for other neuroses. Rayer described a case in which leucoderma appeared in a man soon after he had lost a large sum of money, though he does not tell us how long an interval elapsed between the loss of the money and the appearance of the leucoderma. Other instances are recorded in which it has followed violent mental emotions. Cases have been described in which chorea and hysteria have been present. In most cases the reports are not sufficiently definite to enable us to decide what real nexus there was between the nervous manifestation and the skin lesion. Lastly, it has been claimed that there is a close relation between mental unsoundness and leucoderma. In this connection Hermann Streit examined 1026 cases of mental disease in three asylums and amongst these there were only six of true leucoderma, a percentage hardly above that recorded by some observers amongst all cases seen at dermatological clinics. The pigment granules are absent from the affected spot, both those in the basal epithelium and those which occur between these cells. At the margin of the leucodermic patch, where the, pigmentation is increased, there is no obvious increase of pigment in the epidermis, but in the derma there is a marked increased pigmentation, especially in the papillary layer, but also around the blood-vessels, the hair follicles, and the sweat glands are numerous pigmented cells. Wermann has also shown that there is pigment in the cutis even of the whitened areas, though it has disappeared from the epidermis.

As to the actual mechanism by which the depigmentation is produced, we may obtain an insight from a consideration of the work of Metchnikoff on the bleaching of the hair in age. He has shown that the loss of the pigment granules of the hair is due to the action of a large number of macrophages which, swallowing the pigment, convey it away and leave the hair free from pigment. He is inclined to consider that the super activity of these macrophages is due to the stimulation of some toxin formed somewhere in the body, probably in the alimentary canal. In this way are best explained the pigmentation and the depigmentation of transplanted skin when it is of a different hue from that of the person on whom it has been grafted. The pigment is brought to the skin or removed from it by wander cells. In the same way explains the loss of the pigment of the skin in leucoderma. The excitant is some toxin probably arising from a diseased alimentary canal, but possibly from some other part of the body. This toxin stimulates macrophages to attack the pigment of the skin, the locality of their action being determined by trauma and light. The pigment removed by these macrophages from its own site is carried downwards into the derma and also outwards in a centrifugal direction. In this way is explained the increased pigmentation often seen at the margin of the bleached patches. As the amount of toxin increases or diminishes or the local adjuvants vary in intensity so does the activity of the macrophages wax or wane, so does the patch increase in size or remain as it was. Seldom, indeed, is it that the peccant macrophages can be induced to retrace their steps and to deposit once more the pigment where it should be; but when this happens the whitened patch regains its normal color; but far more commonly the depigmented area remains free from pigment till the end of life. The disease is in all probability due to the action of some toxin, derived from the alimentary canal, assisted by local injury and the action of light; and that the mechanism by which this is carried out is the vital action of peripatetic cells.

8.7 Types of Vitiligo

Vitiligo is a condition that causes depigmentation of patches of skin. It occurs when melanocytes, the cells responsible for skin pigmentation, die or are unable to function. The cause of vitiligo is unknown, but research suggests that it may arise from autoimmune, genetic, oxidative stress, neural, or viral causes.[9] The incidence worldwide is less than 1%.[10] The most common form is non-segmental vitiligo.

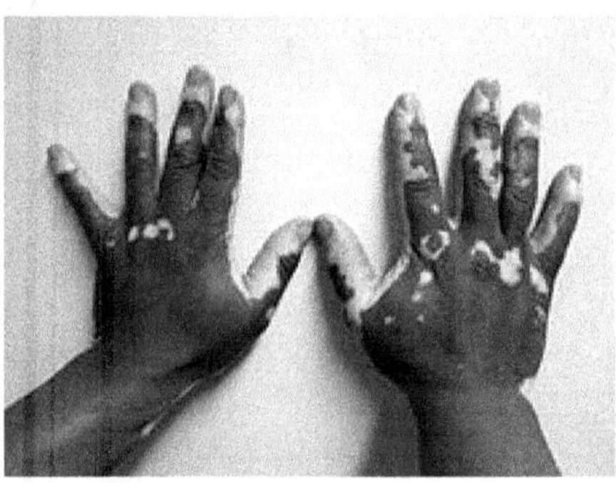

[Colour Fig. on page 406]

The most notable symptom of vitiligo is depigmentation of patches of skin that occurs on the extremities.[11,12] Although patches are initially small, they often enlarge and change shape.[9,11] When skin lesions occur, they are most prominent on the face, hands and wrists.[11,12] Depigmentation is particularly noticeable around body orifices, such as the mouth, eyes, nostrils, genitalia and umbilicus.[11,12] Some lesions have hyperpigmentation around the edges.[13] Patients who are stigmatized for their condition may experience depression and similar mood disorders.[14]

Non-segmental

In non-segmental vitiligo (NSV), there is usually some form of symmetry in the location of the patches of depigmentation. New patches also appear over time and can be generalized over large portions of the body or localized to a particular area. Vitiligo where little pigmented skin remains is referred to as *Vitiligo universalis*. NSV can come about at any age, unlike segmental vitiligo, which is far more prevalent in teenage years.[13]

Classes of non-segmental vitiligo include:

- Generalized vitiligo: the most common pattern, wide and randomly distributed areas of depigmentation[15]
- Universal vitiligo: depigmentation encompasses most of the body[15]
- Focal vitiligo: one or a few scattered macules in one area, most common in children[15]
- Acrofacial vitiligo: fingers and periorificial areas[15]
- Mucosal vitiligo: depigmentation of only the mucous membranes[15]

Segmental

Segmental vitiligo (SV) differs in appearance, etiology and prevalence from associated illnesses. Its treatment is different from that of NSV. It tends to affect areas of skin that are associated with dorsal roots from the spine. It spreads much more rapidly than NSV and, without treatment; it is much more stable/ static in course and not associated with auto-immune diseases and a very treatable condition that responds to topical treatment.[13]

- Vitiligo in a light-skinned individual

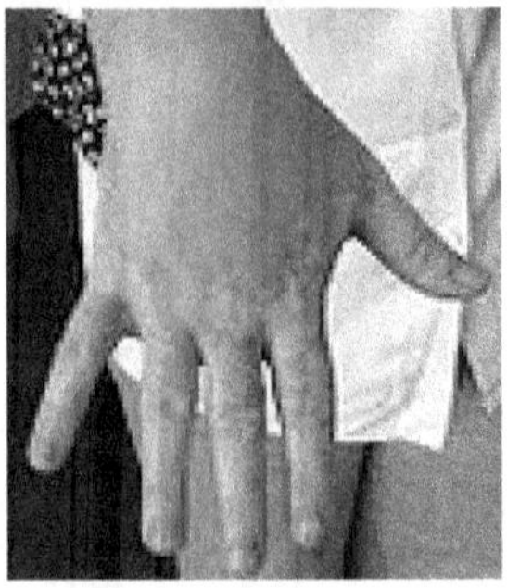

[Colour Fig. on page 407]

- Vitiligo in a dark-skinned individual

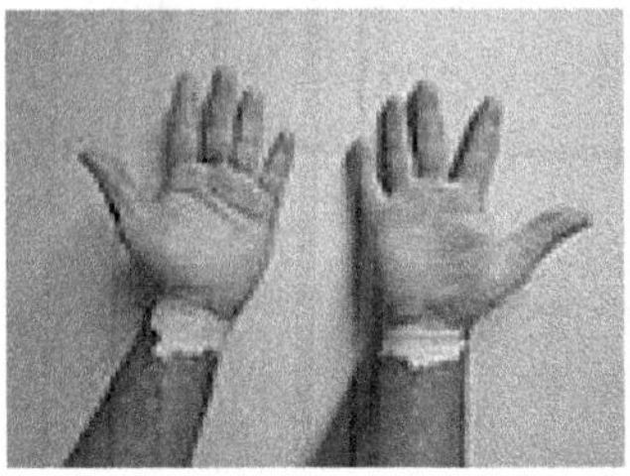

[Colour Fig. on page 407]

8.8 Vitiligo Symptoms

Vitiligo generally called white spots illness as well or Leucoderma, in which the skin loses its pigment due to the annihilation of melanocytes. Melanocytes are such pigment cells which found in the epidermis (the surface layer of the skin) and there are responsible for producing Melanin (a dark pigment that gives skin its color) and protects against ultraviolet radiation., The skin becomes pale when melanocytes stop producing melanin leaving areas of white patches this is called vitiligo. To describe Vitiligo symptoms, the onset of the vitiligo symptoms is very visible in darker and wheatish skinned people as the contrast of white patches looks obvious against dark skin. The manifestation of flat areas of normal-feeling skin with complete pigment loss is sudden or gradual and appearance of vitiligo symptoms the lesions appear as flat areas with no pigment. In common the affected areas are the face, elbows, knees, hands feet, and genitalia. The initial vitiligo symptoms are easily observable with flat white spots or patches on your skin. Vitiligo symptoms usually starts the first white patch appears on the skin area remains exposed to the sun. Vitiligo symptoms do not cause physical discomfort to your skin, such as itching etc. Vitiligo most commonly affects traumatic areas particularly on the face, upper chest, hands and groin. It may be widespread, affecting both sides of the body it may affect only one side of the body or it may affect only one localized area.

If the affected area contains hair, the hair may turn white then vitiligo symptoms sharply distinct white patches are seen rather obviously. Sometimes there may be seen by a circular white patch, resembling a halo.

8.9 Vitiligo Causes

Vitiligo causes or the core for this skin disorder, these are the things which make this skin condition more complex and chronic. Because the information about what are real causes of any disease or condition make it easy to treat. White patches with no pigmentation or coloration in them appear due to the destruction of melanocytes skin cells. Melanocytes cells are the tiny skin color production units in the skin. Which produce a substance which is characterized as skin color called melanin. When melanocytes are damaged in any region of the body, in that part a deficiency of melanin cause depigmentation in skin. What is the factor which attacks on melanocytes and kill them or they themselves destroyed it is still hidden to all of us. Almost all dermatologists have no perfect answer regarding question that what are the causes of vitiligo.

Causes of vitiligo and autoimmunity

A famous autoimmunity expert explaind the activity of a vitiligo antibody which produced due to the internal and external catechol or phenol quantity in patient's body. This antibody attacks on melanocytes cells and damage them. Another negative auto immune response, when a toxic material generated by nerve cells kill skin pigment producing cells or deactivate them to produce pigmentation for skin.

8.10 Pathogenesis

Vitiligo is a disorder characterized by patchy loss of skin pigmentation due to immune attacks on melanocytes, while, there is no significant proof or evidence for this, many doctors believe that[16] it can be caused by defects in many genes. Variations in genes that are part of the immune system or part of melanocytes have both been associated with vitiligo. The immune system genes are associated with other autoimmune disorders. In one case, the gene TYR, which makes the melanocyte more susceptible to the immune system in vitiligo, also makes the melanocyte more susceptible to the immune system in the skin cancer malignant melanoma. So people with vitiligo caused by the TYR gene are less likely to have malignant melanoma.A genomewide association study found 10 independent susceptibility loci for generalized vitiligo, responsible for 7.4% of the genetic risk. Some patients had vitiligo alone; others had generalized vitiligo with other autoimmune diseases. Most loci were associated with both forms. (The exception was PTPN22, which was only associated with generalized vitiligo). In the MHC region, which controls the immune system, major association signals were identified in the class I gene region (between HLA-A and HLA-HGC9) and class II gene region (between HLA-DRB1 and HLA-DQA1). Outside the MHC region, association signals were identified near RERE, PTPN22, LPP, IL2RA, GZMB, UBASH3A and C1QTNF6 genes, which are associated with other autoimmune diseases. TYR encodes tyrosinase, which is not a component of the immune system, but is an enzyme of the melanocyte that catalyzes melanin biosynthesis, and a major autoantigen in generalized vitiligo. The major alleles of TYR are associated with vitiligo, and the minor alleles are associated with malignant melanoma. Vitiligo-associated 402R tyrosinase may be more efficiently presented to the immune system. Melanoma-associated 402Q may fail to be identified by the immune system.[17] The transcriptional profile of melanocytes from vitiligo patients have been studied. Oligonucleotide microarrays containing approximately 16,000 unique genes were used to analyze mRNA expression in melanocytes from vitiligo patients and age-matched healthy controls. In total, 859 genes were identified as differentially expressed.[18]

Vitiligo is sometimes associated with autoimmune and inflammatory diseases,[19] commonly thyroid overexpression and underexpression. A study comparing 656 people with and without vitiligo in 114 families found several mutations (single-nucleotide polymorphisms) in the NALP1 gene. The NALP1 gene, which is on chromosome 17 located at 17p13, is on a cascade that regulates inflammation and cell death, including myeloid and lymphoid cells, which are white cells that are part of the immune response. NALP1 is expressed at high levels in T-cells and Langerhan cells, white blood cells that are involved in skin autoimmunity. Polymorphisms of CD4 were shown to be associated with the vitiligo and other autoimmune diseases like type I Diabetes Mellitus.[20] Among the inflammatory products of NALP1 are caspase 1 and caspase 5, which activate the inflammatory cytokine interleukin-1β. Interleukin-1β is expressed at high levels in patients with vitiligo. There are compounds which inhibit caspase and interleukin-1β, and so might be useful drugs for vitiligo and associated autoimmune diseases. In one of the mutations, the amino acid leucine in the NALP1 protein was replaced by histidine (Leu155->His). The original protein and sequence is highly conserved in evolution, and found in humans, chimpanzee, rhesus monkey, and bush baby, which means that it is an important protein and an alteration is likely to be harmful. Addison's disease (typically an autoimmune destruction of the adrenal glands) may cause vitiligo.[21,22]

8.11 Treatment

The ultimate goal of therapy for vitiligo is regeneration of the epidermal melanocyte population to obtain complete, permanent repigmentation of affected areas. Although this is not always possible and the success of a particular treatment modality cannot be guaranteed, it is important that vitiligo not be viewed as a completely untreatable affliction. A number of therapeutic options are currently available, each with its own advantages and disadvantages. Patience and perseverance are critical, for a trial period of at least 3-4 months is necessary to assess whether any one treatment is effective, and multiple modalities are often attempted before achieving success. The choice of therapy depends on the extent, location, and activity of disease as well as the patient's age, skin type, and motivation to undergo treatment. Some children with skin type I or II and or involvement limited to covered areas may not wish to pursue any treatment other than use of broad spectrum sunscreens. Others with even small lesions in exposed areas, particularly self-conscious adolescents and children who are ridiculed by their peers, may be eager to undergo therapy; however, care must be taken to separate the needs of the child from those of concerned parents. In developing a treatment plan for a child with vitiligo, it is important to determine sites of concern to the patient and explain which areas are more amenable to therapy, be it medical, surgical, or both. This article provides an overview of the treatment options available for children with vitiligo and other disorders of hypopigmentation, including topical corticosteroids, narrow-band UVB, PUVA (topical and oral), and autologous transplantation. For each therapeutic modality, its mechanism of action, indications and restrictions, expected repigmentation rate, side effects, and treatment protocol are reviewed. Experimental and adjunctive treatments as well as depigmentation therapy are also briefly discussed. In addition, factors pertinent to selection of the appropriate patient for each type of therapy are emphasized. The latter, together with clear communication and realistic expectations, provide the basis for a successful approach to the treatment of childhood leukoderma.

8.11.1 Topical Corticosteroids

In general, topical corticosteroids are the first line of therapy for children with vitiligo as well as other disorders of hypopigmentation with an inflammatory component, such as pityriasis alba. Implication of both cellular and humoral immune responses in the pathogenesis of vitiligo provides a rationale for the use of corticosteroids in this disorder. In one series of patients with vitiligo (n = 74), for example, 90% of the biopsy specimens had a dermal lymphocytic infiltrate.[24] Recently, it was also shown that an influx of activated, CD8 skin-homing T-lymphocytes and macrophage paralleled the disappearance of melanocytes from the borders of expanding lesions of generalized vitiligo as well as inflammatory vitiligo.[23,25] Hypopigmentation that accompanies disorders such as seborrheic and atopic dermatitis likewise can be treated by inhibition of the underlying inflammatory process with corticosteroids. Rather than a decreased number or absence of melanocytes, post inflammatory hypopigmentation is thought to result from a decrease in the transfer of pigment from melanocytes to keratinocytes, likely related to factors such as an increase in the distance between cells due to edema or shortened contact time due to an increased proliferation rate.[26]

Advantages of topical corticosteroid therapy for vitiligo include relatively low cost, ease of application, and ability to use at home. Unlike phototherapy (see following section), topical corticosteroids are a treatment option for children of all ages.

Topical corticosteroids are particularly suited for treatment of limited areas, and they are most effective for lesions on the face, elbows, and knees; the proximal extremities and trunk also respond fairly well, while the distal extremities respond poorly.[27,30] Factors potentially contributing to the variation in repigmentation rate by anatomic site include skin permeability, migration of residual melanocytes from uninvolved skin, reversibility of melanocyte damage, and especially preservation and density of follicular reservoirs.[31] In addition, darkly pigmented individuals with vitiligo often have a better response to topical corticosteroids than those with lighter skin.[28]

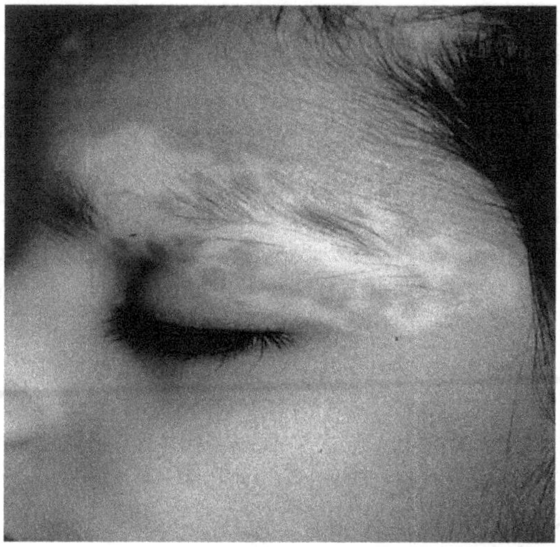

Fig. 8.1 Perifollicular repigmentation within a patch of segmental vitiligo on the left forehead and eyelid following treatment with class V topical corticosteroids.

Limited areas of vitiligo can be treated with daily use of super potent (class I) corticosteroids.[37,38] To decrease local side effects, it is practice to use class I corticosteroids for 6-8 week cycles, alternating with class V corticosteroids (Figure 8.3), or hybrid 2 day/5 day therapy rotating use of class I and class V corticosteroids, respectively. Intertriginous areas are avoided, and strategies for facial lesions include (1) using hybrid therapy; (2) checking for a response of the elbows (Figure 8.4) or knees (if involved) before treatment of the face; (3) doing a small test site on the face; or (4) initially trying medium-potency corticosteroids. In patients with more widespread involvement, one option is to begin by selectively treating patches of vitiligo that are both of particular cosmetic concern to the patient and located on anatomic sites known to respond to therapy.

Superpotent corticosteroids have been used safely in children as young as 3-5 years of age in several studies.[28,29,36] Patients should be monitored closely for early evidence of telangiectasias, cutaneous atrophy, or striae; the former often precede atrophy. Other potential adverse skin reactions include hypertrichosis and acneiform eruptions, especially in older children and adolescents. Treatment with superpotent corticosteroids should be reserved for limited areas of involvement to avoid suppression of the hypothalamic-pituitary-adrenal axis and other systemic side effects. Medium-potency topical corticosteroids are more appropriate for treatment of extensive disease or very young children, and are often tried first in facial lesions because a clinical response may be seen (avoiding the use of class I corticosteroids). Due to the potential side effect of increased intraocular pressure, topical corticosteroids should be used with caution in the periorbital region. Patients can be monitored with Wood's lamp examination at 6-8 week intervals during corticosteroid treatment, and if no response is seen after 3-4 months or 2 "cycles," therapy should be altered. However, multiple cycles are often required to achieve maximal repigmentation (Figure 8.2), and depigmentation may recur upon cessation, requiring additional courses of therapy.[28] Due to a high rate of systemic side effects and inconsistent results, we and others do not recommend the use of oral corticosteroids for the treatment of vitiligo. In most studies, a response to systemic corticosteroid therapy has been limited to patients with rapidly progressive generalized vitiligo.[39] A recent open trial of oral dexamethasone mini-pulse therapy (10 mg on 2 consecutive days weekly) in lightly pigmented patients with vitiligo[30] found that while progression was halted in 88% of those with active disease (39/42), overall, only 7% of patients (2/29) had 50% repigmentation after a mean treatment period of 18 weeks. The majority of patients in this study had side effects, including weight gain, insomnia, acne, and hypertrichosis.

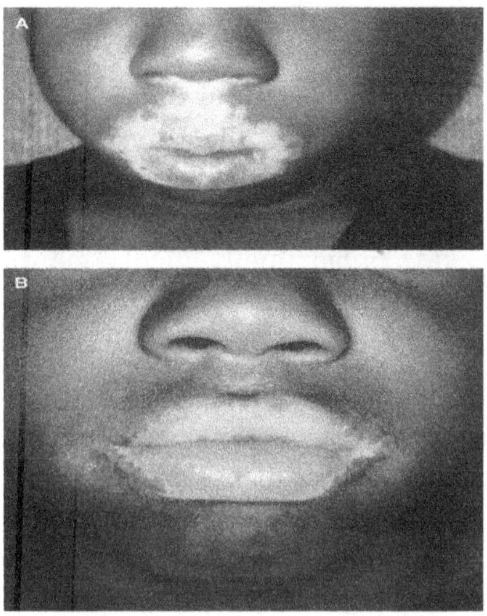

Fig. 8.2 Periorificial vitiligo in a young boy (A) before treatment and (B) with almost complete repigmentation after 2.5 years of therapy of alternating 8 week cycles of class I topical corticosteroids with class V corticosteroids, for a total of 7 cycles. [Colour Fig. on page 407]

8.11.2 Topical Immunomodulators

Topical immunomodulators such as tacrolimus ointment, a formulation of the immunosuppressive macrolide FK506, represent an additional treatment option for childhood vitiligo. In a recent double-blind, randomized, half-side comparative trial (*n* = 20), 23a 0.1% tacrolimus ointment was found to be almost as effective as a class I topical corticosteroid in the treatment of childhood vitiligo (45% vs 65% with 50% repigmentation after 2 months of therapy), with the best response observed for facial lesions. In one series of patients with generalized vitiligo treated with 0.1% tacrolimus ointment, 83% achieved 50% repigmentation. A temporary burning sensation was the most common side effect in these studies. Because it does not produce cutaneous atrophy, tacrolimus may be particularly useful for facial vitiligo, especially in sensitive areas such as the eyelids.

8.11.3 Phototherapy

Although oral and topical psoralens followed by UVA (320-400 nm) irradiation (PUVA) have been two of the most frequently used treatment modalities for vitiligo, they will probably be replaced by narrow-band UVB. Modern photochemotherapy began in 1948, when El Mofty24 reported the successful treatment of vitiligo with an extract from the plant *Ammi majus Linnaeus*, applied topically and/or taken orally, together with either UV light or natural sunlight. Bergapten (5-MOP) and 8-MOP were shown to represent 2 of the major active compounds derived from this plant. Treatment of vitiligo was further optimized in the 1970s with the evolution of high-intensity UVA phototherapy units, 25 then in 1997 with the use of a narrow-band UVB (311 nm) light source.[26,27] The earliest sign of response to phototherapy or topical corticosteroids is perifollicular repigmentation (Figure 8.4) or a hyperpigmented rim. Cytokines and inflammatory mediators released from cells such as keratinocytes as a consequence of UV radiation or PUVA are thought to stimulate inactive melanocytes in the outer root sheath of hair follicles to proliferate, mature, and migrate to repopulate the interfollicular epidermis.[28-32]

The immunosuppressive action of UV-radiation on T-lymphocytes may also have a role in preventing autoimmune mechanisms of melanocyte destruction.[33] A recent left-right comparison study[34] (*n* = 135) showed that combination therapy with UVA and a medium potency topical corticosteroid was 3 times more effective than either treatment alone ($P = 0.001$), suggesting synergy between melanocyte stimulation and immunosuppressive effects (Figure 8.6).

Although phototherapy is considered one of the most effective methods for the treatment of vitiligo,[35] its use requires a highly motivated child and family. There are visits to the light-treatment center approximately twice a week for a period of at least 3-4 months to determine if the therapy is effective, and, if repigmentation occurs, a year or more of therapy is often required to achieve maximal results. As with topical corticosteroid therapy, rates of repigmentation vary depending upon the anatomic site. The face has the highest response rate, the trunk and proximal extremities are intermediate, and the distal digits and lips represent the most treatment-resistant areas. For example, while overall 30-50% of patients achieve cosmetically significant (i.e., 75%) repigmentation with PUVA therapy,[15] the chance of significant repigmentation of the distal fingertips is 5%. Furthermore, when the hairs within a vitiliginous area are depigmented, repigmentation must occur from the periphery of the lesion; this requires 1–1.5 years for an area the size of a 50-cent piece and must be kept in mind when discussing medical therapies.

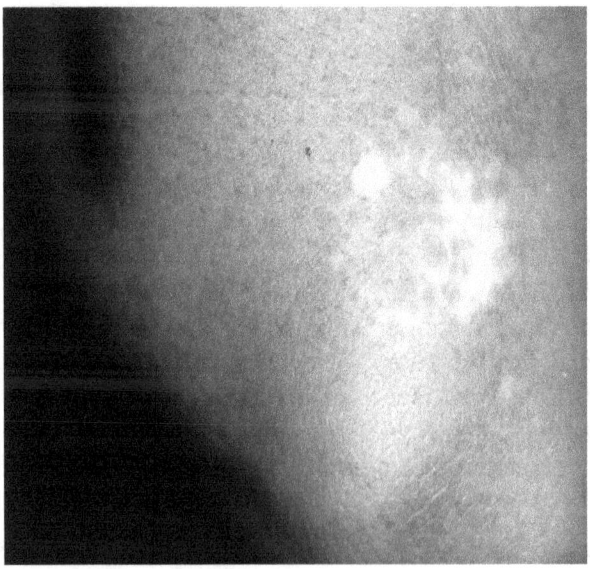

Fig. 8.3 Perifollicular repigmentation of vitiligo on the elbow following two 8 week cycles of therapy with class I topical corticosteroids, alternating with use of class V topical corticosteroid.

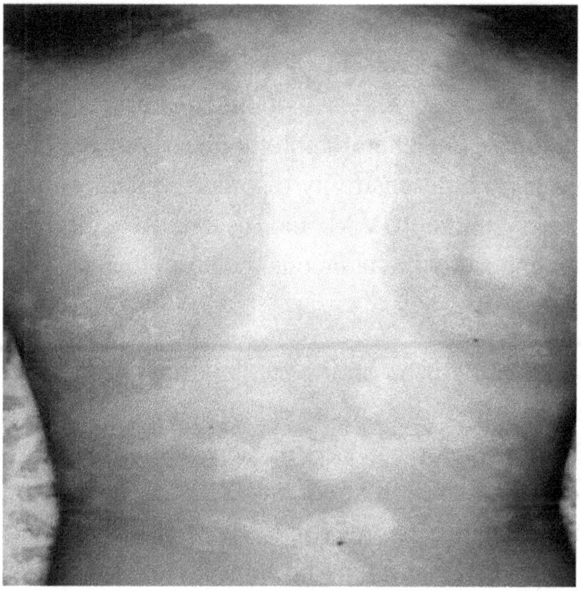

Fig. 8.4 Perifollicular repigmentation of vitiligo following exposure to natural sunlight.

PUVA photochemotherapy

Children with vitiligo tend to respond somewhat betterto PUVA therapy than adults. A recent study 37 showed a mean repigmentation of 70% in children 15 years of age (n = 105) treated with oral and/or topical PUVA, compared to 58% in adults (n = 323). In addition, darkly pigmented patients tolerate higher UVA doses and often achieve more repigmentation with PUVA therapy than those with lighter skin. Repigmentation following PUVA therapy is usually permanent. Two studies have reported retention of 90% of the PUVA-induced pigment in 90% of patients (101/108) 1.5 to 14 years after the conclusion of therapy, with retention nearly always seen in areas of complete repigmentation.[39,40] PUVA therapy also has been attempted for other disorders of leukoderma. The extensive form of pityriasis alba, typically involving the trunk as well as extremities of young adults with no history of atopy, has been shown to respond to oral PUVA;[41] whether this disorder represents pityriasis lichenoides chronica is still a matter of debate. PUVA can induce significant repigmentation in postinflammatory hypopigmention and chemical leukoderma.[26] Lastly, although PUVA has been tried for the leukoderma of piebaldism, only 2 patients have been reported to respond with a slight decrease in the area of hypopigmentation.[26,42] General contraindications to PUVA therapy include pregnancy, photosensitivity disorders, cataracts or retinal disease (particularly for systemic PUVA), and (usually in adults) a history of skin cancer, arsenic exposure, or cutaneous radiation therapy.

Topical PUVA

Topical PUVA therapy is an option for children older than 2 years of age with localized vitiligo that involves 20% of the body surface area. Children treated with topical PUVA have a mean clinical response of 60% repigmentation,[37] which of course varies depending on the anatomic site. Side effects include phototoxicity (erythema and blistering) as well as a rim of hyperpigmentation on the adjacent uninvolved skin; risk of the latter can be reduced by applying broadspectrum sunscreen to surrounding skin before application of topical psoralen. Advantages of topical PUVA include lower cumulative UVA doses than oral PUVA and lack of ocular or systemic toxicity.[37] The commercially available 1% 8-MOP (Methoxalen®) lotion should be diluted 1:10 to 1:100 in alcohol:propylene glycol, acid mantle cream, or Aquaphor; we avoid the former to decrease "running" leading to streaks of hyperpigmentation. A 0.1% concentration of 8-MOP has the same effectiveness as higher concentrations (0.5% or 1%) but a lower risk of phototoxicity.[44] Thirty minutes before UVA exposure, 0.1% to 0.01% 8-MOP is applied to affected areas with a cotton-tipped applicator by a physician or nurse, taking care to avoid surrounding normally pigmented skin. Therapy is typically initiated with UVA doses of 0.12– 0.25 J/cm^2, depending on skin type. Treatments are scheduled once to twice a week, never on consecutive days, and the UVA dose is increased by 0.12–0.25 J/cm^2 per week until a mild erythema is produced. The UVA dose is then held, with adjustments made as necessary to retain a response of asymptomatic erythema. Following each treatment, the area is washed, a broad-spectrum sunscreen is applied, and excessive sun exposure is avoided for at least 24 hours to prevent phototoxic reactions. If severe erythema or blistering occurs, treatments are held until the reaction subsides and then restarted at half of the previous UVA dose. Due to the risk of severe blistering reactions, a 0.1% or higher concentration of 8-MOP should never be used with natural sunlight as a UVA source, and many authors do not recommend any form of topical photochemotherapy outside the office setting.[31,60,62] Considering the inconvenience and costs of in-office topical PUVA, however, Grimes[37] has proposed a home topical PUVA protocol using very dilute 8-MOP (0.001%). This regimen, which is reserved for patients with vitiligo involving 10% of the body surface area, entails applying a thin coat of 0.001% 8-MOP ointment to lesions, waiting 30 minutes, and then exposing the sites to sunlight for 15-30 minutes. Affected areas are treated twice weekly to every other day between 10 am and 4 pm, and exposure time may be increased to 45-60 minutes if mild erythema has not occurred after 2 weeks. As with in-office topical PUVA, washing the sites and applying sunscreen after each treatment are important to prevent phototoxicity. In a series of 125 patients treated with this approach, only 3% had blistering reactions, and the mean repigmentation was 71% of treated areas.[54]

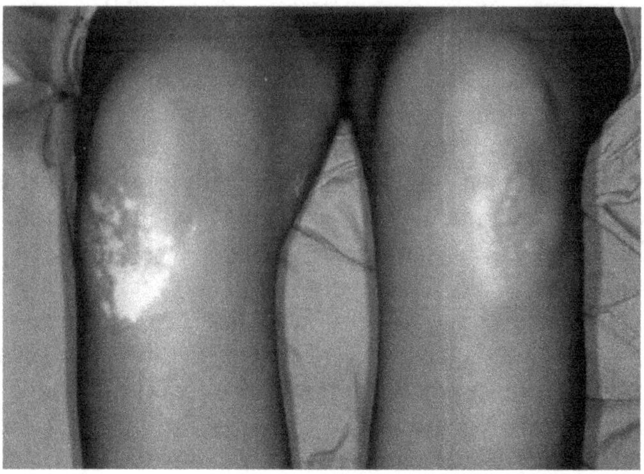

Fig. 8.5 Repigmentation of vitiligo after 75 treatments with oral PUVA and two 8 week cycles of therapy with class I topical corticosteroids (patient's left knee) compared to oral PUVA alone (patient's right knee).

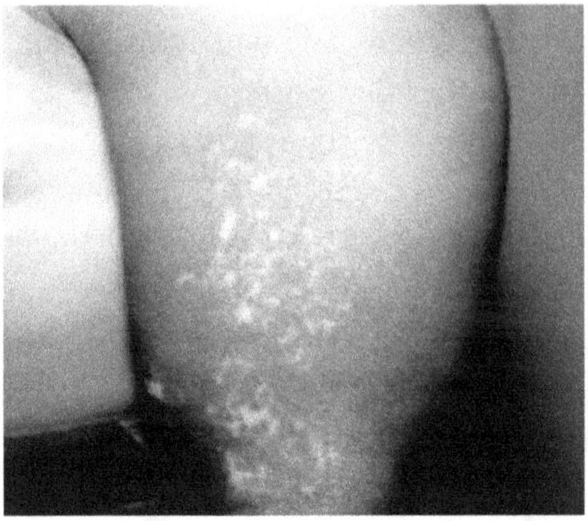

Fig. 8.6 Segmental vitiligo on the left arm showing perifollicular repigmentation after 8 months of treatment with oral PUVA.

Oral PUVA

Oral PUVA may be used for patients with more extensive vitiligo (20% of the body surface area) or those who do not respond to topical therapy. Although oral 8-MOP is not usually recommended for children younger than 12 years of age,[60,63,64] some experienced dermatologists frequently treat children as young as 9 years of age.[54] Approximately 70-80% of patients experience some repigmentation with oral PUVA (mean, 60-70% repigmentation), but 20% achieve complete repigmentation.[54] Phototoxic reactions are less likely with oral as compared to topical administration of 8-MOP. However, other acute side effects of oral PUVA include nausea, vomiting, pruritus, and fatigue. Protective eyewear (e.g., NOIR wrap-around sunglasses) must be worn during sunlight exposure for up to 24 hours after each treatment. This is to prevent the theoretical risk of cataract formation and is particularly critical in children, as protective retinal chromophores do not develop until 12 years of age. Although long-term PUVA therapy for psoriasis has been associated with an increased risk for nonmelanoma skin cancer, in particular squamous cell carcinoma, to date only 2 patients have been reported to have developed squamous cell carcinoma after PUVA therapy for vitiligo.[48] This is likely related to the much lower cumulative UVA doses received by patients with vitiligo compared to those with psoriasis.

The laboratory work-up before initiating oral PUVA therapy includes a complete blood count, liver function tests, and antinuclear antibody testing. An ophthalmologic examination is also recommended at baseline and usually yearly thereafter. Oral PUVA treatments are given twice weekly, with 0.3-0.5 mg/kg of 8-MOP (Oxsoralen Ultra®) taken 1.5 hours before UVA exposure. The initial UVA dose, usually 0.5 J/cm^2, is increased in increments of 0.5 J/cm^2 every other treatment and then held once a mild, asymptomatic erythema is produced. Genitalia, which have a poor therapeutic response and possible increased risk of PUVA-induced skin cancer, are usually shielded during UVA exposure. As with topical PUVA, a broad-spectrum sunscreen should be applied and sun exposure minimized for the first 24-48 hours after treatment. If responsive, perifollicular pigmentation typically should develop within a course of 24 "pink" treatments.[26] Before its withdrawal from the United States market in 1997, we rarely used the synthetic furocoumarin trimethylpsoralen (Trisoralen) because it was less effective than 8-MOP due to its poor absorption from the gastrointestinal tract. Clinical trials suggest that 5-MOP, a naturally occurring psoralen, is comparable to 8-MOP in efficacy but is associated with less nausea, vomiting, and phototoxicity.[49] The use of 5-MOP, however, has not been approved by the US Food and Drug Administration. Khellin is a furanochromone that has been used in conjunction with UVA in the treatment of vitiligo. Although it produces less phototoxicity than 8-MOP, therapy with oral khellin is less effective, has been associated with elevated transaminases in 25% of patients, and is usually not recommended.[32,67]

Water bath PUVA

The most recent model in phototherapy is water bath PUVA, in which the patient lies in a bath tub containing psoralen water for 15 minutes so that the drug gets absorbed on the skin and then goes for light therapy. This kind of therapy is especially beneficial in children for whom oral medicines are not safe.[75] Another method of psoralen treatment, used rarely for pediatric patients with small, scattered vitiligo patches, involves the application of a very dilute solution of the drug directly to the affected skin area. This is then exposed to sunlight. Such topical treatment makes a person very liable to severe burn and blisters following too much sun exposure whereas water bath PUVA has the advantages of being done at home, and does not damage the entire skin surface.

8.11.4 Narrow band UVB therapy

Narrow band UVB therapy or TL-01 therapy is the latest in phototherapy for the treatment of vitiligo. In this therapy there is no need to take oral psoralen or apply psoralen. The therapy is very safe and can be safely administered even to children. Narrow band UVB light is at a wavelength of 311 nm. Narrow band UVB is much safer than full spectrum UVB.

Narrow band UVB is the faithful wavelength that vitiligo responds to best.[76] It's a fact that if exposure to natural sunlight is equal to 100% UV radiation exposure, using a narrow band UV light is roughly 1% UV radiation exposure. Advantages of narrow-band UVB therapy over PUVA include avoidance of psoralens and their side effects, less contrast between pigmented and depigmented skin, and possibly, less long-term photodamage. The 308 nm xenon chloride excimer laser represents another treatment option for localized vitiligo, with the advantage of targeted delivery that does not expose unaffected skin.

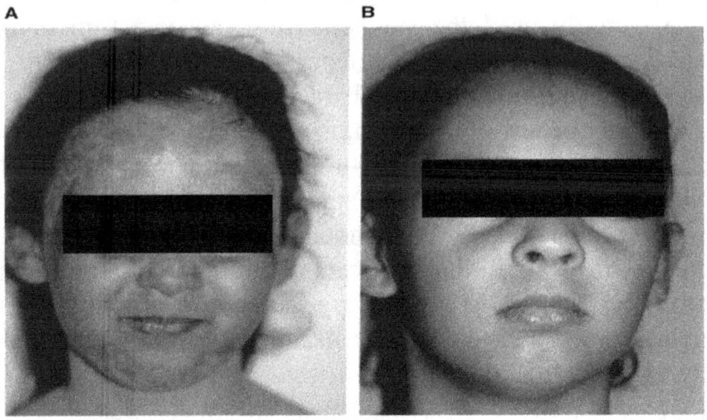

Fig. 8.7 Six-year-old girl with 75% repigmentation of vitiligo involving the face and neck following therapy with narrow-band UVB (from Njoo et al., *J Am Acad Dermatol* 2000;**42**:245-53.).

8.11.5 Autoimmune vitiligo T-cells

The skin is made up of keratinocytes and melanocytes. The keratinocytes make up the bulk of the skin. The melanocytes are the cells that make the skin color. In people with vitiligo, the immune cells which fight infection, attack the melanocytes and damage them.[69] When the melanocytes in a certain area die, the skin turns white. Vitiligo sometimes runs in families, meaning that a genetic factor may be involved. Vitiligo sometimes occurs at the site of an old injury. Even though the condition cannot be cured drastically, medical treatments target the immune system, and try to reverse the destruction.[71] The goal is to restore the skin's color by restoring healthy melanocytes to the skin (repigmentation) allowing the skin to regain its normal appearance.[72] T-cells are more common in vitiligo skin and remains in lesional area but most of the infiltrate appears to migrate with the depigmenting epidermal border. The infiltrate consists not only of CD8 but also of CD4 T-cells. Skin infiltrating T-cells can be isolated and propagated without antigen selection in the presence of IL-2 and anti-CD3/anti-CD28 antibody coated beads. T-cells have been isolated from perilesional skin of a vitiligo patient. These T-cells were found to have similar reactivity towards vitiligo patient melanocytes. Autoimmune response may be allowed to grow and develop in the absence of functional T-regulatory cells. These cells actively mediate suppression of the immune system generally by secreting IL-10 and TGF-β to prevent autoimmunity. Polyclonal cytotoxic T-cells derived from vitiligo skin are highly reactive towards melanoma cells and may serve as a superior source of high affinity TCR genes to treat melanoma.[73]

Tissue grafts

The grafts will be implanted into perforations made at the recipient site using a biopsy punch under local anaesthesia. The grafts should be placed 4-8 mm apart because apparently pigment cells seem not to migrate beyond 5 mm. The grafted area will then be covered with petrolatum gauze or a transparent adhesive tape and secured with bandages to give compression and fixation for at least one week. The success rate of this technique depends upon the individual skin type.[77-79] Difficult areas like lips can also be treated using this technique. Repigmentation is based on the pigment spread phenomena by the grafted piece of normal skin. Pigment spread occurs gradually after grafting within 1 month and full repigmentation can be achieved in 3-6 months.[80]

Split thickness skin grafts

This technique has a high success rate of 78-91%. After obtaining a split thickness skin graft using a dermatome it can be applied directly to the derma braded recipient area. Temporary small epithelial milia like cysts can be observed in the recipient area during the first months, especially on the face and neck. Scar or keloid formation at the donor site is reported in 12% of the patients treated with split thickness grafts. As donor tissue is limited more than one split skin grafting session can be necessary.[81]

Suction blister grafts

Grafts are carefully removed with sharp scissors and forceps after harvesting the graft. This epidermal sheet is then grafted onto the denuded recipient site. The success rate is 73-88%. Pigment spread after epidermal blister grafting can be enhanced by pre operative radiation therapy of the donor site using PUVA. Temporary hyper pigmentation can be seen in the grafted sites in 2-65%.[81]

8.11.6 Non Cultured Keratinocytes and Melanocytes

Transplantation technique with a suspension of non cultured keratinocytes and melanocytes in the treatment of depigmented lesions is effective. Donor skin is obtained from the occipital area and immersed for 18 hours in 0.25% trypsin solution. The following day the epidermis of the donor skin can be separated from the dermis *in vitro* using fine forceps. After several procedures a cellular suspension is obtained.[82] Liquid nitrogen is used to induce blisters in the recipient area. The cellular suspension from the donor site is injected into each blister at the recipient area after aspiration of the viscous blister fluid. The intact blister top is a natural dressing that holds the transplanted cells in place. It is important not to separate keratinocytes from melanocytes before grafting because factors furnished by keratinocytes sustain melanocyte growth.[81]

Transplantation of cultured melanocytes

Lerner et al., first described the use of cultured pure autologous human melanocytes. They explained pigment cells of a shave biopsy from normally pigmented skin *in vitro* with the addition of several growth factors and chemical media.[83]

Cultured epidermal grafts

A shave biopsy of normally pigmented skin is the source for epidermal cell culture. After separating the epidermis from the dermis the cells are seeded in a medium that allows co-cultivation of melanocytes and keratinocytes. After a week a cultured sheet is obtained, released by treatment with dispase and attached to petrolatum gauze as support. Subsequently the gauze to which the epithelium adheres will be applied onto the derma braded recipient site and covered with occlusive dressing.[84] The greatest advantage of this technique is the potential expansion of the cells in culture, which permits treatment of a wide area of hypomelanosis with a small sacrifice donor skin. Because only superficial dermabrasion is performed, the procedure is non-scaring.[84]

Stability in surgical repigmentation of vitiligo

Even after almost thirty years of implementing surgery in vitiligo, there seems to be little consensus among workers regarding the optimal required period of stability. After several years of experience in surgical repigmentation of vitiligo, some interesting observations are raising up. The observation is that even after grafting, the pigment spread from successive sessions of grafting can be unpredictable; perigraft spread of pigment may be minimal or absent and in some cases even depigmentation of grafts is noted.[85]

Autologous skin grafts

This type of skin grafting is often used for patients with small, stable patches of vitiligo (recipient sites). Normal unaffected skins from the thigh or buttocks area of a patient's body (donor sites) were taken and fixed it to an area of vitiligo. The treated area responds almost 90% of the time, but may develop a cobblestone appearance, or a spotty pigmentation, or may fail to re-pigment at all.[86]

Fake tanning products

Cover creams or self tanning products are special drug cosmetics that can be used to match most skin patches when medical treatment is not successful. All patients with vitiligo should always protect their depigmented skin against excessive sun exposure by wearing protective clothing. Tattooing is rarely recommended. It works best for the lip area, particularly in people with dark skin. However, it is difficult to perfectly match the skin, and tends to look worse over time. The remaining skin will be an even white color, which can then be covered with the cosmetics. Cosmetics can be used to improve the appearance of the white areas not covered by clothing. Sunscreens give coolness to the affected areas and also prevent the normal skin around the patches from becoming darker. Bleaching or depigmentation of the normal skin and autologous transplantation of skin are an option for those who are severely affected.[87]

Vitamin D analogues

Combination of PUVA (psoralen-sun therapy) and calcipotriol is highly effective and may be used for shortening the therapy with PUVA in the treatment of patchy areas of vitiligo depigmentation.[88] Topical calcipotriol appeared to be an effective and well tolerated treatment for vitiligo and it can be safely used in conjunction with PUVA.[89]

Pseudocatalase

Narrow-band UVB-activated topical pseudocatalase is another proposed treatment modality for vitiligo. It is hypothesized that overproduction of hydrogen peroxide in patients with vitiligo results in both direct melanocyte toxicity and further disruption of the cellular redox state via inactivation of various enzymes, including catalase as well as those involved in the recycling of 6-BH4, a cofactor for the hydroxylation of phenylalanine to tyrosine. Pseudocatalase acts as a substitute for impaired catalase, degrading excessive hydrogen peroxide and thereby allowing recovery of enzyme activities. Although some repigmentation has been observed in 60% of patients treated with this method, the degree to which the narrow-band UVB irradiation, alone an effective treatment for vitiligo, contributed to these results is not clear.

8.11.7 Other Medical Therapies

A number of other medical therapies for vitiligo have been described, usually in conjunction with exposure to some form of UV radiation. Studies of oral and topical administration of l-phenylalanine followed by exposure to UVA or sunlight have shown variable effectiveness.[93] It has been postulated that in patients with vitiligo, abnormalities in tetrahydrobiopterin (BH4) metabolism interfere with the conversion of l-phenylalanine to tyrosine (the initial precursor in the melanin biosynthetic pathway) and that excess l-phenylalanine may overcome this inhibition.[94] Paradoxically, l-phenylalanine is also known to act as a competitive inhibitor of tyrosinase activity. Reports of hyperpigmentation of calcipotriol-treated areas in patients receiving PUVA for psoriasis, together with evidence of perturbed calcium homeostasis in vitiliginous skin and the known expression of 1,25-dihydroxyvitamin D3 receptors by melanocytes, provided the basis for use of calcipotriol in patients with vitiligo.

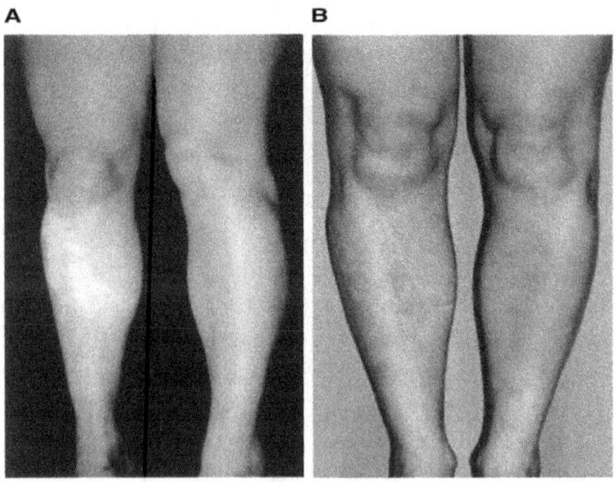

Fig. 8.8 Leukoderma on the right lower leg of a patient with piebaldism (A) before transplantation and (B) showing almost complete repigmentation after 7 sessions of split-thickness skin grafting and 2 sessions of minigrafting (From Njoo et al., *Br J Dermatol* 1998;**139**:829-33.).

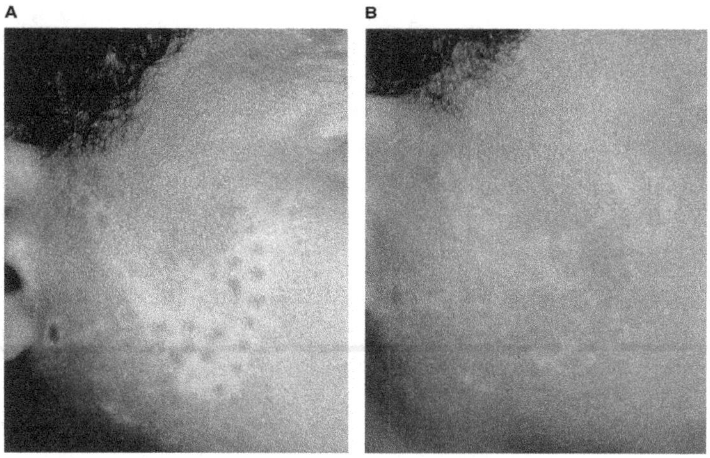

Fig. 8.9 Stable segmental vitiligo of the cheek (A) 1 month and (B) 9 months after placement of multiple 5-6-mm suction-blister epidermal grafts (from R. Falabella, *Dermatol Ther* 2001;**14**:7-14.).

8.11.8 Adjunctive Therapies

The use of sunscreens by patients with vitiligo is important to prevent sunburn of susceptible depigmented areas or induction of the Koebner phenomenon. In addition, sunscreen use minimizes tanning of uninvolved skin and thereby decreases the contrast with lesional skin; this can improve the appearance of vitiligo as well as disorders of hypopigmentation such pityriasis alba. In particular, broad-spectrum sunscreens alone can be an effective therapy in vitiligo patients with skin type I or II.20 sunscreening agents are divided into 2 groups: (1) chemical sunscreens that absorb UVB and/or UVA (e.g., para-amino benzoic acid, para-amino benzoic acid esters, cinnamates, and salicylates); and (2) physical sunscreens that block or scatter both UVB and UVA (e.g,, zinc oxide and titanium dioxide). A broad-spectrum sunscreen protects against both UVA and UVB radiation; UVA protection (which is not reflected in the sun protection factor) is provided by certain chemical sunscreens (e.g., benzophenones and avobenzone) as well as by physical sunscreens. All children with vitiligo should use a waterproof, broad-spectrum sunscreen with a sun protection factor of at least 15 on all exposed skin, both pigmented and depigmented. Use of sunprotective clothing such as wide-brimmed hats should also be recommended. Cosmetic products are an option for camouflage of vitiligo (Figure 8.10) and other forms of leukoderma in some patients, in particular, adolescent girls with limited facial involvement. However, the use of cosmetic cover-ups is not ideal in children. It may be apparent that the patient is wearing a cosmetic, which can result in embarrassment and teasing by peers. Furthermore, conventional cosmetic products (e.g., Dermablend® and Covermark®) may rub off during play activities. Other options such as topical stains and self-tanning products (most containing dihydroxyacetone as the active ingredient) can sometimes be difficult to match to the natural skin color. Lastly, synthetic melanins have been incorporated into cover-ups that may be useful in patients with vitiligo.[95]

Depigmentation therapy

In adolescent patients with widespread and extensive vitiligo (50% of the body surface area) that is resistant to treatment, depigmentation therapy represents an important option. The ultimate goal of this treatment modality is uniformly depigmented skin. The most commonly used technique involves once- to twice-daily at-home application of monobenzyl ether of hydroquinone to areas with residual pigment, which results in gradual lightening of the skin via destruction of epidermal melanocytes. Depigmentation of a particular site typically requires 4-12 months of therapy.[96] Recently, the sequential use of 4-methoxyphenol and the Q-switched ruby laser has been reported as another option for depigmentation therapy.[97] Before instituting treatment with monobenzyl ether of hydroquinone, the patient must be aware of the aforementioned time course, the risk of distant sites of depigmentation, side effects such as contact dermatitis and conjunctival melanosis, potential for repigmentation via follicular melanocytes (Figure 8.11), requirement for life-long photoprotection (which may limit outdoor activities), and the probable permanency of depigmentation. Discussion of the latter aspect of monobenzyl ether of hydroquinone depigmentation is particularly important with young patients, for it is possible that more effective therapies for vitiligo will be discovered in the future. Lastly, the social ramifications of depigmentation therapy must be discussed, especially for patients with skin types IV and V, and the patient should fully accept the concept of a permanently altered body appearance.[96]

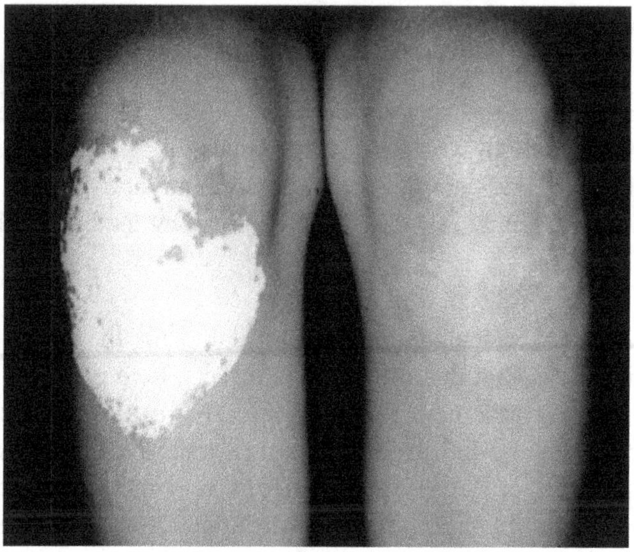

Fig. 8.10 Comparison of vitiligo with (patient's left knee) and without (patient's right knee) cosmetic cover-up.

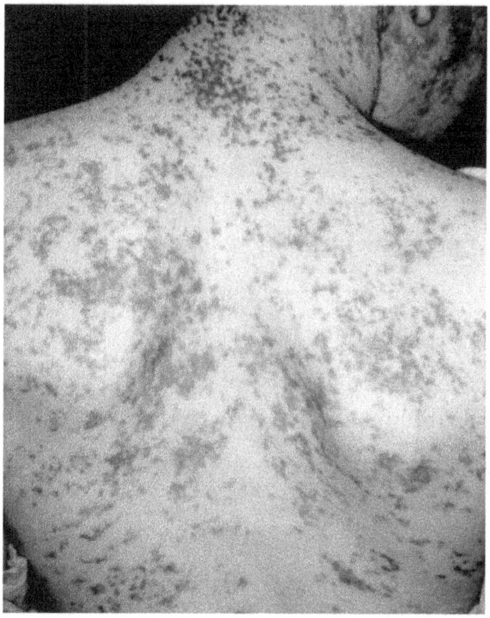

Fig. 8.11 Numerous perifollicular macules of repigmentation following unprotected exposure to the sun in a patient with extensive vitiligo who previously underwent depigmentation therapy with monobenzyl ether of hydroquinone (from JL Bolognia et al., *Dermatol Ther* 2001;**14**:29-34.).

8.11.9 Herbal Medicine for Vitiligo

Vitiligo is skin problem in which due the lack of skin pigment in white spots of irregular shape appears on skin. Vitiligo is such disease which exact origin, such like how it occurs in a person, is it a genetic disorder or such other questions are not fully known to anyone. Except something like it is neither a contagious disease nor spread by the bacterial attacks.

Vitiligo and psoralens

Different latest treatment options are available for the treatment of this vitiligo skin disease but due the negative effects, long period of treatment, very high pricing treatment many people are in search of some other affective treatment option. In this regard psoralens are the best thing for treatment of vitiligo. A useful substance with some tanning by sunlight for repigmentation in of the vitiligo white spots. It is herbal medicine and there for it is necessary to describe some benefits of herbal medicines.

Herbal treatment

The most ancient treatment option for men is herbal medicine. It would be not wrong to say that history of medicine is start from the herbal medicine. The aim of this entry is to provide the info about the importance and effectiveness of the herbal medicines. Importance and use of herbal medicines had been obscured in last few decade due the involvement of latest technologies in medical fields. But today once again the popularity of this medicine is increasing rapidly.

There is much reason for the increasing use of herbal medicine among them someone discussed in this post.

1. These are available at very reasonable price as compared to the other prescribe medicines.
2. There is very rare chance of negative reaction associated with herbal medicines.
3. Easy to use, kike for vitiligo most of the natural treatment based on topical form which apply only in affected area.
4. Solution oriented approach: Traditionally the herbalist use the mixture base remedy for example 12 different people with same diseases, would each receive a different mixture. This diagnosis based on factors that are no longer used by latest medicine.

Organic remedy for vitiligo

Organic remedy for vitiligo should contain following active ingredients:

- Coconut oil
- Black cumin
- *Psoralea corylifolia*
- Barberry root

People with Vitiligo need a product that can modulate their immune system rather boosting (over-active) or weakening (under-active) the immune system. Therefore, one wrong agent/ingredient can cause undesirable reactions. For this reason, don't take the risk of using any vitiligo treatment product without first knowing what the active ingredients the product has.

What make vitiligo oil stand out distinct among the rest are its 100% pure herbal ingredients that include black cumin, *Psoralea corylifolia*, coconut oil, and barberry root.

Coconut oil

Coconut oil is slow to oxidize and thus resistant to rancidity. Coconut oil is the only type of oil that one should use on one's skin for it is absorbed easily and keeps the skin soft. Coconut oil contains vitamin E alpha tocopherol. This kind of vitamin is a well-known potent antioxidant and is beneficial to the skin. With coconut oil as its agent, our organic remedy for vitiligo cure vitiligo oil will make your skin smoother, softer, and moist.

Black cumin

Black cumin refers to seeds derived from a plant called *Nigella sativa*. These are effective to stimulate melanocytes that initiate repigmentation of the skin cells.

Psoralea corylifolia

Psoralen occurs in the seeds of *Psoralea corylifolia* and is a photo-sensitizing agent. It reacts with ultraviolet light and causes darkening of the skin.

Barberry root

The herb includes such alkaloids as berbamine, berberine, oxyacanthine, resin and tannins, and chelidonic acid. Barberry root also constituents the B-vitamin thiamine, vitamin C, lutein, zeaxanthin, the carotenoids beta-carotene, chromium, zinc, and cobalt. The herb has antioxidant and cytoprotective properties.

Herbal products

Anti-vitiligo® (True Herbals, Lahore, Pakistan) Anti-vitiligo® (True Herbals, Lahore, Pakistan) is a traditional herbal formulation which was available internationally since November 2003. It is effective both in disease of recent onset as well as long standing established cases. Formulation contains the following ingredients.

Psoralea corylifolia

It is a rich source of naturally occurring psoralen. It sensitizes human skin to the tanning effect of UV and sun light. *P. corylifolia* has been traditionally used both orally as well as in the form of topical preparations. Oxidative stress is widely believed to be one of the likely causative factors in the initiation of white skin patches of vitiligo. Hence, the protective, anti-oxidative and anti- stress properties of *P. corylifolia* may contribute to the improvement in the hypopigmented white skin patches of vitiligo.

Black cumin

Seeds of *Nigella sativa* have also been having an immunomodulatory as well as anti cancer effect, which is due to augmentation of T-cell and natural killer cell mediated immune responses.[90]

Barberry root

Barberry root or the root of *Berberis vulgaris* contains numerous chemicals and bioactive compounds of medical significance. It contains for example the alkaloids like berbamine, berberine, and oxyacanthine. Other compounds include tannins, chelidonic acid and resins. It is also quite rich in B-vitamin thiamine, lutein, vitamin C, beta-carotene, zeaxanthin, zinc, chromium, and cobalt. This herb has also been shown in scientific studies to possess antioxidant and cytoprotective properties.[90]

Kalawalla® (American Life Style, New York, USA)

Kalawalla® (American Life Style, New York, USA) is a herbal product that works as a natural immunomodulator with proven immunomodulating effect. The product contains *Polypodium leucotomos* standardized extracts. *P. leucotomos* is a fern plant extract that has been used in Europe to treat vitiligo for over 10 years with encouraging results. Vitiligo is characterized by skin depigmentation and is commonly associated with the immune system. The extract can help to regulate the immune system bringing it to its healthiest, strongest and balanced levels. Repigmentation results can be seen within the first month of taking the product. *P. leucotomos* standardized extract has been known to increase the lymphocyte levels. It is also known to regulate the CD4/CD8 ratios to their normal values.[91] This product contains (per capsule): *P. leucotomos* extract 120 mg and *P. leucotomos* rhizome 280 mg.

Piperine

The synthetic derivatives of piperine can stimulate pigmentation in the skin especially when combined with UVR treatment.[92] The studies have compared the effects of piperine and its analogues tetrahydropiperine (THP), cyclohexyl analogue of piperine (CHP) and reduced CHP (rCHP) when applied to the skin of mice, either alone or followed by UV treatment. CHP did not show significant results while piperine, THP and rCHP did induce pigmentation in the skin. When used alone, the compounds stimulated pigmentation to an even, light brown color within six weeks. However, by accompanying the use of piperine or THP with UV, the skin became significantly darker, and within only seven weeks as compared to other treatments which take a year or so.[92]

Herbal anti-leucoderma cream

Herbal Anti-Leucoderma cream contains

Psoralia corilifolia
Chaulmoogra oil
Tulasi oil
Neem oil
Vanishing cream Base

8.12 Marketed Products

Pigmento cream

[Colour Fig. on page 408]

Description

Pigmento cream is a herbal preparation to treat skin pigmentation disorders, acquired white patches, vitiligo, and leucoderma. The re-pigmenting formula that acts from deep within to treat pigmentation problems naturally and safely.

Benefits

1. Stimulates melanogenesis.
2. Promotes transfer of melanin to the skin.
3. Helps in Conjunction with UV therapy.

Dietary discipline

During therapy, the patients should consume boiled vegetarian food with a minimum of condiments. Curd, sour fruits, foods containing combinations of milk with jaggery and fruits should be avoided during, and for 3 months after therapy.

Herbal anti-vitiligo cream

It is a herbal research based formulation of herbs in form of powder or cream for application over the white patches. It starts re-pigmentation immediately after penetrating through skin pores over the vitiligo white patches. Pattern will be brown spot formation or sidewise squeezing or pink conversion of a patch.

- Acts superficially by penetrating through skin pores
- Activates melanocyte cells to produce melanin
- Helps to start repigmentation over white patches immediately
- Helps in covering a white patch
- Application - daily over affected areas only

Ayurhealthline [Colour Fig. on page 408]

Herbal anti-vitiligo capsules

Herbal Anti-vitiligo Capsules starts repigmentation over white patches areas within 3-5 weeks

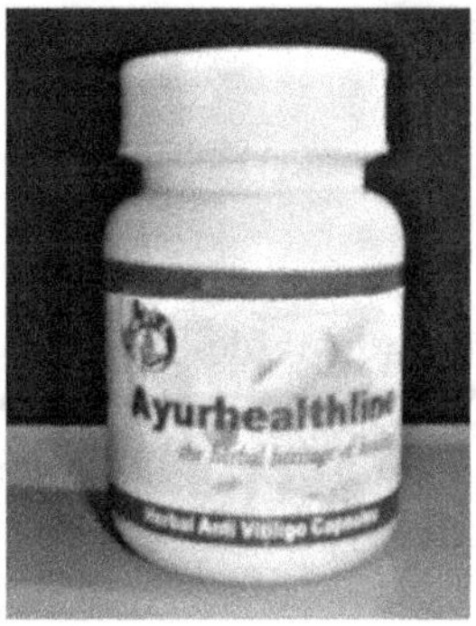

Ayurhealthline [Colour Fig. on page 408]

Anti-vitiligo kit

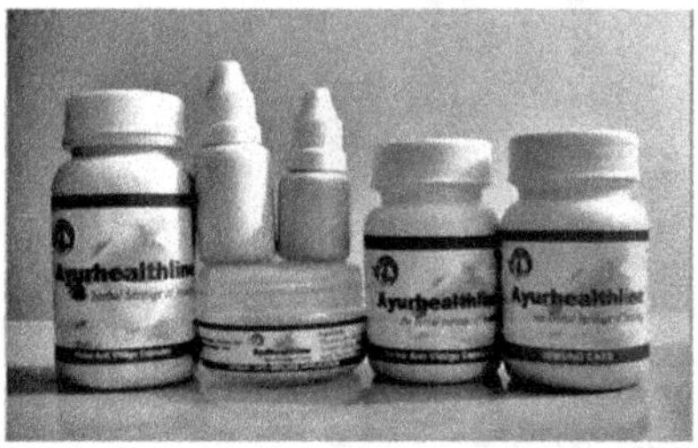

[Colour Fig. on page 408]

Ayurhealthline has the specialty to repigment the vitiligo leucoderma patches with permanency in result. It has researched & developed its unique Anti Vitiligo kit treatment to treat vitiligo & leucoderma.

Kalawalla vitiligo dietary supplement

[Colour Fig. on page 408]

Anti-vitiligo cream – dermablend cover creme

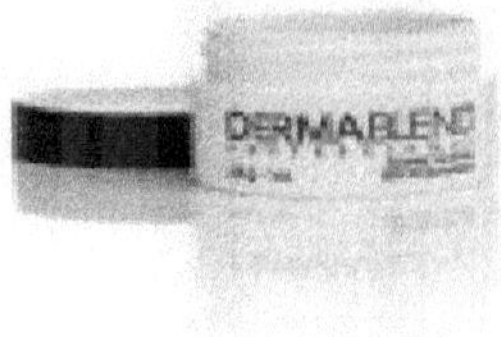

[Colour Fig. on page 408]

Active ingredients : Titanium dioxide 3%. Other ingredients mineral oil, talc, beeswax, isopropyl palmitate, stearyl stearate, kaolin, mannesium carbonate, *Copernicia cerifera* (carnauba) wax, allantoin, microcrystalline wax, lauroyl lysine.

Anti-vitiligo oil

[Colour Fig. on page 409]

Novitil

Novitil gel a vitligo product which tries to naturally support the skin pigmentation production function. Its manufacturer claims that it has no side effects and take up to 6 months to completely cure vitiligo.

Vitiligo protopic

Basically Protopic is used for treatment of eczema it suppress the immune response of the skin. Vitiligo is an autoimmune disorder and Protopic used to decrease the immune reaction against the pigment producing cells. According to Vitiligo Society about Protopic "The ointment is showing very good success in many (but not all) people who are using it."

Drula pigment cream against vitiligo

It is self tanner which tone the vitiligo spots and brown color substance cover the white patches. Slowly it moderate the dark and white skin.

Pigmento tablet for leucoderma treatment

[Colour Fig. on page 409]

Ingredients

Pigmento is made from the most renowned Ayurvedic herbs that are known for their actions in tearing the skin related disorders. Below are the ingredients of Pigmento tablets Abhrak 0.225 mg, Loh 0.225 mg, Tamra 0.225 mg, *Emblica officinalis* Amla 0.375 mg, *Terminalia belerica* Baheda 0.375 mg, *Terminalia chebula* Harde 0.375 mg, *Hingul shuddha* 0.75 mg, Purified *Asphaltum Shilajit* Shuddha 0.9 mg, Kajjali 1.125 mg, *Caesalpinia bonducella* Latakaranj Beej 1.875 mg, Shankha 3.75 mg, *Plumbago zeylanica* Chitrak Mool 3.75 mg, *Sapindus mukorossi* Aritha bhasma 3.75 mg, *Acacia catechu* Katha (Kanpuri) 3.75 mg, *Nardostachys jatamansi* Jatamansi 3.75 mg, Sonageru 6.5 mg, Navayas Loh 6.5 mg, *Myristica fragrans* Jaiphal 7.5 mg, *Caryophyllus aromaticus* Lavang 7.5 mg, *Elettaria cardamomum* Elaichi 7.5 mg, Purified *Ferula foetida* Hing Shuddha 7.5 mg, *Cuminum cyminum* Jeera 7.5 mg, *Cinnamomum iners* Tamalpatra 7.5 mg, Saindhav 7.5 mg, *Piper nigrum* Mari 7.5 mg, Yavakshar 7.5 mg, *Cyperus rotundus* Nagarmotha 7.5 mg, *Cinnamomum cassia* Taj 7.5 mg, *Carum copticum* Ajmo 7.5 mg, *Zingiber officinale* Sonth 7.5 mg, *Lawsonia alba* Mendi Paan 11.25 mg, *Swertia chirata* Chirata 11.25 mg, Yashad 15 mg, *Piper longum* Pippali 15 mg, *Picrorrhiza kurrooa* Katuki 18.5 mg, *Acorus calamus* Vaj 30 mg, Panchamrit Parpati 37.5 mg, *Melia azadirachta* Neem Paan 3.75 mg, *Aloe barbadensis* Kunvar Patha 11.1 mg, *Ipomoea turpethum* Nishotar 11.25 mg, *Embelia ribes* Vayvidang 11.25 mg, *Butea frondosa* Palash

Pushpa 11.25 mg, *Lawsonia alba* Mendi Paan 16.8 mg, *Melia azadirachta* Neem Chhal 22.5 mg, *Amoora rohituka* Rohitak 22.5 mg, *Picrorrhiza kurrooa* Katuki 22.5 mg, *Tinospora cordifolia* Galo 22.5 mg, *Boerhaavia diffusa* Punarnava 22.5 mg, *Tephrosia purpurea* Sharpunkha 22.5 mg, *Solanum nigrum* Kakmachi 22.5 mg, *Eclipta alba* Bhangra 33.6 mg, *Andrographis paniculata* Kalmegh 45.0 mg, *Psoralea corylifolia* Bavchi Beej 93.75 mg

8.13 Conclusion

Vitiligo is an autoimmune disease which targets pigment cells and constitutes a huge research innovation for those interested in melanocyte biology and pigmentation disorder. A number of treatment options are available for vitiligo, ranging from topical corticosteroids to narrow-band UVB and PUVA (topical and oral) phototherapy to autologous transplantation techniques. Although they share the goal of restoring pigment, each modality has distinct advantages and disadvantages, and selecting the right patient is critical. It is important to consider factors such as the extent, location, andactivity of disease as well as the patient's age, skin type, and motivation. With the exception of postinflammatory hypopigmentation, the treatment of other disorders of hypopigmentation is limited. Topical steroids are probably first line therapy for most patients. There are a number of other therapies such as surgical techniques that seem promising. However, further studies are necessary. But now the time has come to offer patients hope for therapy by identifying suitable antibody targets in vitiligo. T-cells from vitiligo skin are highly reactive towards melanoma cells and serve as an effective source to treat melanoma. This could also provide a basis for the development of diagnostic tests. Antigens recognized by vitiligo antibodies could serve as markers for important T-cell responses in patients with the disease.

Steroid creams are the first line treatment for vitiligo. Oral medications of psoralen and phototherapy by ultraviolet rays (PUVA) can be tried for extensive vitiligo. Combination of PUVA (psoralen-sun therapy) and calcipotriol is highly effective. Black cumin has an immuno-modulatory effect due to augmentation of T-cell and natural killer cell mediated immune responses. *P. leucotomos* is a fern plant whose extract has been used in Europe to treat vitiligo for over 10 years with encouraging results Piperine can stimulate pigmentation in the skin especially when combined with UV treatment.

References

1. Nair BKH. Vitiligo-A retrospect. *Int J ikrmatol* 1978;**17**: 755-7.
2. Koranne RV, Sachdeva KG. Vitiligo. *Int J Dermatol* 1988;**27**:676-81.
3. Goldman L, Moraites RS, Kitzmiller KW. White spots in biblical times. *Arch Dermatol* 19h6;93:7U-S.
4. Ortonne JP, Mosher DB, Fitzpatrick DB. editors. *Vitiligo and other hypomelanoses of hair and skin.* New York/ London: Plenum, 1983:129-310.
5. Kaposi M, editor. Pathologie und Thrrapie der Iiautkrankheiten. Berlin/ Wien: Urban und Schwarzcnberg (1st edition 1879) 5th edition, 1899:624,703
6. Sutton RL. On definition of vitiligo (letter). 4rch Dermatol 1965;91:288. Brocq L, editor. Traitement des malad & dcs la peau. Paris: Doin, 1892:85
7. Neumann I, editor. Lehrbuch der Hautkrankheitm. Wien: Braumiiller, 1880:436.
8. Ltwwr 48. Vitiligo. *J Invest Dermatol I* 2115-310.
9. Halder, RM; Chappell, JL (2009). "Vitiligo update.". *Seminars in cutaneous medicine and surgery* **28** (2): 86–92.
10. Nath SK, Majumder PP, Nordlund JJ (November 1994). "Genetic epidemiology of vitiligo: multilocus recessivity cross-validated". *American Journal of Human Genetics* **55** (5): 981–90.
11. National Institute of Arthritis and Musculoskeletal and Skin Diseases (March 2007). "What Is Vitiligo? Fast Facts: An Easy-to-Read Series of Publications for the Public Additional". http://www.niams.nih.gov/Health_Info/Vitiligo/vitiligo_ff.asp#c. Retrieved July 18, 2010.
12. Halder RM, et al. (2007). "72. Vitiligo". In Wolff K, Freedberg IM, Fitzpatrick TB (eds). *Fitzpatrick's dermatology in general medicine* (7th ed.). New York: McGraw-Hill Professional..
13. Huggins RH, Schwartz RA, Janniger CK (December 2005). "Vitiligo". *Acta Dermatovenerologica Alpina, Panonica, et Adriatica* **14**(4): 137–42, 144–5..
14. Picardi A, Pasquini P, Cattaruzza MS, Gaetano P, Melchi CF, Baliva G, Camaioni D, Tiago A, Abeni D, Biondi M (2003).

"Stressful life events, social support, attachment security and alexithymia in vitiligo. A case-control study". *Psychotherapy and Psychosomatics* **72**(3): 150–8.

15. Halder RM, et al. Vitiligo. In: Wolff K, et al. *Fitzpatrick's Dermatology in General Medicine.* 7th ed. New York, N.Y.: McGraw-Hill Professional; 2007

16. http://www.skincell.org/vitiligo.shtml

17. Jin Y, Birlea SA, Fain PR, et al. (May 2010). "Variant of TYR and autoimmunity susceptibility loci in generalized vitiligo". *N. Engl. J. Med.* **362** (18): 1686–97.

18. Strömberg S, Björklund MG, Asplund A, et al. (April 2008). "Transcriptional profiling of melanocytes from patients with vitiligo vulgaris". *Pigment Cell & Melanoma Research* **21** (2): 162–71.

19. Hedstrand H, Ekwall O, Olsson MJ, et al. (September 2001). "The transcription factors SOX9 and SOX10 are vitiligo autoantigens in autoimmune polyendocrine syndrome type I". *The Journal of Biological Chemistry* **276** (38): 35390–5.

20. Mashaghi A et al. Possible association of the CD4 gene polymorphism with vitiligo. *Clin Exp Dermatol.* (2010) **35(5)**:521-4.

21. Gregersen PK (March 2007). "Modern genetics, ancient defenses, and potential therapies". *The New England Journal of Medicine* **356** (12): 1263–6.

22. Jin Y, Mailloux CM, Gowan K, et al. (March 2007). "NALP1 in vitiligo-associated multiple autoimmune disease". *The New England Journal of Medicine* **356** (12): 1216–25.

23. van den Wijngaard R, Wankowicz-Kalinska A, Pals S, et al. Autoimmune melanocyte destruction in vitiligo. *Lab Invest* 2001;**81**:1061–7.

24. Gokhale BB, Mehta LN. Histopathology of vitiliginous skin. *Int J Dermatol* 1983;**22**:477–80.

25. Van den Wijngaard R, Wankowicz-Kalinska A, Le Poole C, et al. Local immune response in skin of generalized vitiligo patients: destruction of melanocytes is associated with the prominent presence of CLA_ T cells at the perilesional site. *Lab Invest* 2000;**80**:1299–309.

26. Bolognia JL. Therapeutics in pigmentary disorders: medical, surgical and physical approaches. In: Levine N, editor. *Pigmentation and pigmentary disorders.* Boca Raton, Fla: CRC Press Inc, 1993:502–7.

27. Koga M. Vitiligo: a new classification and therapy. *Br J Dermatol* 1977;**97**:255–61.

28. Kumari J. Vitiligo treated with topical clobetasol propionate. *Arch Dermatol* 1984;**120**:631 5.

29. Liu XQ, Shao CG, Jin PY, et al. Treatment of localized vitiligo with ulobetasol cream. *Int J Dermatol* 1990;**29**: 295–7.

30. Khalid M, Mujtaba G, Haroon TS. Comparison of 0.05% clobetasol propionate cream and topical PUVASOL in childhood vitiligo. *Int J Dermatol* 1995;**34**:203–5.

31. Halder RM, Brooks HL. Medical therapies for vitiligo. *Dermatol Ther* 2001;**14**:1–6.

32. Njoo MD, Spuls PI, Bos JD, et al. Nonsurgical repigmentation therapies in vitiligo. *Arch Dermatol* 1998;**134**:1532– 40.

33. Njoo MD, Das PK, Bos JD, et al. Association of the Ko¨ebner phenomenon with disease activity and therapeutic responsiveness in vitiligo vulgaris. *Arch Dermatol* 1999; **135**:407–13.

34. Njoo MD, Westerhof W. Guidelines for treatment of vitiligo: is an update pending if recomm

35. Endations for children are not followed?: in reply. Arch Dermatol 2000;136: 1173–4.Scherschun L, Kim JJ, Lim HW. Narrow-band ultraviolet B is a useful and well-tolerated treatment for vitiligo. *J Am Acad Dermatol* 2001;**44**:999–1003.

36. Khalid M, Mujtaba G. Response of segmental vitiligo to 0.05% clobetasol propionate cream. *Int J Dermatol* 1998;**37**:705–8.

37. Grimes PE. Vitiligo: an overview of therapeutic approaches. *Dermatol Clin* 1993;**11**:325–38.

38. Morelli JG. Vitiligo in children: treatment options. *Dermatol Ther* 1997;**2**:93–7.

39. Seiter S, Ugurel S, Tilgen W, et al. Use of high-dose methylprednisolone pulse therapy in patients with progressive and stable vitiligo. *Int J Dermatol* 2000;**39**:624–7.

40. Radakovic-Fijan S, Furnsinn-Friedl AM, Honigsmann H, et al. Oral dexamethasone pulse treatment for vitiligo. *J Am Acad Dermatol* 2001;**44**:814–7.

41. Lepe V, Moncada B, Castanedo-Cazares JP, et al. A doubleblind randomized trial of 0.1% tacrolimus vs 0.05% clobetasol for the treatment of childhood vitiligo. *Arch Dermatol* 2003;**139**:581–5.

42. El Mofty AM. A preliminary clinical report on the treatment of leucoderma with *Ammi majus Linn. J Egypt Med Assoc* 1948;**31**:651–60.

43. Parrish JA, Fitzpatrick TB, Shea C, et al. Photochemotherapy of vitiligo: use of orally administered psoralens and a high-intensity long-wave ultraviolet light system. *Arch Dermatol* 1976;**112**:1531–4.

44. van Weelden H, De La Faille HB, Young E, et al. A new development in UVB phototherapy of psoriasis. *Br J Dermatol* 1988;**119**:11–9.

45. Westerhof W, Nieuweboer-Krobotova L. Treatment of vitiligo with UV-B radiation vs topical psoralen plus UV-A. *Arch Dermatol* 1997;**133**:1525–1528.

46. Morelli JG, Kincannon J, Yohn JJ, et al. Leukotriene C4 and TGF-alpha are stimulators of human melanocyte migration *in vitro. J Invest Dermatol* 1992;**98**:290–5.

47. Archambault M, Yaar M, Gilchrest BA. Keratinocytes and fibroblasts in a human skin equivalent model enhance melanocyte survival and melanin synthesis after ultraviolet irradiation. *J Invest Dermatol* 1995;**104**:859–67.

48. Imokawa G, Miyagishi M, Yada Y. Endothelin-1 as a new melanogen: coordinated expression of its gene and the tyrosinase gene in UVB-exposed human epidermis. *J Invest Dermatol* 1995;**105**:32–7.

49. Horikawa T, Norris DA, Johnson TW, et al. DOPA-negative melanocytes in the outer root sheath of human hair follicles are positive for premelanosomal antigens, but negative for a melanosomal antigen or melanosome associated glycoproteins, tyrosinase, TRP-1 and TRP-2. *J Invest Dermatol* 1996;**106**:28–35.

50. Abdel-Naser MB, Hann S-K, Bystryn J-C. Oral psoralen with UV-A therapy releases circulating growth factor(s) that stimulates cell proliferation. *Arch Dermatol* 1997;**133**: 1530–3.

51. Fitzpatrick TB. Mechanisms of phototherapy of vitiligo. *Arch Dermatol* 1997;**133**:591–2.

52. Westerhof W, Nieuweboer-Krobotova L, Mulder PG, et al. Left-right comparison study of the combination of fluticasone propionate and UV-A vs either fluticasone propionate or UV-A alone for the long-term treatment of vitiligo. *Arch Dermatol* 1999;**135**:1061–6.

53. Pathak MA, Mosher DB, Fitzpatrick TB. Safety and therapeutic effectiveness of 8- methoxypsoralen, 4,5_,8-trimethylpsoralen, and psoralen in vitiligo. *Natl Cancer Inst Monogr* 1984;**66**:165–73.

54. Le Poole C, Boissy RE. Vitiligo. *Sem Cutan Med Surg* 1997;**16**:3–14.

55. Grimes PE. Psoralen photochemotherapy for vitiligo. *Clin Dermatol* 1997;**15**:921–6.

56. Grimes PE, Minus HR, Halder RM, et al. Vitiligo: racial variations in the response to topical photochemotherapy. *J Invest Dermatol* 1983;**80**:367.

57. Kenney JA, Jr. Vitiligo treated by psoralens: a long-term follow-up study of the permanency of repigmentation. *Arch Dermatol* 1971;**103**:475–80.

58. Theodoridis A, Tsambaos D, Sivenas C, et al. Oral trimethylpsoralen in the treatment of vitiligo. *Acta Dermatol Venereol* 1976;**56**:253.

59. Zaynoun S, Jaber LA, Kurban AK. Oral methoxypsoralen photochemotherapy of extensive pityriasis alba: preliminary report. *J Am Acad Dermatol* 1986;**15**:61–5.

60. Hayashibe K, Mishima Y. Tyrosinase-positive melanocyte distribution and induction of pigmentation in human piebald skin. *Arch Dermatol* 1988;**124**:381–6.

61. Drake LA, Dinehart SM, Farmer ER, et al. Guidelines for care of vitiligo. *J Am Acad Dermatol* 1996;**35**:620–6.

62. Grimes PE, Minus HR, Chakrabarti S, et al. Determination of optimal topical photochemotherapy for vitiligo. *J Am Acad Dermatol* 1982;**7**:771–8.

63. Antoniou C, Katsambas A. Guidelines for the treatment of vitiligo. *Drugs* 1992; **43**:490–8.

64. Grimes PE, Kelly AP, Cline DJ, et al. Management of vitiligo in children (a symposium). *Pediatr Dermatol* 1986; **3**:498–510.

65. Njoo MD, Westerhof W, Bos JD, et al. The development of guidelines for the treatment of vitiligo. *Arch Dermatol* 1999;**135**:1514–21.

66. Takeda H, Mitsuhashi Y, Kondo S. Multiple squamous cell carcinomas in situ in vitiligo lesions after long-term PUVA therapy. *J Am Acad Dermatol* 1998;**38**:268–70.

67. Ortel B, Tanew A, Honigsmann H. Treatment of vitiligo with khellin and ultraviolet A. *J Am Acad Dermatol* 1988;**18**:693–701.

68. Njoo MD, Vitiligo Westerhof W. Pathogenesis and treatment. *Am J Clin Dermatol* 2001;**2(3)**:167–81.

69. Bystryn JC. Immune mechanisms in vitiligo. Clin Dermatol 1997 Dec;15(6): 853–61.

70. Kemp EH, Gavalas NG, Gawkrodger DJ, Weetman AP. Autoantibody responses tomelanocytes in the depigmenting skin disease vitiligo. *Autoimmun Rev* 2007;**3(3)**:138-42.

71. Kovacs SO. Vitiligo. *J Am Acad Dermatol* 1998;**38**(5 Pt 1):647–66.

72. Schallreuter KU. Basic research: an update. In: Lotti T, Hercogova J, editors. *Vitiligo Problems and Solutions.* New York: Marcel Dekker Inc.; 2004. p. 65–78.

73. Valencia KO, Van den Boorn JG, Denman CJ, Li M, Carlson JM, Hernandez C, et al. Therapeutic implications of autoimmune vitiligo T cells. *Autoimmun Rev* 2006;**5(7)**: 486–92.

74. Kwinter J, Pelletier J, Khambalia A, Pope E. High-potency steroid use in children with vitiligo: a retrospective study. *J Am Acad Dermatol* 2007 Feb;**56**(2):236–41.

75. Aragane Y, Kawada A, Maeda A, Isogai R, Isogai N, Tezuka T. Disseminated scleroderma of a Japanese patient successfully treated with bath PUVA photochemotherapy. *J Cutan Med Surg* 2001;**5**:135–7.

76. Kanwar AJ, Dogra S. Narrow-band UVB for the treatment of generalized vitiligo inchildren. Clinical dermatology. *Clin Exp Dermatol* 2005 July;**30**(4):332–6.

77. Khunger N, Kathuria SD, Ramesh V. Tissue grafts in vitiligo surgery — past, present and future. *Indian J Dermatol* 2009;**54**(2):150–8.

78. Geel NV, Ongenae K, Naeyaert JM. Surgical techniques for vitiligo: a review. *Dermatology* 2001;**202**(2):162–6.

79. Parsad D, Gupta S. Standard guidelines of care for vitiligo surgery. *Indian J Dermatol Venereol Leprol* 2008;**72**:S37–45.

80. Van Geel N, Ongenae K, Naeyaert JM. Surgical techniques for vitiligo. 2001;**202**(2):162–6.

81. Ozdemir M, Cetinkale O, Wolf R, Kotogyan A, Mat C, Tuzun B, et al. Comparison of two surgical approaches for treating vitiligo: a preliminary study. *Int J Dermatol* 2002 Mar; **41**(3):135–8.

82. Mysore V, Salim T. Cellular grafts in management of leucoderma. *Indian J Dermatol* 2009;**54**(2):142–9.

83. Lerner AB, Halaben R, Klaus SN, Moellmann GE. Transplantation of human melanocytes. *J Invest Dermatol* 1987;**89**:219–24.

84. Barclay L. Cultured epidermis effective in vitiligo. Arch Dermatol 2003;139: 1303–10.

85. Lahiri K. Stability in vitiligo? What's that? *J Cutan Aesthet Surg* 2009;**2**(1):38–40.

86. Lahiri K. Evolution and evaluation of autologous mini punch grafting in vitiligo. *Indian J Dermatol* 2009;**54**:159–67.

87. Berti Samantha, Lotti Torello. Recent advances in the treatment of childhood vitiligo. *Expet Rev Dermatol* 2008;**3**(6):691–9.

88. Parsad D, Sainio R, Verma N. Combination of Puva sol and topical calcipotriol in vitiligo. *Dermatology* 1998;**197**(2):167–70.

89. Ameen M, Exarchou V, Chu AC. Topical calcipotriol as monotherapy and incombination with psoralen plus ultraviolet A in the treatment of vitiligo. *Br J Dermatol* 2001;**145**(3):476–9.

90. Antivitiligo- Herbal treat for repigmentation of vitiligo. http://www.antivitiligo. com/vitiligo-cure/index.html (Accessed on 20 June 2009).

91. kalawalla. http://www.aragonproducts.com/theproducts.cfm?master=6918 (Accessed on 12 June 2009).

92. Gutierrez D, Writer S. Skin Pigment Disease Reversed with Piperine Nutrient From BlackPepper. http://www. naturalnews. com/025302_disease_piperine_ultraviolet_radiation.html (Accessed on 16 June 2009)

93. Camacho F, Mazuecos J. Treatment of vitiligo with oral and topical phenylalanine: 6 years of experience. *Arch Dermatol* 1999;**135**:216–7.

94. Schallreuter KU, Zxchiesche M, Moore J, et al. In vivo evidence for compromised phenylalanine metabolism in vitiligo. *Biochem Biophys Res Commun* 1998;**243**:395–9.

95. Levy SB. Tanning preparations. *Dermatol Clin* 2000;**18**: 591–6.

96. Bolognia JL, Lapia K, Somma S. Depigmentation therapy. *Dermatol Ther* 2001;**14**:29–34.

97. Njoo MD, Vodegel RM, Westerhof W. Depigmentation therapy in vitiligo universalis with topical 4-methoxyphenol and the Q-switched ruby laser. *J Am Acad Dermatol* 2000;**42**:760–9.

Websites:

http://pigmentation.wordpress.com/

http://www.vitiligoguide.com/white-spots-on-skin/

http://www.vitiligoguide.com/vitiligo-causes/

CHAPTER 9

HYPERPIGMENTATION AND ITS TREATMENT

Y. Madhusudan Rao, Shayeda, D. Sathish

Center for Biopharmaceutics and Pharmacokinetics, University College of Pharmaceutical Sciences, Kakatiya University, Warangal-506 009, Andhra Pradesh, India.

9.1 Introduction

In dermatology, hyperpigmentation is the darkening of an area of skin or nails caused by increased melanin. Rapid production of melanin in the skin is responsible for Hyperpigmentation. Skin pigment melanin determines the color of the hair and skin. Less amount of melanin is present in fair-skinned people when compared with dark-skinned people. So ultimately high amount of this substance results in dark, uneven patches of the skin. Geography also plays an important role in getting darker skin. Those who live on regions with more exposure to sunlight acquires darker skin than those who live in the northern regions. Overexposure to ultraviolet rays present in sunlight will cause the skin to tan itself. It is a natural mechanism wherein the dark skin produces more melanin to shield and protect itself from the harmful rays of the sun.

It can also be caused by various drugs, including some antibiotics, anti-arrhythmics, and anti-malarial medication. Skin diseases such as acne and Lichen Simplex Chronicus causes severe itching that leave the skin thick, dark and patchy. Picking and squeezing of Papulo-pustules leads to excessive pigmentation after acne infection. Most hyperpigmentation is caused or aggravated by sun exposure, but some is also caused by a pigment-producing reaction in the skin caused by irritation. This type of hyperpigmentation, called post-inflammatory hyperpigmentation is most common in darker skin types.[1]

The diseases or conditions responsible for hyperpigmentation are:

- Acanthosis nigricans - hyperpigmentation of intertriginous areas (such as skin folds of the groin, axilla) associated with insulin resistance.
- Adrenal insufficiency - which is responsible for several diseases like Addison's disease in which melanin synthesis is stimulated by hormones, like melanocyte-stimulating hormone (MSH).
- Excessive adrenocorticotropic hormone (ACTH) production- Cushing's disease.
- Smoker's melanosis
- Melasma, which is also called as chloasma - patchy hyperpigmentation often found in pregnant women.
- Cronkite-Canada syndrome
- Linea nigra - a hyperpigmented line found on the abdomen during pregnancy.
- Nelson's syndrome[2]
- Exposure to certain chemicals such as salicylic acid, bleomycin, and cisplatin.
- Celiac disease
- Porphyria
- Tinea fungal infections such as ringworm
- Haemochromatosis - Haemochromatosis or iron overload disorder, is a condition where the body contains too much iron. This is usually because of an inherited faulty gene that causes to absorb excess amounts of iron from food.

- Mercury poisoning - particularly cases of cutaneous exposure resulting from the topical application of mercurial ointments or skin-whitening creams.

  Hyperpigmentation can sometimes be induced by dermatological laser procedures.

9.1.1 Colour Development to the Skin

The primary determinant of skin color is the amount and type of melanin produced in the skin. Melanin biosynthesis occurs in specialized organelles called Melanosomes, which reside within the melanocytes. Cutaneous melanocytes are dendritic cells that originate from the embryonic neural crest cells and migrate during embryogenesis to reside at various sites: the eye, the ear, the central nervous system and the skin. In the skin melanocytes reside at the dermal-epidermal junction of the interfollicular epidermis and at the bulb of hair follicles. Each cutaneous melanocyte transfers pigmented melanosomes into a definite number of neighboring keratinocytes. Melanocytes in the skin are surrounded by approximately 36 keratinocytes to form what is called 'epidermal melanin unit'. Once melanosomes are transferred to keratinocytes of the interfollicular epidermis and the hair, they are deposited within the cytoplasm to protect the genome from the harmful effect of incident UV light. The manner by which melanosomes are transferred to and distributed within keratinocytes regulates the skin color exhibited by various races. Keratinocytes in dark skin contain molanosomes that are relatively large and exist individually. Keratinocytes in light skin contain melanosomes that are relatively smaller and clustered into membrane bound groups of four to eight. This distinct distribution patterns causes the diversity in skin pigmentation and photoprotection.[3]

The process of biosynthesis of melanin is an elaborate and regulated process (Figure 9.1). Melanin can be categorized into two groups: black to dark brown, insoluble eumelanins and yellow to reddish brown alkali soluble pheomelanins. Both types of melanins are derived from the same precursor substrate, the aminoacid tyrosine, which is not freely permeable through melanosomal membrane and require a tyrosine transporter. The presence of a specific transporter in the melanosomal membrane has been demonstrated by a number of studies.[4] Tyrosine undergoes many regulated and spontaneous steps to form different types of melanin.

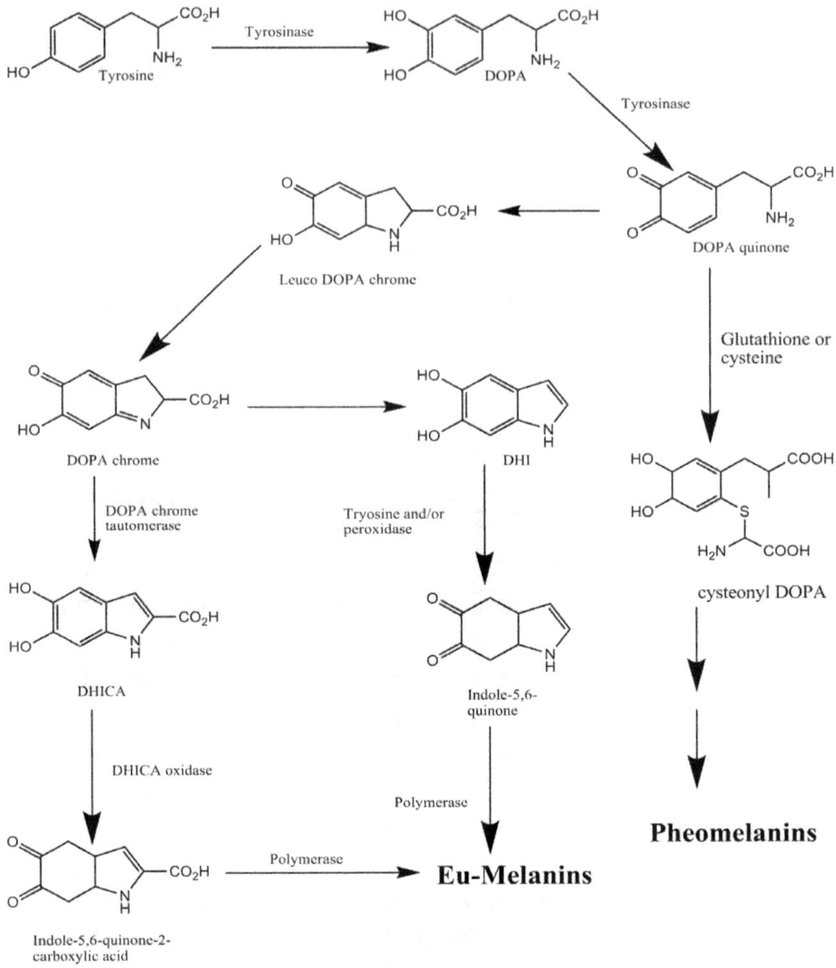

Fig. 9.1 Synthesis of melanin.

Tyrosinase, a copper containing enzyme, initially catalyzes the oxidation of tyrosine to 3,4-dihydroxyphenylalanine (DOPA) and the subsequent oxidation of DOPA to DOPAquinone. DOPAquinone appears to spontaneously progress to DOPAchrome through leuco DOPAchrome. The reaction then branches into two possible pathways. In the presence of Tyrp2 (DOPAchrome tautomerase), DOPAchrome will be converted into dihydroxyindole carboxylic acid (DHICA). In the absence of Tyrp2, DOPAchrome can spontaneously oxidized to 5,6-dihydroxyindole (DHI). Subsequently, DHI and /or DHICA undergo oxidation to form black insoluble eumelanin (DHI-Melanin) and brown, poorly soluble eumelanin

(DHICA-Melanin) respectively. The nature of the enzymes involved in the subsequent oxidation of the two indoles to eumelanin is still under debate.

An alternate but less understood pathway is that of pheomelanin synthesis. Genetically elevated levels of glutathione and or related sulphhydryl compounds in the melanosomes result in pheomelnization. Under these conditions, cysteinyldopa isomers are formed from DOPAquinone. The reaction subsequently proceeds to benzothiazinyl-alanines and then pheomelanins. However, since glutathione (GSH) but not cysteine is the major SH compound in the cells, an alternate route has been proposed in which, glutathionyldopas are formed from DOPAquinone. This reaction also proceeds to benzothiazinyl-alanines and then pheomelanins.

Melanin synthesis is highly regulated, relatively complex biochemical scheme, with several enzymatic steps. Tyrosinase, the rate-limiting enzyme in this process, catalyze the initiating steps of this pathway. Tyrosinase related proteins (Tyrp1 and Tyrp2) are also involved in the regulation of melanogenesis. As their name imply, they are related structurally to tyrosinase. Tyrosinase, Tyrp1 (gp-75 in humans; b protein in mice) and Tyrp2 (DOPAchrome tautomerase, DT) are expressed by three distinct genes and have remarkable sequence homology.[5] Tyrp2 converts DOPAchrome to dihydroxyindole-2-carboxylic acid (DHICA). In contrast, the function of Tyrp1 is unknown. Tyrp1 is responsible for black hair coloration in mice. Mutations in Tyrp1 result in brown hair coloration.[6] Many enzymatic activities have been demonstrated for Tyrp1, these include: catalase[7], DOPAchrome tautomerase (DT)[8], tyrosine hydroxylase[9], and DHICAoxidase.[10] Tyrp1 also appear to interact with other melanogenic proteins (i.e. tyrosinase) to stabilize its catalytic function. In fact, tyrosinase, Tyrp1 and Tyrp2 interact *in vivo* to form a high molecular-weight complex that diminishes the activity of tyrosinase compared to free tyrosinase.[11]

The differences in the expression and the activity of the melanogenic proteins (Tyrp1, Tyrp2, and Tyrosinase) are a major determinant for the variations in melanin content / skin color in human. A direct correlation exists between melanin content, tyrosinase activity and the expression of the three melanogenic proteins in melanocyte cultures established from different skin types. In addition, tyrosinase, Tyrp1 and Tyrp2 are more abundant in darkly as opposed to lightly pigmented melanocytes.[12] Melanocytes derived from dark skin also exhibit higher tyrosinase activity and produce more melanin than melanocytes derived from light skin. However, levels of tyrosinase mRNA are approximately equal between light and dark skin melanocytes.[13]

Human melanins are a mixture of pheomelanins and eumelanins in different proportions. Studies showed that dark skin individuals have higher total melanin and eumelanin and a higher ratio of eumelanin to pheomelanin than light skin individuals.[14] Melanin, mainly eumelanin, plays a photoprotective role in the skin. This photoprotection relies on the ability of melanin to act as a barrier that absorbs and scatters incident UV rays. Another protective function of melanin, particularly, eumelanin is its ability to scavenge reactive oxygen species such as superoxide radicals, hydrogen peroxide and singlet oxygen.[15]

Despite its crucial photo-protective role, melanin in excessive amount and/or disposition is the basis for a large number of skin diseases. For example acquired hyperpigmentation such as melasma, postinflammatory pigmentation and solar lentigo are common skin diseases, permanent in middle-aged women. This additional pigmentation is attributed to an increase in either number of melanocytes or activity of the melanogenic enzymes. Acquired hyperpigmantation disorders have psychosocial and cosmetic importance since they are common on sun-exposed areas of the face and the neck.[16] In addition, hyperpigmentation of skin grafted on burn patients that is a consequence of wound healing and post-inflammatory processes constitute a challenging problem.

Hyperpigmentary diseases, especially when occurring in the head and the neck, frequently results in loss of confidence and self esteem. Therefore many efforts have been made to develop and recognize compounds that act as depigmenting agents. Different treatments for acquired hyperpigmentation are available in the market, but none are completely satisfactory. In addition, maintaining a basal skin tone is an important global concern. Therefore the development of an effective, controllable and safe agent to regulate melanin synthesis in the skin is required. HQ marketed in the U.S. as Rx (Lustra Cream) and as an over the counter cream (Porcelana Cream). Shiseido Whiteness® and Vichy anti-taches Mains® are the commercial product names for arbutin and kojic acid respectively.

Due to the number and variety of maturation steps involved in melanogenesis, pigmentary regulation can be controlled at various levels. Main strategies employed to reverse hyperpigmentation and/or induce hypopigmentation include compounds that can:

1. modulate the activity of enzymes involved in melanogenesis, particularly by using chemicals that can act as a substrate and or inhibitors for tyrosinase
2. regulate transfer and distribution of melanosomes within keratinocytes
3. regulate melanin and melanosomes degradation and
4. regulate turnover of keratinocytes.

9.1.2 Genomics and Proteomics of Pigmentation

In melanosomes (all developmental stages) approximately 1500 gene products (proteins) are expressed, among them 600 gene products being expressed at any given time and 100 of them apparently unique to the melanosome.[17] Many other proteins like membrane-associated, cytoskeletal, transport are involved in pigmentation in both the melanocyte and the keratinocyte. The basic process of stimulation of melanocytes and conversion of tyrosine to melanin involves in signaling, in the transport of melanosomes within the melanocyte and the transfer of melanosomes to the keratinocyte (Figure 9.2).

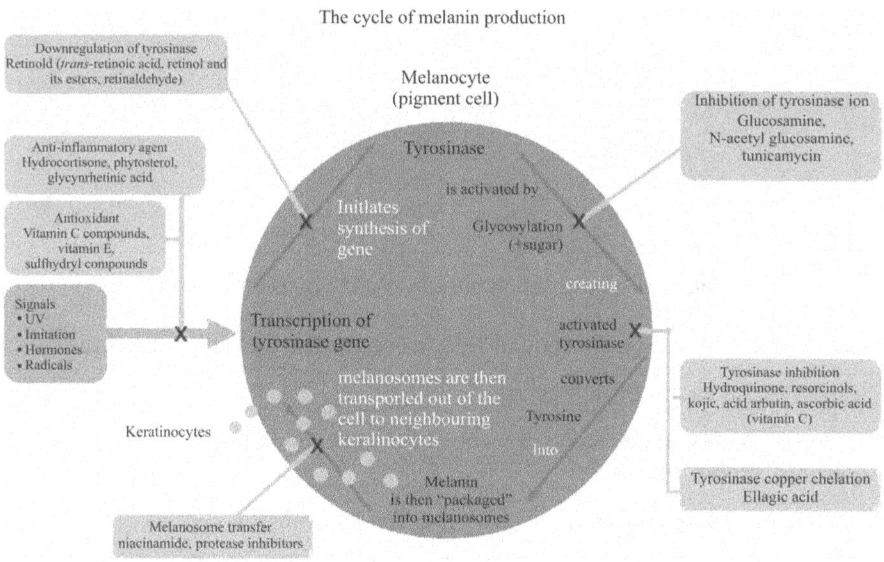

Fig. 9.2 Cross section of skin showing melanocyte. [Colour Fig. on page 409]

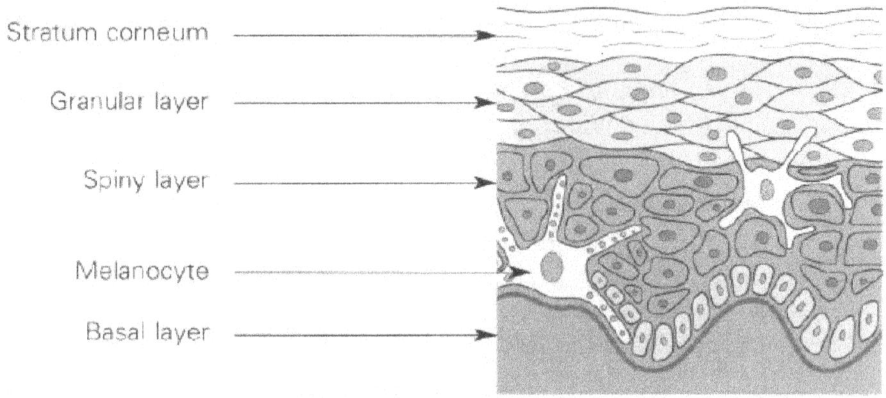

Fig. 9.3 Cross section of skin showing different layers.
[Colour Fig. on page 410]

9.1.3 Types of Melanins

Melanins are quinonoid polymers and can be divided into two groups.

1. Pheomelanins: Pheomelanins are yellowish and reddish brown pigments containing sulphur.
2. Eumelanins: Eumelanins are black or brown insoluble pigments.

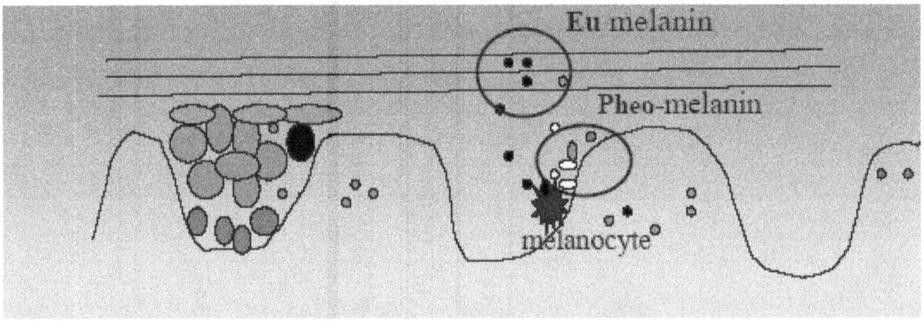

Fig. 9.4 Types of melanins. [Colour Fig. on page 410]

As for facial blotches, 5 types of leisons sometimes exist on the face.

Some typical facial blotch types.

Lentigos: Many are sized from about 0.5 mm to 3 mm. There are black ones and brown ones.

Pigmented nevus: Black spots which exists from birth.

Melasma: On the cheek and forehead, symmetrical, flat, light brown macules.

Freckles: Many small brown spots scattered on both cheeks and nose.

Café au lait macules: From birth or adolescence, light brown, rather dense, there are also some which accompany black hairs.

Solar (senile) lentigiens: Appear after 30 years old and increase with age. Dark or light brown, flat blotches whose outline can be clearly seen.

Verruca senilis: Wart which appears with age. Raised, dark brown. Also called seborrheic keratosis.

Post-inflammatory hyperpigmentation: Pigmentation after inflammation of scratches, burns, acne, etc.

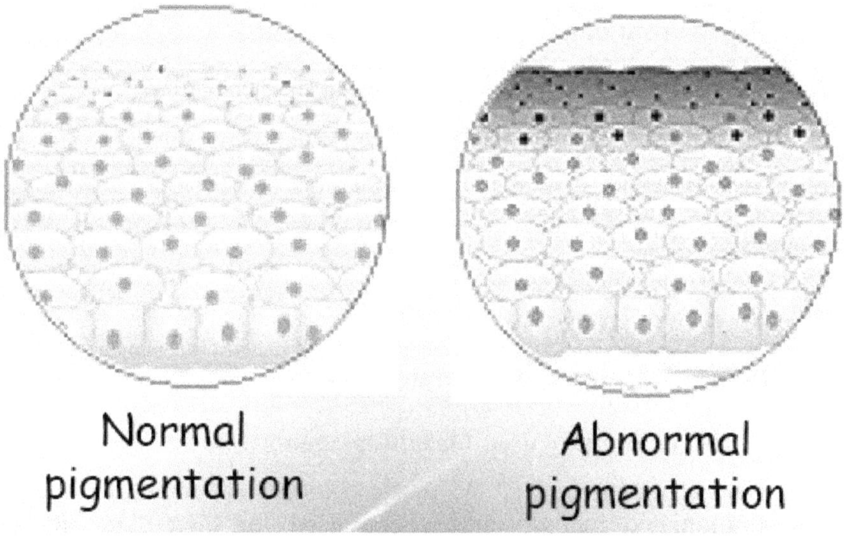

Fig. 9.5 Difference between normal and abnormal pigmentation.
[Colour Fig. on page 410]

9.2 Treatment Options

- Bleaching agents
- Chemical peels
- Intense pulsed light
- Microdermabasion
- Physician formulas
- Laser resurfacing
- Home remedies / natural treatment

9.2.1 Bleaching Agents

Skin bleaching agents interfere with various stages of melanin production thereby producing their bleaching action.[18]

1. Selectively they destroy the melanocytes.
2. Inhibit the formation of melanosomes and alter their structure.
3. Inhibit the biosynthesis of tyrosinase.
4. Inhibit the formation of melanin.
5. Interfere with the transfer of melanosomes.
6. Have a chemical effect on melanin or enhance the degradation of melanosomes in keratinocytes.
7. Decolourization of melanin already present.

Table 9.1 Mechanism of melanogenesis inhibition.

Mechanism	Example
Supression of melanogenesis	Kojic acid, ascorbic acid, hydroquinone, arbutin, ellagic acid
Other mechanisms	
a) Decrease in tyrosinase synthesis	Biomein
b) Cytotoxicity to melanocytes	Hydroquinone monobenzylether, n-2, 4-acetoxy phenyl thioethyl acetamide.(APTA)
c) Decrease in tyrosinase transfer	Glucosamine, tunicamycin

9.2.1.1 Most commonly used bleaching agents

1. *Mercury compounds*:[19] Mercuric chloride, red mercuric oxide and ammoniated mercury have been used for their skin bleaching effect. Out of these ammoniated mercury was extensively used. Mercuric compounds cause appreciable skin lightening in part due to exfoliation. It is likely that mercury will replace copper necessary for tyrosinase activity and thereby inactivate this enzyme. But now, the mercury compounds are prohibited for use in cosmetics.

2. *Hydroquinones*:[20,21] Hydoquinone is a hydroxyphenolic chemical, has been the gold standard for treatment of hyperpigmentation for over 50 years. It acts by inhibiting the enzyme tyrosinase, thereby reducing the conversion of DOPA to melanin. Some of the other possible mechanisms of action are the destruction of melanocytes, degradation of melanosomes, and the inhibition of the synthesis of DNA and RNA. Hydroquinone is the most commonly used

material in bleaching creams. A concentration of 1.5-2% cream is in the market as OTC product, which produces temporary lightening of the skin. A concentration of 4-5% cream should be used under the supervision of a physician. It may produce redness and burning, the skin lightening effect of hydroquinone can be reversed by exposure to sunlight, hence its cream is used at night time.

3. *Hydroquinone mono benzyl ether*: Hydroquinone monobenzylether interferes with formation of pigment and also causes bleaching of the skin. But a large number of people are sensitive to it. It is effective in both low concentrations as well as high concentrations. The reported concentrations vary from less than 1% to 33%. Prolonged use of monobenzylether of hydroquinone leads to leucoderma. In view of this, use of this material has been banned in some countries.

Regulatory update: FDA and hydroquinone[22]

On August 29, 2006, the FDA withdrew the September 3, 1982 tentative final monograph on over-the-counter (OTC) skin-bleaching products and proposed that no OTC skin-bleaching active ingredients be categorized as generally recognized as safe. Of course, prominent among such products is hydroquinone. A final ruling has not yet been handed down. Should the FDA follow through, thus changing the status of hydroquinone and other skin-bleaching agents, the effect would be to reclassify such products as "new drugs," permitting them to be used by prescription until approval of a new drug application. Until such a ruling, however, hydroquinone products remain available OTC, as this ingredient remains an important first line therapy for pigmentary disorders. As of the date of publication, a ruling by the FDA does not appear imminent, but no timetable for a decision has been made clear.

4. *Monomethyl and monoethyl ether of hydroquinone*: This is also a potent depigmenting agent. Electron microscope studies reveal that epidermal melanocytes are destroyed and subsequently removed by macrophages. These are also potent depigmenting agents but have disadvantages similar to that of monobenzyl ether of hydroquinone and therefore did not become popular.

5. *Catechol and its derivatives*: Some catechols exhibited skin lightening effect but these were less effective than hydroquinone. Out of these 4-isopropyl catechol is the most potent depigmenting

agent. However, concentrations of 3% or more caused irritation and sensitizing reactions.

6. *Ascorbic acid and its derivatives*: Ascorbic acid, though very safe, do not seem to be very effective as depigmenting agent. Ascorbic acid, however, has been used in skin bleaching cream containing hydroquinone as stabilizer (anti-oxidant). Use of ascorbyl oleate has been reported in concentrations of 3% and 5% in creams for bleaching freckles in human skin. Ascorbic acid can also inhibit melanogenesis by preventing oxidation of the intermediate dopa-quinone. Ascorbic acid also kept melanin in its reduced and light coloured form.

7. *Azelaic acid*: Azelaic acid is a naturally occuring non-phenolic, saturated, nine-carbon dicarboxilic acid. Its use originated from the finding that Pityrosporum species can oxidize unsaturated fatty acids to dicarboxylic acids, which competitively inhibit tyrosinase. Azelaic acid was initially developed as a topical drug with therapeutic effects for the treatment of acne. But it has effect on tyrosinase, it has also been used to treat melasma, lentigo maligna and other disorders of hyperpigmentation. Azelaic acid has been reported to be effective for hypermelanosis caused by physical or photochemical agents, and lentigo maligna melanomaas well as other disorders characterized by abnormal proliferation of melanocytes. Its mechanism of action is to inhibit DNA synthesis and mitochondrial enzymes, thereby inducing direct cytotoxic effects toward the melanocyte.

   Topical azelaic acid has no pigmentation effect on normally pigmented skin, freckles, senile lentigens, and nevi. This specificity may be attributed to its selective effects on abnormal melanocytes. Azelaic acid can be used for postinflammatory hyperpigmentation in acne.

   In the treatment of melasma, a 24-week study in south America found that a 20% concentration of azelaic acid was equivalent to 2% hydroquinone. In the Philippines, a study found that 20% azelaic acid was better than 2% hydroquinone.[21]

8. *Oxidizing agents*: Hydrogen peroxide has been used in skin bleach creams. Zinc peroxide has been used in anhydrous ointments as bleaching agents but its properties have not been proved.

9. *Opaque covering agents*: Make-up products containing white or pale pigments such as titanium dioxide, zinc oxide, talk, kaolin,

bismuth pigments can achieve remarkable change in the color of skin and hence these materials have been mentioned here.

10. *Kojic acid*: Kojic acid (5-hydroxy-2-(hydroxy methyl)-4-pyrone), a naturally occuring hydrophilic fungal derivative evolved from certain species of Acetobacter, Asperigillus and Penicillium, is used in the treatment of hyperpigmentation disorders. It is a tyrosinase inhiibitor. The 1% cream of kojic acid shows better results.

11. *Arbutin*: Arbutin is the β-D-glucopyranoside derivative of hydroquinone, is a naturally occuring plant derived compound that has been used for postinflammatory hyperpigmentation. The action of arbutin is dependent on its concentration. Arbutin was found to be less toxic than hydroquinone. The reduction in tyrosinase activity depends on concentration of arbutin, as well as melanin content in melanocytes. Arbutin has stronger depigmenting action than kojic acid, ascorbic acid and linoleic acid.[23]

12. *Liquorice extract*: Liquorice or licorice is the root of *Glycyrrhiza glabra* from which a somewhat sweet flavour can be extracted. The main component of the hydrophobic fraction of liquorice extract is glabridin, which has an effect on the skin. Glabridin inhibits tyrosinase activity of melanocytes.

13. Melanogenesis inhibitor from paper mulberry[24] : The mulberry extract from *Broussonetia kazinoki* and *B. papyrifera* has tyrosinase inhibitor effect and it is identified as Kazinol F. This material has the same level of tyrosinase inhibition activity at a lower concentration when compared with kojic acid, ascorbic acid and hydroquinone. Reports shown that Kazinol F had a good free-radical scavenging activity compared to tocopherol. Kazinol F is chemically 5-(3'-(2,4-dihydroxyphenyl)propyl)-3,4-bis(3-methyl-2-butenyl)-1,2-benzenediol. The extract of Paper Mulberry containing 5.0% of this active compound would be sufficient to show a fairly potent lightening effect when used at a concentration as low as 0.1-1.0% in the final product.

Active compounds isolated from plants, such as arbutin, aloesin, gentisic acid, flavonoids, hesperidin, licorice, niacinamide, yeast derivatives and polyphenols inhibit melanogenesis without melanocytotoxicity by different mechanisms were used as topical treatments for hyperpigmentation disorders.[25]

Citrus family contain large amounts of bioflavonoids, *Citrus limonum* was found to give the best results. The aqueous extracts were spray-atomized and then fractionated to obtain a high concentration of hesperidin eriodictyol and naringenin, whose structure is similar to that of hydroquinone. When concentrated in the nano-capsules, they are protected until they reach the active site of melanin synthesis, where they exert a powerful reducing action, anti-radical activity and act as a substrate competitor for the tyrosinases.[26]

14. Deoxyarbutin also inhibits the tyrosinase enzyme thereby acting as a depigmenting agent. Deoxyarbutin inhibition was reversible whereas Hydroquinone showed less or no reversibility.[27]

    Tyrosinase catalyses melanin synthesis, tyrosinase inhibitors are important in cosmetic skin-whitening.

9.2.2 Combination Therapy

Combination therapy is more effective than single agents used alone. The etiology of melasma is not completely understood, thus, therapies that can act at different stages of pigmentation can produce better clinical results than a single therapy acting at a single stage.

The addition of tretinoin eliminates pigment and increases keratinocyte proliferation by preventing the oxidation of HQ and improving epidermal penetration. Further, adding topical corticosteroids reduces the irritative effects of hypopigmenting agents, and inhibits melanin synthesis by decreasing cellular metabolism. This combination, HQ 5%, tretinoin 0.1%, and dexamethasone 0.1%, was first introduced in 1975 and termed the Kligman formula after its inventor. It has been the most extensively used combination therapy for melasma worldwide.

More recently, a new combination of HQ 4%, tretinoin 0.05%, and fluocinolone acetonide 0.01% (Tri-Luma®, Galderma) proved better than any combination of two of the above agents, with 77% of patients showing complete or nearly complete clearing. The most common adverse effects were mild local irritation, erythema, and skin peeling. The mixture should be applied to the entire affected area to avoid blotchiness. The recent 2006 consensus of the Pigmentary Disorders Academy (PDA), a group of international dermatologists and leaders in pigmentary disorders who receive sponsorship from Galderma, supported the use of triple therapy.

The PDA consensus suggested that first-line therapy for melasma should consist of fixed topical therapies and only when triple combination therapy is unavailable or patients have a sensitivity to the ingredients, should dual ingredients or single agents be considered.[28]

9.2.3 Marketed Preparations

Most of the marketed fairness or depigmentation preparations contain herbal axtracts of vetivert (*Vetiveria zizanoides*), Citrus (*Citrus lemon*), Saffron (*Crocus sativus*), Nutmeg (*Myristica fragrans*), Manjista (*Cardia ruarbbifolia*), Red chandan (*Santalum album*), Aloe vera (*Aloe barbadensis*) were used.

Extracts of black plum, almond, turmeric, rose, manjishtha, lemon also have natural skin lightening effect and they were used in depigmentation preparations.

Extrapone Nutgrass Root is one of the most successful natural ingredients which work day in and day out to eliminate those dark ugly patches from the skin. They not only make the skin clean and clear but also make sure that these pigmented patches never re-occur at anytime in future.

Phytessence Wakame is another miraculous natural agent which forms a thin invisible layer on top of the skin and protects it from the potential harm caused by the external factors including the sun and wind. This also helps in preventing the formation of pigmentation.

Examples

Fair & Lovely anti-marks cream [Colour Fig. on page 411]

Ingredients: Biswatulasi, neem, manjistha, yastimadhu, nyagropadhu, chandana, brahmi, ghrit kumari.

Depigmenting Cream 50 ml from Naturalia [Colour Fig. on page 411]

Ingredients: Melfade, a bearberry leaf extract-based compound that prevents the hyperpigmentation of the skin while carrying out a whitening action. The fruit acids reinforce the depigmenting action, helping to unify skin tone while smoothing wrinkles and giving skin a new radiance. Naturalia Depigmenting Cream also contains a deep moisturising formula enriched with D-Glucoronic and vitamin E.

LADYMAX™ Depigmentation cream [Colour Fig. on page 411]

Ingredients: Aloe vera, Avocado extract, Pineapple extract, Licorice extract, diacetyl boldine, trilaurin, BHT, polysorbate 20, cetyl hydroxyethyl cellulose, polyme-thylacrylate, titanium dioxide, capric triglyceride, isopropyl palmitate, glyceryl monostearate, mineral oil, propylene glycol, dimethicone, carbomer, triethanolamine, methyl paraben, propylparaben, deionized water, fragrance.

Natural Depigmentation Cream [Colour Fig. on page 411]

Ingredients: Enriched with natural rapeseed and liquorice extracts.

Biotique skin whitening and depigmentation Cream [Colour Fig. on page 411]

Ingredients: Contains extracts of coconut, dandelion, manjistha and natural oils that help in lightening skin blemishes and in depigmentation.

Oxidation of hydroquinone is affected by the pH of the product, heavy metals and oxygen. pH of aqueous solution of hydroquinone is 4.5. Oxidation increases with increase in pH. pH of hydroquinone preparations should be between 3 and 5.5. Heavy metals, if present catalyze oxidation process. Oxygen available from entrapped air during manufacturing process will add to the oxidation process.

Hydroquinone solutions darken on exposure to light. Therefore manufacture of hydroquinone containing creams should be carried out under subdued light.

Every ingredient of hydroquinone preparation should be tested for compatability with hydroquinone. This may be conducted in the following manner.

1. Prepare an aqueous solution of same concentration as that of formulation.
2. Subdivide so prepared hydroquinone solution into number of portions equal to the number of ingredients to be used plus one.
3. Add one ingredient in one portion. One portion will remain extra. Do not add anything to this. Use this as control.
4. Expose all the portions (in tightly sealed bottles) to 60 degrees for 24 hours.
5. Compare the darkening in each bottle with the control.

Darkening more than present in control indicates decomposition of hydroquinone due to presence of the ingredient.

9.2.4 A Brief Description of the Plant Products used in the Formulation of Depigmentation Creams is given below

Orange essential oil

Botanical source: Orange oil is extracted from *Citrus aurantium* var. belonging to family Rutaceae.

Oil properties: Sweet orange oil has a sweet, fresh and tangy smell, is yellow to orange in colour and watery in viscosity.

Extraction: Orange oil is extracted from the orange peel by cold-pressing and yields 0.3-0.5%.

Fig. 9.6 Orange fruits. [Colour Fig. on page 412]

Chemical constituents: The main chemical components of orange oil are α-pinene, sabinene, myrcene, limonene, linalool, citronellal, neral and geranial.

Uses: The first and most basic use of orange essential oil is aromatherapy. Here, it is extensively used to treat anxiety by acting as a sedative. The oil is known to soothe nerves and eradicate stress and hypertension. It has antidepressant activity (due to the capacity of the oil to make the surroundings pleasant and happy), anti-allergic, antiseptic activities.

Orange oil blends well with Black pepper, cinnamon, cloves, ginger, frankincense, sandalwood and vetivert.

Frankinsense essential oil

Botanical source: Frankinsense oil is extracted from resin from the *Boswellia carteri* tree belonging to family Burseraceae and also known as Olibanum and gum thus.

Oil properties: Frankinsense oil has a woody, spicy, haunting smell, a little bit camphoric, just more pleasant.

Fig. 9.7 Frankinsense resin. [Colour Fig. on page 412]

Extraction: Frankinsense oil is extracted by steam distillation from the oleo gum resin and yields about 3-10%. An absolute is also produced, mainly used as a fixative.

Chemical constituents: The main chemical components are cardinene, camphene, olibanol, dipentene, pinene and phellandrene.

Uses: Frankinsense oil is said to help rejuvenate an ageing skin, is a skin tonic and is effective with sores, carbuncles, wounds, scars and skin inflammation (essential oil.net).

Frankinsense oil blends well with benzoin, sandalwood, lavendor, myrrh, pine, orange, bergamot and lemon.

Lemon essential oil

Botanical source: Lemon oil is extracted from *Citrus limonum* belonging to family Rutaceae.

Oil properties: Lemon oil has a sharp, fresh smell, is pale greenish-yellow in color and is watery in viscosity.

Fig. 9.8 Lemon fruits. [Colour Fig. on page 412]

Extraction: Lemon oil is extracted from the fresh fruit peel by cold expression.

Chemical constituents: The main chemical components of lemon oil are α-pinene, camphene, β-pinene, sabinene, myrcene, α-terpinene, linalool, β-bisabolene, limonene, trans-α-bergamotene, nerol and neral.

Uses: Lemon oil soothes and relieves headaches and migraines and is helpful for rheumatism and arthritis. It is also used for clearing acne, cleaning greasy skin and hair, as well as removing dead skin cells, easing painful cold sores, mouth ulcers, herpes and insect bites (essential oil.net).

Lemon oil blends well with lavender, rose, sandalwood, benzoin, eucalyptus, geranium, fennel, juniper, neroli.

Lavender essential oil

Botanical source: Lavender oil is extracted from the tree *Lavandula angustifolia* of the Lamiaceae family.

Fig. 9.9 Lavender flowers. [Colour Fig. on page 396]

Oil properties: Lavender oil has a light fresh aroma, is clear in color and watery in viscosity.

Extraction: Lavender oil is extracted by steam distillation from the flowering tops and yields 1.4% - 1.6%.

Chemical constituents: The main chemical components of lavender oil are Alpha-pinene, linalool, linalyl acetate, limonene, 1,8-cineole, cis-ocimene, trans-ocimene, 3-octanone, camphor, linalool, linalyl acetate, caryophyllene, terpinen-4-ol and lavendulyl acetate.

Precautions: This oil may have allergic reactions.

Uses: On the skin, lavender oil tones and revitalizes and it is useful for all types of skin problems such as abscesses, acne, oily skin, boils, burns, sunburn, wounds, psoriasis, lice, insect bites, stings and also acts as an insect repellent.

Lavender oil is one of the few essentials oils that can be used neat on the skin, and this is especially useful when treating a minor burn wound.

Lavender oil blends well with cedarwood, clary sage, geranium, pine, nutmeg and all the citrus oils.

Rose oil

Botanical source: Rose oil is extracted from the damask rose- *Rosa damascena* of the Rosaceae family.

Oil properties: Damask rose oil has a deep, rosy, fresh aroma, the color ranges from clear to a pale yellow or greenish tint

Extraction: Rose oil is extracted from the fresh flowers, picked before 8 am in the morning, by steam distillation and the yield is 0.02-0.05%. The heat used in the distillation process is carefully controlled, as the aroma can be damaged if the heat is too high.

Fig. 9.10 Rose flower. [Colour Fig. on page 412]

Chemical constituents: The chemical composition of rose oil is one of the most complex and contains more than 300 known compounds, yet the main chemical components of rose oil can be listed as- citronellol, phenyl ethanol, geraniol, nerol, farnesol and stearpoten with traces of nonanol, linalool, nonanal, phenyl acetaldehyde, citral, carvone, citronellyl acetate, 2-phenylmenthyl acetate, methyl eugenol, eugenol and rose oxide.

Uses: On the skin it is most effective for moisturizing and hydrating the skin, while having a general stimulant and antiseptic action, which is good for all skin types, but especially so for dry, mature and irritated skin. It is used to repair broken capillaries, inflammation as well as skin redness and is useful in eczema and herpes. Rose water can be used for conjunctivitis.

Rose oil blends particularly well with other oils, such as geranium, jasmine, clove and palmarosa.

Saffron oil

Botanical source: Saffron oil is extracted from stigmas of the *Crocus sativum* L. belonging to family Iridaceae.

Oil properties: Saffron oil has a characteristic odour.

Extraction: Saffron oil is extracted by solvent extraction using methanol, ethanol, petroleum ether, acetone etc.

Chemical constituents: The stigmas of *C. sativus* are rich in riboflavin, a yellow pigment, and vitamins. The crocus zeaxanthin-cleavage dioxygenase gene codes for the chromoplast enzyme that starts the production of the 3 major carotenoid derivatives crocetin, picrocrocin, and safranal, are found in saffron. In addition, saffron contains crocin (a water-soluble carotenoid), the major source of yellowish-red pigment. Upon drying, a hypothetical protocrocin of the fresh plant is decomposed into one molecule of crocin (a colored glycoside) and two molecules of picrocrocin (a colorless bitter glycoside). Crocin is a mixture of glycosides: crocetin, a dicarboxylic terpene lipid, and alpha-crocin, a digentiobiose ester of crocetin. In addition, cis- and trans-crocetin dimethylesters have been identified. Similar compounds have been isolated from other members of the Iridaceae family. Gardenidin, a compound obtained from gardenias, has been shown to be identical to crocetin. The characteristic taste of the spice is attributed to the glycoside picrocrocin. Following hydrolysis, the compound yielded glucose and safranal, the main odiferous constituent. The essential oil derived from saffron is a complex mixture of more than 30 components, mainly terpenes and their derivatives.

Fig. 9.11 Saffron flower. [Colour Fig. on page 413]

Potential uses

US patents have been issued for the proposed use of crocetin in the treatment of skin papillomas, spinal cord injuries.

Saffron oil blends well with cedarwood oil.

Tulasi oil

Botanical source: Tulasi oil is extracted from the herb *Ocimum basilicum* of the Labiatae family.

Fig. 9.12 Tulasi plant. [Colour Fig. on page 413]

Oil properties: Tulasi oil has a watery viscosity and is pale greenish-yellow in colour. The aroma is clear, light and peppery and gives a sweet, green top note to blends.

Extraction: The oil is extracted by steam distillation from the leaves and the flowering tops.

Chemical constituents: Basil oil has various chemical compounds that include a-pinene, camphene, β-pinene, myrcene, limonene, cis-ocimene, camphor, linalool, methyl chavicol, γ-terpineol, citronellol, geraniol, methyl cinnamate and eugenol.

Uses: When used on the skin, it helps to control acne. In general it refreshes the skin and can also be used on insect bites (essential oil.net).

Tulasi oil blends well with bergamot, black pepper, cedarwood, fennel, ginger, geranium, grapefruit, lavender, lemon, marjoram, neroli and verbena.

Peppermint oil

Botanical source: Peppermint oil is extracted from *Mentha piperita* of the Labiatae family and is also known as brandy mint and balm mint.

Oil properties: Peppermint oil has a fresh, sharp, menthol smell, is clear to pale yellow in color and watery in viscosity.

Fig. 9.13 Peppermint leaves. [Colour Fig. on page 413]

Extraction: Peppermint oil is extracted from the whole plant above ground just before flowering. The oil is extracted by steam distillation from the fresh or partly dried plant and the yield is 0.1 - 1.0 %.

Chemical constituents: The chemical components of peppermint oil are menthol, menthone, 1,8-cineole, methyl acetate, methofuran, isomenthone, limonene, β-pinene, a-pinene, germacrene-D, trans-sabinene pulegone hydrate.

Uses: On the skin, peppermint oil is used to relieve skin irritation and itchiness and also helps to reduce skin redness, where inflammation is present. It is used for dermatitis, acne, ringworm, scabies and pruritus and also relieves itching, sunburn and inflammation of the skin, while at the same time having a cooling action.

Peppermint oil blends well with benzoin, eucalyptus, lavender, marjoram, lemon and rosemary.

Neem oil

Botanical source: Neem oil is extracted from the seeds of *Azadirachta indica*, belonging to family Meliaceae.

Oil properties: Neem oil is a brownish yellow colour liquid, with smell of a Garlic. Neem oil is slightly soluble in water and have 6.5 to 7.5 pH value, it boils at more than 200°C and freeze at 13°C.

Fig. 9.14 Neem plant. [Colour Fig. on page 414]

Extraction: The oil is extracted by steam distillation from the seeds and the seed kernels.

Chemical constituents: Neem oil contain active ingredients like azadirachtin, salanin, nimbin, meliantriol, meldenin, azadiradione, azadirone, isonimolicinolide, mahmoodin, vepinin, nimbidinin, nimbonin.

Uses: On skin it is used as depigmenting agent, anti-acne agent. It is used in antidandruff preparations for their antiseptic action. It stimulates hair growth also hence used in hair oils. It is also have anti-inflammatory action.

Neem oil blends particularly well with other oils, such as bergamot, black pepper, fennel, ginger, geranium, grapefruit, lavender, lemon, marjoram.

We have prepared depigmentation cream in our lab by using the tentative formula

Depigmentation Cream

Lavender oil	5 to 10 ml
Neem oil	5 to 10 ml
Wheatgerm oil	1 to 2 ml
Cucumber gel	10 gm to 25 gm
Saffron oil	5 to 10 ml

9.2.5 Manufacture

Skin lightening creams using covering agents are made using a vanishing type cream base. These creams are manufactured according to the general method of manufacture of creams.

Creams containing hydrogen peroxide are generally manufactured by adding oily phase to aqueous phase with stirring, cooling the cream to 45 degrees and then adding hydrogen peroxide with slow stirring. After addition of hydrogen peroxide pH of the cream is adjusted to 3.5 to 4 with the help of phosphoric acid. A high grade stainless steel equipment should be used when manufacturing hydrogen peroxide creams.

Choice of equipment in the manufacture of hydroquinone creams is also important. Only stainless or glass lined vessels should be used in the manufacture of hydroquinone creams. If possible the equipment used for hydroquinone cream should not be used for manufacture of other products. Use of alkaline soaps for cleansing the equipments should be discouraged. Some persons may be sensitive to hydroquinone, precautions must be taken in handling hydroquinone. Bright light can darken hydroquinone. Therefore, creams containing hydroquinone should be manufactured under subdued light.

9.2.6 Evaluation of Skin Bleach Creams[29]

Preliminary screening tests

Preliminary screening is done by using black-skinned guinea-pigs which do not pose very great problems in rearing, handling and testing. It is also generally agreed that the skin of the guinea-pig has enough similarity to human skin to make comparisions meaningful.

Black swine can also be used as an alternative test animal.

Tests on black guinea-pigs

Animal models, the guinea-pig has been found to be most useful for screening topically applied chemical compounds for their depigmenting effect. Creams containing concentrations of 1 to 10% of various test chemicals have been applied to the epilated skin of pure black guinea-pigs for 5 days each week for periods of one month and their depigmenting potency assessed and compared with control areas treated with the cream base only. The assessment has been made visually, but also can be measured using a reflectance spectrophotometer.

Tests on black-skinned swine

Though the guinea-pig is a suitable animal for screening large numbers of compounds, it was considered advisable to obtain comparative data on at least one other black-skinned species other than man.

The pig appeared to be a satisfactory choice for a number of reasons.

1. The anatomy of the skin is similar to that of man.
2. The hairs are more sparse than on the guinea-pig.
3. A large area of skin is available for application of materials.

One drawback with pig is the physiology of pig skin may be completely different from that of human skin in that the barrier properties of the stratum corneum may be different, resulting in differing rates of penetration of active ingredients. The sensitivity of the melanocytes to skin depigmenting agents may also be different.

In the beginning of the experiment the pigs were shared and the pigmented area of the back and flanks divided into sites about 5 cm square using a magic marker. Sites had to be frequently remarked during the experiment. The skin reflectance was measured using an EEL reflectometer which in this case was considered to be more useful than the stepped wedge since the color of the pig skin was less grey than that of the guinea-pig. The instrument consisted of a reflectance head comprising a photocell and a light source connected to a Unigalvano 20 galvanometer. Reflection readings of the skin were expressed as a percentage of the reflectance of a standard magnesium carbonate block (the reflectance of which was set at 100%).

The creams were packed in tubes and applied daily for 38 days, 6 mm of cream being applied to the relevant site on the animal. Measurement of skin reflectance were made at weekly intervals, after washing the skin with water to remove traces of dirt and old cream.

The results were expressed as the change in reflectance of the skin compared to its initial reflectance before treatment. Positive values indicate lightening whilst darkening was shown by negative values.

Tests on humans

The creams are applied to 4 test sites on each person, namely the outside upper forearm and the outside of the wrist on each arm, by means of a cardboard template. In this way the central portion of the outside forearm could act as the control site for each arm. If volunteers agreed apply on the face i.e. on forehead. Approximately 0.25 g of cream was applied to each test site on each occasion.

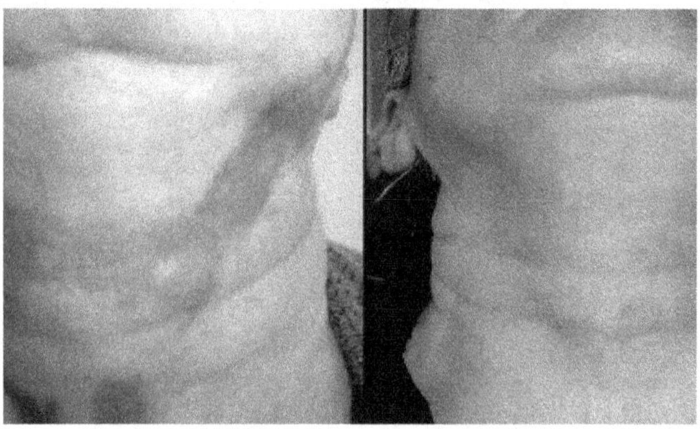

Fig. 9.15 Before and after the treatment for hyperpigmentation.
[Colour Fig. on page 414]

Examination

The volunteers are examined before the test began using a variety of subjective and objective evaluation techniques. In addition the panel members were examined by a consultant dermatologist to ensure that they were suitable for the test. (i.e. had no existing diseases or history of allergy/sensitization), and also during the test in order to detect any signs of primary irritation that might develop.

Evaluation technique

Both subjective and objective methods for assessing the degree of skin lightening effect.

1. Grey Scale wedge assessment.
2. Visual assessment

   The colors of the treatment sites were visually compared with the control site on each arm and the degree of lightening was assessed using the following simple numerical scoring system.

Score	Degree of Lightening
0	No difference
+1	Slightly lighter
+2	Noticeable lighter
+3	Markedly lighter

3. ***Photographic assessment:*** Photographs were taken of the forearms and faces of all subjects initially and of the forearm on each examination.
4. Reflectance skin: By EEL Spectrophotometer.
5. Color of skin: By reflectance Lovibond tintometer.

9.3 Chemical Peel

A professional peel will penetrate and strip away the top layer of hyperpigmented skin to reveal new, clear skin beneath. Alpha hydroxy acids, such as 8% glycolic acid, are exfoliants and can help remove hyperpigmentation.

Beta hydroxy acids, such as salicylic acids, are also exfoliants that can help address hyperpigmentation.

Spot Peel and Cream [Colour Fig. on page 414]

9.4 Intense Pulsed Light (IPL)

IPL is a type of laser that leaves no scars, can sometimes heal freckles or other mild sun spots without using peels or hydroquinone creams beforehand

9.5 Microdermabasion

This nonsurgical, painless procedure "sands" the top layer of skin with tiny crystals to erase discoloration.

9.6 Physician Formulas

These are more expensive skin pigmentation treatments but are very effective (Kinerase, Retin A, Renova, Avita etc).

9.7 Laser Resurfacing

If the hyperpigmentation doesn't respond to the treatments listed above, laser therapy may be the answer. During the procedure, the practitioner uses a laser to create microscopic "wounds" within the targeted areas, well beneath the outermost layer of skin. This in turn triggers the body's natural healing process, accelerating the production of collagen and new, healthy skin cells.

The physiological benefits that have been either experienced or foreseen are:

- Decreased pain levels
- Reduced inflammation

- Increased tissue regeneration
- Enhanced nerve regeneration and repair
- Increased microcirculation and vasodilatation

9.8 Home Remedies / Natural Treatment[30]

There are a number of home remedies that a person can use to treat hyperpigmentation. Of course, there is no guarantee that these remedies will work at all. There is also no guarantee that the effects will be permanent. Still, the good news is, these treatments had proven to be useful in some people. Also, they are cheap and can be easily created.

Some home remedies include:

Avocado

It is understood that the rich sources of unsaturated fatty acids, oleic acid, vitamin E will help in soothing as well as healing the skin. This can help in treating hyperpigmentation. Incase it is allergic to latex then one may want to avoid avocado. One has to peel the avocado and mash it up and apply the juice on the skin that is affected daily.

Cocoa butter

One can massage the skin that is affected perhaps once or daily for about 2 to 3 weeks. Apart from being an antioxidant, it is also an effective skin moisturizer. The massage boosts the skin blood circulation as well as breaks the scar tissues.

Lime or Lemon as well as Honey for promoting natural hyperpigmentation

Lemon or lime can treat the free radical damage caused to as well as honey can moisturize the skin. This can also help in lightening the skin and thus treating hyper pigmentation. One can mix lime as well lemon equally with honey and apply it on the affected area for about 10 minutes daily.

Raw potato juice for hyperpigmentation treatment

The presence of starch as well as mild bleaching property in potatoes can help in the treatment of hyper pigmentation. One may apply the juice of raw potato on the affected area for 10 days.

Gram: Mix 1 tablespoon of gram flour, 2 teaspoon of fresh milk, and 2-3 drops of lime juice. Apply mixture on the skin and leave it for 15 minutes. Rinse well. Do it for 4 weeks and follow up with once a week.

Mint: Make a paste out of grounded mint leaves. Apply on the skin and leave it for 20 minutes before rinsing off with cold water. Do it for 15 consecutively.

Tomato: Grate fresh tomatoes and mix it with 2-3 drops of juice. Apply on the face and leave it for 20 minutes. Rinse well. Do it twice a day for 15-20 days.

- One can apply sun screen lotion on a regularly basis before going out to prevent hyperpigmentation.
- One can drink lots of water and eat plenty of fresh fruits, cereals, vegetables regularly to keep the skin supply as well as healthy.
- One could take about 20 volume of hydrogen peroxide to which one must add about two tablespoonful of some milk powder and then mix it few drops of glycerine. Apply this mix on the pigmented areas and let it remain for 20 minutes. Then rinse the skin with water and subsequently apply moisturizer.
- Take same amount of vinegar as well as vinegar and use for cleansing the skin. Rinse the skin and let it dry naturally by air. The acetic acid in the vinegar will help in getting rid of the dark color and also allows the skin to remain radiant as well as smooth. Apple cider vinegar as well as natural vinegars are beneficial for treating this health condition.
- Mix a vitamin E capsule with some drops of castor oil and spread the content over the affected parts.
- Onion juice is also very good. Cut the onion into pieces and the blend them. Squeeze it in muslin cloth and get hold of the juice. Mix equal amount of apply cider vinegar in the vinegar and apply the content on the face. One can also slice an onion and dip it in vinegar and apply it on the affected part.

9.9 Conclusion

Hyperpigmentation, most commonly melasma and postinflammatory hyperpigmentation remain a therapeutic challenge. Many types of skin are susceptible to pigmentation disorders. Such conditions can appear especially prominent in people with dark skin. There are several types of products both synthetic and natural and home remedies are available for solving the problem of hyperpigmentation. Many of them act by different mechanisms and it is very difficult to say which is the best for an individual. The etiology is bit complicated and hence several products have been tried and still are coming into the market. Multiple topical modalities can be used, and combination topical therapies are the current first-line approach. Currently the focus is on polyherbal cosmetic products which are generally considered to be safe.

References

1. Dr.Shayeda, Design and evaluation of anti-acne, depigmenting and anti-perspirant herbal cosmeceuticals, Ph.D thesis submitted in University college of pharmaceutical sciences, Kakatiya University, Warangal (2010).
2. www.hyperpigmentation-Wikipedia-free-encyclopedia.com
3. Thong HY, Jee SH, Sun CC, Biossy RE. The patterns of melanosome distribution in keratinocytes of human skin as one determining factor of skin colour. *B J Dermatol* 2003;**149**: 498-505.
4. Saga K, Shimojo T. Effect of theophylline on the transport of tyrosine in cultured B-16 mouse melanoma cells. *Arch Dermatol Res* 1984; **276**: 165-169.
5. Kwon BS, Haq AK, Pomerantz SH, Halaban R. Isolation and sequence of a cDNA clone for human tyrosinase that maps at the mouse c-albino locus. *Proc Nat Acad Sci* USA 1987; **84**: 7473-7477.
6. Jackson IJ. A cDNA encoding tyrosinase-related protein maps to the brown locus in mouse. *Proc Nat Acad Sci* USA 1988; **85**: 4392-4396.
7. Halaban R, Moellmann GE. Murine and human b locus pigmentation genes encode a glycoprotein (gp75) with catalase activity. *Proc Nat Acad Sci* USA1990; **87**:4809-4813.
8. Winder AJ, Wittbjer A, Rosengren E, Rorsman H. The mouse brown (b) locus protein has dopachrome tautomerase activity and is located in lysosomes in transferred fibroblasts. *J Cell Sci* 1993; **106**:153-166.
9. Zhao H, Zhao Y, Nordlund JJ, Biossy RE. Human TRP-1 has tyrosine hydroxylase activity but no dopa oxidase activity. *Pigment cell res* 1994;**7**: 131-140.

10. Kobayashi T, Urabe K, Winder AJ, tsukamoto K, Brewington T, Imokawa G, Potterf B, Hearing VJ. The DHICA oxidase activity of TRP 1 and interactions with other melanogenic enzymes. *Pigment Cell res* 1994;**7**:227-234.

11. Orlow SJ, Zhou BK, Chakraborty AK, Drucker M, Pifko-Hirst S, Pawelek jm. High-molecular-weight forms of tyrosinase and the tyrosinase-related proteins. Evidence for a melanogenic complex. *J. Invest. Dermatol.*, **103**:1196-201, 1994.

12. Abdel-Malek Z, Swope V, Collins C, Biossy R, Zhao H, Nordlund J. Contribution of melanogenic proteins to the heterogeneous pigmentation of human melanocytes. *J cell Sci* 1993;**106**:1323-1331.

13. Lozumi K, Hoganson GE, Pennella R, Everett MA, Fuller BB. Role of tyrosinase as the determination of pigmentation in cultured human melanocytes. *J Invest Dermatol* 1993;**100**:806-811.

14. Kadekaro AL, Kavanagh RJ, Wakamastsu K, lto S, Pipitone MA, Abdel Malek ZA. Cutaneous Photobiology. The melanocyte vs. the sun. who will win the final round?.(Review). *Pigment Cell Res* 2003;**16**:434-447.

15. Lang G. Melanin in protection from sunlight. Proceedings of the IFSCC, Yokohama, 1992; 1072-1083.

16. Perez-Bernal A, Munoz-Perez MA, Camacho F. Management of facial hyperpigmentation. *Am J Clin Dermatol* 2000; **1**(5): 261-268.

17. Jean-Paul Ortonne and Donald L Bissett. Latest Insights into Skin Hyperpigmentation *Journal of Investigative Dermatology Symposium Proceedings* 2008; **13**:10–14.

18. Radhakrishnan N, Vijayachandra K, Ranganathan S. Changing skin colour: Evolution and modern trends. *Indian J dermatol* 2007; **52**(2).

19. Nealon DF, Ammoniated mercury and the skin. *Drug cosmet Ind* 1943;**52**: 159.

20. Hemsworth BN, Biological Changes due to topical application of skin lightening compounds. *J Soc Cosmet Chem* 1973;**24**:727-733.

21. Halder RM, Richards GM. "Topical agents used in the management of Hyperpigmentation". Skin therapy letter.com 2004; vol. 9.

22. André O. Barel, Marc Paye, Howard I. Maibach. *Handbook of Cosmetic Science and Technology* 3rd Edition 2009; pp 600.

23. Debr E Brooks. In vitro effectiveness of several whitening cosmetic components in human melanocytes. *Journal of the Society of Cosmet.Chemists*,42,(Nov-Dec); P361-368,199.

24. Jang DI, Lee BG, Jeon CO, Jo NS,Park JH. Cho SY, LKee H, Ko, JS. Melanogenesis inhibitor from paper mulberry. *Cosmetics and Toiletories* 1997; 59-62: 112.

25. Wenyuan Zhu and Jie Gao. Review on the use of botanical extracts as topical skin- lightening agents for the improvement of skin pigmentation disorders. *Journal of Investigative Dermatology symposium proceedings*, 2008, vol.13.

26. Dr.Tiedtke Jane, Mr.Jacques Morel, Dr.Olaf.Marks. Depigmentation Factor Bioflavonoids- A safe and effective skin lightener based on encapsulated Citrus bioflavonoides. *Cosmetic Science Technology*, 2004.

27. Hamed Saja H. Efficacy and mechanism of action of a new tyrosinase inhibitory agent. Thesis submitted to University of Cincinnati for the degree of Doctor of Philosophy, 2004.

28. *Skin Therapy Letter*. 2006;**11**(9):1-6. © 2006 SkinCareGuide.com

29. Curry KV. Evaluation of skin bleach creams. *J Soc Cosmet Chem* 1974;**25**, 339-354.

30. www.herbal-home-remedies.com

CHAPTER 10

MEDICATED AND ANTI-DANDRUFF SHAMPOOS

10.1 Introduction

The term shampoo comes from the Hindi word Champi, which referred to head massage, usually with some form of hair oil. The british loved the massage so much, they started calling Champi as Shampoo. For many years, shampoos were nothing more than Soaps to mean the action of washing the hair and scalp. Although potent cleansers, they had poor lathering capabilities in hard water and led to dull deposition of insoluble calcium-magnesium salts on the hair. In some cultures, bar soaps are curiously still preferred. In dermatological practice 30 years ago, shampoos with harsh surfactants were used to remove messy treatments applied to the scalp. Retail shampoos were originally simple products comprising aqueous solutions of surfactants designed to clean the hair by emulsifying oils and dispersing solid material. The ultimate aim of any shampoo is to reduce the hair fall along with desired action.

10.2 The Hair Growth Cycle

Hair follicles can grow in several repeated cycles. One cycle contains three phases.

1. **Anagen phase - growth phase**

   At any particular time 85% of all hair comes across this growing phase which vary from two to six years. Hair grows approximately 10 cm per year and any individual hair is unlikely to grow more than one meter long normally.

2. **Catagen phase - transitional phase**

   After Anagen phase the hair enters into a Catagen phase which lasts about one to two weeks. During this phase the hair follicle shrinks to about 1/6 of the normal length. The lower part is destroyed and the dermal papilla breaks away to rest below.

3. **Telogen phase - resting phase**

   After Catagen phase the hair enters into a resting phase which lasts about 5-6 weeks. During this phase the hair does not grow but stays attached to the follicle while the dermal papilla stays in a resting phase below. At any particular time 10-15% of all hair comes across this phase.

   At the end of the Telogen phase the hair follicle re-enters the Anagen phase. The dermal papilla and the base of the follicle join together again and a new hair begins to form. At the time of growth of new hair if the old hair has not already been shed the new hair pushes the old one out and the growth cycle starts again.

10.3 Ideal Requirements of a Shampoo

- The shampoo should remove dust or soil, excessive sebum or other fatty substances and loose corneal cells from the hair effectively and completely. It should also remove any applied hair preparations like oil, cream, gel etc.
- It should produce a good and abundant amount of foam to satisfy the psychological requirements of the user.
- It should be easily removed when it is rinsed with water. It should work effectively even with hard water.
- It should leave the hair non-dry, soft, lustrous with good manageability and minimum fly away.
- It should impart a pleasant fragrance to the hair for specified period of time.
- It should not cause any irritation or side-effects to the skin or eye.
- It should not make the hand rough.
- It should be stable in temperature range 2°C-45°C.
- Intensity of color should not be very high. Mainly eye catching and bright colors are used.

Product ingredients

Table 10.1 The raw materials used in the manufacture of shampoos.

The raw materials used	Examples
Surfactants	
Anionic	Sodium laureth sulphate
Cationic	Polyquarternium-10
Nonionic	Laureth-3 or 4, cocamide dea
Amphoteric	Cocamido propyl betaine
Foaming agents	Sarcosinate, lactylates
Conditioning agents	Quaternium 80 and 87
Viscosifying agents	
Electrolytes	NH_4Cl, NaCl
Natural gums	Gum Karaya, tragacanth, alginates
Cellulose derivatives	Hydroxy ethyl cellulose, methyl cellulose
Carboxy vinyl polymers	Carbopol 934
Others	PVP, phosphate esters
Opacifying agents	Glycol stearate, glycol distearate
Stabilizing agents/ Additives	
Clarifying agents	EDTA, citric acid
Preservatives	Phenyl mercuric salts
Buffers	Citric and tartaric acid
Sun-screen agents	Benzophenones
Colors	Green, blue, yellow, etc.,
Pearlescence agents	Ethylene glycol monostearate
Antioxidants	BHT, BHA
Perfumes	Sandle, musk, rose, etc.,

10.4 Classification of Shampoos

Shampoos may be classified based on consistency and characteristics.

Classification based on consistency

1. Clear liquid shampoo
2. Liquid cream/ lotion shampoo
3. Cream shampoo/ shampoo pastes
4. Jelly shampoo

5. Powder shampoo
6. Dry shampoo
7. Aerosol foam shampoo

Classification based on characteristics

1. Conditioning shampoo
2. Egg shampoo
3. Baby shampoo
4. Two layer shampoo
5. Herbal shampoo
6. Nutrient shampoo
7. Medicated / Anti dandruff shampoo
8. Anti-aging shampoo
9. Family shampoo
10. Shower shampoo

This chapter deals with only medicated / anti dandruff shampoos and the remaining will be discussed in 'General Cosmetics' Volume.

10.5 Medicated Shampoos

We need not to use a medicated shampoo frequently until and unless the scalp may be the site of an associated psoriasis, dandruff alone, or, in its severe form, seborrheic dermatitis. Occasionally the scalp may be the site of a folliculitis, so these shampoos are used to correct any disorder of secretion in the scalp.

Medicated shampoos include specialized formulations that incorporate one or several agents that alleviate the underlying scalp problem. Crude coal tar containing shampoos for psoriasis are popular with the consumer but are under attack because of the teratogenic potential associated with their use.

Classification of Medicated shampoos

- Medicated shampoos to combat dandruff
- Medicated shampoos to combat bacterial infection
- Medicated shampoos to combat psoriasis
- Medicated shampoos to combat pediculosis

10.5.1 Medicated Shampoos to Combat Dandruff

Dandruff ("Pityriasis simplex") is a common embarrassing disorder, affecting a large chunk of population (5% of the global population). The yeast, *Pityrosporum ovale* (*Malassezia ovalis*) is the contributing organism of dandruff which is there in the scalp of every person's body and its lipase activity releases proinflammatory free fatty acids, causing dermal inflammation and tissue damage. Dandruff is not a disease in itself. It is only a symptom of some other disorder that our body is suffering from. The best way to get rid of dandruff would be to cure the actual ailment first. This is the only way of hair loss prevention.

Symptoms of dandruff

Itching and too much flaking of the dead skin of the scalp is the sign of dandruff. After the dandruff attack the scalp may be extremely dry or extremely oily. Impaired health, inappropriate diet, low functioning of the person's immune system (due to communicable diseases) are responsible for dandruff.

Causes of dandruff

- Impaired health, growth of a lethal condition primarily because of taking of incorrect foods, constipation, and a low liveliness because of infectious ailments or lack of strong immune system are the major reasons for dandruff.
- Dandruff is caused by a fungus called *Malassezia globosa*. This fungus is found floating in the atmosphere and can infect anyone.
- Approximately more than seven species of Malassezia (i.e., *M. globosa*, *M. restricta*, *M. obtusa*, *M. sloofiae*, *M. sympodialis*, *M. furfur*, and *M. pachydermatis*) exist, and their growth may be encouraged by the hypersecretion of sebum and hyperproliferation of the stratum corneum.
- The species *M. globosa* and *M. restricta* are most closely associated with dandruff in humans.
- Malassezia may stimulate cytokine production by keratinocytes, further providing to the inflammatory component of seborrheic dermatitis and dandruff.
- Another reason for dandruff is the excessive use of hair care products.
- Generally a consequence of oiliness of the skin in excess instead of dryness is responsible for dandruff.

- The dead skin accumulation in the scalp is responsible for dandruff but in most of the cases germ similar to yeast aggravates it. However this microorganism is usually present on every person's scalp, it can generate irritation if it develops heavily on the scalp.
- Dandruff generally starts subsequent to puberty so hormones are another important cause of dandruff.
- Dandruff is more commonly found in men when compare with women. But people with diseases like Parkinson's disease, are more probable to possess dandruff for which the reasons are unknown.
- Another reason is irregular shampooing and improper washing of scalp.

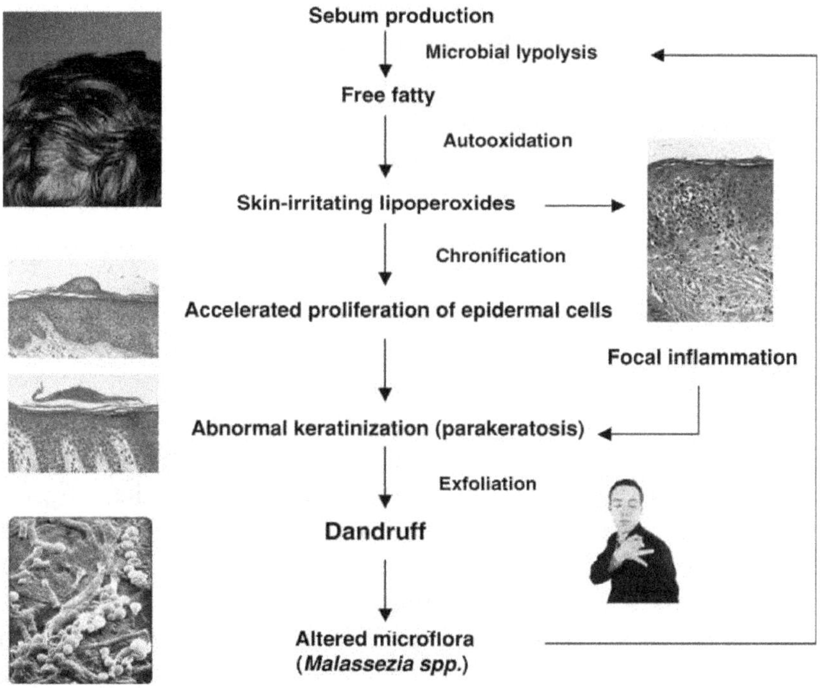

Fig. 10.1 Pathogenesis of dandruff[1]. [Colour Fig. on page 415]

The characteristics of antidandruff shampoo

- It should clean both the scalp and hair.
- It should not irritate the scalp
- It should not sensitize the sebaceous gland

- It should reduce the degree of itching and scaling.
- Any substance can work effectively as antidandruff only if it can function in presence of sebum.

Note: *We should not use antidandruff shampoos repeatedly like normal shampoos which causes abnormal hair loss.*

Active ingredients used to combat dandruff

The agents which are used in the treatment of dandruff as follows:

- Agents that inhibit overproduction of keratinizing cells, e.g., coal tar[24] (now it is banned in Germany for use in cosmetic shampoos) and ammonium bituminosulfonate (pale sulfonated shale oil as a coal tar substitute).
- Keratolytic agents which break down cell aggregations, e.g., colloidal sulphur and salicylic acids.
- Antimicrobial substances which inhibit *Malassezia* spp. yeasts, e.g., selenium disulfide, zinc pyrithione, piroctone olamine, ketoconazole, and ciclopirox olamine, etc.
- Combinations of these agents.

Ketoconazole

It is now generally accepted that *P. ovale* active in the pathogenesis of seborrheic dermatitis. During treatment, *P. ovale* levels are reduced or eliminated. The antifungal properties demonstrated by ketoconazole have made it a leading contender for the treatment of seborrheic dermatitis. It inhibits the ergosterol biosynthesis, the main sterol in the fungal cell membrane. At higher concentrations it causes accumulation of saturated fatty acids which further destabilizes the cell membrane and results in cell death. It has a low relapse rate during the post-treatment follow up. The use of ketoconazole 2% in a shampoo formulation has been demonstrated to be both safe and efficacious. Most of the studies showed that ketoconazole was more effective than zinc pyrithione or selenium sulfide in terms of reducing *Pityrosporum* counts, it is more effective *in vitro* against *Pityrosporum* than other azole derivatives, such as fluconazole, econazole, clotrimazole, and miconazole. It had longer-lasting antidandruff effects. But the disadvantage of monotherapy with ketoconazole is a relatively slow onset of anti-inflammatory effect compared to steroids. Combining ketaconazole with a cortico steroid has been shown to provide faster relief because of the steroid effect and a prolonged post treatment antifungal effect allowing for an overall reduction I intermittent use of the drug.

Pyrithione zinc

Pyrithione zinc is available from 1960s. Early reports suggested a significant reduction in cell turnover rate. More recent studies using radioactive labeling have failed to show any significant reduction in mitosis after the use of zinc pyrithione. Neverthless, the numbers of yeast organisms were markedly reduced in those investigations, indicating that the mechanism of action is more likely to be antimicrobial than cytostatic. The zinc pyrithione molecule is present as a crystalline suspension in glycol distearate and is not water soluble. The formulation allows even distribution of zinc pyrithione crystals in shampoo and the use of non-spherical crystals measuring only 2.5 μ allows better adsorption and more even distribution on the scalp. This is particularly effective in inhibiting *Malassezia* spp. yeasts, even with a short contact time and rinsing. 1% zinc pyrithione is a membrane transport inhibitor in fungi and bacteria. It acts to induce a dose dependent electrical depolarization of cell membrane through a direct or indirect effect on the primary proton pump that energises transport. The combination of zinc pyrithione with zinc carbonate leads to reduced dissociation of the active ingredients into zinc and pyrithione, which alone have a lower anti-dandruff effect. The pyrithione moiety is the active part of the molecule, and its clinical performance is associated with the fact that it binds both to the hair shaft and to the external skin. The usefulness of pyrithione zinc shampoo is enhanced with longer contact time (5 to 10 minutes). Despite its low risk of sensitization, cases of allergic contact dermatitis still occur because of the popularity of such products.[2]

Fig. 10.2 Deposition of micro-fine crystals of zinc pyrithione on the scalp.[3]

Selenium

It is available since the 1950s, selenium in the form the mixed sulphides, including selenium monosulphide and a suspension that incorporates solid selenium with sulphur, is used in the treatment of dandruff and seborrheic dermatitis. Although the exact mechanism of action of selenium sulfide is still not clear, the antimicrobial properties associated with this combination may play a role. It is usually supplied as a 2.5% concentration. Few scientists believe that it is contraindicated for seborrheic patients because of its stimulating effect on sebaceous gland secretion. This shampoo must be rinsed thoroughly from the hair, to avoid discoloration. Patients may complain of a residual odor and oily scalp after using selenium sulphide suspension shampoo.

Sulphur

Sulphur has been used extensively in dermatology for its keratolytic effect and its supposed antimicrobial effect and because it is safe even when used on small children. The keratolytic effect of sulphur is probably due to the reaction between the sulphur and the cysteine in keratinocytes. The supposed antimicrobial effect depends on the conversion of sulfur to pentathionic acid by the normal skin flora or the keratinocytes. This has not been proved in humans. Some *in vitro* tests showed that sulfur itself was unable to inhibit growth of the microorganisms tested. When used to treat skin diseases, sulfur is usually employed in combination therapy.

Piroctone olamine

In several studies, piroctone olamine has proved to be highly effective against dandruff and the itching associated with dandruff. Its mechanism of action is attributed to both its antimicrobial and its antioxidative action. The concentration used should be between 0.5% and 1.0%. A comparative study of piroctone olamine and zinc pyrithione, both at concentrations of 0.5%, showed that piroctone olamine was more effective in the treatment of dandruff.

Tar

Although tars have been classically used to treat psoriasis, they offer an effective therapy option in treating dandruff as well. Problems with staining, odor, and messiness in its application make tar a second-line therapy for most patients. Tar gels contain coal tar extract, and they are generally less messy and smelly than tar itself. *Tar shampoos* work through antiproliferative and cytostatic effects, although definitive analyses are difficult because of the large number of biologically active components in coal tar products. Tar products disperse scales, which may reduce *Malassezia* colonization.

Along with the above mentioned agents Lithium gluconate and corticosteroids were reported in the treatment of dandruff. Lithium gluconate can act by inhibiting the production of free fatty acids necessary for the growth of *Malassezia* spp. Other agent reported is pimecrolimus which is a member of new class of non steroidal agent.

Herbal ingredients like tea tree oil, rosemary oil, coleus oil, clove oil, pepper extract, neem extract, and basil extract also recorded anti-pityrosporum activity, but their MIC are much higher than the synthetic ingredients. These ingredients can be exploited for its antidandruff activity individually or in combination in antidandruff shampoos. The commercial shampoos with tea tree oil, rosemary oil, henna, lemon also recorded good anti-pityrosporum activity *in vitro* but not better than shampoos with synthetic ingredients in both MIC and ZOI assays. But for regular usage even shampoos with herbal antidandruff ingredients may suffice the purpose.[4]

Dietary Treatments to treat and cure Dandruff

- Milk, dairy items, animal proteins, sea foods and foods containing fats are on the catalogue of foods which should be avoided by the people having problems related to dandruff.
- Vitamin C is not considered to be good for people having dandruff. The majority of sour tasting foods contain vitamin C. For that reason, oranges, tomatoes, tamarind, lemons etc. which contain vitamin C, must be avoided.
- Fresh and clean vegetables must be incorporated in the food chart. Green vegetables and fruits have excellent effects.

Home Medications to treat dandruff

- To control the dandruff lemon peel may be rubbed on the scalp and massage gently, leave it for half an hour, then wash and rinse.
- 3 tbsp of henna powder, one egg, 1 tbsp spoon of curd/yogurt and the lemon juice were mixed to make a paste and apply it on the scalp and massage gently. Leave it for 15 minutes, wash and rinse. For better results this procedure can be repeated monthly.

- To control the dandruff daily cleaning of the comb or hair brush with soap is necessary. It is better to soak the comb in a mixture of lemon juice and warm water (1:1) for 1 hour.
- Egg white mixed with 2 tbsp of lemon juice leave it for half an hour, then apply it on to the scalp and leave it for one hour before shampooing.
- Lemon juice is mixed with vinegar (1:1) and apply it on to the scalp, leave it for 15 minutes and wash.
- Warm coconut oil is used to apply and massage over the scalp. Wrap a hot steamed towel over the head so that the oil gets absorbed. Leave it on for 1 hour. Then apply lemon juice on the scalp. Shampoo after 15 minutes.
- Rinse the hair thoroughly with plenty of water after shampooing. For fast results, add peppermint oil to your shampoo and conditioner. It is known for its anti-dandruff properties and excellent aroma.
- Protect your scalp from harmful sun rays by covering the head with a scarf or a hat.
- Do not scratch the scalp. It would worsen the dandruff and can even result in inflammation and infection by other pathogens
- ***Fenugreek Seeds:*** 2 tablespoons of fenugreek seeds are soaked in water throughout the night. The next morning, pour the yoghurt/curd, lemon juice and grind the seeds into a fine paste. Apply this paste on to scalp and leave it for 30 minutes, wash the hair with cold water properly. This is very effective.
- ***Aloe vera*:** Apply the *Aloe vera* gel onto the scalp. Leave it overnight and the next morning, shampoo regularly.
- ***Apple Cider Vinegar:*** Apple cider vinegar is poured into the scalp and massage. Take a clean cotton towel and wrap it tightly around the head. Leave the towel on for 1 hour and then wash the hair with warm water.

10.5.2 Medicated Shampoos to Combat Bacterial Infection

Active agents which are used in antibacterial shampoos are triclosan, chlorhexidine, benzoyl peroxide, salicylic acid, poviodine-iodine, and sulphur. Although the surface of the scalp consists of bacteria, they are usually members of the normal resident aerobic and anaerobic scalp flora. Bacteria present on the hair shafts are easily removed by shampooing but are restored to their original level within 24 hours. Bacteria on hairs are usually inconsequential, but under certain circumstances bacteria such as *Staphylococcus aureus* may involve the follicle, resulting in a staphylococcal folliculitis. Antibacterial-containing shampoos are of limited benefit in the management of scalp folliculitis.

10.5.3 Medicated Shampoos to Combat Pediculosis

Active agents which are used in shampoos to combat pediculosis are lindane, malathion, permethrin, and pyrethrin. *Pediculus humanus* var. *capitis*, the head louse, has been a companion of humans since long times. Head lice infestations remain a major public health concern worldwide. Recent studies reveal that lice have become firmly established in public schools.

Lindane

Lindane became available in the 1940s for the treatment of pediculosis capitis and scabies. Children are considered to be particularly at risk, and percutaneous absorption may cause central nervous system toxicity. The use of lindane shampoo has decreased due to availability of other effective, safer treatment agents.

Malathion

Eventhough it is classified as an organophosphorous pesticide, malathion has an excellent safety profile. In some countries, malathion has displaced lindane for the treatment of pediculosis and scabies. Unfortunately, patients complain of the unpleasant odor associated with malathion shampoo. Malathion is not currently available in some countries.

Permethrin

Permethrin is one of the most suitable of the pyrethroids because of its stability, low mammalian toxicity, and high insecticidal activity. Permethrin 1% cream rinse has been approved for use on prescription by the FDA since April 1986. It is available as a mixture of 25% cis- to 75% trans-isomers and formulated as 1% permethrin in a standard commercial cream hair rinse to which is added 20% isopropanol. The cis-isomer has a higher potential for mammalian toxicity than the trans-isomer, which is more rapidly metabolized. The 25:75 cis:trans ratio was preferred for human use because of the lower levels of &-isomer.

Pyrethrins

Pyrethrum is an extract from chrysanthemums that provides a naturally occurring insecticide effective for the treatment of scabies and pediculosis. Pyrethrin's action is enhanced when the agent is combined with piperonyl butoxide. With the introduction of the synthetic pyrethroid permethrin, the use of the pyrethrin shampoo formulations has diminished.

10.5.4 Medicated Shampoos to Combat Psoriasis

Active agents which are used in shampoos to combat psoriasis are crude coal tar, salicylic acid, sulfur, and selenium.

Coal tar

Coal tar is a byproduct that follows the destructive distillation of bituminous coal and is a complex mixture of aromatic hydrocarbons and phenols. Tar-containing shampoos are frequently used for the treatment of psoriasis and seborrheic dermatitis. The exact mechanism of coal tar's action is unknown, but it exhibits a cytostatic effect after long use (40 days) at a 5% concentration. Research studies have shown that commercial coal tar suppresses epidermal cell DNA synthesis in the hairless mouse model. Coal tar shampoo is the most useful in the treatment of scalp psoriasis. It has been demonstrated that human exposure to PAH (in coal tar) is associated with an increased risk of cancer. Wood tars, oil of Cade, and pine tars were removed from shampoos on the recommendation of the FDA in 1990 because their efficacy had not been established.

Salicylic acid, sulphur and selenium

Some clinical data suggests that shampoos that include one or a combination of these agents have some effectiveness in the management of mild to moderate scalp psoriasis. 0.05 % clobetasol propionate has recently become available in short-contact shampoo formulations for scalp psoriasis. It presents a superior alternative to coal tar shampoo in terms of efficacy and product appeal and results have shown that it does not produce unwanted corticosteroid effects on the skin, adrenal axis, or eyes.[5] We have discussed this topic in the chapter 'Psoriasis'.

10.6 Examples for Formulations

Anti dandruff shampoos

Formula 1

Ingredient	% by wt
SLS	20
Ethylene glycol	
monostearate	5
Lauric	5
diethanolamide	1
Empicryl APD	5.5
Selenium disulphide	pH 4-4.5
Citric acid	
Perfume, dye,	Qs
preservative	Balance
Water	

(Empicryl APD - Aqueous pigment dispersant)

Formula 2

Ingredient	% by wt
SLS	18
Ethylene glycol	
monostearate	5
Lauric diethanolamide	5
Laponite XLS	6
Selenium disulphide	5.5
Citric acid	pH 4-4.5
Perfume, dye, preservative	Qs
Water	Balance

Laponite XLS- it may be used as a pre-dispersed liquid concentrate and added to formulated products as required. It is used to impart a shear sensitive structure to a wide range of personal care products. Its chemical composition includes

SiO_2	54.5%
MgO	26.0%
Li_2O	0.8%
Na_2O	5.6%
P_2O_5	4.1%

Medicated shampoo

Ingredient	% by wt
Sodium lauryl ethoxy sulphate	45
Coconut diethanolamide	3
Irgasan DP 300	0.5
Citric acid	pH 4-4.5
Sodium chloride	Qs
Perfume, dye, preservative	Qs
Water	Balance

Irgasan DP 300 - 5-Chloro-2-(2,4-dichlorophenoxy)phenol

10.7 Marketed Preparations

Johnson's Nizoral Anti-Dandruff Shampoo [Colour Fig. on Page 415]

Key ingredients: Ketoconazole, sodium lauryl ether sulphate, brilliant blue FCF, water.

Coal Tar Shampoo to fight Psoriasis [Colour Fig. on Page 415]

Mediker Anti-lice Treatment Shampoo [Colour Fig. on Page 416]

Renref - Anti Lice Shampoo [Colour Fig. on Page 416]

10.8 Evaluation of Shampoos

Evaluation of Shampoos include the following tests

- Foam and foam stability
- Detergency and cleaning action
- Effect of water hardness

- Surface Tension/wetting action
- Surfactant content and analysis
- Rinsing action
- Conditioning action
- Determination of pH
- Softness
- Luster
- Lubricity
- Texture and set retention
- Irritation and toxicity
- Stability studies
- Microbiological assay
- Eye irritancy test
- Fragrance
- Color
- Consistency
- Package

All the above mentioned tests will be discussed in 'General Cosmetics' Volume. This chapter describes only evaluation tests for antidandruff shampoos.

Because of unavailability of standardized schedules, reliable modes of assessment and the lack of meaningful animal models all the tests are performed on human panellists. Most of the methods are based on corneocyte counting and measurement of the amount, size, and thickness of dandruff scales.

Eberhard Futterer[6] described the experimental design in the half-head technique, which allows the direct comparison of two products preferably shampoos in the same subject at the same time on a double blind basis. The application of the products involves one product on each half of the head. They have selected the subjects with moderate or severe dandruff and the assessment of dandruff was done before treatment started, during the test period, and after the last treatment. To satisfy the regulatory requirements they have used placebo (vehicle control) formulation. Subjects must not have used an active agent for 1 month.

The amount of scaling is estimated by scraping the scalp at multiple sites with a wooden tongue blade. The following simplified scoring system based only upon severity is used:

+ + + = 3 = severe dandruff

+ + =2 = moderate dandruff

+ = 1 = slight dandruff

(+) = 0, 2 = dandruff no longer detectable for test persons the grader still occasionally find some scales

0 = completely free from dandruff

Quantitative clinical criterion also includes evaluation of the following

- Loose dandruff
- Adherent scale
- Hair brittleness
- Hair oiliness
- Scalp cleanliness
- Scalp looseness
- Scalp redness

Corneocyte Counting

1 ml of buffered 0.1%-Triton-X-100 is placed in a 3.8 sqcm glass cup placed on a small area of the scalp from which the hair has been clipped. The surface is rubbed 1 minute with a teflon rod, the wash fluid is aspirated, and after repeating this procedure, the two samples are pooled. The cell suspension is agitated mechanically and counted in a hemocytometer. Statistical significance for reduction of corneocyte counts is measured by the students' T-test.[7]

10.9 Conclusion

Shampoos are the most frequently prescribed treatment for the hair and scalp. A shampoo is composed of 10 to 30 ingredients. Selection of medicated shampoo depends on the scalp condition whether it is attacked by dandruff, bacterial Infection, psoriasis or pediculosis. Dandruff is a chronic and recurrent disorder and repetitive treatment courses are necessary. Unlike corticosteroids, antifungal agents do not carry a risk of skin atrophy with prolonged use. Recent developments in shampoo technology have led to increased efficacy of anti-dandruff agents, allowing shorter contact time, and reducing irritation.

References

1. Ralph M.Trüeb, *Shampoos: Ingredients, efficacy and adverse effects Clinic for Dermatology*, University Hospital of Zurich, Switzerland JDDG; 2007; **5**:356–365.
2. Chih-Wei Hsieh, Mei-Eng Tu*, Yu-Hung Wu, Allergic contact dermatitis induced by zinc pyrithione in shampoo: a case report, *Dermatologica Sinica*; 2010; **28**: 163–166.
3. John Gray, *Clinics in Dermatology*. 2001;**19**:227–236
4. M Prabhamanju, S Gokul Shankar, K Babu, MS Ranjith, Herbal vs. chemical substances as antidandruff ingredients: which are more effective in the management of Dandruff? - An overview, *Egyptian Dermatology Online Journal* **5**(2): 8.
5. Jerry Shapiro, Stuart Maddin, Medicated Shampoos, *Clinics in dermatology*, 1996; **14**: 123-128.
6. Eberhard Futterer, Evaluatioonf efficacy of antidandruff agents, *J. Soc. Cosmet. Chem*, 1981; **32**: 327-338.
7. James J. Leyden, M.D., Kenneth J. Mcginley, Albert M. Kligman, Shorter Methods for Evaluating Antidandruff agents, *J. Soc. Cosmet. Chem.*, 1975; **26**: 573-580.

CHAPTER 11

MEDICATED TOOTHPASTES

Y. Madhusudan Rao, D. Sathish, S. Himabindu

Center for Biopharmaceutics and Pharmacokinetics, University College of Pharmaceutical Sciences, Kakatiya University, Warangal-506 009, Andhra Pradesh, India.

11.1 Introduction

Oral health problems remain one among the most common problem faced by mankind. The impact ranges from a minor inconvenience, a situation which can be reversed by maintaining good oral hygiene, to excruciating pain and loss of masticatory function.[1] Regular and proper usage of a suitable dentifrice checks for the development of dental caries. Dentifrice is any preparation used in the cleansing of the teeth, e.g., a tooth powder, toothpaste, or tooth wash. The primary purpose of brushing the teeth with a dentifrice (*dens* - tooth, *fricare* - to rub)[2] is to clean the accessible tooth surfaces of dental plaque, stains and food debris.

11.1.1 Structure of Tooth

A healthy tooth can broadly be described in three parts: crown, neck and root.

Crown: It is that part of the tooth which is visible above the gum (gingiva).

Neck: The region of the tooth that is at the gum line, connecting the root and the crown.

Root: It anchors the tooth within the gum. It lies below the gum line and is not visible outside.

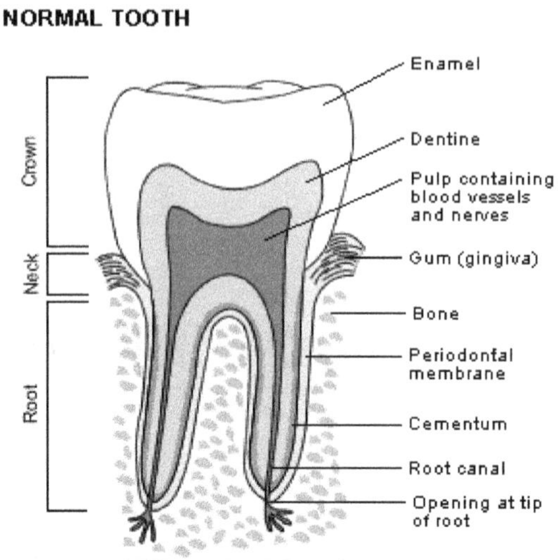

Fig. 11.1 Structure of Tooth. [Colour Fig. on page 416]

The half-way section of the tooth shows the following parts:

Crown

The coating of enamel is found on the crown of each tooth, which protects the underlying dentine. The hardest substance in the human body is enamel, which is made up of tightly packed rows of calcium and phosphorus crystals within a protein matrix structure. Once the enamel has been completely formed, there is little turnover of its minerals during life and is no longer considered to be a living tissue.

Dentine

Dentine is found beneath the enamel. Dentine is comparatively softer than enamel, with a structure more like bone. It is elastic and compressible in contrast to the brittle nature of enamel. It contains tiny tubules throughout its structure that connect with the central nerve of the tooth within the pulp. Dentine is a 'live' tissue.

Cementum and the periodontal membrane

The dentine of the root is covered with a thin layer of cementum, rather than enamel. Cementum is a hard bone-like substance. Over the cementum is the periodontal membrane that bonds the root of the tooth to the jaw bone.

Pulp

The central portion of the tooth is pulp. It is richly vascularized soft tissue. The blood vessels supply nutrients while the small lymph vessels carry white blood cells to exert their phagocytic action and help tooth fight bacteria. The pulp is also supplied with nerves to enable the tooth sense heat and cold.

Root canal

The extension of the root within the jaw bone is called the root canal. The nerve supply and vascular supply from the surrounding tissue enter the pulp through a small opening at the tip of the root canal.

11.2 Toothpaste

11.2.1 History

Toothpaste is an old phenomenon. In 3000-5000 BC Egyptians made a dental cream by mixing powdered ashes of oxen hooves with myrrh, burned egg shells, pumice, and water and used chew sticks to apply their dental cream.

In 1000 AD Persians added burnt shells of snails and oysters along with gypsum so toothpaste was reserved for the rich only. In 18th century in England a tooth cleaning "powder" containing borax was sold in ceramic pots but the problem was that they were often very abrasive, causing damage to teeth.

Modern toothpastes were developed in the 1800s. In 1824, a dentist named Peabody added soap to the toothpaste. John Harris first added chalk as an ingredient to toothpaste in the 1850s. In 1873, Colgate mass-produced the first toothpaste in a jar. In 1892, Dr. Washington Sheffield of Connecticut manufactured toothpaste into a collapsible tube. In 1896, Colgate Dental Cream was packaged in collapsible tubes imitating Sheffield. Advancements in synthetic detergents made after World War II allowed for the replacement of the soap used in toothpaste with emulsifying agents such as sodium lauryl sulphate and sodium ricinoleate.

Before World War II, toothpaste was packaged in small lead or tin alloy tubes. The inside of the tube was coated with wax, but later they discovered that lead was leached into the product from the tubes. So there was the shortage of lead and tin during World War II that led to the use of laminated (aluminum, paper, and plastic combination) tubes. At the end of the twentieth century pure plastic tubes were used.

The breakthrough that transformed toothpaste into the crucial weapon against tooth decay was the finding that fluoride could dramatically reduce cavities. Dr. William Engler tested 400 pre-school children and discovered a dramatic reduction in dental cavities among children treated with fluoride. Later the research was carried out world wide during 1950s, led to the widespread introduction of fluoride in to toothpastes.

11.2.2 Basic Toothpaste Ingredients

Abrasives

In order for a dental paste or gel to be referred to as a tooth paste, it must contain an abrasive. The primary purpose of an abrasive is to remove plaque from the teeth. Abrasives scrub the outside of the teeth to get rid of plaque and loosen particles on teeth. Abrasives also contribute to the degree of opacity of the paste or gel. The most commonly used abrasives are hydrated silica (softened silica), calcium carbonate (also known as chalk), and sodium bicarbonate (baking soda). Other abrasives include dibasic calcium phosphate, calcium sulfate, tricalcium phosphate, and hydrated alumina. Each abrasive also has slightly different cleaning properties, and a combination of them might be used in the final product.

Detergents

Foaming action is created by detergents which is associated with toothpastes. Foam keeps the toothpaste in the mouth, and aids in suspending and removing the debris. SLS (sodium lauryl sulfate) is the detergent most commonly used. Unfortunately, SLS and other detergents have been linked to the promotion of canker sores (mouth ulcers) in susceptible individuals; therefore care should be taken not to exceed the concentration of surfactant above 2%. Sodium lauryl sulphoacetate, sodium dioctyl sulphosuccinate and N-lauroylsarcosinate are other surfactants which may be used in toothpastes (3).

Binding agents

Binding agents are necessary to maintain the physical stability of the paste and prevent separation into component phases. Natural or synthetic gums or hydrophilic colloids are the typical binders used in toothpastes. Carboxymethyl cellulose is one of the preferred gelling agents used in toothpaste. Hydroxy ethyl cellulose, carrageenan, natural processed bentonites, cross linked acrylic acid polymers are some of the other compounds which are used as binders. Usually they are used at 0.9%-2.0% concentration range in toothpaste formulations.

Humectants

Humectants give toothpaste its texture and retain moisture so that the toothpaste will not dry out. At the same time they give shine and some plasticity to the paste. Glycerin, sorbitol, and water are commonly used humectants. Glycerin and sorbitol also have a role in preventing microbiological growth and add sweetness to the taste of the toothpaste. Xylitol is a superior humectant, which also boosts fluoride's cavity-fighting power. Generally the total humectant loading is in the range 10%-30% by weight.

Preservatives

Most of the ingredients used in toothpastes are susceptible for microbial attack. Preservatives are used to prevent the growth of microorganisms. Common preservatives include sodium benzoate, methyl paraben, and ethyl paraben. They are employed at a concentration range of 0.05%-0.2%.

Flavoring agents

Toothpastes have flavors to make them more palatable. Mint is the most common flavor used because it imparts a feeling of freshness. Mint flavors contain oils that volatize in the mouth's warm environment. This volatizing action imparts a cooling sensation in the mouth. The most common toothpaste flavors are spearmint, peppermint, wintergreen, and cinnamon. Some of the more exotic toothpaste flavors include bourbon, rye, anise, clove, caraway, coriander, eucalyptus, nutmeg, and thyme. Depending upon the formulation, e.g. the abrasive nature and level, the gelling agent used and the presence of therapeutic ingredients which may impact taste perception, the flavor level may vary from around 0.5%-1.5%by weight.[4]

Sweeteners

Sweeteners improve the taste of toothpaste. Most toothpaste sweeteners are artificial and contribute very little to cavity formation. Saccharin is a common toothpaste sweetener, generally used at a level between 0.05%-0.5% by weight.

Coloring agents

Coloring agents provide toothpaste with pleasing colors. Now a days red, green, and blue toothpastes are becoming famous and attractive. To create such toothpaste, artificial dyes are used. Titanium dioxide is used to make some tooth pastes white.

Example 1

Ingredient	% by wt
Dicalcium phosphate	60
Sorbitol	15
Gum tragacanth	1
Sodium lauryl sulphate	1
Sodium saccharine	0.1
Water	to 100

Example 2

Ingredient	% by wt
Calcium carbonate	40
Glycerin	30
Propylene glycol	5
Gum tragacanth	1.2
Saccharin sodium	0.05
Mineral oil	1
Sodium lauryl sulphate	1.1
Water	to 100

11.3 Medicated Toothpastes

Dentifrices and mouth rinses are routinely used as a delivery system for therapeutic agents such as antimicrobials and anti-sensitivity agents. Therapeutic oral care products are available to assist the patient in the control of dental caries, calculus formation, and dentinal hypersensitivity to name a few. Many attempts have been made at various times to add therapeutic agents with the object of interfering with oral flora, limiting plaque formation and making teeth more resistant to caries.

11.3.1 Anti-Caries / Anti-Cavity Toothpastes

The most important ingredient to look for when choosing toothpaste is fluoride to stop tooth enamel decalcification and protect teeth from tooth decay and cavities. Fluoride is a naturally occurring mineral. Its use has been instrumental in the dramatic drop in tooth decay and cavity occurrence that has taken place over the past 50 years.

Teeth are hard, and this hardness is caused by a form of calcium called hydroxyapatite. Bacterial processes change carbohydrates like sugar in food left on teeth to acid that demineralizes hard tooth structure. Hydroxyapatite is very susceptible to this acid attack. If the speed of demineralization exceeds the speed of remineralization, a carious lesion will eventually form.

Fluoride plays a significant role in this ongoing process. Hydroxyapatite is also quite susceptible to attack by free fluoride ions, but instead of causing destruction of the hydroxyapatite crystals, it causes their transformation into fluoroapatite. The fluoride ions essentially substitute themselves for the hydroxyl groups in the hydroxyapatite. Fluoroapatite has similar characteristics as hydroxyapatite, but is quite resistant to acid attack. Thus, using fluoride containing toothpastes coats the outside of the teeth with a new layer of acid-resistant fluoroapatite.[5,6]

The effectiveness of anti-cavity toothpastes is influenced by the concentration of fluoride, i.e., toothpastes with a higher concentration of fluoride, 1500 ppm (0.15 %F-) have a greater cariostatic effect than toothpastes with 1000 ppm (0.1 % F-).

One problem with young children's use of toothpaste is that they often swallow considerable amounts with a subsequent risk of dental fluorosis Fluoride toothpaste may be responsible for up to 80% of the daily fluoride intake[7] and the first 3 years of life seem to be the most critical. Therefore, parents should be strongly advised to use only a pea-size of toothpaste for very young children and assist or supervise tooth brushing until at least 7 years of age[8].

If the sole source of fluoride exposure is toothpaste containing fluoride between 1000-1500 F ppm, used as recommended, there is a minimal concern that children under the age of 6 will develop fluorosis since the amount absorbed would be less than half the accepted adequate intake of 0.7 mg/day fluoride intake for children between the ages of 1 and 3, that maximally reduces dental caries without causing unwanted side effects.

Non-fluoride anti-caries agents

Phosphate containing agents

These include simple inorganic salts ranging from sodium and potassium to the more complex polyphosphates, such as tri-meta-phosphate and pyrophosphate. Organic phosphates such as glycerophosphate and phytate have also shown cario-static activity in animal studies. Possible mechanism of action of phosphate agents is that, the inorganic phosphates could act directly by promoting either remineralization, or reducing demineralization. Phosphates in high concentrations have also been shown to decrease acid production by oral streptococci, possibly by preventing the activation of lactate dehydrogenase by fructose diphosphate.

Calcium containing agents

Calcium containing agents like calcium lactate and calcium carbonate have been demonstrated to raise calcium and phosphorous levels in plaque and thereupon are available to buffer plaque acids produced by bacteria.

Ingredient	% by wt
Glycerine	22
CMC	1.1
Sodium saccharin	0.2
$Na4P_2O_7$	0.5
MFP	0.76
Sodium fluoride	0.1
Dicalcium phosphate	48
Sodium lauryl sulphate	1.5
Flavour	0.8
Water	to 100

CMC Carboxy Methyl Cellulose
Na4P2O7 Sodium Pyrophosphate
MFP Monofluorophosphate

11.3.2 Anti-Plaque/ Anti-Gingivitis Toothpastes

Among the number of microorganisms present in our mouth bacteria are common. Enzymes produced by these bacteria convert all foods, especially sugar and starch into acids. Bacteria, acid, food debris, and saliva combine in the mouth to form a sticky substance called plaque that adheres to the teeth.

Among the several oral/dental diseases gingivitis is the most common and mildest form. Gingivitis is characterized by inflammation and bleeding of the gums. In early stages gingivitis rarely painful, if it is not observed in the early stage, it causes severe irritation or receding of the gums. If left untreated, gingivitis may lead to a more serious condition called periodontitis, in which the inner gum and bone pull away from teeth and form pockets. These pockets harbor bacteria and debris, and become infected or abscessed. Bacterial toxins eventually break down the underlying bone and connective tissue that hold teeth in place finally leading to tooth loss.[9]

Anti-plaque toothpastes have antibacterial ingredients to fight the growth of bacteria and the formation of dental plaque. Compounds with anti-microbial properties have been tested in toothpastes in order to develop products that can retard plaque formation and thereby prevent gingivitis. The most important agent is Chlorhexidene. This is a broad-spectrum anti-bacterial agent which has been shown to be highly effective in reducing plaque and gingivitis when delivered in simple forms to the oral environment. The speciality of this compound is that it bound and retained in the mouth for several hours because of its positive charge. But the disadvantage is that it reacts with many of the ingredients used in normal toothpaste and it causes side-effects such as staining of the teeth, increased calculus formation, and alteration in taste perception. By considering all these parameters it is used in the commercialization of mouth rinses which are prescribed for specialist uses or sold under the supervision of the pharmacist. Clinical trials have evaluated toothpastes with different abrasives in their ability to control and remove extrinsic chlorhexidine stain. Toothpastes with a variety of abrasives including dical, baking soda, and alumina, have been shown to effectively reduce chlorhexidine staining of the natural dentition.[10]

Now a non-cationic anti-microbial, triclosan, 2,4,4'-trichloro-2'-hydroxydiphenyl ether is widely used in toothpastes. Even though triclosan does not have a high affinity for the oral tissues and several approaches have been utilized to improve its efficacy. In some formulations, it has been combined with such ingredients as zinc citrate, which has anti-bacterial properties. Alternatively, adding the organic copolymer Gantrez® (copolymer of methyl vinyl ether and maleic acid) has increased the retention of triclosan in the oral environment for long periods of time.

Chlorophyll

Chlorophyll is still present in some tooth-pastes and it was one of the earliest agents added to the paste. Although *in vitro* tests showed that chlorophyll- containing tooth pastes limits bacterial growth, but clinical trials have not shown any anti-caries effects.[11] Chlorophyll is bacteriostatic, and only slightly bactericidal. It is particularly effective against anaerobic bacteria, those which do not require oxygen. Dentists and physicians have successfully used chlorophyll to control mouth infections such as pyorrhea and Vincent's angina. Chlorophyll solutions provide significant relief of pain, reduction of inflammation, and the control of odor for patients with serious mouth diseases.[12,13]

Ammoniated tooth-paste

It contains urea, and developed in an attempt to control the acid production in plaque. A number of clinical trials were carried out, but all gave very little positive or inconclusive results. Ammoniated pastes have been superseded by more effective agents, Antibiotic toothpastes containing penicillin, triclosan or topical anti-biotic such as tyrothricin have also been tried. It was based on the assumption that if acidogenic bacteria are destroyed, caries will be controlled.

Anti-enzyme paste

These toothpastes were introduced on the basis of a mechanism that they interfere with enzyme systems of the bacteria and thus with their growth and function. Still their effectiveness has not been evaluated by clinical trials.[11]

Herbal treatment

Toothpaste containing sage oil, peppermint oil, chamomile tincture, Echinacea purpurea juice, myrrh tincture and rhatany tincture are also employed to treat gingivitis.[14]

Example 3[4]

Ingredient	% by wt
Sorbitol (70%)	45.5
Silica abrasive	10.0
Silica thickener	8.0
Sodium lauryl sulphate	2.4
SDBS	0.8
CMC	0.8
Zinc citrate trihydrate	1.0
Triclosan	0.3
Flavour	1.2
Sodium chloride	1.0
NaMFP	1.12
Sodium saccharin	0.3
Water to	100.0

SDBS Sodium dodecyl benzene sulphonate
CMC Carboxy methyl cellulose
NaMFP Sodium monofluorophosphate

Example 4[4]

Ingredient	% by wt
Sorbitol (70%)	25.0
Silica abrasive	20.0
Glycerin	10.0
Silica thickener	5.5
Sodium lauryl sulphate	2.5
Gantrez	2.0
Sodium hydroxide (50%)	2.0
Flavour	1.1
Ethyl alcohol	1.0
Iota carrageenan	0.6
Titanium dioxide	0.5
Sodium saccharin	0.4
Triclosan	0.3
Sodium fluoride	0.243
Water to	100.0

11.3.3 Tooth Pastes for Sensitivity[4,15]

Usually tooth sensitivity (dentin hypersensitivity) presents as temporary tooth discomfort or pain after eating cold food, drinking cold liquids, or breathing cold air. Several theories have been proposed to explain the mechanism involved in dentinal hypersensitivity which include the transducer theory, the modulation theory, the gate control and vibration theory and the hydrodynamic theory.

Among these theories most widely accepted one is hydrodynamic theory which was developed in the 1960's. Assumptions of the hydrodynamic theory conclude that the problem begins when the gums recede exposing the underlying tooth roots. The exposed roots contain small pores or tubules which lead directly to the nerve of the tooth. When the fluids within the dentinal tubules are subjected to temperature changes or physical osmotic changes, the movement stimulates a nerve receptor sensitive to pressure, which leads to the transmission of the stimuli and trigger the tooth nerve causing pain and discomfort.

The radius of the tubule is the most important variable affecting the fluid flow in dentin. If the radius is reduced by one-half, the fluid flow within the tubule falls to one-sixteenth of its original rate. Consequently, blocking the tubule even partially can greatly increase the effectiveness of the treatment. Treatment can be invasive in nature or noninvasive. Invasive procedures may include gingival surgery, application of resins, or pulpectomy. Non-invasive treatment options are topical agents and dentifrices that contain a desensitizing active ingredient. These are considered to be the simplest, cost-effective, and efficacious first line of treatment for most patients.

Most of the currently available anti-sensitivity toothpastes use soluble potassium ions as desensitizing agents. The potassium ions are thought to block the synapse between nerve cells, reducing nerve excitation and the associated pain. Ingredients used in these types of dental creams typically are:

- Potassium nitrate
- Potassium chloride
- Potassium citrate

Other ingredients which are incorporated into toothpaste for sensitivity are those which are believed to block the open dentine tubules, either by deposition of mineral salts or precipitation of proteins in the tubules. These include:

- Strontium chloride
- Strontium acetate
- Hydroxyapatite

Toothpastes containing strontium ions not only prevent sensitivity in teeth, but also helps build tooth structure. Strontium ions make the minerals of the saliva to crystallize and cover the pores in the exposed roots of teeth, so that cold stimuli do not reach the tooth nerve. Hydroxyapatite nano-crystals have chemical composition similar to the main structure of tooth enamel and can effectively enhance the mechanism of regeneration of tooth enamel, and tangibly reduce the sensitivity of tooth. Other active agents like dentin sealers (resins), sodium citrate, and sodium monofluorophosphate have also been proven to be effective as desensitizing agents.

11.3.4 Tartar Control Toothpastes[16]

These toothpastes contain pyrophosphates that reduce new tartar build-up (but they can't remove the existing tartar). The tartar cycle begins with food. When food particles are allowed to remain on the teeth after eating, bacteria begin to feed on them. These living organisms excrete acids that leach out calcium from tooth enamel, a process called demineralization. This compound of calcium and acid combines with oxygen to form a substance called calcium phosphate. Calcium phosphate tends to bond with existing enamel along the gum line to form tartar. This is the hard, yellowish material which must be scraped away with metal tools. Calcium phosphate will continue to form as long as the cycle of acid production and demineralization remains unchecked. Brushing with regular toothpaste removes the acid deposits and food particles, but the tartar will remain.

Calcium phosphate is an insoluble form of phosphate. This means that existing tartar build-up cannot be dissolved in water. So creation of a foam of phosphate is necessary which is soluble and combines chemically with the destructive calcium phosphate. This active ingredient in tartar control toothpaste is sodium pyrophosphate. When tartar control toothpaste containing the soluble sodium pyrophosphate is applied to the teeth and gums, a chemical bonding process occurs. Any calcium phosphate which has not yet bonded to teeth is attracted to the sodium pyrophosphate. When the new compound mixes with water, it is completely dissolved. This means that the destructive calcium phosphate destined to form more tartar is instead removed with the rinse of water. Tartar control toothpaste cannot dissolve tartar which has already bonded with the enamel, but it can stop future deposits from forming.

Example 5[4]

Ingredient	% by wt
Sorbitol	50.7
Silica	20
$Na_4P_2O_7$	3.4
$Na_2H_2P_2O_2$	1.4
Sodium lauryl sulphate	1.4
Flavour	1.3
Xanthan gum	0.6
Dye solution	0.4
Sodium saccharin	0.3
Sodium fluoride	0.243
Carbopol 940	0.2
Water	to 100.0

$Na_2H_2P_2O_2$ Sodium acid pyrophosphate

$Na_4P_2O_7$ Sodium pyrophosphate

Example 6[4]

Ingredient	% by wt
	30
Sorbitol (70%)	10
Glycerin	0.8
Iota Carrageenan	20
Silica abrasive	3
Silica thickener	1
Flavour	3
PEG 600	2
$Na_4P_2O_7$	1.5
Gantrez	1.2
Sodium lauryl sulphate	
NaOH (50%)	1
Titanium dioxide	0.5
Sodium saccharin	0.3
Sodium fluoride	0.243
Water	to 100.0

$Na_4P_2O_7$ Sodium Pyrophosphate

PEG Polyethylene glycol

NaOH Sodium hydroxide

11.3.5 Whitening Toothpastes

Whitening Toothpastes have either higher abrasion value than normal toothpastes to mechanically remove food, smoking and other stains from teeth, or/and special ingredients as Peroxide for teeth bleaching and whitening. The primary mode of action of teeth whitening toothpastes is one of abrasion. So the whitening toothpaste includes minute, abrasive particles (usually aluminum oxide, dicalcium phosphate dihydrate, hydrated silicas or calcium carbonate) in its formulation. The scrubbing motion of the bristles of a toothbrush in combination with the presence of these small particles create an action that can have an effect where it scours debris off the surface of teeth. So, as opposed to peroxide-based teeth whiteners where the whitening effect is produced by a chemical change that occurs within a tooth, whitening toothpastes produce a whitening effect solely by way of removing accumulated debris off a tooth's external surface. For this reason, teeth whitening toothpastes are sometimes referred to as "non- bleaching" whitening products.

Some teeth whitening toothpastes include peroxide compounds, however only at low levels. Studies have suggested that a whitening toothpaste with an added peroxide compound will only deliver a 1% (or less) exposure of hydrogen peroxide to a tooth's surface. Because of this low level of peroxide exposure and the relatively brief exposure time teeth have to toothpaste in general, the whitening effect of the peroxide additives found in the formulations of whitening toothpastes is considered to be negligible

11. 3.6 Smoker's Toothpaste

These toothpastes contain ingredients to tackle stains that are a result of the intake of nicotine and tar. The toothpaste may be more abrasive in an attempt to wear away the stains. Toothpastes with a combination of baking soda and hydrogen peroxide are frequently used to remove tobacco stains. Other bleaching agents which can be employed include sodium perborate, sodium benzoate and magnesium peroxide

11.3.7 Toothpastes for Dry Mouth

Dry mouth (xerostomia) can be a consequence of many medications and of cancer therapy especially when there is irradiation of the head and neck because it can result in permanent damage of the salivary glands. Even if not permanent there are residual effects that can seriously affect comfort and result in oral and dental complications.

Dry mouth (xerostomia) can also result from Sjogren's, which is a disorder of the immune system. This disorder causes the immune system to attack healthy tissue. The mucous membranes and moisture secreting glands of the mouth and eyes are usually the first affected leading to decreased production of saliva and tears.[17]

Many types of toothpaste designed to help with xerostomia do not contain sodium lauryl sulphate, a compound used for cleaning and lubrication because it may cause mouth ulcers or canker sores, especially in conditions of dry mouth. Alternately, some toothpastes may incorporate salivary enzymes that moisturize mouth and reinforce the normal properties of saliva. Certain anti-xerostomia dentifrices (Biotene® toothpaste and Oralbalance® gel) contain three salivary enzymes, lactoperoxidase, glucose oxidase and lysozyme, specifically formulated to stimulate saliva and activate intra-oral bacterial systems.[5,18]

11.3.8 Natural Toothpastes/Herbal Toothpaste

Alternative medicine seems to have reached every area of healthcare and oral hygiene is no exception.

There are now a growing number of natural toothpastes in market. Makers of the natural pastes use a wide range of different herbs which they claim, mimic the functions of traditional toothpastes - the ability to fight plaque, freshen breath and prevent gum disease. Many of the herbal toothpastes in the market also claim they are 'fluoride free'. Although fluoride has been championed for years as the best way of combating tooth decay by increasing the resistance of enamel to the acid produced by bacteria in the mouth, there has been some controversy over its use in recent years. A growing body of experts claims that if children take too much fluoride when they are young they can suffer a condition called fluorosis whichcauses teeth to become mottled. Neem and Aloe vera extracts are widely used in herbal toothpastes. Neem extracts fight dental plaque and aloe vera is used to help fight disease-causing bacteria. Other herbal ingredients include myrrh, propolis, and pine resin. Anti-microbial ingredients include sage, oak apples and tormentil. Finally, for dental immunity boosts, toothpastes can also include echinacea and baptisia.

Dabur India Limited markets a good number of herbal tooth preparations such as Dabur Red Toothpaste (active ingredients like Laung, Pudina and Tomar), Babool Toothpaste (packed with the medicinal benefits of Babul tree '*Acacia Arabia*'), Meswak (containing extracts of the Miswak plant '*Salvadore Persica*', the famous 'Toothbrush Tree')

[Colour Fig. on Page 416]

Vicco Vajradanti is one another example of herbal toothpaste which claims to combine the actives of twenty Ayurvedic herbs known for their value in dental hygiene and invigorating the gums.

11.4 Conclusion

While our knowledge of the dental caries process and its prevention has greatly advanced over the past fifty years, it is fair to state that the management of this disease at the level of the individual patient remains largely empirical. Fluoride dentifrices remain the most widely used method of delivering topical fluoride. The efficacy of this approach in preventing dental caries is beyond dispute. However, the vast majority of currently marketed dentifrice products has not been clinically tested and has met only the minimal requirements of the FDA monograph using mainly laboratory testing and animal caries testing. The use of remineralizing agents (other than fluoride), directed at reversing or arresting non-cavitated lesions, remains a promising yet largely unproven strategy. Most of the recent innovations in oral care products have been directed toward making cosmetic marketing claims. There continues to be a need for innovation and collaboration with other scientific disciplines to fully understand and prevent dental caries.

References

1. www.ncbi.nlm.nih.gov/pmc/articles/PMC2147065/
2. www.encyclo.co.uk/webster/D/37
3. Marcel Dekker, Disperse systems volume 2
4. Poucher's Perfumes, Cosmetics and Soaps 10th Edition.
5. Search DoctorSpiller.com
6. Dr. Kathy Phipps, June/July 2004 Journal of the AZDA (http://www.azda.org/).

7. Almeida BS, Silva Cardoso VE, Buzalaf MAR. Fluoride ingestion from toothpaste and diet in 1- to 3-year-old Brazilian children. *Community Dent Oral Epidemiol* 2007;**35**: 53-63
8. Guidelines on the use of fluoride in children:an EAPD policy document.
9. www.lef.org/protocols/dental/gingivitis_01.htm
10. http://d3e9u3gw8odyw8.cloudfront.net/toothpaste_ingredients.pdf
11. KG Chhabra, Preetha J Shetty, Prasad K V V, Chaya S Mendon, and Ramya Kalyanpur *Journal of International Oral Health* The beyond measures: Non flouride preventive measures for dental caries 2011; **3**(2): 1-7.
12. Chlorophyll as Therapy (http://chlorophyllplus.com/Chlorophyll_Plus/Studies.html).
13. H.E. Kirschner, M.Dhttp://www.pines.net/cgbook/chapter4.htm
14. www.fatfreekitchen.com/teeth/gingivitis-gums-treatment.html
15. Dentinal Hypersensitivity: A Review *The Journal of Contemporary Dental Practice*, Volume 6, No. 2, May 15, 2005.
16. http://www.wisegeek.com
17. http://oralcareaustralia.com.au/info_pages.php/pages_id/36_Sjogrens--dry- mouth
18. http://www.livestrong.com/article/306680-toothpaste-to-help-dry-mouth/#ixzz1c4WK87OB

Colour Photographs of All Chapters

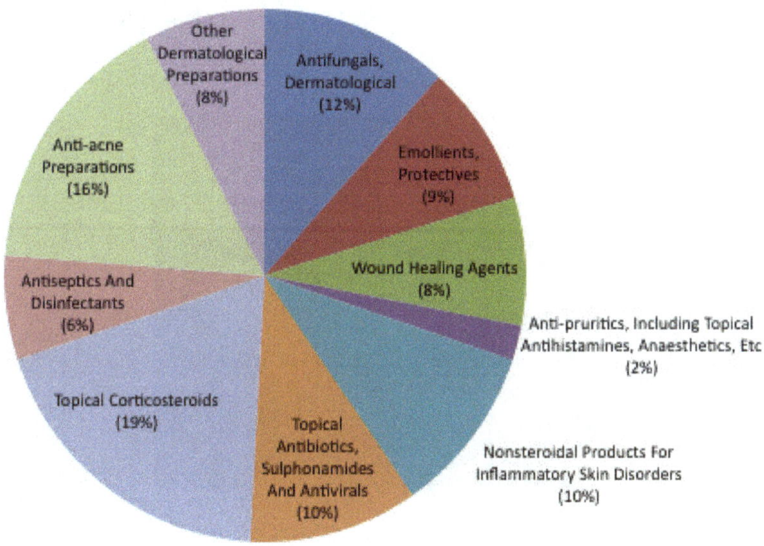

Fig. 1.1 Global Therapeutic Dermatology Marketsplit by Product Class.

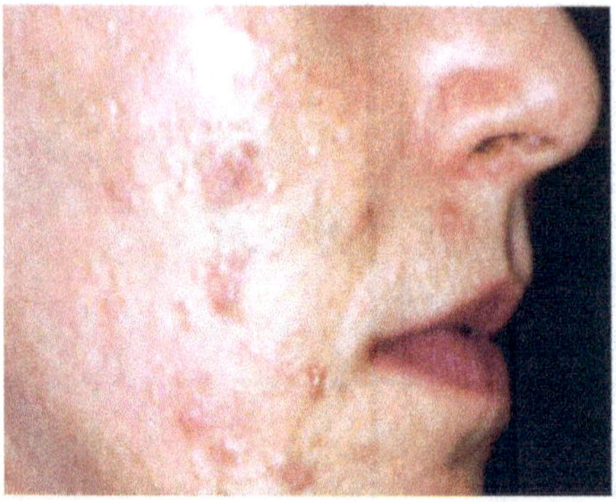

Fig. 2.1 Multiple closed comedones (white heads).

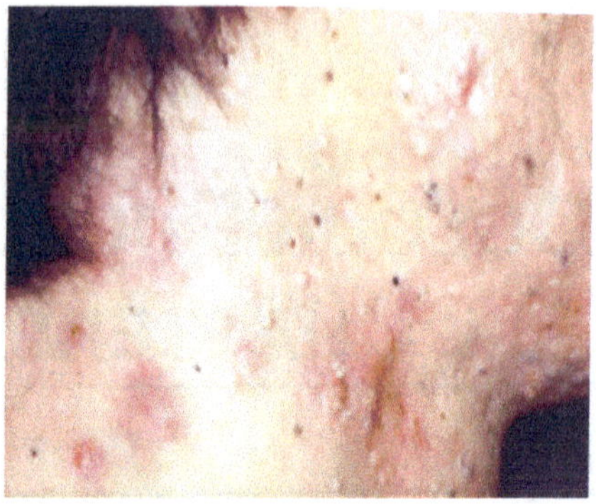

Fig. 2.2 Multiple open comedones (Black heads).

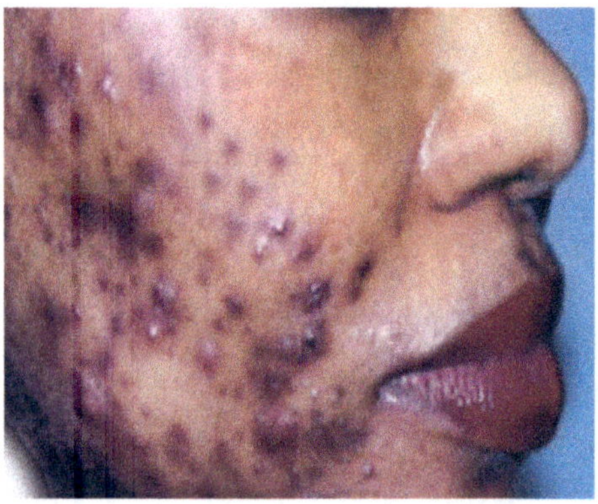

Fig. 2.3 Papular and cystic acne and the figure also shows post inflammator hyperpigmentation.

Fig. 2.4 Sandal Wood Plant.

Fig. 2.5 Sandal Wood Chips.

Fig. 2.6 Ylang ylang oil.

Fig. 2.7 Tea tree plant.

Fig. 2.8 White Camomile Plant.

Fig. 2.9 Yellow camomile plant.

Fig. 2.10 Bergamot Plant.

Fig. 2.11 Lavender Flowers.

Fig. 2.12 Patchouli Plant.

Fig. 2.13 Jasmine Flower.

Fig. 2.14 Jasmine Plant.

Fig. 2.15 Geranium Plant.

Fig. 2.16 Sage Plant.

Fig. 2.17 Sage Flower.

Fig. 2.18 Aloe leaf.

Fig. 2.19 Aloe vera plant.

Fig. 2.20 Cross section of Aloe leaf.

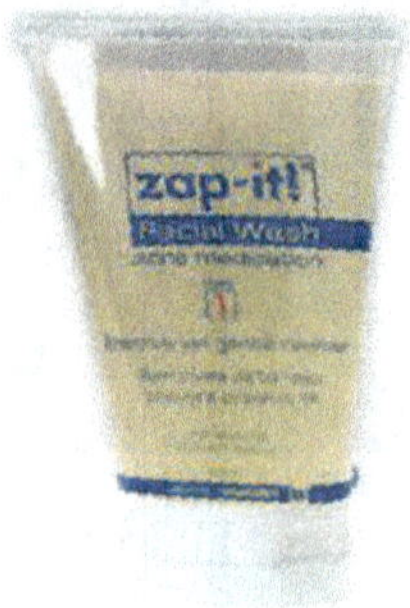

Facial Wash

Deep Cleaning Astringent

Pore Clarifying Cream

NATURA BISSE
Diamond Extreme Anti Aging Bio
Regenerative Extreme Cream.

PAYOT Benefice Soleil Anti-Aging
Protective Cream SPF 30 UVA/UVB.

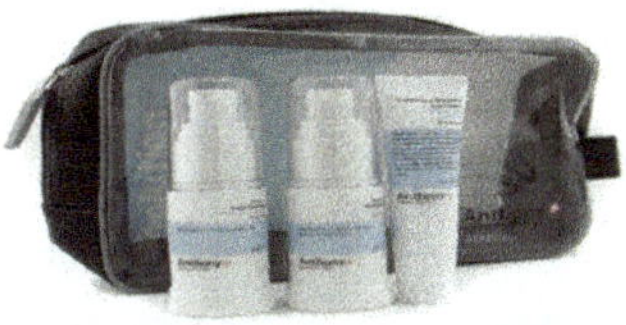

ANTHONY Logistics for men the Anti-Aging Starter Kit: Facial Treatment + Facial Serum + Eye Cream.

ORLANE B21 Anti-Aging Sun Cream SPF 30 for Face and Body

Revitol Anti Aging Solution

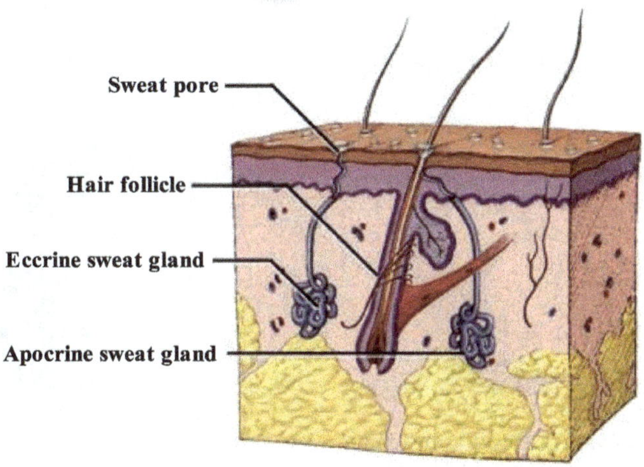

Fig. 4.1 Structure of sweat glands.

Hindustan Unilever Limited manufactures Clinical protection Anti-Perspirant Energizing Deodorant.

Nivea roll on for men

Oriflame India Refreshing Sensitive Deodorant Wipes for All Skin Types

Oriflame India Roll-on Anti-perspiring Deodorant with Lime and GingerExtracts

Hindustan uni lever Rexona deo

Adidas Body Care

Soapwalla's Deodorant Cream

Lemongrass Rosemary Deodorant Spray (Natural)

Spearmint and Tea Tree 'Pit Putty

Lavera Body Spa with Baking Soda

Calendula Blossom Natural
Deodorant Spray

Men's Stock Natural Dry
Herbal Pine Deodorant

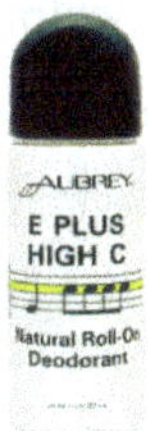

E Plus High C Roll-On Deodorant

L`Oreal India Pvt. Ltd.

Lakmé Ultra Matte Sun Protection Cream

Mary Kay Cosmetics Pvt. Ltd.

Blue Lizard Regular Suncream 30+

Sunblock SPF30 with Chamomile extract

Sensitive SPF 20 Lotion

Lotus herbals safe sun

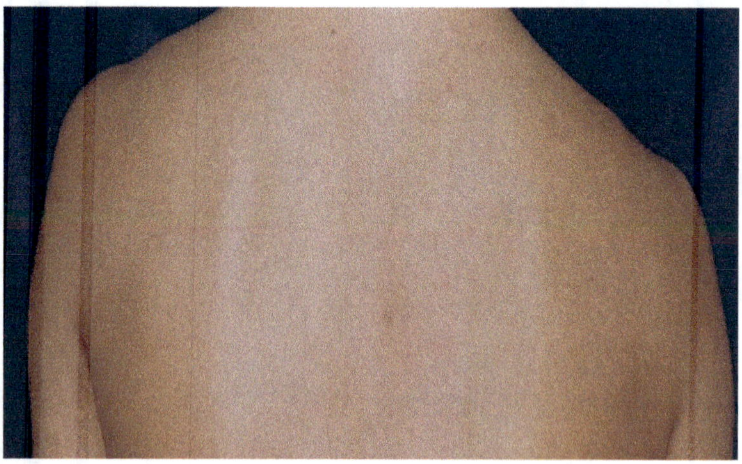

Fig. 5.1 photograph showing Erythema produced after exposure to sunlight.

Grecian Plus Gradual Haircolor Foam 5 oz (142 g)

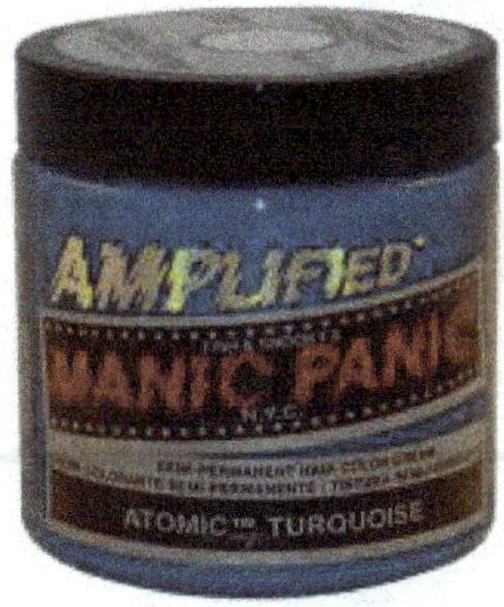

Manic Panic Amplified Semi-Permanent Hair Color Cream.

Herbal Hair Color and Henna hair color dye.

Wella Color Charm Demi-Permanent Hair Color # 4/0 Medium Natural 60 ml

Profession by Indola.

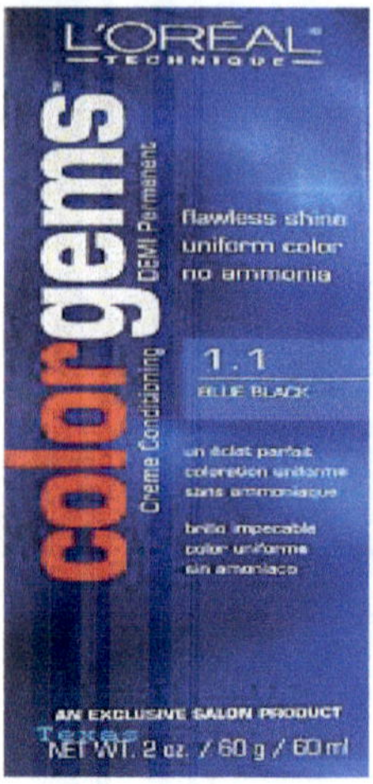

Color Gems Creme Conditioning DEMI Permanent.

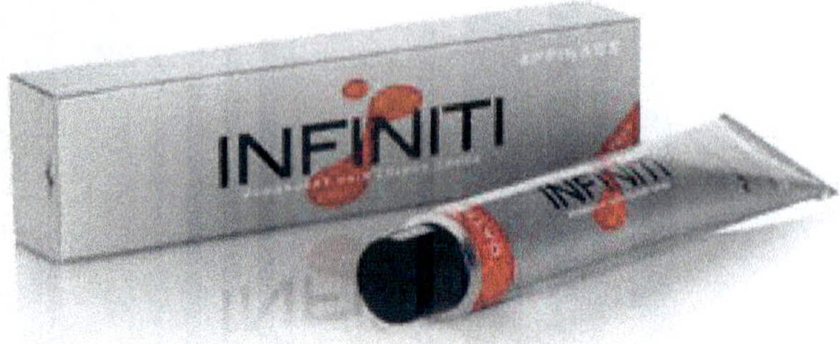

Infiniti Permanent Haire Colour Creme by Affinage.

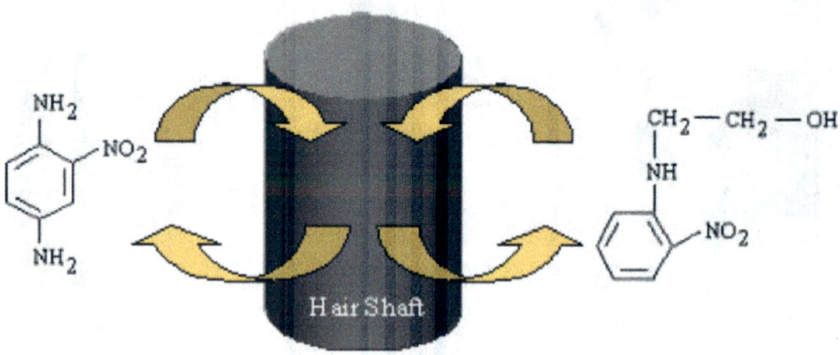

Fig. 6.7 Semi-permanent dyes are small enough to enter and exit the hair shaft. As the hair is being washed, the dye leaves the hair shaft as the hair returns to its original color.

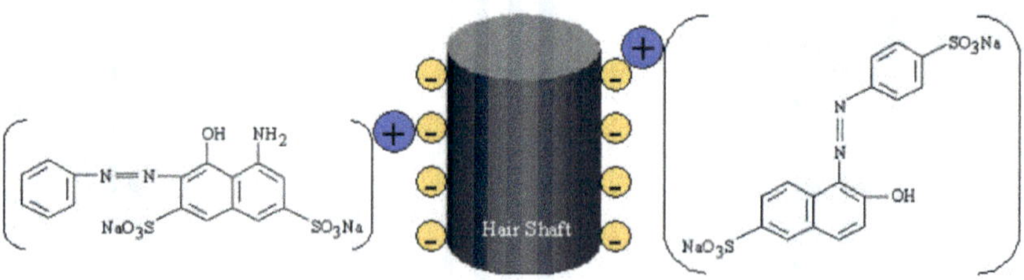

Fig. 6.8 Schematic of the cationic basic dye attracted to the surface of the hair shaft. After a few wash, the dye will leave the hair surface.

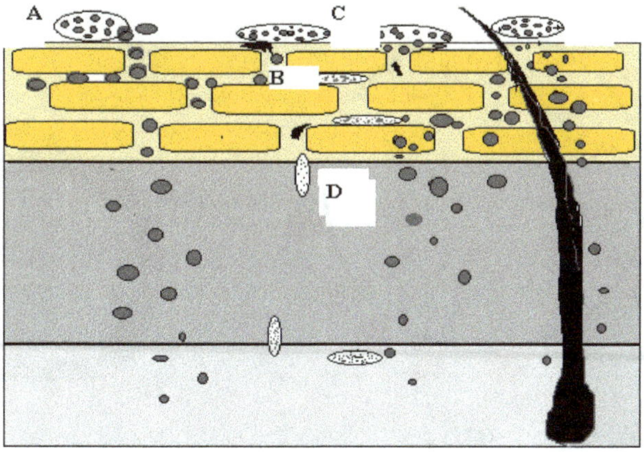

A- Free drug mechanism
B.Penetration enhancing process of liposomal components
C.Vesicle adsorption and/or fusion with Stratum corneum
D.Vesicle penetration into or into through the intact skin

Fig. 7.2 Possible mechanism of liposome through skin.

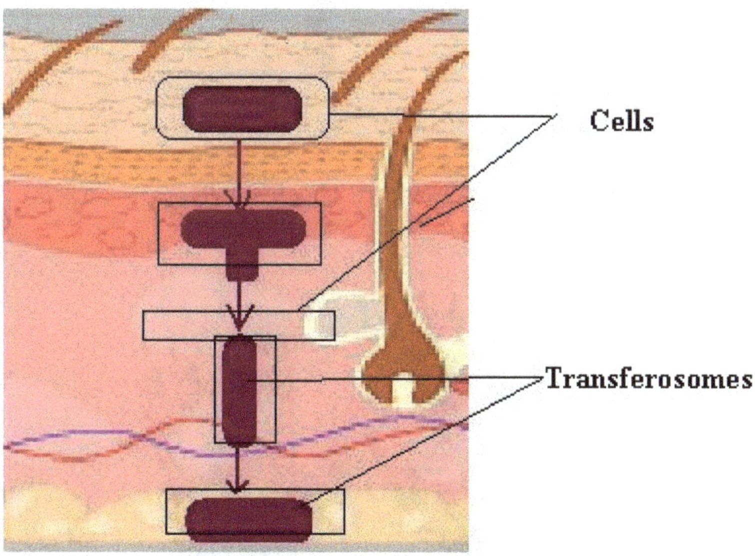

Fig. 7.3 Mechanism of permeation of transferosome through skin.

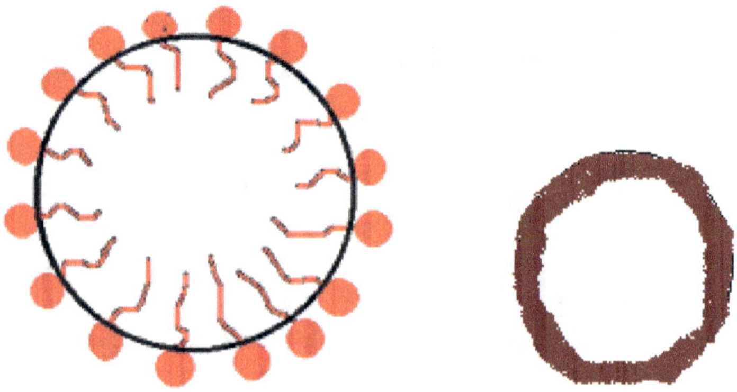

(a) (b)

Fig 7.4 Cross-section of (a) nanoemulsion and (b) biopolymeric nanoparticle.

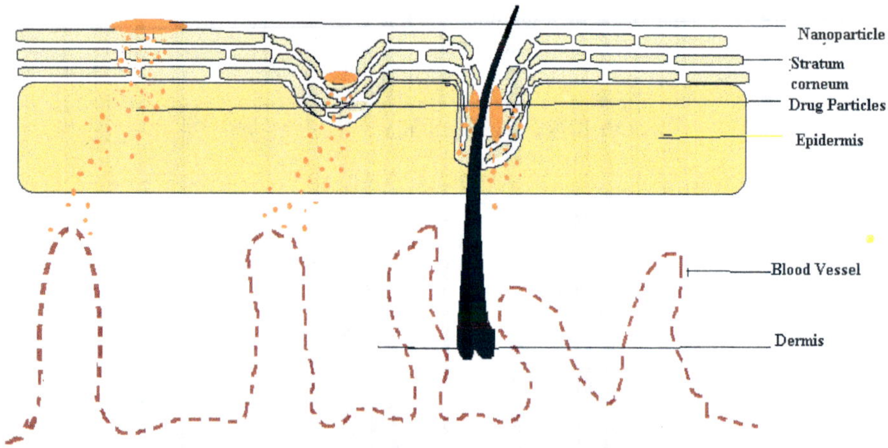

Fig. 7.5 Topical nanoparticle delivery through skin.

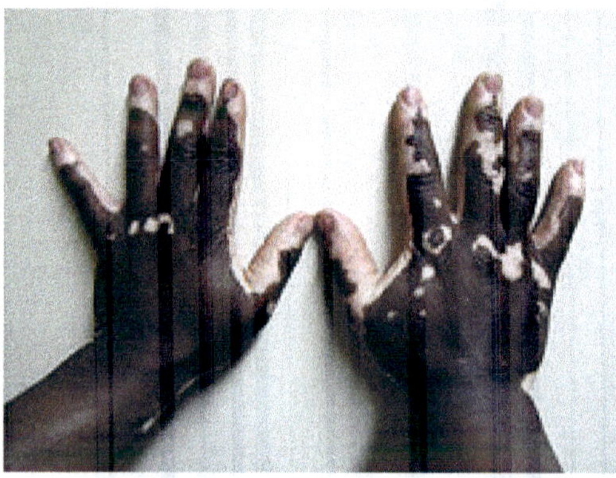

Non-segmental vitiligo

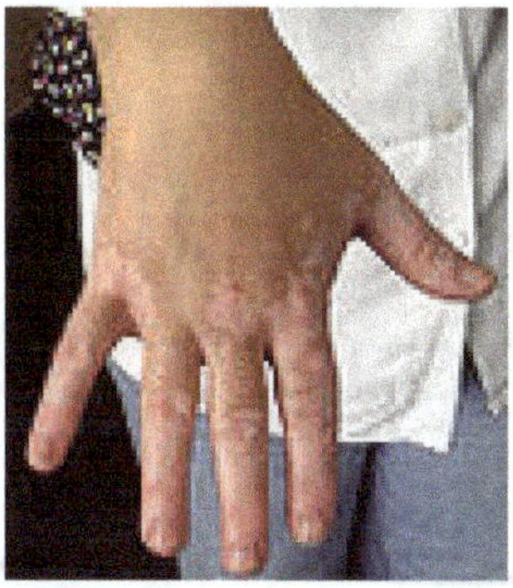

Vitiligo in a light-skinned individual

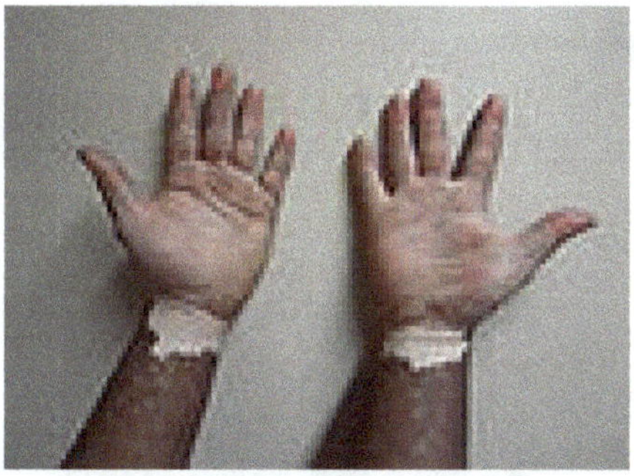

Vitiligo in a dark-skinned individual

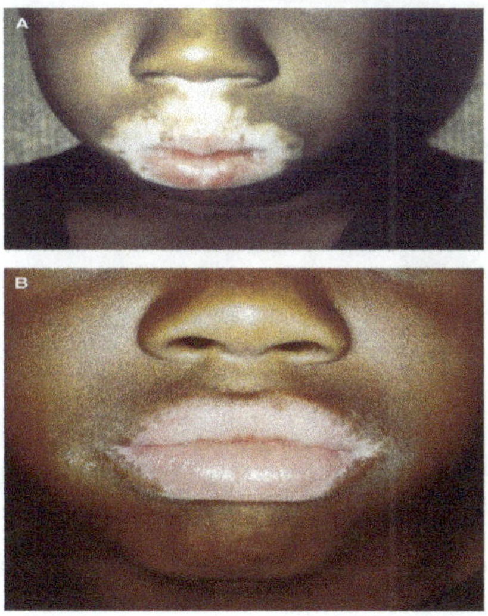

Fig. 8.2 Periorificial vitiligo in a young boy (A) before treatment and (B) with almost complete repigmentation after 2.5 years of therapy of alternating 8 week cycles of class I topical corticosteroids with class V corticosteroids, for a total of 7 cycles.

Kalawalla vitiligo dietary supplement

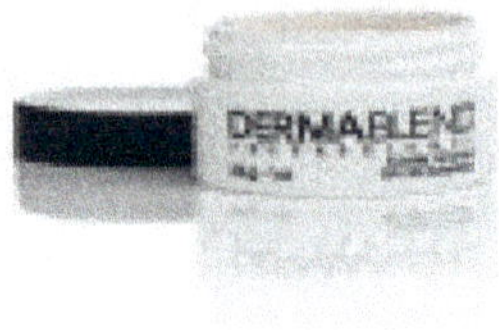

Anti-vitiligo cream – dermablend cover creme

Pigmento cream

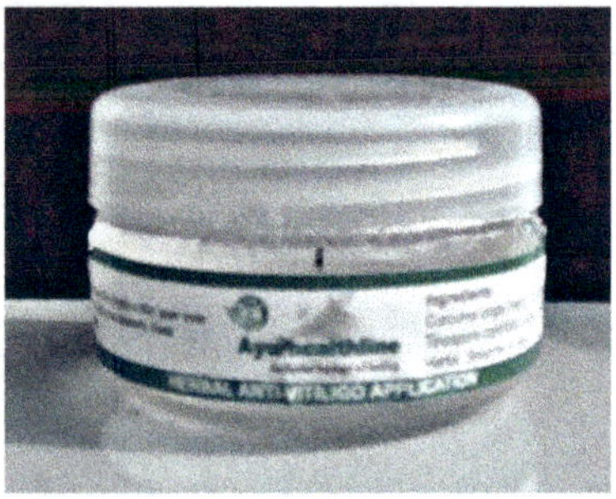

Ayurhealthline

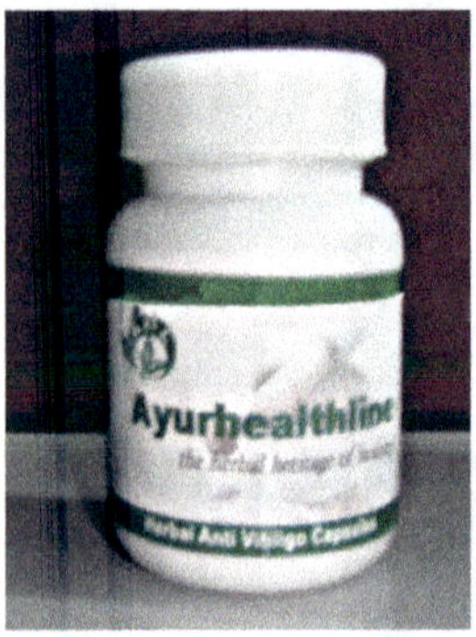

Ayurhealthline

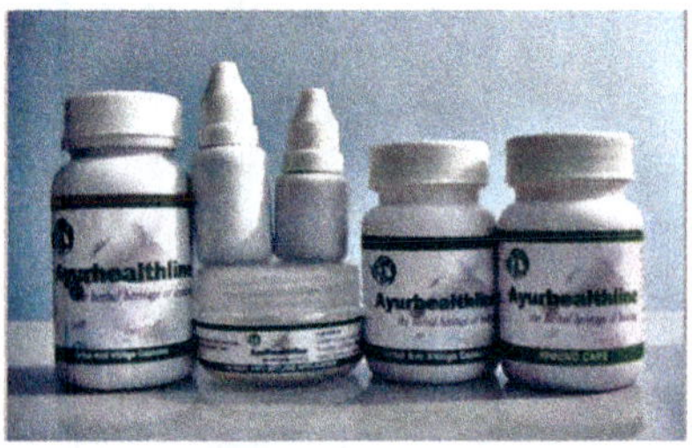

Anti-vitiligo kit

Anti-vitiligo oil

Pigmento tablet for leucoderma treatment

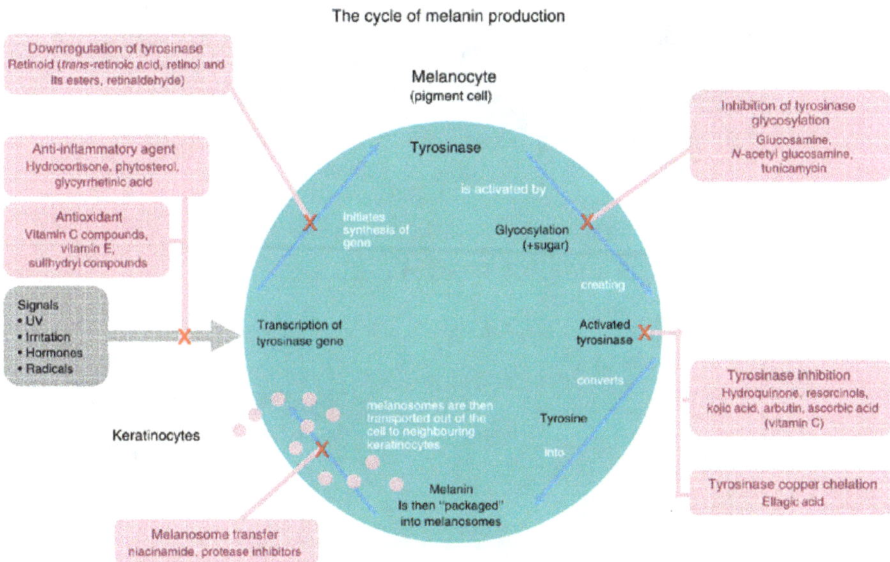

Fig. 9.2 Cross section of skin showing melanocyte.

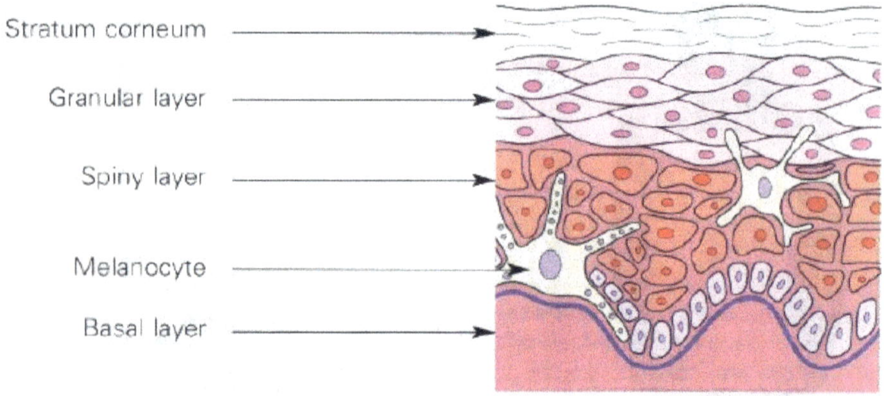

Fig. 9.3 Cross section of skin showing different layers.

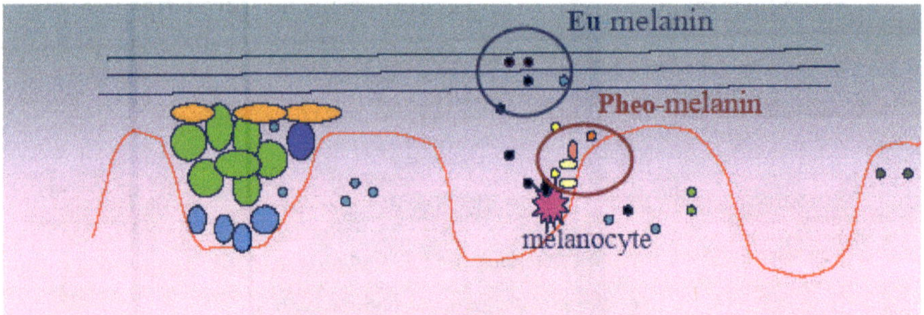

Fig. 9.4 Types of melanins.

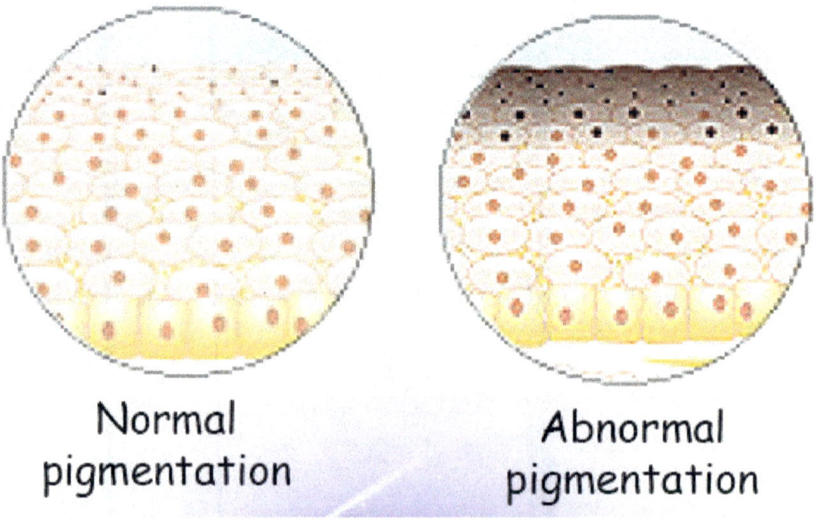

Fig. 9.5 Difference between normal and abnormal pigmentation.

Fair & Lovely anti-marks cream

Depigmenting Cream 50 ml from Naturalia

LADYMAX^{TM} Depigmentation cream

Natural Depigmentation Cream

Biotique skin whitening and depigmentation Cream

Fig. 9.6 Orange fruits.

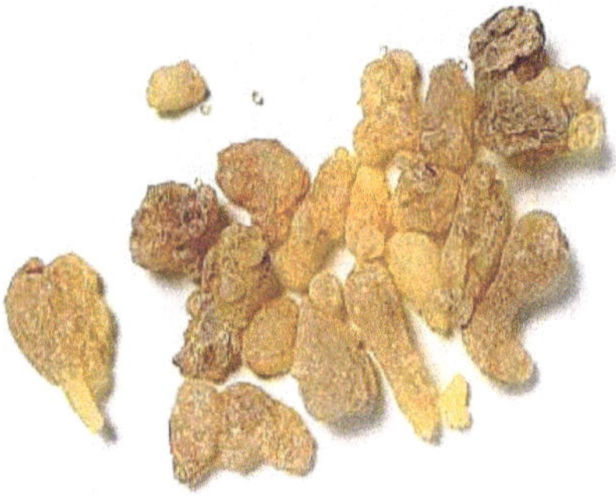

Fig. 9.7 Frankinsense resin.

Fig. 9.8 Lemon fruits.

Fig. 9.10 Rose flower.

Fig. 9.11 Saffron flower.

Fig. 9.12 Tulasi plant.

Fig. 9.13 Peppermint leaves.

Fig. 9.14 Neem plant.

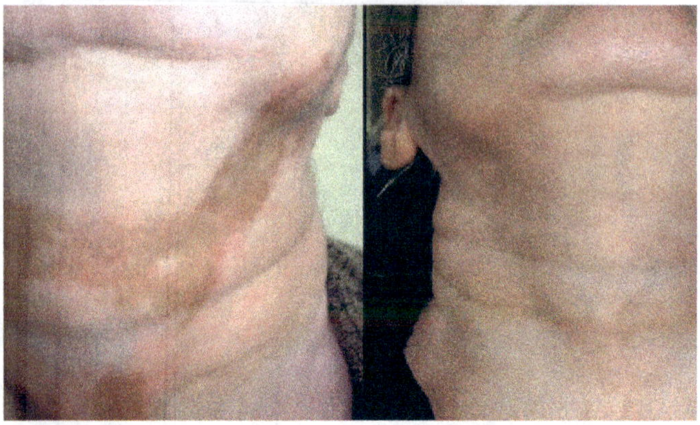

Fig. 9.15 Before and after the treatment for hyperpigmentation.

Spot Peel and Cream

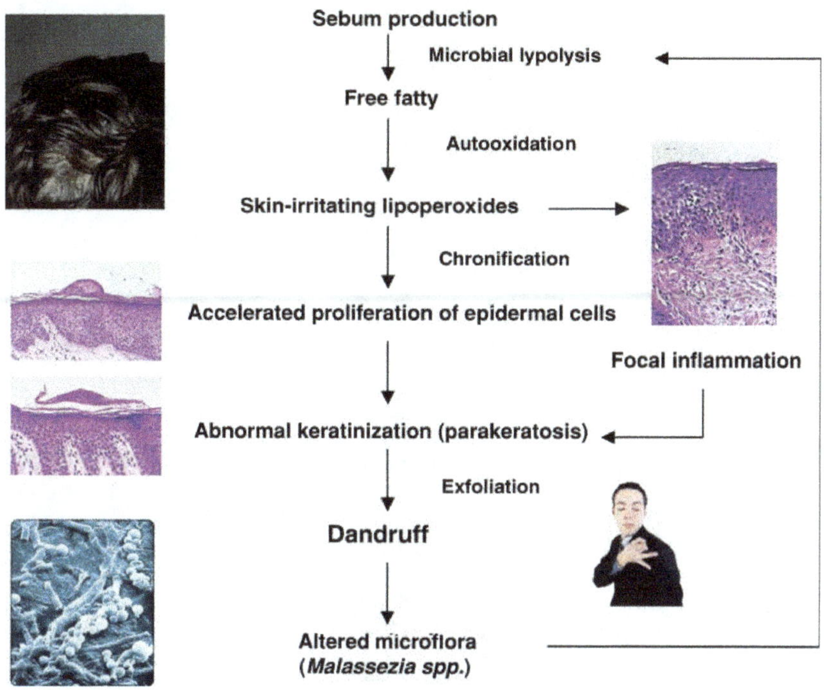

Fig. 10.1 Pathogenesis of dandruff.

Johnson's Nizoral Anti-Dandruff Shampoo

Coal Tar Shampoo to fight Psoriasis

Mediker Anti-lice Treatment Shampoo

Renref - Anti Lice Shampoo

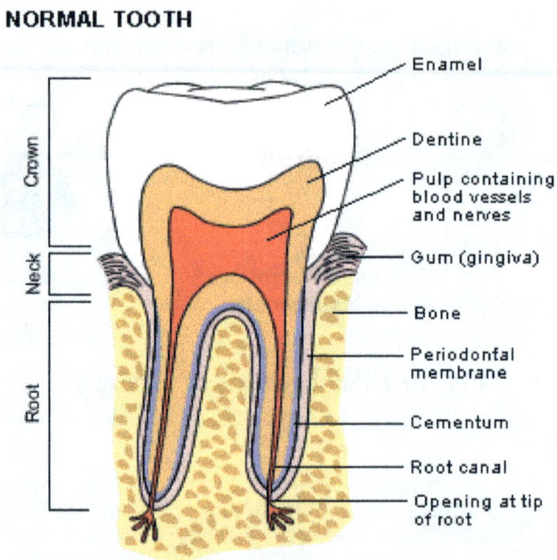

Fig. 11.1 Structure of Tooth.

Herbal Toothpaste

INDEX

L

M

N

O

INDEX

F

G

H

I

J

K

L

M

N

O

P

Q

R

S

V

W

X

Y

Z

www.ingramcontent.com/pod-product-compliance
Lightning Source LLC
Chambersburg PA
CBHW071329230926
51849CB00002B/346